The Wrong Side of Murder Creek

The Wrong Side of Murder Creek

*A White Southerner
in the Freedom Movement*

BOB ZELLNER

WITH CONSTANCE CURRY

FOREWORD BY JULIAN BOND

NEWSOUTH BOOKS
Montgomery

NewSouth Books
105 South Court Street
Montgomery, AL 36104

Library of Congress Cataloging-in-Publication Data

Zellner, Bob.
The wrong side of Murder Creek : a white southerner in the freedom movement /
Bob Zellner, with Constance Curry.
p. cm.

ISBN-13: 978-1-58838-222-1
ISBN-10: 1-58838-222-2

1. Zellner, Bob. 2. Civil rights workers—Southern States—Biography. 3.
Whites—Alabama—Biography. 4. African Americans—Civil rights—Alabama—
History—20th century. 5. African Americans—Civil rights—Southern States—
History—20th century. 6. Civil rights movements—Alabama—History—20th
century. 7. Civil rights movements—Civil rights—Southern States—History—
20th century. 8. Alabama—Race relations—History—20th century. 9. Southern
States—Race relations—History—20th century. 10. Alabama—Biography. I.
Curry, Constance, 1933- II. Title.
E185.98.Z44A3 2008
323.092—dc22
[B]

2008025962

Design by Randall Williams

Printed in the United States of America by
Maple Press

Second Printing

With love to

Dad and Mom, who prepared me for the journey;

to my brothers, Jim, Doug, David, and Malcolm;

to my daughters, Margaret and Katie;

to my wife, Linda;

and to Maggie Donovan.

Contents

FOREWORD

JULIAN BOND

Although his life's journey eventually would take him to New York, Bob Zellner was as Southern as MoonPies and RC Cola when we first met in Atlanta in 1961.

At the time, I was the Communications Director for the Student Nonviolent Coordinating Committee (SNCC), an organization born from the ferment created by sit-in demonstrations in early 1960.

From the first, SNCC was an interracial organization. Bob Zellner was its first white field secretary, but Jane Stembridge, daughter of a white Baptist minister and a student at Union Theological Seminary, was the organization's first employee. SNCC's workers were "the new abolitionists" historian Howard Zinn described in the first book written about the group.* Zinn called SNCC "more a movement than an organization."

Having surveyed the backgrounds of one-third of the SNCC staff in late 1963, Zinn wrote:

> Of the six white staff members two were from the Deep South. The white youngsters and most of the Northern Negroes came from middle-class homes; their fathers were ministers or teachers or civil service workers . . . These are young radicals. The word "revolution" occurs again and again in their speech.

Like many other black and white Southerners drawn into the movement,

Zellner's inspiration came from his religious faith.

Born in "L.A."—lower Alabama—John Robert Zellner was the son of a Methodist minister. Bob attended Huntingdon College in Montgomery, Alabama. He and four fellow students at the all-white Methodist-related school became locally notorious as the "Huntingdon Five" when they outraged school authorities and state officials by daring to attend a civil rights meeting. Bob and his four friends took seriously a sociology class assignment to research solutions to racial problems. Despite their professor's adamant orders not to do so, they attended a meeting with black students from what was then called Alabama State College for Negroes, and later an anniversary celebration of the 1955–56 Montgomery Bus Boycott.

Their "research" brought them to the attention of Alabama's Attorney General, MacDonald Gallion, who warned them that they were "falling under communist influence."

"Are there communists in Alabama?" Zellner asked incredulously. "No," answered the Attorney General, "but they come through here."

Bob Zellner was one of relatively few white Southerners engaged in the activist Southern civil rights movement of the 1960s literally from the beginning. The grant to hire him came to SNCC from the Southern Conference Education Fund (SCEF), a progressive organization whose newspaper, *The Southern Patriot*, was frequently the only outlet for news from the civil rights battlefield.

It was Zellner's good fortune that his guide and mentor in the world of anti-racist activism was a courageous white Alabama woman, Anne Braden, SCEF's director. Anne and her husband Carl nurtured many young whites like Bob in the intricacies and difficulties of fighting rigid American apartheid in a world where almost all whites were hostile and many were dangerous.

It was also Bob's good fortune that Connie Curry, another Southern white woman who knew and supported the student civil rights movement

---

JULIAN BOND has been chairman of the NAACP Board of Directors since February 1998. He is a Distinguished Scholar in the School of Government at American University in Washington, D.C., and a professor in the Department of History at the University of Virginia.

from its inception, agreed to work with Bob on this book. An accomplished writer who knows the territory, Connie has helped Bob tell his story in a compelling way. And he has a compelling story to tell.

THE STUDENT NONVIOLENT COORDINATING Committee that Bob joined organized nonviolent direct action against segregated facilities. We conducted voter registration projects in Alabama, Arkansas, Maryland, Missouri, Louisiana, Virginia, Kentucky, Tennessee, Illinois, North and South Carolina, Georgia, and Mississippi. We built two independent political parties and organized labor unions and agricultural cooperatives. SNCC gave the movement for women's liberation new energy and inspired and trained many of the activists who began the "New Left." SNCC helped expand the limits of political debate within black America and broadened the focus of the civil rights movement.

The son and grandson of Ku Klux Klan members, Bob initially was hired by SNCC to conduct outreach to Southern white students, explaining the civil rights movement to them and soliciting their involvement and support.

The Wrong Side of Murder Creek is a travelogue of civil rights hot-spots that Zellner frequented, from his inauguration into the movement in Montgomery, Alabama, the Cradle of the Confederacy; to Mobile and Talladega, Alabama; McComb and Greenwood, Mississippi; Albany, Georgia; Danville, Virginia; and other towns large and small, where the battles were fought.

In McComb, a small town in southwestern Mississippi—the most racially recalcitrant state in the South—he joined his black colleagues in a violence-plagued campaign against entrenched segregation. Bob was arrested and beaten into unconsciousness—not for the last time—when an enraged white mob, encouraged by the eerily coincidental presence of a racist schoolmate who had tormented Zellner at Huntingdon College for his racial liberalism, turned on him with lead pipes and baseball bats.

White civil rights activists faced unique torments. While Zellner's black colleagues won respect and admiration in their communities, he and other white Southerners earned the hatred and contempt of their contemporaries. It took a special brand of commitment and courage to do this work, and Bob never lacked for either.

When his minister father broke with the Klan, Bob's mother made white

Sunday school shirts for Bob and his brothers from their father's Klan robe. Bob writes that when things got tough for him and his name became well-known, drawing disapproval from many Alabama whites, his brothers all agreed to say—"Yes, he's my brother, and I'm proud of it."

Bob Zellner has been my brother since 1961, and I'm proud of it, too.

The New Abolitionists by Howard Zinn, Beacon Press, Boston, 1964.

Preface

Constance Curry

I recently spoke to a meeting of a black women's sorority at Emory University, here in Atlanta. I talked about my time with the Student Nonviolent Coordinating Committee (SNCC) in the early 1960s and the courageous black families across the South with whom I later worked as Southern field secretary for the American Friends Service Committee. These families, trained and taught by SNCC workers, were involved in school desegregation after the 1964 Civil Rights Act and voter registration after the 1965 Voting Rights Act. The Emory students were absolutely floored to hear that white people like me had been involved in the freedom movement. I assured them that we had been there to support a movement that young black people started and led—a movement that lasted a short time but changed this country forever. As I have traveled to other campuses these days, I have found the same thing—very little knowledge of the violence that pervaded such a short time ago and the history of the enormous student participation in the movement. All of this has reminded me of what Bob Moses said at the thirtieth anniversary of SNCC—that we needed to start writing our own stories, because history and historians will either not tell about it or will get it wrong.

Here is one such first-hand account, and it is unusual because it is from one of the few white Southerners who were directly involved with the student movement. I first heard of Bob Zellner when he submitted an application to attend the Southern Student Human Relations Seminar of the United States National Student Association in the summer of 1961. By then he had been at Highlander Folk School for a program and had been involved in student protests in Alabama. He brought an unerring dedication to freedom and justice to our group of eighteen Southern students, black and white, determined to break down segregation. We continued our friendship when he came to Atlanta later that fall to work with SNCC as a field secretary and to visit white schools in particular. He made it clear from the beginning that he was not there to further the "Negro" cause since he had learned from his own experience that violence and repressive laws were also a threat to whites' choices in life.

Bob and I have continued our friendship here and there over forty-seven years. When he asked me four years ago to help him with his memoirs, I almost said "no," because I know him well and knew it would not be an easy job. But I also knew it would be an exciting, worthwhile story.

In looking at our country today, it is hard not to be discouraged. Despite the astonishing gains made by the freedom movement of the 1960s, we are now facing a more sophisticated version of racism that thrives on the motivations of power and greed. The face of that continuing racism thrives in the schools-to-prison pipeline, in the criminal justice system, the health care system, and on and on.

We see stirrings among young people and students here in the fall of 2008 that certainly can give us hope. I sincerely hope that Bob Zellner's story will be an inspiration for them to get out there and fight for the values that they know are just and right. I also hope it will be a trip down "memory road" for some of the well-known sisters and brothers who are mentioned in the book, by episode if not always by name, and will urge them on in telling their own stories. Many movement folks—too many to list—helped Bob and me so much with fact-checking, research materials, moral support, and in other ways; I thank all of you.

THE WRONG SIDE OF MURDER CREEK

1

Growing Up in L.A. (Lower Alabama)

I was born in Jay, Florida, on April 5, 1939, at home in our small wood frame parsonage. I grew up in south Alabama with my Dad, my mother, Ruby, and four brothers—Jim, Doug, David, and Malcolm. My father, the Reverend James Abraham Zellner, was a Methodist preacher, which meant that we moved to a different church every three or four years. Daddy was raised in Birmingham, and he joined the Ku Klux Klan there in 1928 when he turned eighteen.

[handwritten: -18 / 1910]

My grandfather, Daddy's father, J. O. Zellner, was also a Klansman. Granddaddy worked in Birmingham for the Gulf, Mobile, and Ohio Railroad. Starting out as a telegrapher, J. O. eventually retired as a dispatcher. Maybe his work on the railroad, a place where segregation was strictly enforced in both the work force and on the trains, made Granddaddy a likely candidate for the terror and hatred preached by the Klan.

The Klan in Birmingham in the 1920s was an interesting combination of people and interests. With the railroad, the mines, and the steel mills, union-organizing, protests, and strikes were always a threat to the power structure. Klan violence against these demonstrations was historic and widespread. At the same time, the Kluxers held a wide appeal for many working-class whites as well as white ministers, judges, and lawyers who believed they could express their varied needs by joining the fluid organization.

When I was older and an activist, I thought it was ironic that leaders on both sides of the race divide often worked for the railroads. A. Philip Randolph was a sleeping car porter, as was E. D. Nixon, one of Martin Luther King Jr.'s mentors. Eugene V. Debs, the great socialist union organizer, was a railroader. I like to daydream about my grandfather, a white Birmingham

Klansman, and E. D. Nixon, a black Montgomery revolutionary, working on the same trains.

As a child I knew nothing about the Klan and race hatred. I loved Granddaddy Zellner and Grandmother Bessie. She was a Carmichael before she married my Dad's father, and I knew and loved my Great-Grandmother Carmichael, who I think was born during the run-up to the Civil War in the 1850s.

When Dad reached high school age he was sent off to the backwoods mountains of Toccoa Falls, Georgia, for boarding school. It was hard enough growing up in a Klan household—now he would be sent to Dr. Forrest, founder of the Toccoa Falls Institute, for training as a street-corner evangelist. The Institute was known as a place in the Bible Belt South that prepared God's people to flesh out the call. Pupils were required on weekends to walk or hitch into "downtown" Toccoa and preach on the streets. Daddy shoveled coal into the heating furnace and worked in the hot kitchen making corn bread to help pay his way at the school.

It didn't matter that Georgia only accredited the high school after Daddy graduated in 1928. He was headed to Bob Jones College in Lynn Haven, Florida, and they cared only that James was saved and preached the gospel on the streets. The college, founded in 1927, was an extremely conservative, fundamentalist, religious institution. My future mother, Ruby Rachael Hardy, oldest daughter of a Methodist minister, was one of the first students to arrive at the college and one of only two to graduate four years later in the depths of the Depression. Mom joked that she was valedictorian of the class, having "edged out" the other graduate.

Going to college amid the sandspurs, saw grass, and piney woods forest of Bay County in the Florida panhandle, the raw new campus could not have been nearly as foreign to Mom as it must have been for Dad. He grew up in the cold, dank, smoky steel town of Birmingham, and Preacher Boy Zellner must have thought College Point, as the campus area was called, was quite exotic.

Mom, born in 1910 not far away in Blountstown, Florida, located due south of the junction between Alabama, Georgia, and Florida, felt quite at home among the mosquitoes and palmettos. Her mother was a Spivey, before she married Granddaddy J. J. Hardy. She was thought to be a Cherokee, but since everybody in the South seemed to have a "Cherokee" grandmother, I always thought that Grandma Hardy's Indian blood was mostly hyperbole. There was a story passed down of my grandmother Hardy getting on a mule and taking hams to my grandfather. He lived close enough that she could ride there. She had heard that his family had rotten meat and not too much of anything to eat. Another part of that family legend is that when he was young he attached himself to the Confederate Army as a drummer boy. I also found Zellners, most of whom were related, in Confederate history. One was a colonel from Forsyth, Georgia. Another was in Company H in Tennessee, and he was one of the few Zellner men to survive the war. Then there's a gap in family history through the 1920s. It was during this period when a nationwide KKK resurgence occurred, and that's when my father's father joined.

When I grew up and became interested in the family tree, I was always puzzled that most any older family member could recite Daddy's side all the way back to two Zellner brothers landing from Germany in Savannah in 1775. On Mom's side things became fuzzy just past her mother and father!

"What about your grand- and great-grandparents, Mom?" I would ask.

One day Mom took me aside and said in a hushed voice, "Well, Bobby," (she and everybody else called me Bobby until I was in college, and most still do back home), "since you insist on knowing about these things, I guess I'll just have to tell you."

Looking around like someone might be trying to listen, she whispered, "don't you go around trying to pry into these things with anyone else in the family . . . but . . . your great grandfather, on my side, was a . . ." she paused to indicate how important this was.. "He was a woods colt."

"Now are you satisfied?" she said, exasperated with herself. "You've wheedled the secret out of me. Don't tell anybody I told you."

I confess I didn't know exactly what she had told me, but I understood clearly that it was all I was going to get out of her, at least at this sitting. I'd have to give it another shot later, or figure out on my own what a "woods colt" was.

I only hoped I had heard Mother correctly. She inadvertently gave me a hint when she walked off shaking her head and muttering something under her breath about Southerners always being "so dad-burned interested in the blood lines."

Apparently, Mom and Dad didn't think it was odd for us boys to have a grandfather and uncles in the KKK. Having a woods colt in the family, however, was kept a deep dark secret.

DR. BOB JONES SR. thought so much of his little preacher boy, James Abraham Zellner, that after graduation, he picked my Dad to go with him to Europe on a mission from God to spread the true gospel to the Jews. Dr. Bob's cockamamie scheme was to convert Europe's Jews to Christianity to save them from Nazi gas chambers. Doctor Bob had returned after a month or two, but where was that pretty little preacher boy, James?

Dad stayed on in Europe, but his conversion to integrationist-internationalist was not what Bob Jones had in mind. The young Reverend James Zellner was interrogated by the Gestapo in Berlin while delivering messages and money to the Jewish underground. My father began to question the beliefs that had attracted him to the Ku Klux Klan. I don't know how much training, if any, Dad had to be a spy, but he was certainly primed by the government to keep his eyes open for information which might be useful in the coming struggle with the Axis powers. Patriotism and nationalism vied in Dad's soul with the racist beliefs he had actively espoused since boyhood. The fascists would soon be enemies of his country, yet their ideology was close to his own. The process of differentiation between himself and the fascists was speeded along by the sobering realization that he risked execution or life imprisonment for what he was doing.

As the train pulled into the Berlin station, Daddy frantically pondered how to conceal the letters and the packet of cash he had been instructed to deliver to the man with the white carnation whom he would meet on the platform. A sharp rap on the compartment door made Reverend Zellner and his British compartment-mate jump. "Passport please," the Gestapo officer barked in English to the Englishman, who stood closest to the door. Seeing the British passport, he methodically took the man's luggage apart. Then without a word he turned to my father. Dad casually placed the letters and the money in the back cover of his passport, snapped it shut and handed it to the German. With the faintest of smiles the Gestapo agent handed back the passport along with all its contents. "American," he mused, "Welcome to Berlin, Herr Zellner." With his riding crop, the officer turned one shirt over on top of Dad's open luggage, stepped out and closed the door to the sleeper. It was lucky the Third Reich hated the British so much while holding out some hope for Joseph Kennedy's America. Joe Kennedy, the father of future president JFK, was a renowned bootlegger and a notorious admirer of Hitler.

After a while in Berlin, Dad was so little enamored of Germans and their leader that he passed up an opportunity to see Hitler. When he told the story I would always fuss at him that he could have at least looked. Dad said Hitler was not worth walking down to the corner to see. He had been sitting in a café and someone had run by saying that the Fuehrer was passing in the next street. Everybody rose and ran to look, while Dad kept his seat.

The defining experience for Dad in Europe, however, occurred one winter in Russia. He'd been traveling for several months on the underground circuit without encountering a single English-speaking person. It was the dead of winter and my father traveled in deep snow, mostly by horsedrawn sled, with no one but a guide and a Latvian interpreter. Going from one little secret church to another scattered across the Russian hinterland, my father's small band of outlaws joined up with a group of gospel singers from the United States, who were making the same underground rounds. It had been so long since Dad had heard any native English spoken, he was transported with delight. What is more, they spoke with Southern accents. Daddy said, "Bob, it was so wonderful seeing people from home."

The only trouble was that the singers were all black. It was the first time in his life, Dad told me, that he spent whole days and nights with black people. "We preached together and sang, we ate together in the homes of the poor people, many times using our fingers as there were few utensils, reaching into the common pot of potatoes with small pieces of salt-meat, and maybe some cabbage. We even slept together, either in one big bed or huddled together on the floor for warmth beneath some thin and ancient blankets. We talked about home and food and a warm fire and the most disconcerting thing kept happening. I forgot that they were black!"

Dad said the first time it happened he thought he was having a nervous breakdown, like he woke up suddenly and didn't know where he was or even who he was. "It wasn't their fault; they weren't trying to make me forget my place, I was sure of that. But that pesky thing started happening more often. It got to where there were large parts of the days when I would forget my new friends and comrades were black. And they didn't treat me like a 'white man.' Of course they had no need to, here in Europe. It finally got to bothering me so much I just determined to make it light on myself and forget about color while I was here and just go back to the old way when I got back home. But, you know, things never were the same after living with my friends and not thinking about what color we were," he said. "It certainly ruined me as a Klansman, that's for sure.

JAMES'S JOYOUS HOMECOMING TO Alabama in the mid-1930s was unmarred by the revelations about race from his trip abroad. The born-again street preacher was prepared to come out from under the hood, but first he had to find the woman who had occupied many of his daydreams when he'd been stranded in Russia in the dead of winter for months on end. Ruby Rachael, the beautiful oldest daughter of the Reverend J. J. Hardy, had promised back at Bob Jones that she'd wait for him to get back from Europe. Dr. Bob Jones performed the wedding ceremony for Ruby Hardy and James Abraham Zellner in Fort Deposit, Alabama, in the middle of the Great Depression, on December 31, 1935.

After the wedding, Mom and Dad served their first charge in a mission church in Mobile, Alabama, working with the homeless and the seamen on the waterfront. To get closer to Granddaddy and Grandma Hardy, they moved to Dixie, Alabama, where their firstborn entered the world as James (after Dad) Hubert (after Mom's brother). I was born next on April 5, 1939, after they had moved to the Jay, Florida, charge. Then in quick succession Richard Douglas was born in Century, Florida; David Otis in Newton, Alabama; and the baby, Malcolm Cary, in Slocomb, Alabama.

Each time I asked Dad why our family had different attitudes than most Southerners, he always came back to that experience in Russia when being struck blind to color ruined him as a Klansman. Being an intelligent man and a real believer in the gospel of Jesus, Dad was forced to wrestle with the deep beliefs from his childhood. In the final analysis he could not reconcile his belief in white supremacy with the high ideals of his country, the teachings of his church and Bible, his innate intelligence, and, now, his own experience in Europe.

I don't think Mother had ever been as enthusiastic about the KKK as Daddy. Maybe Mom was only a lukewarm racist because having a bastard for a grandfather had bent her in a more liberal direction. When Dad finally broke with his Klan brothers in the mid-1940s, Mom happily cut up his Klan robes and made white shirts for us boys to wear to Sunday school. Mom's dad, Reverend J. J. Hardy, was one of the last of the old horseback circuit riders in the Alabama-West Florida Conference of the Methodist Church. He had already alienated the Klan when he had refused their "love offering" at one of his small country churches. The KKK—in full regalia—had marched unannounced down the center aisle of the church to hand Granddaddy an envelope full of money. Eyeing their dirty boots and the ridiculous hoods covering their faces, the right Reverend Hardy made a simple but truthful statement, "My church no longer accepts donations from unidentified persons." Grandfather, who could look awfully stern, handed back the money. The Klan did not come back.

She also must have known, growing up in Blountstown, that it was named in honor of John Blount, chief of the Apalachicola Creek Indians. She may not have known of their forceful removal in April 1834, when Chief Blount led them away from their ancestral home in Florida to Mabank, Texas, the present site of their tribal council house. History like this was hidden from most white Southerners in school.

From the time I was born in Jay, Florida, until we moved to Loxley, Alabama, in 1947, we lived in an area that relied on oysters from Apalachicola Bay. Daddy used to smack his lips reaching for a frosty Apalachicola oyster on the half shell. "These are the best raw oysters on earth—this is the life!" he'd exclaim. As an adult I wondered if Daddy ever thought how much the Southeastern Indians who had been removed to the west missed those great oysters and clams, once the very basis of their diet and money.

WE MOVED EVERY FOUR YEARS to a new church assignment, and memories of the various towns remain so clear. I was not quite two when we moved to Newton, Alabama, at the edge of Fort Rucker. The base boomed during the war, and every available room was taken up by soldiers flooding in from all over the country. We always had a smartly dressed officer living in the parsonage, and I remember Dad's cardinal rules—no women and absolutely no drinking in the officer's quarters. Two "family stories" cling to my little boy's mind. One time, Daddy ordered a drunken soldier out of the house, and he marched solemnly off the porch into Mom's favorite rose bush. Another officer, posted overseas, left the "apartment" in seemingly spotless condition, but when Mom opened the closet door, empty Four Roses bottles cascaded to the floor. The officer, after carefully stacking the bottles from floor to ceiling, had tacked a friendly note to the door, "Thanks for the good times. I'm off to fight the Hun. Love, Col. Tricky."

In 1945, we moved to Slocomb, Alabama, a little town just east of Dothan, where Dad served the Slocomb Methodist Church as well as eight country churches. Zion Hill, Pinkard, Malvern, Hurricane, Headland, Mars Hill, and Oak Grove remain branded in my memory, redolent of a rural existence known today mostly through film and literature. They evoke a delicious nostalgia of planks on sawhorses lined up under the trees along the cemetery fence, loaded with country food—sliced fresh tomatoes from the garden, not the store, slightly wilted in the afternoon heat, blue bowls of green and yellow butterbeans next to fried okra and fried green tomatoes, mounds of fragrant fried chicken—yard chickens with real meat on them, done according to grandma's recipe—anyone's grandma. One lady invariably made a platter of sandwiches with sliced white bread, a great treat because it was store-bought. I loved tomato and mayonnaise on white bread, or sliced pineapple or sliced banana made the same way.

Back to the oysters. Slocomb was famous for Brink Barnes's salty winter oysters, and when older brother Jim and I were little we'd accompany Dad there. The ancient mahogany bar at the oyster house, where the shucking went on right in front of us, occupied half of the Gulf filling station, smack in the middle of town, on Highway 52 between Hartford and Dothan. Enterprise, just up the road in Coffee County, was known for a giant bronze boll weevil on a pedestal in the middle of town square, erected in recognition that the weevil had forced cotton farmers to plant corn, peanuts, and that new "Jap" bean, the soy. Dothan, meanwhile, was noted for peanuts.

At Barnes's oyster house, Daddy would pay ten cents a dozen, and he always reminded us that when he first starting eating oysters there, they were a nickel a dozen. Today, oysters cost a dollar or two apiece. The bill was figured by Brink counting the half-shells left in front of us. The top half of each shell had already gone in the waste barrel, so each half-shell represented one oyster. When Barnes opened the fresh, dripping oysters, he'd flip the top shell into the shell tub, cut the muscle with a flick of his oyster knife and place the plump morsel in front of us, nestled in its own dish. It was not uncommon for Daddy and us two little ones to eat twelve or fourteen dozen of the briny bi-valves, which Brink would "round down" to ten dozen—"Pay up, Rev., one dollar."

The whole time we were growing up, Mom taught school to supplement Dad's meager minister's pay. Truth be told, she probably earned as much or more than he did. Mom was a gifted country cook; she had to be good in the kitchen to feed seven hungry mouths on those small salaries. Dad always grew a garden, and he often experimented with new seeds. We were introduced to fennel as a vegetable, which never caught on so well, and once he planted an exotic type of vine spinach that grew to fifty-two feet long. The more you picked the leaves, the more the vine grew. We couldn't eat or can everything Dad grew, so when we lived in Loxley he made a deal with our school lunchroom to supply produce in exchange for free lunch for the Zellner kids. Jim and I would trudge the six blocks to school each morning pulling our red wagons full of collards, turnips, okra, tomatoes, lettuce, and onions. One day we brought artichokes and fresh fennel which nobody knew what to do with.

Mom loved flowers and cultivated them as often as possible. When I finished hoeing and weeding the vegetable garden, I often helped Mom in her little flower beds. She taught me the names and the nature of each one—snap dragons, monkey lilies, pansies, daises, peonies.

I almost always had a pig to fatten, and Dad made wonderful barbecue and often cooked strange and wonderful things. We always kept a cow for milk, butter, and cheese, which Jim, my older brother, and I milked every morning and night. Mother canned a lot, and the church would give the preacher's family a "pounding" (food packages). We always had huge bowls of vegetables, cottage cheese made by Mom, ham from Uncle Harvey's smokehouse, along with rabbits from the pens and chickens from the yard. Daddy liked to hunt and fish and cooked us squirrel, quail, wild ducks, and venison when he could get it. We boys learned to fish and hunt and we brought game to Mom's kitchen as often as possible.

Dad and Mom had invented Zellnerinies, toasted home-baked bread covered with chopped lettuce and scallions from the garden. This was topped with hot soft scrambled eggs fresh from the nest, and finally crowned with Mom's famous bubbling hot white sauce flecked with black pepper and specks of butter from our own cow and Mom's churn. The hot eggs and white gravy wilted the onions and lettuce. Dad said it reminded him of food he had eaten in Russia and Poland.

Despite this bucolic life, our stint in Slocomb was a rough time for me. I couldn't seem to do right no matter hard I tried. One time I released the captive crows of an important parishioner. The man lived way out in the country, where he had a large cage in his back yard. I stood by full of amazement as the church member explained to Dad how he had trapped the crows and split their tongues. He was teaching them how to talk. There must have been a dozen or more of the huge black birds, and they made a lot of noise when the farmer came close to their cage. I couldn't make out any words they were saying, but they didn't seem very happy to me. Their owner, on the way into the house for Sunday dinner with the preacher's family, bragged that the flock was so tame by now that they would not leave even if he left the cage open. I decided to see if he was telling the truth so I hung back and darted toward the cage when Daddy and the man disappeared into the dogtrot of the house.

I stood on a box and quietly opened the cage door. The birds began to squawk loudly but they would not go near the open door. Now I was afraid the farmer would come back so I tried to hush the crows or shoo them away by beating on the back of the cage. Suddenly, they all flew out of the cage and perched on the center ridge of the old farm house and started yelling like someone was beating them to death. I ran up and down in the cleanly swept, grassless backyard flapping my arms and yelling for them to leave before the grown-ups came back. The crows wouldn't leave and they wouldn't shut up. I sat down in the sand frustrated at the stupidity of a bunch of birds being given their freedom and not having the sense to leave. Out of nowhere, Daddy suddenly picked me up by the collar and promised me, through clenched teeth, a whipping when we got home. That was always the worst kind, the kind you had to wait for. I always preferred punishment on the spot. Back home in the woodshed Dad give me a whipping. It may have been my imagination but it seemed that any misbehavior involving parishioners always resulted in the harshest punishment.

I started school in Slocomb in 1945, at six years old, and I failed the first grade. That really put the hurt on me—whoever heard of failing the first grade? My teacher and Mom were concerned that it might be bad for me but they agreed that it might be worse on me in the second and third grades if I still could not read. So I repeated the first grade in 1946, and in June 1947, we moved to Loxley where I went to second and third grades.

THEN THE SUMMER OF 1949, when I was ten, everything changed. In those days few people understood dyslexia, and in my early grades, my teachers must have thought I was retarded. Every assignment I handed in came back with a huge zero on it for everybody to see. I had the misfortune to follow two grades behind my brother. Jim was a gifted student and my teachers tormented me with questions of why I couldn't be more like him.

Luckily I lived in a family full of school teachers. Mom was a teacher as was her sister Lavada Pope, the one we called Aunt Peg. Mom's sister Rosetta Hardy was also a lifelong school teacher in Roanoke, Alabama. Aunt Rose was so dedicated to teaching that she never married. My mother didn't know exactly what was wrong with me, but she knew I was not stupid. She and her sister Peg consulted on why I couldn't learn and Peg suggested that I go to summer school at Barton Academy in Mobile. She had heard that they were experimenting with teaching methods to aid the learning disabled (if that was a phrase then). Most classroom teachers had not the mistiest idea about learning disabilities. If you got zeros, then you were terminally lazy or an imbecile. It did not occur to me, or to my teachers, for that matter, that in order to make consistent zeroes the problem might be that I did not even understand the instructions. I blanked on every task. If I had no idea where or how to begin, then I was doomed.

So that summer of 1949, I lived in Mobile with Aunt Peg and Uncle Doug, while my family lived in Loxley, Alabama. Going to live with Aunt Peg and Uncle Doug was a life-changing experience for me in a number of ways. I had an early taste of city life and I learned to read well enough to skip a grade and catch up with my group in school, going that fall from the third grade in Loxley to the fifth.

Mobile and the fancy house on Old Government Street were a millions miles from Mom and Dad, Jim, Douglas, and baby David, back in the dusty little Alabama crossroads of Loxley. It was a novel experience to walk along the street in Mobile and not know anyone. In all the country towns we had lived in, you couldn't do anything bad and get away with it. If you got into a fight, everybody knew about it. One time I went in a lady's yard and picked some flowers for Mom who was sick in bed. I had to go back and apologize and the lady said, "I know your mom is sick so take some more, I'll help you pick them."

My new home for the summer in Mobile was all hustle and bustle, compared to Loxley, where the biggest excitement was the occasional escaped criminal from the chain-gang shed just west of town, or the biggest potato or cucumber weighed-in down at the grading shed. The clean, neat look of the Mobile house and yard, and having the undivided attention of my uncle and aunt, combined with their upscale way of living, made me feel slightly ashamed of our existence back home. The moment I was aware of this feeling, I was ashamed of being ashamed.

Loxley was agriculture and Mobile was post-war boom. To reach Mobile from Baldwin County and Loxley we had to drive through the Bankhead Tunnel, one of the Seven Wonders of the World, we children thought. Just before the tunnel we crossed Mobile Bay and just before that we drove through Malbis, Alabama, a Greek settlement. Daddy took us to the restaurant there sometimes because he had developed a taste for exotic foods when he was in Europe. The salad was divine with black olives and crumbly cheese and robust with vinegar and little green onions. I lusted after the rice wrapped in grape leaves and the thin pastry layered with honey and walnuts.

All food paled, however, in the presence of my first steak. It was a small, tender, bacon-wrapped morsel of filet mignon grilled by Aunt Peg. Accustomed to making them each week for herself and Uncle Doug, she now added another for me. I simply could not believe that anyone could taste something this delicious without jumping up and down. It was red in the center and had blood running out of it! The Douglas Popes of Old Government Street, Mobile, Alabama, though, ate their steaks with one hand in their laps like it was the most natural thing in the world.

I loved the new experience of rare steak, but sometimes I did miss Mom's mounds of fresh vegetables. Aunt Peg cooked more like Yankees when she put three undercooked green beans and a spoonful of mashed potatoes next to the filet mignon. Well, one can't have everything in life, and right then life was good.

School was fun for the first time in my life. At Barton Academy, I learned to read by seeing a picture and the word next to it. I think the theory was to recognize whole words rather than break them into parts. My visual and auditory memory is strong and I can still see in my mind's eye a picture of a "pegion" and the word "bird." I guess that's why I can't spell pigeon. I am still a horrible speller. Thank you, Jesus, for spell check!

As late as eighth grade I remember a teacher making me write the word "family" one hundred times so I would stop spelling it "fambly." Part of the problem, I now realize, is that the Southern English of the street is far different from the King's.

Once I learned to read, I couldn't get enough of it, but never to the extent of older brother Jim who had long since been dubbed a bookworm. "Always got his head in a book," the old country people would say of Brother. "That boy will never amount to anything."

I loved Jack London, never knowing he was a lefty. His *White Fang* and *The Call of the Wild* and Bret Harte's *The Luck of Roaring Camp* gave me untold hours of pleasure. And I never knew that Samuel Clemens was another iconoclast subverting unsuspecting boys and girls with his stories about Tom Sawyer, Huckleberry Finn, and the racially subversive Pudd'nhead Wilson, and his book *A Connecticut Yankee at King Arthur's Court*. Aunt Peg took me to the library and introduced me to *Moby Dick, Little Women, Rebecca of Sunnybrook Farm, Robinson Crusoe*, and *The Grapes of Wrath, The Old Man and the Sea,* and other classics. I had no idea I was beginning my education, I was just having fun reading.

Each summer afternoon I got off the city bus and walked home along Government Street with its centuries-old live oak trees bowing low with necklaces of Spanish moss, turning slowly onto Old Government, past the park at the fork on down to Aunt Peg's house on the right. I did not realize at the time that I was becoming the little boy that she never had. I wondered why she and Uncle Doug did not have little children but I was happy that she met me after school with cookies or a small sandwich before I did my homework. That was a chore I had to complete before going out to play with the neighbor kids.

At home we never went to summer school and we could do our homework after it got dark. Another difference was the fastidious way Aunt and Uncle kept the house and the yard. There also was not a single thing to eat in Aunt Peg's garden. Dad's victory garden at home was a survival necessity for our family while the Popes' garden was for beauty alone.

During that summer of school in Mobile, Uncle Doug and Aunt Peg drove me over to Loxley every Friday afternoon. Arriving with them in their new Nash to a hectic weekend of washing clothes and canning confirmed the relative chaos of home. The backbreaking work Mom performed as a matter of routine became painfully visible as she and we boys did the washing on the back porch in an old wringer machine.

Dad's and Mom's work clothes for church and school and the mountains of dirty boys' clothing were beaten by the agitator, rinsed twice, and wrung out a final time into the wash tub to be hung out to dry on clotheslines— people in those days were using solar energy before anyone had ever heard the term. Sheets alone from four or five beds each week filled several machine loads. Mom ironed most of this mountain until she taught Jim and me how to iron.

Then there were beds to make, floors to sweep, and restaurant-sized batches of dishes to wash, dry, and put away. Jim and I milked Janie the cow morning and evening and the rabbits and chickens had to be fed. Doug and later David and Malcolm did the feeding.

The events of the day seemed to happen in Loxley by chance and very slowly, but the schedule in Mobile was exactly the same every day. Up at the crack of dawn, the fragance of night-blooming jasmine still drifting through the house, and breakfast at exactly the same time. Uncle Doug and I taking turns in the shower (at home we had never, ever had a shower), and then stuffing ourselves into our clothes. We had a contest of who could dress first. Uncle said I had an unfair advantage because, "My Peg has fitted you out in nothing but short pants and that silly jacket that says 'Barton Academy'. Pretty fancy for a country boy like you, don't you think?"

"Yes," I hollered back to my favorite uncle, "but you got out of the shower first and had a head start."

"Yeah, Bobby, but I got to put on a whole suit, with shirt tie and all."

Fleeting memories of living in Mobile that first time include the smell of diesel as the huge buses pulled off after letting me out at Barton or back home in the afternoon. It reminded me of the kerosene scent of Mom's kitchen stove back in Slocomb. At other times Mobile simply stank from the International Paper and Scott Paper Company paper mills situated just north of town. The smell was hard to get used to but native Mobilians seemed never to notice it. Much later, when voters became more environmentally conscious, they asked Governor George Wallace to do something about it. Rather than require the mills to invest in anti-pollution equipment, George said, "What do you want me to do? That's just the smell of money."

The odor could be so powerful it sometimes made people do funny things. Mother told a story that became part of our family lore. When she first moved to Mobile to live with Daddy, they had been married only a few days. She joined Dad in his ministry to the seamen and the homeless—"tramps," we called them—along the wharfs and the dives of the old Mobile waterfront.

The Salvation Army Commander's wife, Evelyn, took Mom under her wing, trying to prepare her for that life. A country girl with a strict upbringing, Mom knew that the cloistered confines of Bob Jones College had hardly prepared her for life in a rowdy port city. One day Mom and Evelyn were walking arm-in-arm past Bienville Square with its moss-covered oaks and flowing fountain when Mother was struck by an overpowering stench. She reflexively moved away from her new best friend who laughed, "That's all right, Ruby, it's just the paper mill. The wind must have changed. It ain't me babe."

WITH A MOVE EVERY three or four years, it was not easy being the new kid in town with four brothers and a school teacher mom and a preacher daddy. Jim and I had to fight our way into every little town. The South has a culture of violence—the honor code. It is much like that of our national ethic. It just seemed Southern boys had to fight a lot, but I never knew when my fighting would "get Daddy in trouble" with the powers in the church. My older brother Jim was as slim as a dragon fly and more refined than most boys his age. He read a lot and listened to music. Jim liked lure casting, for instance, while most south Alabama fishermen used stink bait for catfish or plain old worms for bream and bass. Jim was pretty fast with his fists. We were best friends and we watched each other's back when we had to fight. When I started first grade at Slocomb in 1945, it seemed like I had to fight every morning and afternoon on the way to and from school. Jim was bigger and more experienced and he told me that we would have to fight for the rest of our lives, at least for the first few weeks in each new town. He said new guys in town didn't have to be good at fighting, they just had to be willing. "I'm willing," I said, "but I don't like to do it because it always makes me cry. If it's so natural to have to fight why do I always cry?"

My brother told me that he didn't know—that was just the way it was. He said it was better not to cry but the main thing was to put up a good fight. After you fight someone, then they know you have heart. You may not have to fight them again; you can become good friends and help each other in fights with other boys. I told Jim that he and I were good friends, and that I appreciated it when he helped me fight. Jim said he didn't help me fight—that he just told the other boys that if more than one at a time got on me, they would have to deal with him.

When Brother and I fought our way into Loxley, Alabama, he gave me pointers aimed at improving my fighting style. "You're good," he told me, "and you'll soon be better than me. I can barely handle you now. You are getting bigger, and I can tell you'll be heavier than me, and stronger."

That was quite an admission for an older brother, and I remembered it some years later when Jim went out for football at W. S. Neal High School in East Brewton. He was desperate to play ball and spent several years sitting on the bench in blue and gold waiting for a chance to get into the game. It was ironic because the coach had tried to convince me to try out. My shrewd mother, however, had other ideas. She bought a brand new gold-plated trombone with the understanding that because it was so expensive and such a sacrifice for the family, I would have to promise to stay in the band. I could march on the field at half time but not play football where I could get seriously hurt. Maybe she was right, but when I saw Burns Blackwell, the halfback, bull his way up the field tossing defensive backs out of the way like they were dried corn stalks, ripping off fifteen yards at a time, I thought to myself, "I could do that." But a promise is a promise.

To fight or not to fight became an obsession when my father was appointed by the Bishop to serve the church in Daphne, Alabama. We moved from Loxley in June and I started the fifth grade that fall in Daphne. Jim was a sixth-grader and our little brother Doug was in the first grade. Mother was the first-grade teacher.

Before school started, I told Jim that I didn't plan to fight at the new school. "I just cry," I explained again, "and it doesn't make sense to fight if all I'm going do is cry. They'll just have to accept me the way I am. I'll tell them I don't believe in fighting and it's not because I'm chicken."

"I don't know, little brother, that doesn't sound like a real good plan to me. I don't think they'll understand; you won't get away with it. They'll just think you are a coward and they'll make your life miserable until you show them you got heart."

"I got heart, Jim, you know I got heart."

"I know you're not scared," Jim said. "The problem is, those bullies don't know that. I suggest you think about this some more."

I suggested that maybe there weren't any bullies in Daphne but my big brother didn't agree. "There's bullies in every town," he said, "and they'll all have a try at you. The more you don't fight, the more bullies there'll be. Shoot, even the scared ones'll start picking on you."

My stomach was tying in a knot and I was dreading the start of school. There has to be a better way, I thought. Brother said maybe there was and maybe I'd find it, but he doubted it. For what seemed like weeks after school started I was brutalized before school, after school, and at recess. I didn't tell anyone and my brother looked on in agony for me. Finally, Mother asked if anything was going on at school that she should know about. She noted that four out of five mornings I had a stomachache and begged to stay home. My eyes started squirting tears while I begged her not to make me go to school, but I didn't intend to tell her what was happening. This didn't do any good because she had seen for some time that I was black and blue. She said she'd been waiting for me to say something to her. "Is someone bothering you at school?"

"Someone?" I blurted. "They're all beating me up. Every day at recess."

"Aren't your teachers doing something?" she asked.

I told Mom that I had made up my mind not to fight and I told her the reasons why. Even before she could answer, I started my arguments, pointing out that she and Dad had always told us not to get into fights. As preachers' kids we have to set a good example for others, I reminded her.

Mother was outraged. She said I should have told her about this a long time ago. She'd take it up with the principal and have a stop put to this misbehavior instantly. Now I was truly terrified. If she did that, I'd never be able to hold my head up in the school. Struggling to control my rising panic, I pleaded with Mother not to talk to the principal. "If you don't want me to go to the principal," she said, "then you're just going to have to fight those boys."

That was a proposition I could understand. Out went my nascent non-violence. When Mother started with the pep talk, however, about not having to win the fight but just proving you would fight, I decided to try again to convince her. I informed her that I had fought plenty of times—that Jim and I always fought our way into every new town but now I had decided not to fight. I assured her that Jim supported me in my decision, that it was harder on him to see me punished every day than it was for me to actually be punished. Mother obviously didn't understand that I had made a decision. She said she would get Daddy to give me fighting lessons.

That night when Dad came home from his pastoring rounds, he agreed to give me some lessons. He said the most important thing in fighting was to be sure when the fight started to hit the other person as hard as possible on the nose. That method assured, he said, that even if the person went on to beat you up, at least you have done damage to them and they don't get off scot-free. They may wind up beating you, he said, but they paid a price. But most of the time, if you managed to get in a good sock to the nose, Dad assured me, you can go on and clean their plow. Cleaning plow was always big in my family. Daddy ended my fighting lesson with the story of the chairman of the official board. Once during a heated session of the board of his church stewards, a right-wing, very important deacon had threatened to throw my father "out that window, preacher or not."

My father's response was the stuff of family legend. "Deacon so and so, you may indeed throw me out that window, but if you manage to do it, you'll sure enough know you've been in a fight, Chairman of the Board or not."

It is telling that my father's fighting lesson did not demonstrate how to stand or how to hold one's hands or even to make a fist. Dad apparently believed that technique would take care of itself if one's attitude was correct. First things first, and of course Dad was a minister and therefore much better at telling than showing.

So, Dad on one side and Mother on the other, Jim looking on, little brothers lurking outside the door, they all assured me that I would have to fight, principles or not, otherwise my life would remain miserable. I told them once again that I always cried when I had to fight and I didn't see why it was necessary. "Well, it is necessary," Dad said, "so get on with it, Bobby. Jim you watch him tomorrow and if more than one gets on him at a time, then you get in there, too."

My brother looked hurt that Dad would think it necessary to tell him that. Later when we got to bed, Jim told me he was looking forward to tomorrow. I was not at all looking forward to tomorrow.

The next morning I timed my arrival to coincide with the bell so I got to my room without incident. The shoot-out at the O.K. corral would have to wait till morning recess at ten o'clock. At recess I walked onto the long front porch of the grammar school. By that time I had forgotten that I had sneaked into school just before the bell. I strolled along in the middle of a Gary Cooper daydream. Word had gotten out that Bobby was a changed man . . . boy, and not to mess with him. To do so would mean instant death. Just then one of the bigger boys grabbed me from behind. The element of surprise, however, shifted to my side because heretofore I had never resisted. They had gotten used to treating me like a rag doll. I caught a glimpse of my big brother just as I made a mighty heave, throwing the boy who had me around the neck past me on the left. As the startled bully hurtled by me, I swung at his nose with my right fist. Missing his nose, my fist bounced off his cheek and smashed into the post holding up the porch. I looked at my knuckles and saw white bone but very little blood. That made me mad so I advanced on the still-stricken boy with both fists landing solid blows. I must have hit him twelve times in half that many seconds.

The kid managed to gasp, "Somebody take him for a while."

My brother stepped over close to me and shouted, "One at a time, please, otherwise you'll have to deal with me, too." Then Jim added, somewhat ir-relevantly, but I thought with a touch of pride, "He's my brother."

I had time to be thankful he hadn't said "little brother," before another big boy stepped in front of me. I felt like a bull, and Jim said later that I never stopped walking forward and I never stopped swinging. As each boy would tire, another took his place until everybody who felt froggy had jumped. When there was nobody else in front of me, I figured that I had at least demonstrated that I was willing to fight—as silly as it was, and as pointless. So I had a good cry and Jim walked with me back to my class-room. Recess was over.

2

BISCUIT MAN

I did my real growing up in East Brewton, Alabama, a small town across the creek from Brewton, once called America's richest little town. We moved there in 1955, when Dad was finished with his ministry serving the church in Daphne.

People in East Brewton, where we lived, didn't own much. I know we didn't. The sister towns were separated by Murder Creek. In the 1800s, legend and history say that a group of settlers traveling west—and supposedly carrying a lot of money, were ambushed, robbed, and murdered on the banks of this creek by three bandits, two white men and an Indian. The solid citizens of Brewton let you know in no uncertain terms and as often as possible that if you lived in East Brewton, you lived on "the wrong side of Murder Creek." I found that this didn't bother most people in East Brewton; it had always been that way. Mother being a school teacher, and Dad a minister, I was in contact with people on the "right side" of Murder Creek, but I quickly learned where my place was. It struck me more forcefully, no doubt, because I had come from outside. My family, as explained, was a bit unusual anyway, and we would, after all, be moving on in another three or four years. Also, we may have been on the wrong side of the Creek, but we were closer to the coast and our delicious oysters.

In the meantime, I began to learn consciously about race and class. I started to work for "King Tut" Edwards who ran a little country store. He hired me to wait on customers, clean the store, and deliver groceries to our "charge" customers. One day, after an old black couple left the store, Mr. Edwards said to me with a worried look, "You can't do that, Bob." I asked what I had done wrong and was told that I had said "Yes, sir" and "Yes, ma'am" to the old people who had just left and not to do that if there were white people in the store at the same time. I was puzzled, and told my boss that my daddy and mother had taught me to be courteous, especially to old people.

"Well, that's right," said Tut with a pained expression, "and I'm sorry to have to teach you this, but you can get in trouble saying yes sir and no sir to a colored person, and I can get in trouble, too. They all know I'm a Unitarian, so I'm in enough trouble already."

King Tut got his name when he worked in the brick yard in Brewton, and he was always covered in red brick dust. This was around the time that King Tut's dusty remains were dug from the tomb in Egypt. He taught me about the state of Alabama being run by the "Big Mules" for the benefit of the rich people. He told me that Huey P. Long was the greatest politician of all time and that he would soon unite all the poor people, including the colored, to kick out the Morgans, Vanderbilts, Rockefellers, and the Tennessee Coal and Iron Company, which owned most of the state. Tut repeated that Brewton was the richest little town in America and East Brewton was the poorest.

Then he told me about the bloodlines and how the rich families— the Bloedels, McGowins, Millers and MacMillans had intermarried for generations so that they could own everything in sight—the T. R. Miller Company, a huge lumber outfit, and the new Bloedel and MacMillan paper mill. Most of the timber land was owned by them along with TCI (which later became United States Steel). The Robbins and McGowins and Hainjes owned the department stores and the Luttrells owned the biggest hardware store in south Alabama and with the L&N railroad here, "they shipped all over the state."

I asked Tut what he meant by "Big Mules" and he said it was like the way big mules, being taller and stronger, ate the hay off the wagons being pulled by the little mules. He said the image came from former Alabama Governor Bibb Graves, a Montgomery Kluxer. Then I was even more confused and told Tut I thought the Klan were bad people. He told me, "They are, but politics makes strange friends sometimes. It will take some time before you understand any of this, Bobby. I'm not sure I understand it myself." The best I could make out, at my young age, was that populism was good and the idea of poor whites and blacks helping one another was good, but difficult and unlikely to happen—that the rich guys liked to keep poor white and black people alienated. Where the Klan fit in, I was not at all sure. I knew that my daddy had left them and that our family was happy about it. The fact that I was even thinking of this, at age fourteen, was a testament to the passions and teaching ability of my improbable mentor, the Unitarian King Tut Edwards.

WHEN I WAS IN HIGH SCHOOL, my Dad was moved from the East Brewton Methodist Church to the Broad Street Methodist Church in Mobile, where I had lived for that summer with Aunt Peg and Uncle Doug. I know that Daddy was happy about the move and Mom was glad to be close to "The Seven Z's," our little cabin in the woods across the bay from Mobile. Daddy called our little homemade house the "Seven Z's" because there were seven of us Zellners.

If East Brewton had set me on a path of discovery concerning race and class, our sojourn in Mobile proved pivotal in leading me toward the emerging civil rights movement. It also seemed that the pace of life suddenly picked up. My new high school was so big that it had sororities and fraternities. I pledged the first fraternity that asked me. Mercifully, I have forgotten its name. One of my new friends was Tommy Adkins, "Mr. Everything" at Murphy High, Mobile's only public high school—for whites. Tommy's dad owned United Fruit Company and many of his ships made port calls at the Mobile docks.

I guess it was ironic that the Klan would contact me at the same time I am hanging out with the offspring of the local ruling class, but that is what happened.

All the high school boys who could afford it were getting souped-up jalopies and killing each other drag racing and playing chicken, or going at top speed over thrill hill up on Wolf Ridge. The point was to make all four wheels leave the ground at the same time. Some cars ended up upside down in the kudzu or wrapped around a loblolly pine.

The mayhem caused the city fathers to institute a nightly 9 P.M. curfew applying to everyone under eighteen. When I had just turned eighteen, Daddy had helped me buy a canary yellow Dodge convertible, sporting a raccoon tail and a shrill wolf whistle. Daddy was a Chrysler man his whole life. He made me promise not to use the whistle, explaining that the sound was produced by cold air hitting the hot motor block when the string was pulled. "You can bust your block like that and it would cost more to fix than this thing is worth," he warned.

Soon after the curfew was imposed and I got the car, I was hanging out at Johnny's Drive-In eating a burger and talking to girls. Suddenly a bright light hit the girls hanging on my door and they parted to reveal a TV cameraman and someone holding a microphone. There were giggles and gasps as the reporter stuck his mike in my face and started firing questions about the curfew. Television was so new that I had seen my first telecast just two years before and we had gotten our first set just the last Christmas, a gift to Mom and Dad from the church.

I was flattered to be questioned about the curfew and it happened so unexpectedly that I did not have time to be nervous.

"What's your name young man?"

"Zellner."

"What school and what grade?"

"Murphy, Senior."

"Is it a good idea to have a curfew for young people in Mobile?"

"No, I don't think it's a good idea."

"Why?"

"It seems to be arbitrary—what if someone is seventeen and a half? Do they still have to be home by nine?"

"Any other reasons you oppose the curfew, Mr. Zellner?"

"Yes. If sixteen is old enough for a license and some boys are able to get in the Navy at seventeen, why do they have to be in by 9 P.M.?"

I figured later that the TV reporter had picked me because of my yellow convertible and not because I looked particularly intelligent. But that may have been one way I got on the KKK's screen.

Anyway, the bad guys picked me up one night to go for a ride with them. Ralph and Clyde, a couple of my fraternity brothers, were in the car, so I was not overly concerned. They said they wanted to show me their friend's car, a green 1955 Pontiac which they assured me was fast and powerful. Both the boys were also in Demolay with me, the junior version of the Masons—

Daddy was a 33rd degree Mason and Mom was active in the Eastern Star.

The two older guys in the front seat took turns talking to me. The driver said he thought I had "leadership" potential. I asked why he had that opinion and he said, "We have our sources. We've been hearing about you." The other one hinted that I "might better join them."

"Join who?" I asked somewhat belligerently.

"But first," he said, "you have to pass the test."

"What test?" I asked, not feeling very well.

"Don't ask so many questions."

One of the boys in the back with me was putting together something that looked like a long fishing rod, fitting it piece by piece.

"Here comes one," the driver yelled. "Get ready and really let him have it!"

Before I knew what was happening, my "friend" Ralph hove the rod out the back window just as the car swerved to the left side of the dark road. We were in Prichard, a mostly black town on the outskirts of Mobile.

The protruding rod struck something in the darkness with a stomach-churning thud. Inside the speeding car we lurched to the left as the driver swung the big Pontiac back to the right, throwing up a hail of gravel. My "friend" held the pole tight, I realized, in order to deliver the maximum blow to the midriff of an old black man walking in the opposite direction. I barely glimpsed his startled face as we hurtled by.

The glee was instant and sickening, as if the guys in the car had experienced a sudden release of almost sexual tension.

"I'll look for another one," the driver sang out. "Get that stick to Bobby and let's see if he's any good."

Clyde hollered, "Bob, quick, change places with me." I was shunted to the right side of the back seat as Ralph tried to shove the disjointed rod at me. "Put this back together and whack one on that side." I clasped my hands in front of my chest and said, "No, sir, that's not for me, you moron."

"You got to," Ralph hissed, leaning past Clyde in the middle.

"I ain't got to do crap."

"You most certainly do," Clyde said into my ear. "These fools don't play. They might kill all three of us."

I was really weary by now and not willing to play their game anymore.

"What do you mean *us*, man?" I asked loudly. "I am not one of you, whatever the hell you are. You can let my ass out now!"

"Y'all having any trouble back there?" It was the older man in the shotgun seat. I had already silently nicknamed him "Green Teeth." His tone was low and menacing, and he did not look around.

"No, it's all right," Ralph tried to explain. "He'll do something even if I have to kick his ass."

"Okay, look," I said, "I've got this biscuit that I saved from supper. If it will make you happy, Ralph, I will try to hit somebody with it."

Clyde chimed in, "Biscuit?"

"A biscuit," I said, showing them the small piece of bread I had saved to eat later. "That's the best I can do, but I will sacrifice my biscuit for the cause. If that won't satisfy you and your unknown friends up there, then I guess we'll all have to die."

With that I rolled the window down and tossed the scone in the direction of the next pedestrian walking toward us. A muffled whump seemed to give my tormentors some relief, so they delivered me back to the vicinity of my comfortable little convertible.

I often remember that night of testing—testing to see if I had a violent-enough nature to be good Klan material. If things had not been moving so fast, I might have acquitted myself more honorably. But I really make no excuse, because I failed on two counts—I washed out as a future Klansman because I was not mean enough, and I flunked as a decent person because I failed to stand up to the criminals in that car.

In spite of my somewhat cowardly response to the Klan overtures, I had disagreed with my peers on matters of race and segregation prior to that incident, and some of us tried to witness whenever we could. During my junior year, on February 3, 1956, Autherine Lucy enrolled as a graduate student at the University of Alabama, and the demons of race hate descended. That is when the nightmare began.

On the third day of classes, Autherine Lucy faced mobs of students, townspeople, and even groups of outsiders. There were students behind her saying, "Let's kill her! Let's kill her!" She needed a police escort to get to class and crowds chanted outside constantly. Lucy was suspended from the university with the board stating that it was for her own safety. The NAACP filed a contempt of court suit, but Lucy's expulsion took place anyway. In 1988, Lucy re-entered the University of Alabama to earn a master's degree in elementary education, and in 1992, both she and her daughter, Grazia, received degrees.

I am not sure exactly what made me follow Lucy's story so closely in 1956, but I remember being fascinated with what the "adults" would do to keep her out. Before the actual event, I was with a bunch of students who were standing and sitting around the red brick stoop leading up to the main building of Murphy High School—band members and football players and our after-school prayer group. I played second trombone in the marching band. We were discussing the ever-hot topic—the integration of the University of Alabama.

Someone hollered, "If Autherine just wants to get an education, she wouldn't be trying to go the university—she knows she can't. They'd close it before integrating. She knows she should go to one of her own schools and not try to destroy ours. It's a shame that nigger girl wants to destroy our state university."

When I said I thought she had a right to go to any tax-supported school in our state, Sam Culpepper, one of our star football players with a neck as wide as his head whispered to me, "Don't let anyone hear you say that."

"Why do you think she wants to explode the university?" came another question.

"Maybe she just wants to get an education," I said.

An angry rose color spread up Sammy Culpepper's thick neck to his screwed-up face. "Be quiet, because they will hurt you."

"Who is they?" I shot back. "Will you hurt me, Culpepper?"

"No, hell, Bob I won't hurt you. I know you are crazy, but they don't have the slightest idea how screwed up you are, and I'm telling you they will put the hurt on you. Let any of them hear you talking that mess, and I can promise you that I ain't going to help you when they get on your scrawny little ass." Culpepper, all 285 pounds of him, paused and took a huge breath. "Zellner, you know I am planning on playing pro ball, you idiot!"

It was kind of fun, the image of Big Sammy helping me in a fight with the Klan boys, but I pressed the point. "Culpepper, I know you are planning on going to Alabama to play college football, and I know how important it is to you, but you don't need to be so fearful. The University will still be in Tuscaloosa next year when you get ready to go."

"Fearful? You little shit, I ain't fearful of nothing on earth that moves."

"Yes you are," I pointed out. "You just advised me to keep quiet or get hurt."

"Well for your information, I just think it is my duty to protect you from your own stupidity if you believe in something as far out as integration. I'm telling you these old boys will whip you till your ass won't hold shucks. People just don't go around talking like that. I myself ain't got to worry, because I think segregation is just fine. But even if I didn't, I certainly wouldn't let people know." Sammy spun around and skulked off looking around to see if any of the in group had taken offense at him talking to the alien.

I called after him, "I'm not scared of anything either, Culpepper, I refuse to live that way."

Sammy and I had been going at it so intensely that others in the group weren't able to get a word in.

Jamie Cecil, my girlfriend and the leader of our little prayer cell, admonished me for being so argumentative with Sammy. "We'll never make converts beyond the six of us if you don't learn to be more diplomatic. You put people on the defensive."

Our "cell," as we called it, met after school once or twice each week at Dauphin Way Methodist Church, where Jamie and her best friend Glenda Johnson were members. Dauphin Way was high church. Their minister had a "Doctor" in front of his name and he had served the congregation for thirty-five years. My Aunt Peg and Uncle Douglas were members, and they were the richest people among our kinfolks. The Reverend Dr. Adkins liked to fly in Uncle Doug's Piper Cub and to fish with Uncle Doug on his cabin cruiser, *The Flour Peddler*. Until he shot himself with his own pistol, my Uncle Doug made a good living as a flour broker, servicing Gulf Coast bakers. We were never clear about the circumstances of the shooting but believed it was an accident while he was cleaning the gun.

Our prayer circle met sitting on the carpet in an upper room at the church and we liked to think of ourselves as special disciples of Jesus, hiding in the catacombs. Periodically we would sally forth and do battle with evil. I liked that part best and considered racism and segregation to be among the worst evils. My best friend Ray Powell, a frat and Demolay brother, and Gordon Tatum, a member of my dad's lowly working class Broad Street Methodist Church, were not as enthusiastic as me on the race question. Fastidious Gordon was embarrassed with Dad's slogan blazed on the church marquee—"The Working Man's Church, Rev. James A. Zellner, Pastor." Race was taboo and class was too. Most of us in the cell were Murphy High juniors.

By my senior year, 1956–57, our little prayer cell grew to a dozen or more regulars. I was brought up short one day when my French teacher congratulated me on being chosen to be a graduation speaker. I tended to think of myself as a struggling student because of the rough start I had in Slocomb, Alabama, with dyslexia, and not learning to read or spell until third grade.

I thought they had made a mistake. It turned out that the selection committee at Murphy had simply listed the top one percent of the fifteen hundred or so graduating seniors to be speakers. Since those amounted to over a dozen students they announced there would be a speaking contest to select the best four to share valedictory duties. Jamie said that I should enter the contest and try to land a spot as a speaker. "You need to represent the church youth."

I told her that I had no idea I was up for such an honor and besides, I always got sick to my stomach if I had to make a speech, *and,* I finished, "I actually think they've made a mistake in picking me."

She wagged her finger and lectured me about going toward the things you fear. I knew she was reading Ayn Rand, so I asked Jamie if Rand was the one who said, "If it doesn't kill you, it will make you stronger."

"No, genius, it was Nietzsche that said something like that."

"Not true," I kidded her; he was misquoted. What Friedrich actually said was, "That which doesn't kill you can really mess you up real bad."

Well, she talked me into entering and helped me write my speech. The whole cell got in on the project and Gordon, one of the smartest boys in school, came up with the idea that worked.

"The students are going to vote after hearing all of you 'stars,'" Gordon said. "The ones who make it through the first cut will be the ones the audience will remember. If it's alphabetical, Bob, you will be last and that will help. But what will clinch it is that the students will remember the speeches that are funny and not boring."

So, to make my speech funny, I decided to describe a typical day in the life of a Stone Age teenager. Predictably, instead of driving his jalopy to school, as we did, Clyde, my mythical teen, rode to school bareback on his pet pink polka dot dinosaur. With the image of fur-clad Clyde bouncing along to school atop Pinky, trying in vain to hold on to his bulking stone tablets, I had them. They started laughing and didn't stop. They laughed at parts I didn't even consider funny. I could do no wrong. I knew what it meant to be "in the zone!"

Needless to say, I won the first round going away. I don't remember anything else about the contest, but I wound up in the final four. I actually do remember graduation day and the speech I made, a real snoozer, to seven thousand bored-out-of-their-gourds friends and relatives, seated uncomfortably on bleachers at Ladd Stadium. Faculty geniuses had decided it would be exciting to give each of us a verse from the school song to write our speeches around. Mine was:

In days of old when Spaniards bold were sailing Mobile Bay
A dream was born one early morn. That dream's come true today.
Now colleges and high schools too, may have traditions old,
But none can boast the blah blah blah of Murphy's blue and gold.

The memorable first line of my valedictory speech went something like this: "From the very beginning Murphy High School represented the very best quality, blah, blah, blah. . ." It was never explained to us how someone during the days of the Spanish conquest was already thinking about Murphy High School. It was in the song so we thought it must be true. Maybe the song writer was thinking of Bienville and d'Iberville? But no, that couldn't be. Those founders of Mobile were French.

The event that involved all of the prayer group had occurred immediately before graduation. Growing up in small towns in rural south Alabama, I had always looked forward to graduation and the accompanying baccalaureate service. Now that I was to be a graduation speaker for this huge graduating class of some twelve hundred, I took more than a passing interest in the Murphy traditions surrounding commencement. Most of our cell members were native Mobilians, and I had only been there for the eleventh and twelfth grades, so I asked Jamie and Glenda when and where the baccalaureate service would take place.

They replied, almost in unison, "Oh, we don't have one."

Glenda linked pinkies with Jamie. "We said that together, didn't we?" Glenda chortled.

What exactly is a *backalariet*?" Jamie asked.

"Murphy does not have a baccalaureate service in a church?" I was incredulous. "It goes with graduation. Always has," I stated with finality. I had only been at Murphy for two years and had come from the tiny school in East Brewton to Mobile. How could Murphy High not have a baccalaureate? I got together a bunch of kids I knew from the Methodist church and we decided to petition the principal. I didn't go to see the principal; I stayed in the background, and we got the service.

The following fall, our core group—all Methodists—were off to Huntingdon College in Montgomery, which was the church school for our Methodist Conference. In the college, our Mobile group became the backbone of the progressive or liberal forces.

3

RACE RELATIONS 402

In my senior year of college, I was given an assignment to study the racial problem and write a paper proposing some solutions. This was in a sociology course in race relations, and it was not an unusual project even for Huntingdon College in 1960.

Founded in 1852 as a liberal arts college for Methodist women, our school was named for Selina, Countess of Huntingdon, an English follower of Charles and John Wesley. The campus—landscaped by Frederick Law Olmsted Jr.—was green, shady, and cool. Its Gothic buildings gave the college an air of serious learning in the European mode. When I arrived in 1957, men were still few enough to be remarkable. I lived in Massey Dormitory—the sole residence hall for men.

When the professor told us to research solutions to racial problems, we were supposed to understand that research was done in the library. We might look at *Caste and Class in a Southern Town* by John Dollard or at Tom Pettigrew's research from Harvard, and of course there were Gunnar Myrdal's *An American Dilemma* and C. Vann Woodward's *The Strange Career of Jim Crow*. If one were particularly diligent, one could read Frederick Douglass or even W. E. B. Du Bois. But to do original research, with primary sources? Here in Montgomery? No. In Montgomery in 1960, that could be dangerous. Well, if one insisted, one could pay a visit to the local White Citizens Council, and if one really wanted to extend oneself, he could go to the Klan office. They had plenty of literature on the subject, according to our sociology professor.

Five of us decided otherwise. One day we approached Dr. Arlie B. Davidson to discuss our plans for field work. Joe, Townsend, and I were from

48

Mobile. We had graduated from high school together three years earlier and were best friends. Townsend—I called him "Tee"—was my roommate. John Hill, the youngest of our group, was a sophomore from a small Alabama town. William Head, a senior like the rest of us, was the intellectual of the group, an aristocrat from Union Springs, in the heart of Alabama's Black Belt.

"We'd like to interview Dr. Martin Luther King Jr. to ask him about the Montgomery Bus Boycott, which is an approach that has been tried right here to solve the racial problem." We wanted to investigate that particular tactic because it seemed to have worked in Montgomery and might be applicable elsewhere.

As we told him this, Dr. Davidson's eyes got bigger and bigger and he started to sputter.

"That won't be necessary," he said, "I'm sure you have enough material already, and I'm sure you'll all make extremely good grades. No, that won't be required, so you just go and write your papers."

"But we want to do field work," Joe Thomas and Townsend Ellis, said practically in unison, "This is sociology, right?"

"Oh you can do some field work if you want to," the professor bleated, "Haven't some of y'all been to the Citizens Council and the Klan?"

"Yes," Bill Head said quietly, "we've gotten wheelbarrows full of 'literature' from them, but we thought it would be fair if we also go to the Montgomery Improvement Association."

The MIA, under the leadership of E. D. Nixon, the local NAACP president and head of the local Brotherhood of Sleeping Car Porters, had been formed to conduct the bus boycott.

"Go to Martin Luther King, the MIA?" Dr. Arlie B. said in a daze. "You can't do that, why you'll all be arrested!"

Being young scholars and budding sociologists, our interest was piqued by the mention of arrest. Someone asked, "You mean we can be arrested for doing research? Are you saying we can't go and meet with Reverend Abernathy and Dr. King?"

John Hill asked if Dr. Davidson was forbidding us to go meet some students at Alabama State (the local black college) to discuss this "problem" with "the ones who are directly involved?" Our sociological imagination was being aroused.

"No," Davidson pleaded, "I'm not forbidding you . . . they are forbidding you."

"Who?" we asked.

"They . . . the Klan and them . . . I guess," our professor said weakly. "They won't let you."

"Why?" we asked.

"Why?" he said. "Are you asking me why? It's self-evident, isn't it?"

"What's self-evident?" we asked.

"It's evident," he said, "that you can't just go willy-nilly meeting with colored people in Montgomery. It's against the law," he blurted. "Don't you know that?"

"Actually we've already met Dr. King and Reverend Abernathy," I spoke up for the first time, "and we didn't get arrested."

"How on earth did you do that?"—a strangled scream from Dr. Arlie B. "Where did you meet them? When did you do that? I just hope it wasn't on account of this course!"

"In fact," I said, trying to calm him down, "we first met earlier in the year at the federal court building; they were standing in the hall during court recess."

I explained how we had been there during the hearings when black ministers Ralph Abernathy, Solomon S. Seay Sr., Fred Shuttlesworth, and Joseph Lowery, along with Dr. King and the New York Times Company, had been sued for libel by Montgomery officials. The resulting landmark First Amendment case, *Times v. Sullivan,* started with an ad, placed by King and others in the *Times,* that had offended the officials.

I continued, "We introduced ourselves, told them we were from Huntingdon and asked if they'd arrange for us to meet some students at Alabama State."

"Thank God." Arlie B. breathed deeply. "Apparently you haven't yet broken the law; that's vertical integration . . . as long as you are standing up, it's okay. You can stand up and talk to a colored person all day and not break the law. It's when you sit down that you get into trouble."

The professor seemed to have forgotten about us while he rambled on about vertical integration. Regrettably, he trailed off just as he had managed to get our undivided attention; we wanted to hear more from our learned sociology professor about the different kinds of integration, legal and illegal.

"Why?" we asked.

"Because," he started up again, surprised that we were still listening, "when you sit down with a Negro, or any person of color for that matter, the Ku Klux Klan and others may take exception to your sitting down and they will come and beat you up and that will be a breach of the peace, which you have caused, and therefore you will be guilty of inciting to riot."

"Why don't they just arrest the Klan?" we hollered.

"Look," he explained patiently, "they can't arrest the Klan; there's too many of them." Davidson told us that it would be much easier for the cops to arrest the few of us, and besides most of the time the cops and the Klan are the same thing, and he told us we shouldn't expect the police to arrest themselves. Our professor looked like a person who had spoken too freely. I think he wanted to take the last part back but he didn't, probably because he knew that we knew it was true.

We tried briefly to rekindle the conversation but it was no use. I said something about doing a monograph on the different types of integration. I thanked Davidson for explaining that vertical was all right and that sitting was all wrong; then I asked him about horizontal.

"Horizontal? What do you mean horizontal?" he asked.

"Horizontal," I said, "you know, the kind that results in all different shades of Negroes." As he was turning away, I held onto his sleeve while I tried to explain that I had read one theory of race relations from somewhere in South America, Brazil, I thought, where miscegenation was advocated for long enough to do away with black people altogether. When I said it looked like they had been trying that in the South for some time, he pulled his arm away and headed for the door.

Turning his red face toward us as he reached the door he said, "Don't do it. I'm telling you not to do it. You got enough stuff, and God knows you are all taking this more seriously than anybody else. If you insist on going to see the nig . . . Nigras, it's not my responsibility—you are strictly on your own and neither I, the department, nor this college, I'm sure, will take responsibility for you."

WE WERE UNDER THE IMPRESSION that the due process provisions of the

Fourteenth Amendment applied to Huntingdon. We were mistaken. If we had known what we were getting into, we may never have done what we did next. But we were young and naive, so we asked Reverend Abernathy to help us meet some students at all-black Alabama State, less than a mile from our all-white campus.

Abernathy arranged it and told us when and where to meet Joe Louis Reed, a student leader at Alabama State. At the first meeting we were very excited because we knew we were doing something risky. We felt like conspirators.

The meetings with the black students went off without a hitch. One reason these early meetings seemed so peaceful was that we had no idea we were being followed.

The content of the meetings was innocuous. It was clear to the black students and to ourselves that we had no intention of engaging in any "action." Earlier in 1960, the student sit-in movement had erupted in North Carolina and quickly spread across the South. Joe Reed and Bernard Lee had already led the Alabama State students in sit-ins and other protests. This thrilled us, but we considered direct action the job of the black students. We felt it was dangerous enough for us to simply gather information. Getting to know the situation was, on the face of it, strictly research—just school work.

In the first meeting at Alabama State, after Reed introduced us, I explained to the black students, as I had to King and Abernathy, that even though we white students had, as individuals, sympathetic feelings toward the movement, we would limit our activities to carrying out research for our paper. We told the black students that we had been warned not to meet with them and not to seek out the MIA.

Reed, unable to take his eyes off Townsend, who weighed around four hundred pounds, chuckled and said, "Yeah, I can see how you could get in trouble coming here. You all are not exactly inconspicuous."

Townsend spoke quietly, "It's not that we mind getting in trouble, you understand; it's just that we want to be on good grounds when we do get caught. You all have the support of your parents and your community—we don't." As it turned out, Townsend was mistaken about that. We had simply assumed that their parents were as proud of them as ours were embarrassed or outraged at us. We discovered from Joe and the other black students that some of their parents were extremely upset with them for marching and sitting-in. In many cases, our new black friends were the first in their families to attend college, and their parents were making huge sacrifices for their children to get an education. For instance, when John Lewis became a movement leader in Nashville, his sharecropper family in Troy, Alabama, was terrified. They feared economic or physical reprisals against the family.

As THE YEAR WENT along, we learned there was to be an anniversary celebration of the victory of the Montgomery Bus Boycott. Although Dr. King had moved to Atlanta in January 1960, he had stayed in close touch with the MIA and would attend events like the celebration. A week of evening mass meetings at black churches were to be followed by nonviolent workshops on Saturday and Sunday at Reverend Abernathy's church. We talked to the students and later with Dr. King and Reverend Abernathy about attending some of the meetings. Dr. King assured us we were perfectly welcome, but we risked arrest; practically no local white people attended the mass meetings.

I remember Dr. King saying, "Now, Bob, you must remember, meeting with the students in private is one thing. Coming to a mass meeting or to the nonviolent workshop where the police and the press are present is another matter entirely. All the proceedings are tape-recorded by state investigators. The police are inside and all our meetings are completely public."

I'm sure they wanted us to come, but Dr. King was being meticulous in telling us the dangers. They could tell what neophytes we were, and I'm sure they didn't want us to get into trouble and then come crying to them or anybody else that we had been tricked into attending. But we felt we had a right to attend any meeting we wanted, and we were willing to fight for that right. At the same time we wanted to be as inconspicuous as possible and not to do anything as a "demonstration." If we were arrested, it would be the fault of the police—not us. We were terribly naive and found out later that state investigators had followed us to every meeting, even the "secret" meetings with the students.

Our first mass meeting, however, was fantastic. Three of us came rather furtively to the front door and asked for the "deacon" as we had been told to do. The deacon led us to seats on the back row in the corner of the church under the balcony and told us that the cops were in the balcony above and that he would keep us informed of their movements. The church was humming at our presence!

For some reason I had expected *not* to be noticed by the congregation. I guess I had a preconceived notion that I and my friends would be invisible. So it came as a somewhat disconcerting but pleasant surprise that the people in the church began to make eye contact with us. I remember the friendly eyes and the bright smiles. I thought later that black people had never looked at me like that. Maybe they had always thought of me as the enemy, and in this context it was clear that I was not. Maybe it was because I had never looked at *them* like this. Anyway, this was great!

We were just getting into the swing of the meeting, however, when the bottom fell out. I had noticed the large, conspicuous, reel-to-reel Wollensack tape recorder on a table in front of the pulpit with wires running up to a microphone clipped onto the light stand in front of the speaker. We had arrived late, and Reverend Abernathy was introducing Dr. King. I had seen and heard King on television and had been with him in private meetings, but I had not heard him preach to a movement mass meeting. I was really looking forward to this. But it was not to be.

As Abernathy was thundering his introduction, the deacon suddenly appeared, leaned over several people and hissed, "They're coming down; the cops are heading this way and we're afraid they are going to arrest you."

"Can we leave the way we came in?" I asked.

"No. They're out there between you and the door," the deacon said.

"Is there any other way out?"

"You can go out the back way. Follow me."

We trailed the deacon down the aisle, by the pulpit, where a startled Abernathy glanced our way. We hurried through the choir loft while the whole choir and congregation looked at us. Without looking back, we darted out the back door. When the cool outside breeze hit us, we ran. If we had looked back while running down the center aisle of the church, we would have noticed a single cop in the balcony, one who had not come down with the others. He had noted our exit from the church. Later I got to know this state investigator very well. His name was Willie B. Painter.

The next night at the second in the series of mass meetings, Townsend,

Joe Thomas, and I had to leave early because we were actors in a play at Montgomery's Little Theatre. We left the church as quietly as possible. I thought we had gotten away again when suddenly, out of the shadow of a giant magnolia tree on the corner, two figures emerged. I could see the glow of cigarettes remaining under the tree. Two uniformed Montgomery policemen approached us, and one said, "Do you mind if we take your pictures?" The other cop was raising a camera with a flash attachment to his eyes.

"Yes we do!" I said quickly and firmly.

I didn't feel very confident or very firm. Events were happening in slow motion. Maybe that's why I remember these confrontations so clearly.

"Why can't we take your picture?" one asked.

"Why do you want to take our picture?" I asked.

The small one with the camera ignored my question and continued, "What's wrong? Are you ashamed of what you're doing?"

"Why should we be ashamed?" I asked. I regretted asking the question because I quickly realized that they wanted to provoke this kind of give and take—the old police technique designed to get us to talk as if this was just a normal conversation that might happen between people on any street in the city.

The big one, his hand on a black leather slapjack which hung from his belt, chewed his tobacco wad. He spat and said in what I'm sure he thought was a kindly voice, "We'd just like to get your names and ask you a few questions and we really would like to get your pictures, if you don't mind."

"Look, sir," I said, "we definitely do not want you to take our pictures, and if we are not under arrest we would like to go on our way. As for our names and answering questions we won't do that either if we're not under arrest."

"Oh, you're not under arrest. We just thought you wouldn't mind if we took your pictures and asked a few questions."

We slowly walked away. The policemen followed us for a few steps, then stopped. One said, "If you're not ashamed of what you're doing then why . . . ?"

When we were out of earshot, we picked up the pace and headed for Joe Thomas's mother's car. But as he was about to reach for the door of the car Joe said in a loud stage whisper, "Wait! I can't let them get the tag number of my mother's car—she'll kill me! Or worse, yet," he said, with grim humor, "they'll kill her."

"What can we do?" Townsend groaned. "We're going to be late for the play and the director will kill us."

It was opening night of an eight-performance run for the play. Townsend, Joe, and I comprised the major part of a Chinese ensemble that had to be on stage throughout the whole play.

Our problems were complicated and solved with almost the same stroke when it started to pour rain, and a cab came by. We hailed the cab and leaped in as Townsend said to the black cab driver, "Thank God you stopped, man. It's raining like a tall cow pissing on a flat rock out there."

"Yeah, I know, man," said the young driver. "I'm not supposed to pick you guys up, you know, but what with the rain and all, I thought . . ." His voice trailed off and then he said, "I hope it ain't no cops watching—that's all."

We all laughed hysterically just to release the tension. In this rain we couldn't tell whether the fuzz was following us or not.

We found out later that seconds after the three of us dashed soaking into the dressing room to put on our costumes and makeup, four cops chugged into the theater searching the audience for us. We thought it was funny that they didn't recognize us onstage as Chinese musicians. How they missed Townsend, we could never figure out.

The week progressed; we kept going to meetings, dodging the cops, and acting in the play. We relaxed slightly and even felt a little cocky, looking forward to the weekend, so we could attend the workshop at Reverend Abernathy's church on Saturday.

On Friday night while everybody else was out partying, the five of us—Townsend, Joe Thomas, myself, John Hill, and William Head—who had gone to some of the mass meetings got together for a bull session in the room I shared with Townsend. We lived on the fourth floor of Massey Dorm, crammed under the eaves with only a narrow dormer window to give light. The room was cluttered with dirty clothes and Townsend's big stereo and a thousand or so unsheathed records. The Kingston Trio was blasting a calypso song about down Jamaica way where the nights are gay and the dancing girls sway to and fro. The December weather was unseasonably warm; trees had sprouted buds like they intended to skip winter. The breeze through the window was sweet with false spring—light and soft. We felt good talking about the cloak-and-dagger week we had just spent. The conversation turned inexorably to the subject. What would we do tomorrow? Should we press our luck and go to the workshop or leave well enough alone, gather our research, and write those damned papers for Sociology 402?

Townsend was saying, "I say let's go and to hell with them!" Whenever Townsend swore, I always suspected he had been drinking. I had never had a drink, but I could always tell when he had.

"Townsend," I said, "where did you have supper tonight? I didn't see you in the dining hall."

"At the Green Lantern—why?"

The Green Lantern, a local roadhouse, was the stage for one of the most memorable stories about my beloved friend Townsend. He and I liked to go there and order their specialty, a huge steak prepared for two. Townsend would get two orders—one rare, and he'd ask the waitress to line up sixteen stingers, his favorite drink. He explained to me that weighing in at about four hundred pounds, it was hard for him to get good and drunk. I did not drink, but I did understand his problem.

After one of his drinking bouts, Townsend and a Montgomerian named Sonny Kyle Livingston reached the exit door at approximately the same time. Townsend could seem arrogant at times and refused to give way. Sonny Kyle was a local bail bondsman with a vested interest in maintaining his reputation as a Klan enforcer. He was famous for having his picture in the Montgomery papers in the act of smashing a Negro woman in the head with a baseball bat. He had also been implicated in several incidents of violence connected with the bus boycott, and was acquitted each time by all-white juries.

As my roommate brushed by the smaller Klansman, Sonny Kyle blurted out that he was going to kill Townsend's roommate Bob Zellner. Townsend glared down at Sonny Kyle in the roadhouse parking lot. Townsend, pretty well tanked up and standing his full height of six feet five inches, looked around at Livingston and his companions and made them all a proposition.

"If anything should happen to my roommate, anything at all, will y'all explain to this fool that I will personally hold him responsible. If Bob should slip and fall in the shower, Sonny Kyle, I will come looking for you and I promise I will break every sorry bone in your scrawny-assed body."

So far Livingston hadn't bothered me, and on this Friday night in the dorm room, the five of us continued discussing the pending workshop. I warned that we could be arrested if we went to the meeting the next day.

"I know that," Townsend said, "but didn't you say we should be willing to be arrested if it came to that because we, by God, have a right to go to those meetings if we want to?"

I had wondered if I was egging the others on to go to the meetings—that maybe if it weren't for me they wouldn't be doing this. It occurred to me then that I was not influencing them as much as I thought. This freedom stuff was in the air and it was contagious. Joe, John Hill, Bill Head, and Townsend really wanted to go to the workshop even at the risk of being trundled off to jail.

I was relieved. I could make my decision, and they could make theirs. But there was one issue I thought we should discuss—parents. "Townsend," I said, "what is your mother going to say if you wind up in jail? Your father, for that matter, what will he say?"

"My father?" Townsend laughed. "If he's sober enough to speak at all, he'll holler, 'Jail! What'd they get him for? Public drunk? Chip off the old block. That's my boy!'"

Most of us knew about Townsend's father, but it was awkward for us for him to laugh it off with such bitterness.

"I know about your father, Townsend, but what about Delia?"

"Oh, Mother will no doubt be highly pissed. Our business is, as you know, about ninety percent colored, so that's where her bread and butter is. What will really tick her off is the rich white clients who'll never darken her doors again with their tax returns. That will lose her some profit. Personally, she doesn't mind if I consort with Negroes. She does it all the time, and Daddy drinks with them on the corner, but, all in all, they will be highly pissed."

Bill hadn't said much so I asked, "What about you, Head?"

Bill looked at me morosely and sighed, "They'll run me out of Union Springs like an egg-sucking dog, but that won't be any great loss. I don't even go home for holidays now, and my parents haven't spoken to me since I told them I'm an agnostic. Mother knows I spend most of my time writing poetry. Let's go," he said firmly.

"Wait just a minute," Joe said. "I don't know about John Hill's situation, but I'm pretty doggone sure that Zellner here is the only one of us with any support from home. The rest of us are going to be hung out to dry, and we've got to realize that the KKK, if they choose to, can hunt us down like stray dogs. I don't like to be hunted, and I know Bob doesn't either, but at least he's got the support of his daddy and mother."

I tried to say something, but Joe put his hand up and continued, "Reverend Zellner is a for—" Thomas paused and struggled for the word. "Formidable," Bill Head prompted. "Formidable," Joe agreed, "fighter inside the church. He's willing to battle the church and the college, so Bob's got real support."

"But the support is not just for me," I interjected. "It's for all of us."

"I know," Joe agreed, "but it makes a hell of a lot of difference to the way a person feels when he has the support of his family. None of us do." In the spring I would remember Joe's words when I was the only one of our five to graduate.

Finally, John Hill, who didn't talk much, suggested that we had debated long enough and that the time had come to choose whether to knuckle under or rebel. "There's no middle ground in Alabama," he said.

I said I agreed with him and that we had to realize how completely alone we were among white people in supporting civil rights. "Do you wonder how we can be right, and everybody else, the white people at least, are all wrong?" I asked. As we were soon to discover, there were a few white people in Montgomery who were defying the segregationist line. Their numbers were small, but they were there and would soon be bringing us in the circle.

"Wait a minute," Townsend said. "What was that you said about taking action? I'm not talking about taking action. I'm just talking about going to a meeting."

Everybody just looked at Townsend and laughed. Head said laconically, "That seems to be action enough for me."

"Look, Townsend," I said, "Reverend Abernathy said there might be some young people at King's workshop from SNCC. They draw cops like flies."

I had pronounced SNCC the way the movement people said it— "SNICK."

"Who's 'SNICK'?" they all said.

I reminded them that Joe Reed had mentioned the Student Non-Violent Coordinating Committee in our first meeting with the Alabama State students. "SNCC people are supposed to be the most militant of the movement. There's friction between them and King, but they cooperate."

"Okay, okay," Hill said, "I didn't ask for an essay. We just wanted to know who they are, that's all."

"I read about them in *Newsweek*," I explained lamely. I was excited about SNCC because they were determined to eradicate segregation in the South or die trying. My friends might not be interested. I was.

By this time we had discussed the subject so long that we could not think of any valid reason not to go to the workshop the next morning. The decision we made to break the law, defy the college, the state, and in most cases our families, was one of the most fateful of my life.

We would go.

4

The Huntingdon Five

or most of the local black participants, the workshop might have
seemed anti-climatic after a week of soul-stirring mass meetings. But
I soon realized that these working sessions were the nuts and bolts
of the movement. Here were the people who went out and did the actual
work. The meeting began with a brief prayer and a welcome by Reverend
Abernathy. Then the congregation divided into smaller groups which went
to various rooms of the church or corners of the sanctuary to discuss voter
registration, direct action, fund raising, and other subjects. Each session
was led by an experienced person. We five Huntingdon students had a brief
discussion on which workshops we would attend. We all wanted to go to the
direct action session, but we decided to split up and go to different ones, so
we could report their contents to each other.

The others deferred to my desire to go to the session on direct action.
There I met, for the first time, some of the SNCC people. Strangely, I don't
remember who they all were, though they made such an impression on me.
I had known church people strong in the faith, but until then I had never
seen such dedicated soldiers. It was clear that they did not fear death. This
gave them an aura of invincibility and a charisma I had never experienced.
SNCC kids were powerful. I was so new and naive, and the day was so exciting. When the Freedom Riders came to Montgomery the following spring,
in May 1961, and were brutally beaten by a KKK-led mob, I visited the
wounded at St. Jude Hospital. I had the definite impression that I had met
some of them before at the workshops, including Jim Zwerg and Bernard
Lafayette. I know John Lewis was there—the John Lewis who two decades
later became a Georgia congressman.

After the morning session, the ladies of the church furnished an incredible dinner (lunch is called dinner in the South and dinner is called supper) and as we ate we compared notes on the morning sessions and talked with the movement people. I don't know who was more interested in whom—the black students in us young white Southerners, or we in them. Of course the white students from Nashville, like Susan Wilbur, her sister, and others from Scarritt College and Vanderbilt, had been working all along with the black movement and had participated in the sit-ins and nonviolence training. We were delighted to meet some of the characters we had seen on the front pages of our papers and on television—the same students who had dressed themselves neatly in suits and trench coats and gone to sit quietly at lunch counters, reading their books, waiting to be served.

FOLLOWING THE AFTERNOON SESSIONS, the closing plenary turned out to be an inspired worship service with a sermon preached by Dr. King. I welcomed the worship service, relieved that we could truthfully say we had been to church. I learned that church services had historically been used in the black community to facilitate, and sometimes to mask, political activity. The reality that political work was being accomplished in our workshop did nothing to diminish the spiritual dimension. It strengthened the spirit of the occasion, especially for the five of us, having been affected in one way or another by the same social gospel that had nurtured Dr. King. His sermon was particularly inspiring because I realized that this assemblage, here in Montgomery, was part of the heart and the guts of the burgeoning civil rights movement.

This was where it had all started and these were the organizers who had carried out the daily slogging struggle of the bus boycott and the sit-ins. E. D. Nixon, the fearless leader of the local movement before King assumed the role, was present, as was Mrs. Rosa Parks, the gentle soul made of granite, who had helped to ignite the movement in the first place. We were introduced to these great people. We had previously been unaware of them, and even as we were introduced, we didn't know that these were the quiet ones who would live in legend.

I looked at Townsend floating through this, four hundred pounds of him, and then at the face of Joe Thomas. I didn't know this experience would shape Joe's life in the ministry, taking him to far places in the world, and then out of the ministry. I thought of John Hill and Bill Head, realizing that if they never did anything else in the movement, this day would remain with them. We were sky high, and Martin Luther King was soaring to one of his exuberant rhetorical climaxes which would become familiar to the whole world at the March on Washington three years later.

Suddenly Reverend Abernathy approached our little group, motioning for us to follow him. Huddling with us in a small room behind the pulpit, Abernathy explained quickly that the police had the church surrounded and were threatening to come inside and arrest the "white trouble makers" from Huntingdon. We heard the roar as King finished his sermon. Then King was there, his face glistening, concern in his voice. He was breathing in gulps from the exertion of speaking or from anxiety for what was about to happen. "What's the story?" Dr. King inquired. "What's happening, Ralph?"

"The authorities are all excited about Zellner and the students being here; I think they may barge in here and try to arrest them. If they do, I'm afraid our Montgomery people are going to lie down in their path, then we'll have lots of people in jail, and I don't know what we'll do with them."

King grinned and put his hand on Abernathy's shoulder. "Relax, Ralph, I don't think that's going to happen; if it does, maybe it's not so bad an idea. We haven't given this Montgomery power structure a good licking for a while now." King turned to me with a faint smile, "Are you all prepared to go to jail?"

"Well, Dr. King," I said, "you remember we talked about this before when we first discussed coming to these meetings."

"I remember," he said.

"Okay, Dr. King," I said, "we said we were willing to be arrested because we felt we had every legal and moral right to attend any meeting of our choice, but that we did not want to court arrest. We did not intend to 'demonstrate.' We were doing research for our paper. Well, we've talked it over and we are willing to be arrested if it comes to that, but I feel that we owe it to our parents and the school to make an attempt to escape."

The others had been quiet, leaving the talking to Abernathy, King, and me. Now Townsend said, "Look, if we make an effort to get away, and they arrest us, then it'll be their fault. If we walk out the front door with you,

Dr. King, then it will look like we want to be arrested. It'll look like one of those demonstrations."

Joe looked at Abernathy and asked plaintively, "What about using the back door?"

Abernathy said quickly. "I've got an idea. Martin, you go up front with what's left of the congregation. Take the SNCC people and go out the front door. When you do, I'll let Zellner and them go out the back. The cops are back there, but at least these students will be able to say they tried to avoid a confrontation."

"All right, Ralph," King said, "but be sure to give them Attorney Gray's number so they can call him from the jail."

King looked at us and smiled, "It's been great having you. I think this is more than a research paper for you, so if and when they get you, we'll be right down to bail you out. This should be a great test case. Welcome to the movement."

Dr. King started for the front of the church while we stared morosely at the back door. Reverend Abernathy seemed to be counting slowly to himself. There was a sudden sound of movement outside the door, and I thought, "What the hell—here goes nothing." Abernathy opened the back door and we looked up a short flight of steps leading to the sidewalk to see the retreating backs of three city cops.

"Go!" Abernathy said in a stage whisper, while we hurried up the steps. The coast was momentarily clear. A mob of cops, feds, and reporters converged on the front door, so we knew that King had just stepped outside. The cops expected us to come out behind him.

We turned left and walked slowly down the sidewalk, feeling that every eye in the world was staring at our exposed backs. But we had allies. People from the church would drive by and whisper, "Go one more block straight ahead; there's no cops there." Then another car, and someone would say, "Turn right at the next block." They kept us apprised of the moves of the police.

We couldn't believe we were getting away with it! Then someone remembered we had parked across the street from the church.

"Man, we are screwed!" Bill Head said.

"Hold on," I said, "They haven't caught us yet; they must think we're still in the church. We only have to walk in a square until we get to the car on the other side of the street. We can check out the action at the church, get in the car, and quietly leave. We'll be coming from the other direction!"

It was easy. We simply walked in a big square, arrived at the car across from the church, looked at the crowd, got in and drove away.

BACK AT CAMPUS, WE used different doors into the dining hall, and sat in different parts of the room. About five minutes into dinner, I saw Dean of Men Charles H. Owens III dart into the hall, peering in all directions. I watched while he picked out Townsend. Then he scanned for Joe Thomas, Bill Head, then John Hill. Finally his eyes locked on mine.

Owens walked straight towards me. Dean of Students Charles Turner was also zeroing in on me. Dean Owens puffed up to my table. His harried look, eyes bulging and face red with anger, startled the students at my table, as he practically shouted, "Meet me in Dr. Searcy's office in forty minutes."

Dean Turner—"the Silver Fox," students called him—fairly purred into Owens's flushed face, "Have you told the others yet?"

"No," hissed Owens, "but they are all here. I'm going to corral them now."

I had worried the others might bolt at this powerful display of administrative might, but they held their ground as Dean Owens stopped and spoke briefly to each.

When the brass left the hall, we hurried to gather near the exit. Everyone else in the dining hall, by now, wondered what was afoot in our quiet, peaceful old college.

A SHORT TIME LATER, we trudged single file into Dr. Searcy's office. I was exhilarated until despair gained the upper hand. I realized that the entire college administration—President Hubert Searcy, academic deans Stone, Turner, and Owens, Dean of Women Julia Harper, even Librarian Glenn Massengale, and a few others—was crowded into the president's office.

Dean Turner indicated five chairs clustered at the end of the table and we took our seats. Dr. Searcy sat at the other end of the long table, facing us; administrators lined each side. They all stared at us. What followed was like a movie interrogation by a totalitarian dictator and his gang.

Searcy started in on us, his face beet red. He told us we were in big trouble and suggested that we would have been in jail if school officials hadn't intervened. He demanded to know why we went to the church, what we were thinking, how we got away. He had decided I was the instigator and turned to me. "What on earth is happening here, Zellner? Can you please explain it to me?"

The president of our college screamed, practically choking on the words, "Who gave you the right, young Mr. Zellner, to take our students to an integrated meeting and breach the law in Montgomery, Alabama?"

"You did," I said, "in a way." He turned purple. "We went to the meeting for an assignment in Sociology 402. That's Race Relations 402," I reminded him. "Actually I said 'you' to mean Huntingdon College collectively and our teacher Dr. Arlie B. Davidson specifically. We talked to Dr. Davidson about going to the meeting and . . ."

"Dr. Davidson said you could go to the meeting?!" asked President Searcy, practically apoplectic by now.

"Well, not exactly," I said. "He 'suggested' we not go because of the likelihood of our being arrested." I eased up on Dr. Davidson because he could lose his job over this.

"Go on," Searcy said impatiently. "If I didn't tell you that you could go, and Davidson didn't tell you that you could go, then who said you could go?"

He paused to glare at Owens and whisper hoarsely, "Go to his house and tell Arlie B. to come here immediately."

"Where were we?" Searcy asked, looking like a man who was slowly losing control without understanding why.

"It all started," I said, "with a discussion of vertical and horizontal integration." Townsend and the others perked up when I mentioned horizontal integration.

I told Searcy that Dr. Davidson had said vertical integration such as standing in a hall talking to Negroes was all right. Apparently, as long as you didn't sit down there was no breach of the segregation law. The professor, I told him, said please don't cause trouble by going to an integrated meeting.

"Why'd you go then?" Searcy asked.

"Because," I said, "we explained to Davidson that scholars from all over the world journeyed to Montgomery to study the budding civil rights movement. We felt we wouldn't have a decent intellectual product if we failed to investigate the local situation, especially since the bus boycott was right here in our backyard and many of the principals were still here."

I could not be sure that Searcy was taking in all that I said. The most he could manage was, "What was that you said about 'horizontal integration'?"

"Oh that," I said. "That's when you integrate horizontally, lying down, you know, like in bed. That's why, I guess, we have so many different shades of Negroes here in Montgomery—that's what our professor called 'horizontal integration.' I'm still puzzled, though, Dr. Searcy, why the in-between kind of integration causes so much trouble. Why does the simple act of sitting down with a Negro, with or without food and drink, cause so much consternation in Montgomery? We have a lot to learn in this sociology class, Mr. President."

Searcy exploded, "That's quite enough, Mr. Zellner. Thank you for your levity." My compatriots next to me on the dunce seats shook with silent mirth, but Dr. Searcy went on sternly. "What you boys did was very serious, and if you do that again, you will be arrested, the law says, and there'll be nothing we can do for you. Therefore I am immediately restricting each of you to this campus until you resign from this school which I am requesting you to do now. From this time until you resign and are gone, you are not to leave this campus for any purpose whatsoever unless you have written permission to do so or are accompanied by me or one of the other members of the administration."

There it was. They planned to get rid of us.

With that on the table, the meeting turned into a spirited debate about due process and free speech and why these didn't apply on a private school campus. But Bill Head got everyone's attention when he mentioned the American Association of University Professors.

"What's that you're saying about the professors, Mr. Head?" Dr. Searcy asked sarcastically. "Since you're supposed to be the smartest student here at Huntingdon College, I guess we can't be spared the benefit of your wisdom." Several of the more prescient administrators tried to head the president off.

When the hubbub began to die down, Head said quietly, "I just suggested that the American Association of University Professors might be interested in five top students being expelled for carrying out a school assignment."

"Also," I said without missing a beat, "the publicity alone, if we file a complaint, could be very critical for the school."

"Wait just a doggone minute," President Searcy pleaded, "I didn't say you were expelled! I just said you should resign for your own good and the good of the school. That's all—if you don't believe me, I'll have Jan read back that part," looking to Jan Gregory, who was busy taking shorthand notes.

I hadn't realized the meeting was being recorded, but I told Dr. Searcy I was delighted there would be a record of the meeting, because I wanted to make a statement. I was sure the others would also.

"Wait a minute, hold on there. The only statement that will be needed is the one I'm about to make. . ."

Searcy did everything but pound his chest as he said, "The Association of American Professors doesn't mean do-do on this campus. Anyway, this is my ultimatum to you boys. While you remain on campus you are not to have contact with Negroes publicly, privately, directly or indirectly. You are forthwith restricted to campus until further notice. That's all, class dismissed, no more need be said, end of discussion, good-bye, good-bye, good-bye. This meeting is over!"

Nobody moved while Searcy tried to gather up his papers.

Thinking of the record, I took a deep breath and said, "Dr. Searcy, before we go, I need to get something straight."

"Bob, I said this meeting is over. Please listen to me. In the name of all that is decent, are you all completely out of control?"

"Yes," I said, "we are beginning to be out of control. We've been under control much too long now, certainly as far as this subject of race is concerned."

"Race! I didn't say anything about race!"

"Now, Dr. Searcy," I insisted gently, "You are telling us we have no First Amendment rights. What you are saying to us five is that we cannot, in Montgomery, Alabama, at Huntingdon College in 1960, avail ourselves of the most basic rights guaranteed to citizens of the United States—the rights of assembly, freedom of speech, and religion. According to you we can't practice any of our civil rights or liberties—including academic freedom?"

"Right, you can't do that and remain a student at Huntingdon College," Searcy stated finally. "Are you that naive, Mr. Zellner? Don't you realize how you all have embarrassed this institution? We've managed to keep a low profile in all this mess, and now you boys go and do this to us. You have no idea what danger you were in—what danger you are in now. Do you think the Klan will hesitate to march on this campus and get you, especially you, Mr. Zellner? We don't know if we can protect you on this campus, much less off it. I've tried to keep from saying this, but your lives are in danger. The newspapers have already gotten hold of this and they are asking me for a statement of school policy regarding you boys. What am I to tell them?"

John Hill, the youngest of the five now spoke up, "Dr. Searcy, Professor Davidson already tried that one on us. He said if we had a meeting with any colored people, and the Klan found out, then we might be beaten up and charged with disturbing the peace. The threat of violence is no reason to give up one's civil liberties. If that was the case, Dr. Searcy, we would never have won these liberties in the first place."

"Don't be naive, John," Dr. Searcy said. "That's just stuff you read in books. It doesn't work like that out here in the real world. Now you've stirred up a real big-time hornet's nest here, and I'm the one dealing with the buzzing bees!"

When I arrived at church in the Chisholm community the next morning, I found out that Dr. Searcy had given a statement to the newspapers. The little cotton mill community of Chisholm was a Klan stronghold on the north side of Montgomery—not the kind of place you want to be greeted with a cheerful, "I see you made the paper this morning." The Methodist church in Chisholm was pastored by the Reverend Floyd Enfinger, an old friend of Daddy's, and I worked my way through college by helping at Floyd's church. I was the choir director, the Sunday soloist, youth director, and all-round janitor and yard man.

I didn't know the extent of the damage until Reverend Enfinger handed me the Sunday *Montgomery Advertiser-Alabama Journal* and I saw the head-line: "Huntingdon Students Asked to Leave School."

The paper quoted Dr. Searcy saying the five students were trouble-makers.

We were hoodlums who were not representative of Huntingdon College. The paper said the five of us were observed attending a nonviolent workshop held at Reverend Abernathy's church, and that Reverend Abernathy and Dr. Martin Luther King had helped us escape a cordon of police trying to arrest us for violating the segregation laws and causing a disturbance of the peace. Dean Charles Turner had obviously opened his files to the press because the paper listed every infraction any of us had ever committed. We had thrown water balloons from Massey Dorm aimed at pedestrians. We had engaged in fire extinguisher fights. Townsend signed a false name checking out a book, "T. Elbridge," and we had all killed rats at the city dump.

On the way to breakfast Monday morning I passed a burned cross on the green, a large expanse of lawn and trees in the center of campus. I was surprised to see it and wondered what or who it was for. I didn't connect the hideous symbol with myself at all.

I was soon joined by Townsend, who told me there were three other crosses outside the dorm. "Are you happy now?" he said.

"Happy about what?"

"They're meant for you, you know."

"Why just for me? There's five of us involved, in case you've forgotten."

"I haven't forgotten," Townsend said bitterly as we continued across the green toward the dining hall. "Bob, everybody is blaming you. They say you put us up to it and Thomas implied that Dean Turner hinted you called the press so it would be a big story."

I told Townsend I was crushed that he and the others would fall for such divide-and-rule tactics, especially without even talking to me about it. We hushed when we joined the line picking up breakfast trays; everybody had stopped talking to listen to us. I guess we were the number one topic of discussion anyway.

Townsend and I found our way to the table where Joe Thomas, Bill Head, and John Hill sat. They were sticking together, they told us, since hearing that some of the basketball team were planning to beat them up. Joe, the smallest of the five of us, looked at Townsend sadly and said, "You and Bob don't have anything to worry about. Nobody in his right mind would mess with either of you."

Townsend exploded, "Who has threatened you, Joe? I'll just go right now and break every bone in his body." Tee was big on breaking every single bone.

"Hold on, Townsend," Joe said, "nobody has actually threatened me. We just heard there were threats."

I put my hand on Tee's shoulder, "Yes, and Townsend, what about nonviolence? Aren't we trying to be nonviolent? You know, in the spirit of the movement?"

"It's okay for a demonstration," Townsend shot back, "But, Bob, these Mississippi plowboys don't play no nonviolence. It'd be wasted on them. I'm going to tell Doc and Henry Marcus and the rest of that yahoo bunch that if Joe so much as slips down and hurts himself, I'm holding them responsible."

The strain was showing. Since the mass meetings, the workshop on Saturday, and the newspaper articles, events were piling up.

THE NIGHT AFTER OUR breakfast meeting, I was settling in for some much-neglected study, when George Waldron from next door ran into my room out of breath. Waldron, a nephew of grocery tycoon Alfred Delchamps, the Huntingdon board chairman, spoke rapidly, "The Klan is gathering down at the corner. They're burning a big cross and Townsend thinks they're going to come on to the campus to get you."

Thinking he was kidding, I said, "Who told you this? Where is Townsend? I thought he was at the library."

"He was," George gasped, "but, he's coming up the stairs now with Thomas and John Hill. Nobody knows where Head is."

The door burst open. Joe and John propelled Townsend into the room. They had helped him run up the stairs. Tee had a wild look in his eyes, "Don't you think you'd better hide someplace?"

"I'm not going to hide," I said. "There's nothing to hide from. These are just rumors. I think you guys are panicking over nothing. What have you heard exactly, what's this about Head being missing?"

"Bob," Thomas said solemnly, "these are not rumors. They shouted into the library that a cross was burning down the street from campus. We ran to the front arch and looked down Fairview Avenue. There's a hell of a big fire down there, and noise from what looks like a lot of people."

Just then a strange and wonderful thing happened. We looked up to see a small crowd gathering around our door. When Townsend saw John Ed Mathison and big Henry Marcus from the basketball team, he said under his breath, "Oh, hell!"

John Ed looked in and said, "Zellner, can we come in?"

"Yeah, John Ed, y'all come in," I said.

"Bob, they're burning a thirty-eight-foot cross down there on the corner of Court Street, and there's talk of coming on campus to get you."

"How do you feel about that, John Ed?" I asked.

"Well," John Ed drawled, looking at Marcus and the other jocks, "the way we feel about it is that you are a first class son-of-a-bitch, but you're our son-of-a-bitch and no two-bit bunch of Klansmen from off this campus is going to lay a hand on you."

Townsend breathed a sigh of relief, and I joined Thomas and Hill in a big cheer. We were far too gallant to ask these newfound friends how they knew the cross was exactly thirty-eight feet tall.

5

UNDER THE INFLUENCE

The day after the Klan scare, I received an ominous envelope bearing the state seal and the address of the Attorney General of the State of Alabama and containing a terse message: "Meet me in my office at the State Capitol at 10:30 A.M. on Wed., Dec 12th. I have a matter of importance to discuss with you." It was signed by Attorney General MacDonald Gallion.

The others had received the same letter. Townsend was beside himself, "Well, ol' buddy, ol' roomy, the feces have contacted the rotary blade. What the hell are we going to do now?"

"I guess we are about to go see the attorney general," I said, trying to sound calmer than I felt. "Why should this be worse than what we've already been through? What can he do? We haven't really broken any laws you know."

Townsend accused me of having a grin on my face proving that I was enjoying the whole situation. And when I replied that Gallion was probably just trying to scare us, Joe Thomas piped up and said, "Well, he's already got me scared. I don't want to go. In fact, I don't intend to go. It's not like it's a subpoena or something. You go, and let us know what happens, Zellner."

"I intend to," I said. "Y'all can come if you want to. I've already called Daddy, and he is raring to meet with the attorney general."

My father, in fact, was convinced that Gallion was keeping files on him and other Methodist preachers of the Alabama-West Florida Conference who were suspected of not being strict segregationists. Dad had the notion that he might somehow confirm such spying during the meeting with Gallion.

DAD DROVE UP FROM Fort Walton Beach, Florida, where the family was living at the time, to join me for the meeting with Gallion. Before going to the capitol, we stopped for breakfast so we could discuss our strategy. Daddy was big on strategies. Over grits and eggs, biscuits and gravy, he laid out his plan for my approval. I was pleased that Dad was treating me with respect, consulting with me, more or less, as an equal. Under the circumstances, he probably felt more comfortable with me as a co-conspirator than as his son.

"Look," Dad said, not paying much attention to his breakfast, "Fletcher McLeod [one of Dad's close minister friends] and the rest of us have known for some time that Gallion has some of his henchmen investigating us. We think the attorney general pulls out his files to impress visitors or to intimidate people he wants to be his stool pigeons. The [Governor John] Patterson administration has been on a witch hunt and red-baiting our liberal and radical ministers of the conference and many of our congressmen who are for a more enlightened racial policy in Alabama. I'm sure my name has been in the 'Red' files of the state ever since I went to Boston in 1948 to help defend Bishop Oxnam when they called him a Red for serving on the American-Soviet Friendship Committee. That committee was fine in '45 when we were allies; but what was patriotic during the war suddenly became communistic as soon as the Cold War started. But that's ancient history, so if Gallion says anything about Reds, you just play dumb, and see what he does. He's just trying to intimidate you and Townsend and them. I'm sure he just thinks y'all are a bunch of school kids he can scare. He doesn't realize that Huntingdon is a Methodist church school. Some of us crazy preachers have something to say about the way it is run. Searcy and them don't have any guts; we know that. The preachers in our core group do."

Dad took a deep breath and looked at me sheepishly, "Sorry, I guess that was a long speech. I guess I was working on it all the way up here in the car. Anyway, Bob, what do you think? How do you think we should play this?"

I grinned with happiness at the very idea that Dad would ask what I thought. I said, "I think that we should really stick it to them while we have the chance. I haven't had a chance to tell you about the meeting the five of us had last night with Glenn Smiley from a group called the Fellowship of Reconciliation. It was a short meeting; we didn't have much time to talk.

Smiley found us in the Tea Room, and we went for a walk on the green. It was very conspiratorial. He said people in the North had read about us being told to leave school, so it made us feel better that the word is getting beyond the South. Smiley told us not to worry if we are expelled by Huntingdon—that he will guarantee that we can transfer, with scholarships, to any school in the country. That's why I say to push ahead on this question of academic freedom. If we get expelled, we'll just transfer and finish up somewhere else."

But at that Dad reminded me that my mother was upset by all the controversy and was insisting that I finish up at Huntingdon this year.

I admitted I had promised her I would. "I will stay here and graduate, but I don't intend to obey these ridiculous Mickey Mouse rules that Searcy has laid down by fiat. So, it may not be up to me whether I graduate or not this spring," I said firmly. "Your eggs are getting cold," I added, pointing to his plate.

"Never mind the eggs," he said.

I told Dad that Dean Turner had said we'd be killed if we ventured off campus, but that weekend I had gone as usual to my job at Floyd Enfinger's church in Chisholm and didn't have a moment's trouble. Dad replied that he knew we were being restricted to campus because school officials wanted to keep us quiet.

"That doesn't mean there are not real dangers out there," he said. "Remember, Sonny Kyle and those other yahoos are still out there with their baseball bats. Anyway, we'd better go. We can't keep the attorney general waiting, can we?

MacDONALD GALLION STARTED OUT immediately trying to intimidate me. Sitting behind his huge desk stacked with papers, flanked with the U.S. and Confederate flags and backed with a portrait of Governor Patterson, he leaned toward me and boomed, "What made you go out and join those marches and take part in those sit-ins? Don't you know that those types of activities are against the law in Alabama? What do you have to say for yourself, young man?"

Gallion had barely looked at Dad and had shaken hands only reluctantly. When Dad told the attorney general that he was here only to see that his son was treated fairly, Gallion had shot back, "Why wouldn't he be?"

When Gallion asked what I had to say for myself I realized that I really didn't have much stomach for playing dumb, so I looked him in the eye and said, "Mr. Attorney General, I'm sure you are aware, if your informants are giving you accurate information, that I have done none of the things you seem to be accusing me of. What marches? What sit-ins are you talking about?"

"Now, Mr. Zellner, I'm not saying you've done anything illegal. I'm just saying you've fallen in with the wrong crowd. You've fallen under the communist influence," Gallion blurted.

"You mean there's communists in Alabama?" I asked incredulously.

"No, they don't live here," he said, "but they come through here, and it's obvious you've fallen under their influence."

Before I could think of anything to say, Gallion leaned back in his chair, swiveled to his right, and pulled out a file drawer, which revealed a row of 3x5 cards about twelve or fourteen inches deep. Plucking out the first inch of the cards, he began to thumb through them, picking out a half dozen cards.

From the corner of my eye, I saw Dad home in on that file drawer full of cards. He almost got out of his chair to look. I know he was thinking that his card would be at the very back. "Z" was always easy to find.

Gallion was saying, "If any of these people contact you, young man, please call me immediately. I'll have my secretary provide you with a special number you can call night and day. There will always be someone you can talk to. Here's one. Be on the lookout for an Anne Braden or Carl Braden. B-R-A-D-E-N. Also be careful you don't get contacted by Virginia Durr or Clifford Durr. And there's Aubrey Williams . . . there's lots of them."

I had never heard of any of these people, but I was struck that he put the ladies first—Anne before Carl, Virginia before Clifford. Later, I learned why.

Before I could say anything, Dad spoke up. Very innocently he said, "Mr. Attorney General, would it be possible for you to provide us with a list of those names. I don't seem to have a pen and paper on me."

"Reverend Zellner, I'm sorry, but I couldn't possibly put these names in writing for you, but you are free to use this paper and pencil if you want to get them down." Gallion handed Dad a small pad and pencil and then repeated the names, spelling out the surnames. "As I said," he continued, "if any of these people get in touch with you, you are to let me know immediately. Is that understood?"

As fate would have it, before the week was out, I was contacted by two people on the attorney general's list—first Anne Braden and then Virginia Durr. I didn't know whether to be more amazed at the prescience of the attorney general or that of Anne and Virginia. Anyway, I remembered thinking, "Ah, these are the communists; they must be the good guys."

Needless to say, I didn't "immediately" contact the Attorney General.

THURSDAY NIGHT, FOLLOWING THE meeting with Gallion, I was trying to study in my room when George Waldron arrived with a message: "There's a lady on the phone who says she's from some newspaper, and she wants to talk to you. Her name's Miz Braden, or somethin' like that. It's a Southern newspaper and sounds very patriotic. I don't know what side they're on. Do you want to talk to them?"

I said I would talk to them—her—and find out what it was about. I wasn't accustomed to calls from ladies representing newspapers, patriotic or not.

Waldron followed me down and stood near the folding door as I said "hello" into the old pay phone. When I put the earpiece to my ear, static made the caller sound far away—Louisville, Kentucky, it turned out.

Mrs. Braden came right to the point, "I got your name from Reverend Abernathy. I hope you don't mind me calling you at your dorm."

"It's the only phone I've got," I said. "I don't mind." I held the earpiece tight against my ear and leaned as close as I could to the mouth piece on the box on the wall. "I can't hear you very well. This is an old phone," I shouted.

"I could call back and try for a better connection," she shouted back, "but before I risk losing you, let me ask about the letter you wrote to Dr. King and Reverend Abernathy. I'd like to get your permission to use it in our paper—the *Southern Patriot*."

"I don't know," I said.

"Before you decide," she shouted, "let me tell you more about it."

"Okay," I said, "but wait a minute, someone's calling me."

George Waldron was tugging at my sleeve with a suggestion that she call me back on his phone. I gave Mrs. Braden George's number and I thanked George for the use of his phone as we walked to his room. Even though George was an underclassman, he was a handy man to know. His uncle, Alfred Delchamps, was chairman of the Huntingdon College trustees. George thought we "trouble makers" were hot stuff, and more importantly, he had the only private phone in the dorm, one that actually worked. When his phone rang, we started all over.

"Oh, that's much better," Mrs. Braden said.

"Yes, it is, thanks to my friend George. What's the name of your paper again, Mrs. Braden, the *Southern Patriot*? Is that a conservative or, excuse my language, a right-wing paper?"

"Oh, heavens no, and please call me Anne, Mr. Zellner."

"Okay, then you can call me Bob," I said. "Anne Braden. I know I've heard your name recently. Do you mind if I ask if you are famous?"

"Not that I know of," she said, sounding amused.

Then I remembered. "Oh," I blurted, "the attorney general knows you. Is your husband named Carl?"

"Yes," she said.

"Is that with a C or a K," I asked, and we both laughed. Then, as if to say enough of this small talk, Mrs. Braden, Anne, got down to business again.

"Reverend Abernathy was impressed with your letter to Dr. King and the MIA. He showed it to me with the understanding that I would keep it confidential unless I got your permission to use it. One reason I could tell he liked the letter was that when he took it out of his shirt pocket to unfold it, it nearly fell apart. It looked like he had shown it to lots of people. Anyway, I was interviewing Abernathy here in Louisville for a story on the anniversary celebration of the boycott, and he used your letter to illustrate that the movement has support from some whites in Montgomery. Do you mind if we quote your letter in the next issue of the *Southern Patriot*?"

"It's not exactly my letter," I said. "I did draft it, but we all discussed its contents and then approved it. About twenty-three students here on campus signed it and contributed money to help Dr. King and Reverend Abernathy and them."

It seemed months ago, but it must have been only weeks since we had sent the meager collection to the black ministers expressing outrage at the

City of Montgomery for confiscating their cars and homes.

"We didn't even collect much, about fifty dollars, I think. I tried to tell Reverend Abernathy that we realized it wouldn't even make a dent in the millions of dollars they've been fined. We just meant it as a sympathetic gesture. We wanted them to know that all the white people in Alabama are not against them. That's all. But I couldn't give you permission to use the letter. All those names. We didn't mean for it to be a public letter."

I stopped when I realized I was rambling; I didn't want to run up a big phone bill for her.

"Oh, we would never use the names in the paper. I'm from Alabama myself, and I know how much trouble people can get into. Why don't you let me tell you what I have in mind, and then you can tell me what to do," she said. I really liked her voice. She didn't sound at all like a Yankee, and now she had told me she was from Alabama, but I thought MacDonald had said that none of the communists lived in Alabama.

She sensed my hesitation. "If you'd rather not talk about this now, I'd understand. I could call you back later."

"No," I said quickly, "it's not that I don't want to talk about it. It's just that I'm not used to talking to the press, and I'm having trouble thinking this fast."

"Okay, I'll slow down. I read that you and the other students have been asked to resign because you attended the workshop at Reverend Abernathy's church. You must be under a lot of strain. I'm mentioning this because I'd really like to do a story on the Huntingdon Five for next month's issue—the *Patriot* comes out only once a month, so you can see we're not the Big Press. But, right now all I'm interested in is the story of the letter. What I want is a small sidebar using your letter and a comment from Abernathy or King, if I can reach him—he travels so much . . . on what it means to them, and the Negro community in Montgomery, to have even a little support from the white community."

She asked if I could poll the other signers for their consent to use the letter, which she said might inspire other Southerners to break their silence on civil rights. I replied that she didn't sound like the typical "objective" reporter.

"I'm not," she said matter-of-factly. "That's the beauty of working for the non-traditional press. We sometimes call it the alternative press. I'll send you some copies of the paper and you can judge for yourself. We do take a stand, and it's not with the Klan—despite our patriotic-sounding name."

"Great," I said. "The only thing I've seen that takes a stand on social issues or politics is *National Review*; a friend gave me a subscription and I find that it takes the absolutely wrong stand on everything."

"You'll like the *Southern Patriot*," she said emphatically.

"Are you really from Alabama?"

"Yes," she laughed, "I'm from Anniston, as a matter of fact. That's one reason my ears perked up when Abernathy mentioned your letter."

"Our letter."

"Your letter," she agreed, "Your collective letter. When you get out of Alabama, you tend to lose the habit of saying 'y'all' as the plural of 'you.' When I say 'your letter' I don't mean just Bob Zellner's letter. I mean the letter from all of you. Anyway, I was fascinated because you were all from Alabama, attending an Alabama school."

I agreed to ask the others if the paper could print the letter. They agreed as long as their names weren't used. Anne asked if she could use my name, and I agreed after clearing it with the others. I cautioned Braden not to identify me as the leader. I told her we did things by consensus, and that we had no formal organization. "You're going to love SNCC," she said.

The significance of her remark escaped me at the time. Anne later convinced me to join the SNCC staff.

THE SECOND NAME TO surface from Gallion's list was that of Virginia Durr. The Virginia and Clifford Durr part of my life began innocently enough. When I received Anne's phone call, I had no idea how important she was to be in my life. The same could be said of Virginia Durr.

The card was deceptively simple; it was the first formal dinner invitation I had ever received. Simple and elegantly printed, it read:

Mr. Robert Zellner: We desire the pleasure of your company for dinner at our house, 2 Felder Avenue, Montgomery, Alabama. Wed. evening, 8 P.M., December 1960.

It was signed by Virginia and Clifford Durr. Their phone number was included, followed by a request that I please RSVP after conveying the invitation to "your four friends, Messrs. Thomas, Ellis, Hill and Head."

When I showed the card to Thomas and the others, Thomas exploded in his trademark nervous laugh, "Damn, isn't that one of the main communists Gallion told you about?"

"Two of 'em," I replied. "Virginia *and* Clifford Durr."

"How'd they find out about us?" Townsend asked, looking at me somewhat suspiciously.

I looked at my roommate and laughed hysterically, "Oh, how? I guess we're some well kept secret or something. Get your party duds together fellers," I said. "It looks like we're going to dinner."

We went and it was fabulous. I was glad the others came to the Durrs' dinner, because they had a chance to hear sane, reasonable, and erudite people discuss what we had done. Moreover, our hosts and the other guests approved what practically everyone else found reprehensible.

When the five of us walked up the drive to the Durrs' house on Felder Avenue, we bunched together for protection against the Klan and against our nervousness at this "social" occasion. We all wore suits and we had no idea what to expect. I had spoken only briefly to Mrs. Durr when I called to accept the invitation, but it was long enough to recognize the aristocracy in her voice. Most of us were small town or country boys except Bill Head. Though Townsend and Joe Thomas had grown up in Mobile, none of us were long on etiquette.

I was impressed with the home. Occupying a strategic corner in the upper-crust part of town on the corner of Felder and Court, the old house was across the street from Montgomery's society bastion—Sidney Lanier High School, the counterpart to Robert E. Lee High School on the working class side of town. The Durr daughters, Tilla and Lula, I learned later, took a lot of knocks behind Lanier's ivied walls from the city's young blue-blood elite.

As we approached, the gravel on the drive crunched loudly. The lights were off on the long wrap-around old porch, accentuating the brightness from inside. Laughter and the tinkle of ice and glasses came from open windows; a white-aproned black cook approached a long table with a steaming plate of food. Couples faced each other holding long-stemmed glasses, like in the movies, I thought.

We ascended the broad steps, crossed a large expanse of porch and approached the tall screen door. I was about to knock when a rosy-faced woman of somewhat ample proportions, hair tied in a bun, detached herself from a small knot of people to open the door.

"Why, Mr. Zellner, I'm so glad you all could come. Come in. I've been longing to meet you, and I'm delighted all of you came. I'm Mrs. Durr."

She swept the five of us into the room; I wondered how she knew I was Zellner. I didn't ask because she immediately began showing us off like we had won a gold medal at the Olympics.

She asked me to name my companions, then she introduced the people in the room. Mrs. Durr was obviously in her element. We weren't, but I managed to introduce each of us and his place of origin: Joe Thomas, Mobile; Townsend Ellis, Mobile; John Hill, Camden; and Bill Head, Union Springs. At the mention of Union Springs, Virginia brightened. She took Head's arm and asked about his mother and his uncle so-and-so. The names she fired at the three of us from Mobile and poor John from Camden didn't ring many bells with us. I began to suspect that Head's family might be more prominent than he had let on.

"And you, Mr. Zellner, I understand your folks live on the beach in Florida. Valparaiso, I believe."

"Yes, they do, ma'am, but I never lived in Florida, except I was born in Jay, Florida, about fifteen miles from Brewton, Alabama. I graduated high school in Mobile but I guess I'm more or less from East Brewton."

"I know," she said. "Your father's a Methodist minister and you've moved a lot."

"That's right," I said. "How did you know?"

"Mrs. McLeod told me all about your family. But just let me introduce you."

Everybody gathered around us; we huddled together in the middle of the room.

"This is Mr. Durr," Mrs. Durr said as I shook hands with a tall, stoop-shouldered man. "His name is Clifford."

Clifford Durr looked like he'd just stepped out of the pages of *To Kill a*

Mockingbird. Silver hair lapped modishly over gold, wire-rimmed glasses. Mr. Durr's seersucker suit was rumpled but expensive, and his startlingly blue eyes shone through the smoke curling up from a non-filtered Pall Mall cigarette held loosely between his lips. "Looks like you may have stirred things up there at the college—first time in years. Do the place good," he said.

I liked the Durrs immediately, not realizing then that Clifford would become almost a second father while Virginia metamorphosed into a sort of mom-away-from-home; their house, especially during the SNCC years, would serve as a safe home port.

The only guest I remember from the dinner was Mrs. Francis McLeod. Virginia's choice of Mrs. McLeod as a dinner companion was inspired: Francis McLeod was the grande dame of the famous Methodist McLeods. Because she was present, I felt quite at home as did the other Huntingdon men. All of us were Methodists and more or less active in the church. Mrs. McLeod's sons were longtime friends and political allies of my father. Her son Fletcher was my father's best friend; everyone assumed that her oldest, Powers McLeod, would someday be bishop. Francis had two other sons in the Alabama-West Florida Conference of the church, and her forebears, too numerous to mention, had grown old and honored in the church.

Townsend seemed nervous; I saw him looking at the food cooling on the table. In our shyness, we had unconsciously gravitated to his bulk, so when he edged closer to the table, we followed. Just then, the cook arrived with the last dish of food. Virginia assumed her place at one end of the table—Clifford at the other. Mrs. Durr directed me to the chair on her right, and Townsend to sit near the end at Clifford's left, sensing he would need room for his large right arm. It's a good thing Southerners always make too much food because we were all starved for home-cooked food. We found that Virginia kept a legendary pantry and retained the services of an excellent cook.

The food was simply outrageous. Townsend and I had a habit of remembering memorable meals, and this one joined our pantheon of greats! Fried chicken was followed by the most delicate pink roast beef that has ever melted in my mouth. Red meat of any kind was a delicacy in our house, and rare roast beef was a new experience for me. Everyone clamored for more corn bread sticks as a huge basket of them quickly disappeared and was refilled. Every few minutes the cook came back with more hot ones.

A plate piled high with deviled eggs, which had passed John Hill, then Head, almost disappeared as it went by Townsend, arriving in Clifford's hand with just three halves. Clifford gave Townsend a "growing-boys-must-eat look," quietly asking the cook if she had any more eggs. "We're making some more now," she said. "In the meanwhile why don't y'all try some of that delicious English pea salad."

I don't know how they did it in December, but there were plates of okra, sliced tomatoes, and a large bowl of butter beans. A huge mold of tomato aspic decorated the center of the table, and, as usual, nobody ate any. I have always wondered what people did with tomato aspic when the party was over.

The conversation was so good it kept interfering with the eating. I asked Mr. Durr if it was legal for Huntingdon to restrict us to the campus, and what to do if one is casually identified by the attorney general as subversive or communistic. Since I sat at the opposite end of the table, everybody had to listen.

Clifford explained that we had fewer rights at a private school than students at a state school. No institution could, however, without good reason, abridge any of the rights guaranteed under state and federal constitutions such as freedom of assembly, speech, religion, and so forth.

I told Mr. Durr that Dr. Searcy had restricted us to campus supposedly for our own safety. "Searcy maintains the administration is acting in the place of parents while we're away from home and they are responsible for our life and limbs. They say they can't guarantee our safety off campus."

"I'm not sure they can guarantee it on campus," Head interjected.

"That may be true," Clifford said. "What Dr. Searcy is enunciating is the theory, 'in loco parentis.' That's just Latin for—"

"In the place of the parents," Bill Head broke in.

Clifford looked approvingly at Head and continued, "Right, but in the final analysis, according to what Bob said, their position rests on the old segregationist view that people don't have the right to do anything the Ku Klux Klan doesn't want them to do."

Joe Thomas told of the conversation with Dr. Arlie B. Davidson, our sociology professor, who said we'd be arrested if we sat down with Negroes to discuss the bus boycott. Everybody laughed when John Hill explained standing-up and sitting-down integration. Then Townsend described Searcy's face when I added "horizontal" as a third type of integration that seemed to be accepted in Montgomery, as evidenced by the number of light-skinned Negroes.

"It is ironic, isn't it, Mr. Zellner," Mrs. Durr was still being formal with me, "that segregationists will tolerate standing-up integration and even support lying-down integration but will kill over sitting-down integration, don't you think?"

Before I could answer, Clifford said, "I don't think it's ironic at all, Virginia, if you understand the Southern mind . . ."

"I believe I do, Cliff. Why I've got one myself," she replied. "Indeed I do understand the Southern mind, but why do otherwise sane, hardworking, God-fearing people insist on continuing to believe these Southern myths and fantasies that have no other purpose than to prop up—"

"They prop up the Southern way of life which has always been damned good business for those who own the South, a lot of whom now are Yankees," he replied, getting in the last word for once.

THAT MEMORABLE DECEMBER DINNER was a welcome respite from the intensity that faced us on campus. Four of us were due to graduate in a few weeks, while Hill had another year to go. I was becoming more and more aware of the difference between the other four students and me in that I had the support of my family and they didn't. They were devastated by the pressure we faced that spring of 1961. Joe Thomas took an overdose of some medicine and was found wandering around campus in a state of incoherence. My roommate, Townsend Ellis, who struggled with obesity and diabetes all his life, went on a drinking and eating binge. John Hill, youngest of the five who were asked to leave Huntingdon, was relatively unscathed. He simply withdrew from school and left for home.

Most affected was William Head from Union Springs, the intellectual leader of our small group. A poet and the most sophisticated of our five, Bill was seen by the rest of us as highly bohemian. We believed he had actually read *On the Road* while we had only heard about Jack Kerouac and other avant-garde writers. If you hung around with "the Head," people thought you were a heavy-duty brain. Before Head and I were revealed as misfits, we had been selected for Sigma, Sigma, Sigma—the college's highest honor. I was sure I had been included out of benevolence or maybe because of my outgoing personality. The power of society was revealed by what happened to William Head when President Searcy demanded that we resign.

Bill did resign from Huntingdon and returned to Union Springs. Normally at college we learned little of each others' families, but, while discussing the importance of parental support when one is rebelling against society, it was hinted that Bill's family in Black Belt Union Springs was on the prominent side—a planter family with political aspirations. Needless to say, his descent into heresy didn't play well back home. Later there was a rumor that Head had become Catholic and enlisted in the Marines. The significance of this rumor was that such behavior was at the very sad end of the spectrum for Brainy Bill—the personification of the questioning mind and the unfettered spirit. I learned years later that William Head had become mentally ill and died an early death.

Townsend tried to explain to me why the four of them were resigning and going home. "You have support, and that makes all the difference in the world. We not only don't have the support of our families, we'll be lucky to stay alive when we go back home."

I told Townsend I didn't see how it could be that bad. He turned red and shouted, "What are you talking about, Zellner? Head has to go back to Union Springs and that's a hell of a lot more dangerous than Mobile. If you get in trouble with the college or the Klan, your father will be up here with twenty preachers to bail your little ass out. Our parents will help the goddamn Klan hang us to a tree."

I pleaded with them not to resign. "Searcy is not going to expel us," I said. "If the administration intended to throw us out, they would already have done it. They're scared to kick us out because of academic freedom. Don't you remember what Glenn Smiley told us?"

I reminded them of the Fellowship of Reconciliation field secretary's offer. He had told us that if we were expelled for attending an integrated meeting with Dr. King, he could guarantee that we would be admitted to any college or university of our choice, including Harvard or Yale. Townsend got mad all over again and hollered that it was well and good for Bill Head and me, but the others were average and could never go to school outside the South much less to Harvard or Yale. He pronounced the names like they were just too precious for words.

I continued doggedly, "They want y'all to voluntarily resign, Townsend; it lets them off the hook. They'll tell the politicians, the police, and the Klan that we are all gone—no more problem. Huntingdon won't have to take a stand either way and everybody will be happy, except us, out on our ear, with no place to go. If we fight them, though, and get expelled, we'll have somewhere to go. There will still be the cause."

That night the Huntingdon Five and a few others close to us discussed "the problem" late into the night. Joe Thomas, ministerial student, again raised the question of how we knew we were right on the subject of race. Townsend and I had recently dropped out of the ministerial program due to its terminal hypocrisy. Joe Thomas, trying to remain in the ministry, questioned, "Say there are three million people in Alabama, and, you know yourself, there are only a tiny number of us. On campus here, for instance, only five people have sufficient balls—excuse the expression—to go to a nonviolent workshop. Twenty are willing to contribute secretly to the Montgomery Improvement Association when the state is taking homes and the cars of black ministers. You know a preacher can't do without a car, no matter what color he is. What makes us right and the rest of the world wrong? Maybe we are wrong and they're right. In fact, I don't see how we can be right and everybody else wrong—it's not natural. What makes us so conceited to think we are correct?"

We chewed on that, then we went over everything again. The first amendment gives us the right to attend meetings. The concept of academic freedom guarantees the right to investigate any question, including integration versus segregation. We not only have the right to disagree with the majority, but the teachings of the church and the great martyrs of history tell us we have a duty to disagree when we think we are right. The discipline of the Methodist church, and Huntingdon is a Methodist school, obligates us to work for racial harmony in an imperfect society. Then the clincher—we're assigned to study the racial problem and that's what we've been doing. Invariably we came to the conclusion, amazing as it seems, that we were right, and the overwhelming majority of the (white) people are simply wrong. We believed most people would someday agree with us.

I unveiled a theory I had concocted. "The main reason for not resigning college is that ninety-nine percent of threats from authorities are not carried out. Mostly authority is not challenged. They seldom intend to carry out their threats, especially when their authority is shaky, as in our case. Therefore, when you resist illegitimate authority, you achieve a degree of freedom for the small price of being willing to resist. If, on the other hand, you obey, they get you to give up your freedom voluntarily. In other words, they oppress you for free. If you resist, freedom is expanded. If you surrender, freedom is curtailed with no cost to the authority." Nobody said anything.

"Of course," I added as an afterthought, "You should be prepared in case they carry out the threat." I ended with a grand flourish, "After all, men, aren't we sociologists and historians? What's the use of a good education if we can't develop theories while testing them in the great laboratory of society?"

"You test them," John Hill exclaimed. "Me, I'm heading home."

When graduation day arrived, I was the only one of the Huntingdon Five to graduate. Townsend transferred to the University in Tuscaloosa and finished two years later. Joe Thomas returned to graduate later. Hill was readmitted the next year and was present when I was arrested on one of my visits back to the campus. Sam Shirah was also there during that visit. Sam, who later became a SNCC worker, had been expelled from Birmingham-Southern, our sister Methodist college in the North Alabama Conference. I was taking Hill's admonition to test my "authority theory" seriously and to set about challenging Huntingdon's restrictions as soon as I could.

6

Freedom Riders in Montgomery

In the meantime, on May 21, 1961, the Freedom Riders came to town. By the time they arrived in Montgomery they were world famous. People and governments around the globe followed their every move, trumpeting their successes and failures. The rides had begun on May 4 in Washington, D.C., when the Congress of Racial Equality (CORE) organized an integrated group of activists to ride Greyhound and Trailways buses into the South; New Orleans was the final destination. Although the federal Interstate Commerce Commission had stated the illegality of segregated facilities at bus and train stations, the Southern states had maintained "White" and "Colored" waiting rooms and bathrooms.

The riders had proceeded with only minor problems until they arrived in Anniston, Alabama, on Sunday, May 14—Mother's Day. One bus went to the Anniston Trailways station where a waiting mob, especially targeting the white riders, entered the bus and beat and stomped the riders and threw them to the back of the bus. The other bus found a KKK-led white mob waiting at the Greyhound station. The driver managed to pull away, but carloads of thugs pursued and a few miles outside of town gunshots flattened the bus's tires and the driver was forced to pull over on the roadside. Then the attackers knocked out windows and threw home-made "Molotov cocktails" into the bus, setting it on fire. The riders were beaten as they left the bus and some might have been killed but for a plainclothes policeman who was on board.

Meanwhile the Trailways bus proceeded on to Birmingham. By this time, the police certainly knew that attacks had occurred in Anniston and that another mob was waiting in Birmingham. But when the bus pulled into the Trailways station, there was not a police officer in sight, and the white mob—again KKK-led—had a free hand in beating the riders. When news reporters later asked Birmingham Police Commissioner Eugene "Bull" Connor where the police were, he managed to keep a straight face when he answered, "Well, unfortunately for these trouble makers, they arrived heah in Birmin'ham on Mutha's Day and all my police were home visiting their mommas."

Pictures of the bus being burned in Anniston and riders being beaten by jeering white mobs in Birmingham appeared in newspapers around the world the next day—on Russian and Chinese breakfast tables—while our people at the United Nations lamely explained to African diplomats that events in Alabama did not represent the United States, just the South.

Part of CORE's objective for the Freedom Rides had been to test the resolve of new President John F. Kennedy and his brother, new Attorney General Robert F. Kennedy, to enforce civil rights legislation and regulations. After Anniston and Birmingham, the Kennedys tried to get CORE to suspend the rides. But students in Nashville, veterans already of the early sit-in movement, were determined that the rides continue. A group of these young people made their way to Birmingham to replace the riders who had been injured. When it became clear that the rides would go on, the Kennedys reluctantly got involved and it looked like the riders would receive a modicum of protection when they left Birmingham headed for Montgomery.

BETWEEN CLASSES, MY LITTLE group of students at Huntingdon were glued to radio and TV watching the struggle and the violence as the riders got closer and closer to us in Montgomery. Gallows humor spawned jokes and bets on whether the riders would get that far.

A prominent news story showed pictures of Bobby Kennedy on the phone from the White House calling to find out who was in charge of the Greyhound and Trailways bus companies, trying to find a bus driver willing to get behind the wheel on the leg to Montgomery. Finally in frustration Bobby ordered that Mr. Greyhound be brought to the phone, "Maybe he can drive his bus from Birmingham to Montgomery." Above the burble of conversation in the TV room we all heard Townsend say, "Yeah, but Mrs.

Greyhound ain't gonna let Mr. Greyhound get nowhere near that particular bus!"

I stayed busy going from friend to friend to see who was willing to go down to the Montgomery bus station to serve as "observers" when the Freedom Riders arrived. After determining that it was mostly the five of us, I arranged a Saturday morning meeting in the dorm room that Townsend and I shared. Speaking quietly behind our closed door, we talked about what we might do if riders were being brutalized in front of us—would we just take mental notes, or, even though we were untrained in nonviolence, would we try to intervene to protect the protesters in some way?

I thought each of us should act as individuals since we would probably not all agree on a collective course of action. Townsend agreed, pointing out that someone needed to remain above the fray to report back, or get people out of jail, etc. "Report to who?" Joe Thomas asked no one in particular. "Whom," Bill Head corrected. "Who, whom, what the hell difference does it make? Townsend grumbled. "Fact is, we ain't got nobody to report to."

"Mrs. Durr said they'd be at Mr. Durr's law office. It's just across the street from the bus station," I said helpfully. Just then the door flew open. It was George Waldron in tears shouting, "They're already at the station and the mob is killing them, it's terrible, you can hear them screaming over the radio." We all broke and ran for my car, careening down four stories of winding stairs.

We had missed the riders' arrival because the normal two hours to travel from Birmingham to Montgomery was cut in half. All traffic was removed from the road and the bus sped to Montgomery under state trooper escort, up to ninety miles an hour. But at the city limits, the state trooper cars and the state plane overhead peeled away, with the understanding that Montgomery police would pick up the protection. However, the local police did not materialize.

There was no protection at the bus station and forty years later the buck is still passing; each level of government, from the national to the local, continues to blame the other. You'd think, after burned buses and Mother's Day massacres, that federal officials would have had several layers of redundancy in place so that protection would be guaranteed! What actually happened is like Hitler telling the Brown Shirts to protect the Jews. President Kennedy turned it over to Bobby who turned it over to the two Johns, Seigenthaler and Doar. They relied on a dedicated segregationist, Governor John Patterson, who in turn asked his very decent but too trusting Public Safety Director Floyd Mann to take over. Mann, head of the Alabama state troopers, inexplicably took the word of Montgomery Public Safety Commissioner L. B. Sullivan that local police would protect the brave young people. Sullivan, the same hard-eyed racist who sued Shuttlesworth and the *New York Times*, turned the Freedom Riders' safety over to the tender mercies of a local Klan thug, Claude Henley, and fifteen or twenty others from the mob in Birmingham. All of this was dutifully reported back to the Kennedys by J. Edgar Hoover's FBI, completing the circle of neglect and incompetence. Once again, repeating the Birmingham experience, the nonviolent demonstrators were left to a KKK-led mob.

Speeding down Court Street we found streets empty of people and cars. Smoke rose slowly from the direction of the bus station and the Federal Building. There were no Freedom Riders in sight, but as we leaped from our old car we saw a crowd of whites circling the bus station and parking lot with their backs to us. Working my way to the front I saw otherwise normal people dancing crazily around a fire in the middle of the street just outside the station parking lot. Shards of broken glass and pieces of cameras littered the street, which looked like it was covered with isolated puddles of glistening red jelly.

As incongruous as the fire was, I remember being shocked when I saw that the burning pile consisted of the Freedom Riders' busted suitcases, books, note books, and the odd toothbrush or deodorant. "That's Samsonite," I said to myself, "You can't break Samsonite."

BACKING SLOWLY OUT OF the crowd, I wheeled and headed for Mr. Durr's law office. Near the entrance to the building I saw a four by eight sheet of plywood with a brick sticking half way through it. The area looked like it had been hit by a sudden and unexpected Category 5 storm.

Hurtling the stairs I found Clifford on the phone peering down at the bus station. Virginia grabbed both my arms, softly screaming that I had to "find Decca—she's down there, no telling what has happened by now . . ."

"Who's that," I blurted.

"Decca—Jessica, Jessica Mitford, remember I told you she's staying with us while doing a story for *Esquire* . . . "

"Yes, I remember . . . what's she look like? How can I find her?"

"She said she'd stay in sight of the office, over there on the corner . . . I can't see her now. Bob, you've got to save her—if they find out she's a Yankee reporter, they will kill her—she's wearing a pink sweater."

I dashed out to look for "Decca," asking myself somewhat irrelevantly if it was a good idea for her to be wearing pink. Then, there she was, cool as a cucumber, taking notes on the corner right outside the office. I was relieved but it turned out she wasn't as calm as she looked. When I clumsily approached her asking, "Are you Jessica Mitford?" a look of pure terror came over her.

"Why do you want to know? Who told you that?" she asked, backing away from me. I finally stammered that Virginia had sent me to get her, frantically pointing over my shoulder in the general direction of the law office. With a great deal of relief, regaining the British jut of her aristocratic chin, she replied, "Well, carry on, we'll go see Virginia and see what we can get into next. You must be Bob."

At that early stage of my involvement, I had little idea how important the Durrs were to the freedom movement in Montgomery and in the country. Since returning to Montgomery from Washington, where Clifford had served in Roosevelt's New Deal and later as a member of the Federal Communications Commission, the Durrs had organized themselves and a few comrades-in-arms into a reliable rear guard for the front-line civil rights workers. I knew, of course, that Clifford and Virginia had gone down to the jail with E. D. Nixon to bail out Rosa Parks, and I knew they were close to Aubrey Williams and his wife. The State Attorney General had told us that much. Virginia's little circle also included Dr. Swenson, a local dentist originally from Minnesota; the Reverend Bob Graetz, a white minister who served a local black Lutheran congregation, and his wife, Jeannie; and Mrs. Francis McLeod, the grand dame of Alabama Methodism. Rosa Parks served as the group's unofficial mentor and contact with the local and national civil rights troops. Aubrey Williams, possibly the most radical of the group, had convinced a young Antioch student, Peter Ackerburg, to come South on his work-study break to help with the *Southern Farmer* magazine which Williams published each month. Peter had adopted our little group at Huntingdon. I was not surprised, then, to find him in the Durrs' tiny office when I returned with Mrs. Mitford. Virginia gave Decca a rare hug and thanked me for "saving her." It wasn't hard, I told her because Mrs. Mitford was right where she said she'd be.

"But what happened to the Freedom Riders?" I asked. "Did any of them survive?"

Joe Thomas and Townsend Ellis had slipped in quietly. Clifford, cupping his hand over the phone, told us that some of the Freedom Riders had been taken to St. Jude's Hospital and asked if we and Peter could go over there and then come back with a report.

Back through the milling crowd and the debris of an uneven battle, we made our way as inconspicuously as possible to the car and headed for the hospital (St. Jude's was a Catholic charity hospital in black west Montgomery, serving mostly the black community). Nobody wanted to talk about what we had witnessed.

Joe and Townsend had not spent as much time with Peter as I had so they made small talk about how a "Yankee" feels living for a while in a Southern town like Montgomery. Ackerburg, however, would have nothing to do with genteel conversation. He asked how we felt about living in a part of the country which was trying to secede from the union a second time. Listening intently, I tried to pay attention to the driving. Joe and Townsend replied a little defensively that while they obviously didn't feel like the white mob outside the bus station, the situation in the South was more complex than Peter might think.

At the hospital visitors' desk we asked about the Freedom Riders, not knowing any of their names. The nuns made sure we were students from Huntingdon before taking us down a hall. Near the end of the passage we could see several doors opened to the hall. Inside the first room was a bed occupied by a young man in a flimsy gown. Sunlight and breeze on white curtains created a flickering glow behind the bed near the window. The form in the bed, its head and face covered in gauze, was indistinct—so much so, I could not determine race or gender. That bruised body in front of us was the white participant, Jim Zwerg.

Zwerg, along with John Lewis, ended up on the first page of newspapers all over the world. There was a familiar picture of Jim feeling inside his bloody mouth for a missing tooth while blood still dripped onto his white shirt and suit, standing next to John Lewis looking dazed but determined.

The black cab drivers at the bus station had been afraid to carry white passengers so a cab had departed with Lewis and William Barbee, leaving Zwerg behind. Later, a black cab driver risked his life and drove Zwerg to St. Jude. The only thing I could think of to say to Zwerg was, "We are so proud of you—you have fought the good fight, but now your freedom ride is over."

Jim managed to lift himself half up. Looking like Lazarus must have, he croaked, "Oh no, as soon as we are able we will be back on the bus." He explained in abbreviated form what he, John Lewis, Diane Nash, and others would repeat many times in the next days and weeks: If the mobs and the Klan and their masters, the Southern politicians, are allowed to stop the movement with violence and murder, then nobody will ever be safe in the South when they exercise their constitutional rights. He said this is a life-and-death struggle and we are committed to see it through. He said the riders were well trained in nonviolence and they had all written their wills. "Win or lose, we are in it to the end."

I could tell Peter Ackerburg was shocked and deeply moved, especially by his fellow northerner, Jim Zwerg. Almost pleading, Peter said, "But this is way past rhetoric. You are almost certainly going to be killed when you get to Mississippi."

Townsend reminded Zwerg that Jim Peck and his bus load of Freedom Riders were almost killed in Anniston when their bus was burned and the riders on the other bus were brutalized when they reached Birmingham. We didn't have to remind him of what had happened here in Montgomery just hours before.

Jim Zwerg wanted us to find the others. "William Barbee is hurt real bad, but I bet you that he and Bernard Lafayette and the others are all planning to continue."

John Lewis, we learned, was patched up by a local black doctor and then went to the Reverend Solomon Seay's house. William Barbee was badly injured and suffered from it for the rest of his life. Freddy Leonard, Bernard Lafayette, and a few others jumped over a retaining wall and escaped through the adjacent post office. Other riders managed to find safety in the black community.

I had expected to see John Lewis at the hospital. He had been badly beaten at the bus station. I hadn't yet met John, but I knew he was an Alabama homeboy, who, like me, grew up experiencing the bittersweet and very slow life of the farm and small-town South. We share the name John Robert, and we both mumbled badly, tending to mangle the language in a pronounced rural dialect. John was short and stocky, dark and muscular—"built low to the ground for hard work," as my uncle Harvey, who lived not far from the Lewis farm, used to say of a good cotton chopper.

John is now a powerful Congressman from Georgia, high up in the Democratic leadership. But back then, I was embarrassed and humiliated and very sad that my fellow white Southerners had battered him and the others like they were dangerous snakes. I would learn later that there were some small heroic actions by some white Southerners that day. When he learned that the Montgomery police were not stopping the mayhem, State Trooper head Floyd Mann rushed to the Greyhound station. He drew his gun and stood over William Barbee saying, "There will be no killing here today!" Tennessean John Seigenthaler Sr., on the scene as Attorney General Bobby Kennedy's personal representative, also risked his life trying to save Susan Wilbur and other women Freedom Riders.

ONCE WE CAME BACK to campus we tried to concentrate on classes. By now everybody considered our little group to be "movement headquarters" at Huntingdon. All day rumors flew that mobs were continuing to gather at various locations around town vowing to hunt down the Freedom Riders and stop them for good. Radio and TV broadcasts kept repeating the promises of the riders to continue all the way to New Orleans, or die trying.

The next night, crowds of Montgomery's black citizens converged for a mass meeting at the Reverend Ralph Abernathy's First Baptist Church. Dr. King had arrived from Atlanta and was there. This was the same sanctuary the Huntingdon Five had visited for the MIA workshops some months earlier. As soon as I got wind of the gathering I planned to go, so when Mrs. Durr insisted that I stay with her and Cliff at their Felder Avenue house I was somewhat crestfallen but maybe a little relieved at the same time. That church would be a dangerous place to try getting into and out of, especially, I thought, for a white person. Virginia explained that the Durr home was becoming a center for progressives from around the country, who were hurrying to Montgomery to continue the rides. The Durrs needed me there to help with any emergencies that might come up. I wondered what kind of emergencies she had in mind. I had not yet put my feet clearly in the activist camp and I was feeling the pressure from home, especially from Mom. She and Dad promised that if I would stick it out at Huntingdon and graduate, then they would both support me in anything I wanted to do in the burgeoning civil rights movement. In retrospect, that was pretty good advice because I probably never would have gotten my bachelor's degree if I had followed my inclination to drop out and join the Freedom Riders. I would have ended up in Mississippi's Parchman Prison with the others.

With mixed feelings then, I waved goodbye to Jessica Mitford and Peter Ackerburg as they departed for the church in Virginia's old Plymouth. Decca had tapped Peter to accompany her to the church in her role as reporter. The next twelve hours were filled with a mixture of heroism, terror, and craven Southern cowardice. Decca had Peter park near the front of the church so they would not have to encounter too many members of the mob outside.

As more Montgomery Negroes packed into the church, more heat was generated, both literally and figuratively. The local and state police apparently decided that a church full of dead blacks and their few white supporters would not look good for Alabama. Governor Patterson had promised Bobby Kennedy he would maintain order, though he didn't prevent the Montgomery police complicity in the Klan massacre of the Freedom Riders at the bus station. Now began some feeble attempts to protect the people inside the church. However, tear gas intended to ward off the racists outside began to waft through the open windows to the already sweltering people inside. Closing the windows only made the heat soar.

Early in the evening, as Reverends Abernathy, Seay, and Fred Shuttlesworth, along with attorney Fred Gray, tried to keep up the people's hopes with spirited oratory, Dr. King was on the phone with Bobby Kennedy in Washington. King demanded that President Kennedy nationalize the Alabama National Guard as the only force large and strong enough to deal with the enraged racists of Alabama. The Kennedys were reluctant to do so because

Governor Patterson had always been a Kennedy man and they did not want to lose what little support the administration had in the South. Eventually, however, the Guard was mobilized and came to the church, restored order, and escorted the trapped people to safety.

Later, Jessica and Peter were exhausted and still jittery from the night's ordeal, but they said a cheery "good night" to the soldiers who dropped them off at the Durr home. "And a good morning to you," the young Guardsmen shouted as their jeep hurtled off into the gathering light, presumably to ferry another anxious group safely home. Jessica then told Virginia how terribly sorry she was that the Durrs' car had been burned up by the mob. Virginia asked Decca if the hoodlums had known it was her car and Decca said they didn't need to know that that particular one belonged to the Durrs. They were burning all the cars.

I learned more about the car-burning about 1995 when I picked up the ringing phone and heard a vaguely recognizable voice, or was it just the Alabama accent? "You may not remember me," the voice said, "but we were school buddies at Huntingdon. I'm Jim Bishop."

I told him I was delighted to hear from him and of course I remembered him—he was rich, from a local construction family. Bishop told me that he had seen my picture in the *New Yorker* magazine and it made him think of me and he had decided to look me up. I said I was glad but I thought he was mistaken about the *New Yorker*.

"That magazine," I assured him, "does not carry photographs—never has, never will, I suppose."

"That shows how much you know, Bob Zellner, because it certainly does now and you are in there, and looking pretty good if I do say so myself—it's a picture of you and Julian Bond, your wife Dottie, and some other SNCC people."

He explained that "Yes, your picture is in the *New Yorker*. It's a photo essay on Camelot, by Richard Avedon. He's a famous person, you know." Then, of course, I knew what Bishop was talking about because Avedon had taught a lot of the SNCC photographers how to take pictures, me included. Between lessons, he took pictures of us. While he took photos of us, because we understood that he was famous, we took pictures of him taking pictures of us. But I had no idea his pictures of us had ever made it into print except in his own books.

I told Jimmy Bishop teasingly that this was all very interesting, but I didn't know until now that Klansmen read the *New Yorker*. After a lengthy silence, Jimmy said, "Well, look, Bob, about that church that night, and burning up all those cars, I want you to know that I never threw that brick I was charged with throwing . . . I know I was in the wrong place at the wrong time, and that is why I was arrested. I always wanted you to know that I personally never set fire to anything and I did not throw that brick."

He went on to say that he now knew he should have been inside the church with me but he did not know any better at the time. He was relieved when I told him I was not in the church either, but I thanked him for thinking I was.

"Well, the important thing is that you knew what was right at the time and we were just too dumb to know it."

I believe that was about the best compliment I ever got for my work in the movement.

A FITTING ENDING TO the story of the Freedom Riders coming to my town of Montgomery was what happened when the first bus pulled out of the battered station for Mississippi. All week Bobby Kennedy and President Kennedy and other parts of the federal government had negotiated with the bus company and city, county, and state officials to provide buses and protection for interracial interstate travelers. Our friend Peter Ackerburg became more and more fascinated and challenged by the raw courage and quiet commitment of the young movement people. Peter kept repeating, sometimes to us, sometimes under his breath, that the Freedom Riders were the most courageous people on earth and that he himself would never be able to do what they are doing.

As their elders in various organizations maneuvered and jockeyed for position and credit for the "success" of the ride, Diane Nash, John Lewis, and the other youth leaders went quietly about the business of calling home to say good-bye and writing their wills. A few of us from Huntingdon were invited to attend, as observers, some intense sessions of preparation. The Reverend James Lawson of Nashville trained the group using role playing and led philosophical and spiritual discussions which provided a forum for the young Freedom Riders who were preparing themselves for possible death.

We stood against the wall in awe as these young people prepared to penetrate the impenetrable and immovable state of resistance called Mississippi. On the morning of their departure, the local newspaper carried an alphabetical list of the Freedom Riders who had boarded the bus for the one-way trip to the Magnolia state. The first name on the list was "Peter Ackerburg."

7

The Highs of Highlander

I first heard about Highlander Folk School in the spring of my senior year at Huntingdon College, from Anne Braden of the *Southern Patriot* newspaper. Anne was also affiliated with the Southern Conference Education Fund, or SCEF. During a telephone conversation with her about the "Huntingdon Five" being restricted to campus "for our own safety," I told her that my dad was willing to go with me to an integrated meeting to test the college's policies, and she told me about an upcoming meeting at Highlander in Monteagle, Tennessee.

"You and your father might want to come," she said. "Dr. King and Rosa Parks have both been to Highlander."

When Dad and I decided to go to Highlander that spring before I graduated, I wanted to learn as much as possible about the folk school. In 1932, seven years before I was born, Myles Horton and Don West founded Highlander School near Monteagle, in west Tennessee. I learned that over the years, Highlander had sparked or assisted a number of important social movements. In college, I had learned a little about one of them—the labor movement. Books on race and civil rights had touched on the importance of labor organizing, especially the difficulty of getting white and black workers in the South to unite.

I thought of Tut Edwards in East Brewton and my early indoctrination in the efficacy of populism. Malcolm "Tut" Edwards used to say with wonderment, "There are so many poor white and colored people, and so few rich people—how can the few rule the many?" Would Highlander help me understand how populism could be successful after so many failed attempts? I was already beginning to wonder how blacks could trust populist leaders who could, if they chose, double cross their black allies and go back to being "good white people."

Highlander Folk School had worked at the Southern grassroots in the mines, the cotton mills, in the forests with timber and lumber workers, and in the 1950s and 1960s it was taking on segregation. You had to admire their guts and determination to believe that education could provide the necessary cutting edge for social change in the South.

During that period, the school was one of the rare places that black and white Southerners could even meet together. Realizing that I had learned more at Huntingdon through participation and "getting into trouble," I was intensely interested in the Highlander theory of education, "experiential learning." The folk school featured learning in the round, with everyone literally sitting in a circle. There were no teachers and no students. All in the circle were both teachers and learners. Director Horton was fond of chortling, "There are no experts here." Highlander had a reputation of being passionately committed to social justice and racial and gender equality, and its analysis of the South and the nation demanded economic and political justice. An earnest young reporter once asked Myles how he got black and white Southerners to sit down together to eat. Myles told him that the famous adult educational center had a very scientific approach that had worked wonderfully over the years.

"What's that?" the reporter asked.

"Well," said Myles, "We use the two-step process, especially on the first day. First, we prepare really delicious food for our hungry folk, and second, we ring the dinner bell. It never fails to work."

At that spring 1961 gathering of movement folk, I was introduced to more of the Student Nonviolent Coordinating Committee freedom fighters. And I learned from Myles Horton that the school was planning a summer program for Southern high school students who would be entering integrated classrooms that fall. Horton asked if I'd be interested in working at Highlander for the summer as a counselor and lifeguard. I had not had time to think much about what I would do for the summer. Heretofore I had worked summers to earn enough money for the next year's college expenses. But now, with luck, I'd be a college graduate—grown! I'd be "free, white, and twenty-one." The world would be my oyster and I was ready to wail. What better way to prepare myself for a life of crime than a summer at Highlander—a hothouse of subversion, known all over the South as a "Communist Training School." A common billboard seen in the South that summer, besides the one that said "See Rock City," was one with a photograph of Martin Luther King Jr., Aubrey Williams, and Myles Horton in a Highlander workshop. The caption was simply "COMMUNIST TRAINING SCHOOL." I still wasn't sure what a communist was but it was clear they weren't segregationists, and they seemed to be a hell of a lot more exciting than the folks I'd grown up with. Besides, any enemy of George Wallace and MacDonald Gallion couldn't be all bad.

THAT SUMMER ON THE Cumberland Plateau was the most exciting in my young life. It was the perfect bridge between two major sections of my existence—before SNCC and after SNCC. Part of the transition from Alabama life to political life was the fact that my little brother, Malcolm, was among the campers. More importantly, SNCC was looking for a white Southerner to join its staff as a campus traveler to interpret the student movement to other young Southerners.

It is ironic that my first extended up-close look at gracious living should be at Highlander, a place that took pride in its identification with the plain people—the poor and the working class. The whole Horton entourage—Myles Horton; his wife Aimee; Charis and Thorsten, Myles's children with his first wife, Zilphia—was glamorous to my south Alabama eyes. The family lived in a rambling old red split-level farm house they had renovated some years before. Along one side of the large house a spacious patio nestled under an ancient wisteria vine, its trunk as large as a small tree. Next to it a pair of sliding glass doors and a row of picture windows revealed a cool interior where a huge living room was centered around an old-fashioned fieldstone fireplace. The patio, with comfortable wooden lounge chairs covered with brightly colored cushions, was surrounded by a low moss-covered stone wall. A desk and straight-backed chair occupied the back corner of the patio under the eaves of the house. There Aimee was writing a dissertation for the University of Chicago, and I was told that Myles sometimes did some of his writing there.

The patio and the living room, dining room, and den area were serviced by a large country kitchen. Guest rooms ranged down a series of halls fanning out from the patio, the den, and the nearby dining room, which held a table matched in size only by the one I had seen and admired at Virginia Durr's house in Montgomery. Family rooms were upstairs. Myles and family held court in this gracious "mansion." At least in my mind it was quite grand.

The house was in shouting distance of the main meeting hall, kitchen, and dining hall but it was isolated enough to give the family some privacy, which they needed because of the constant flood of people who came through Highlander. Having met Clifford and Virginia Durr in Montgomery before coming to Highlander, I was a recent initiate to the Southern salon, the point of which seemed to be to get interesting people together in comfortable surroundings, fortified with food and drink, for the purpose of talking. That's what happened on the Hortons' patio and in their dining room all that spring and summer of 1961. It was a wonderful time to be alive. The Highlander family made me feel part of something special—in a place where I belonged. Virginia Durr had once asked me if I was kin to "anybody." I said no but she accepted me anyway. Highlander people only wanted to know what you had done and what you planned to do about the condition of the world. Talking, apparently, was how these things were discovered. I had thought that preachers, their wives, families, and friends could talk. That was before I met the radicals—the political people. Now, they could talk.

It took a while for me to realize that when Highlander people mentioned Eleanor Roosevelt, Reinhold Niebuhr, Mary McLeod Bethune, or Jane Addams they actually knew these people—they were friends or colleagues! Myles and Aimee talked about the visit of John Dewey and the merits of Hull House and the Danish folk schools. I learned that Myles had been there and knew whereof he spoke. By example, Myles and the folk school staff taught the value of Mao's admonition, "no investigation, no right to speak."

The Hortons' summer soirees introduced me to activists of the exploding Southern civil rights movement. I met Septima Clark, who would run, with the help of Highlander, the citizenship schools with Andrew Young, Dorothy Cotton, and the Southern Christian Leadership Conference. I met Ella Baker, once acting executive director of SCLC, who became very influential in my life. Mrs. Baker, as the SNCC kids called her, had assured the formation of an independent youth movement inside the civil rights struggle—SNCC. She had become one of the adult advisors of SNCC along with Spelman College professor Howard Zinn and Connie Curry of the U.S. National Student Association in the spring of 1960.

I also met important unsung heroes, like Esau Jenkins, a black bus driver from the Sea Islands of South Carolina, a pioneer in the teaching of literacy and promoting black voter registration. He was continuing the work begun by New England schoolmarms who came South during Reconstruction to address the hunger for education among the newly freed men, women, and children of the former slave states. Jenkins required riders on his bus to learn to read, using the transit time between their island homes and Charleston, where they worked. First, large individual letters were posted in the front of the bus. When everyone mastered the letter, another was added until the alphabet was learned. Then words and later simple sentences were posted, leading to the first "book." The book consisted of requirements and instructions on how to register to vote. The payment each student owed for learning to read was to recruit another person for the literacy class, and everyone had to become a registered voter.

At Myles and Aimee's house I met Modjeska Simpkins, who became the board president of the Southern Conference Education Fund, and I met Candy and Guy Carawan, bards and troubadours of the movement—as of 2008 still singing and living at Highlander. Guy taught us an old Southern hymn that Zilphia Horton had first heard sung by tobacco workers on a picket line. The workers had sung, "I shall overcome," but Zilphia changed it to "we shall overcome." And for that song, as they say, the rest is certainly history.

Candy and Guy were busy spreading the news and wearing big holes in the bottom of their shoes. Along with Pete Seeger, Guy and Candy helped develop the powerful movement culture sweeping the South and later the nation. Candy, a close friend of freedom rider Susan Wilbur, was a student at Fisk, a white "exchange student" from California, and an earlier sit-inner and freedom rider. Guy was from Pomona, California, and they both talked a little funny with hard r's and clipped speech. Candy, a blond, blue-eyed comedienne, had written a very funny song about going to jail called, "The Judge, He Went Wild Over Me." Guy, tall and thin with his banjo, could be mistaken for a slack-jawed mountaineer right out of the Hatfields and McCoys. They were the first full-time movement people I met from the younger generation.

THE 1961 SUMMER PROGRAM was the last act in the existence of Highlander at its Monteagle, Tennessee, location. During the fall and winter the state of Tennessee confiscated Highlander and systematically destroyed the facility, eventually razing the buildings and bulldozing the site. It is not recorded whether salt was sown in the torn-up ground. Myles Horton had always told anyone willing to listen that no organization or institution should last beyond twenty-five years. His theory was that if you can't do what you set out to do in that time, you're not doing something right. At one workshop that summer, billed as how to organize for the long haul, Horton described how in the early days he urged the Folk School board—which included Reinhold Niebuhr, Jane Addams, and Eleanor Roosevelt—to amend the charter to require Highlander to go out of business after twenty-five years. Myles could be very persuasive, but the board refused to go along. "That was all right," Horton laughed, "because every twenty-five years or so the state comes along and destroys us anyway." That was when he told us that our summer camp at Monteagle would be the last for the Highlander Folk School.

As we sat in the traditional Highlander circle, Myles told the life story of his institution. Then he said a new organization, the Highlander Center, would open in a big house on the river in Knoxville. If you're a big overripe seed pod like Highlander Folk School and reactionary powers smash you, then seeds fly everywhere.

Listening to him, it was hard to be sad, but later in the bunk house, talking to my little brother Malcolm and the other boys in my charge, I realized that Myles, his wife Aimee, Guy and Candy Carawan, the staff, and board members had every right to feel flattened, but here they were—grinning, rubbing their hands together—looking forward to the next chapter in an exhilarating life. I tried to find out if Malcolm and his new friends in the bunkhouse were getting the lessons, but they only wanted to talk about girls. Malcolm asked what I thought about Tony Helstein and I said I thought she was pretty.

"Yeah, she's bad," he said. I thought, how extraordinary that my brother, who until now had never been outside of south Alabama, could have a crush on the daughter of Ralph Helstein, the president of the Amalgamated Meat Cutters Union from Chicago, Illinois, a man pilloried as a communist labor leader. Even more remarkable was the new vocabulary Malcolm was picking up from his black bunk mates.

Malcolm and I also learned that [violence is never far beneath the surface in the South, especially when social change is occurring.] Highlander was near the cliffs marking the eastern edge of the Cumberland Plateau. The achingly beautiful campus included a lake which sparkled in the clear mountain air. Swimming, however, was an adventure. The first time strangers appeared across the lake, I thought they were waving to us and maybe skipping stones on the water towards us. It occurred to me soon, however, that the puffs of smoke and the popping sounds meant that they were shooting at the black and white kids in the water. As the Red Cross-certified head life guard, I thought it best to order the campers out of the water till the shooting stopped. At dinner that evening, the summer staff announced amended swimming rules. "When shooting starts, everybody out." In addition we recommended that each swimmer and his/her buddy find a suitable tree or rock to get behind. Snipers became another summer hazard like high wind or sudden electrical storms.

If even the isolated and relatively insulated campus was unsafe, then venturing into town was a trip. Myles and Aimee decided that the entire summer army—campers and staff—needed a break, so they planned a field trip to see Rock City. Many of the campers from the South, black and white, had spent their lives reading the giant slogan painted on the tops or sides of barns, urging that they "SEE ROCK CITY." Some Southern mothers swear the first words their child ever read were, "thee wok thity."

Aimee and Myles loaded up their little red English Ford convertible and the rest piled into an assortment of vehicles for the mountain ride to Chattanooga. Somebody shouted, "I want to see the choo-choo." Another asked if he'd be able to see the shoe shine boy. Another wit asked in a loud voice, "The shoe-shine *what?*" "Sorry, the shoe-shine *man.*"

When our group ascended the mountain, it was clear that we were the first integrated gaggle of tourists to see these wonders. It was not long before some yahoo commandeered the public address system asking what the world was coming to when niggers could barge in where only white people belonged. We took the abuse stoically but when the whites began to organize into fighting groups, we thought it wise to group together for a strategic retreat, the adults forming a circle around the smallest children. Safely in the cars, headed out of Chattanooga, someone thought our feelings would be helped by an infusion of ice cream so we all pulled into a Dairy Queen. Since we were served standing up, the counter people didn't seem upset with our group's salt-and-pepper complexion. The rowdies, however, had other plans and some began harassing us. What we didn't realize was that the more serious Klan types were preparing an ambush for us on the road back to Monteagle.

Just as the last camper grasped her ice cream cone an oily-haired local with rolled up tee-shirt sleeves slammed the child against the ice cream shed and pushed the cone into her face. As Susan Wilbur, another of the counselors, and I took the tearful camper by each arm, the crowd began chanting, "Kill the nigger-lovers, kill the son's a bitches . . ." Beating a second retreat, everyone loaded up in the nearest car. I remember being somewhat torn between wanting to protect my little brother Malcolm and a strange urge to keep a safe eye on my comely new friend Susan.

As our little caravan pulled out slowly from the Dairy Queen, we were careful not to lose any of our cars, even though we were followed by some of the hoodlums who hung out their car windows shouting insults, "Good riddance and don't ever come back. Go back to New York." When one shouted over the noise of the hurrying cars, "No, go back to RUSSIA!" we could hear cackling laughter echoing up the mountain road.

Then, without warning, rounding a curve, we were startled to see pickups and cars partially blocking the road, bright headlights pointed at us. In the lead car, Myles could see there was enough room for one car to get through. He waved us ahead at high speed. I remember shouting, "Roll up the windows and duck." As the right rear window in our car was being raised, a Coke bottle whizzed through and shattered against the left window inside the car. Luckily we were in and out of the gauntlet in seconds. Everybody had their heads down and eyes closed, so, in our car, we were merely drenched with glass particles.

Those country boys proved to be good shots with rocks and bottles so the nurse back at Highlander was up late cleaning glass from eyes and fixing cuts and bruises. Every car in the caravan looked like it had been the loser in a demolition derby. I learned a couple of valuable movement lessons that night. Be cool under fire and make good decisions. Movement cars take a lot of punishment and being in a storm of violence and emotions binds people together—the foxhole effect. If you are being shot at together, you tend to become brothers and sisters quickly.

Another lesson, somewhat more complicated, was repeated frequently in my movement experience. A person with little familiarity with civil rights history might ask, "If you want to make good decisions, why go in an integrated group to see segregated Rock City to begin with?" What is difficult to understand is that the radicals, and especially the young people on the cutting edge of the struggle, made a decision to try to live as if the "beloved community" already existed. In other words we would take great risks to do ordinary things. What, after all, could be more normal than taking a group of young people to the top of Lookout Mountain, where one could see seven states? The only way our group differed from thousands of other pilgrimages to Chattanooga was that we were black and white together. Today, I am sure, not a head turns when tourist buses unload thousands of multicolored travelers to see Rock City.

THE MOST EXCITING EVENT of the summer was falling in love with Susan Wilbur. Already a movement hero, she was a member of the incredible Nashville student group which had such a stunning impact on black and white young Southerners. Nashville kick-started and energized the entire movement, ending the lull which followed the Montgomery Bus Boycott. I had seen but not met Susan earlier in the spring of 1961 when she and the other Susan, Susan Hermann, committing an act of revolutionary near-suicide, were on the first bus of freedom riders to reach Montgomery and the waiting Klan terrorists. The two Susans and Jim Zwerg were the only whites on the bus as the KKK thugs began methodically brutalizing the black, white, male, and female riders. John Seigenthaler Sr., the personal representative of the attorney general of the United States, tried to help some of the women escape. A group of white women with bricks in their purses were pummeling Susan and the other women while chasing them down the street away from the bus station when Seigenthaler pulled his car alongside. Leaping out, he ordered the women to get into his car. "I'm a federal officer," he shouted.

Hesitating a moment, Susan pulled away, "Mister, this isn't your fight—we'll be all right."

In that split second, they could have gotten away. As it was, Robert Kennedy's personal representative was felled from behind by a pipe-wielding citizen of the rebel state of Alabama. Susan and her friends managed to achieve sanctuary of sorts by fleeing into the nearby post office/federal courthouse. Their would-be rescuer, bleeding and unconscious from the nearly fatal blow behind his ear, lay for more than an hour in the bloody, wreckage-strewn street, while the mob tossed broken news cameras, clothes, toothbrushes, suitcases, and college school books into garish mid-street bonfires. When Susan told me this story I thought that Seigenthaler, attorney general's representative or not, was lucky to survive his trip to the Cradle of the Confederacy. I knew Susan and the others were also lucky to be alive and I marveled at her calm assertion that she would do the same tomorrow if it became necessary.

I told Susan my own story from the point of view of a non-terrorist member of the crowd at the bus station that day. This shared adventure got us introduced, but it was hormones and Susan's beauty which took us the rest of the way. I was captivated by her red hair, and her healthy, outdoor complexion spoke of days on horseback in the Tennessee back country. She was ruddy and rosy red and her slightly up-turned pudgy nose with little freckles fit perfectly over her pouty and, I thought, extremely kissable lips. Lithe and shapely, Susan was less self-conscious about her body than any woman I had ever met. She was the first example I'd personally experienced of many women within the civil rights movement who were challenging both gender and racial boundaries. Maybe she came by it naturally; her mother, a working single mom, had obviously instilled in Susan an appreciation of female liberation even before that's what it was called.

Susan had brought her jumping horse to Highlander to augment the folk school's small herd. Soon after we met she invited me to saddle one of the Highlander horses and ride out to the cliffs with her. Deep into the farther pasture, we jumped the fence and rode along the precipice looking into the blue distance of the Cumberland Mountains. With an intense feeling of euphoria, I rode along behind this beautiful woman. That day and over that summer at Highlander, Susan introduced me to a level of relationships and intimacy that was new to me—natural and free from repressed guilt. I could not help comparing the experience of loving Susan with that of my high school and college romance with a girl I had assumed I would eventually marry, because that's how it was supposed to work in those days. My earlier girl friend and I had been inhibited and frustrated, and as our college years ended it became clear that the security of marriage was really more significant to her than the mutual giving of a relationship.

Susan was nothing like that. Guilt and repression were not a part of her love equation. I was even more astounded and delighted when, on our first visit to her home in Nashville, her mother obviously was accepting of our affection for each other. Breathing a silent prayer of thanks for the people of the upper South, I was amazed at how different they were from the ones I'd grown up with in Alabama. The people of the Bible Belt participated in a lot of sex—but they always had to pay. Anything that much fun must be a sin and the wages of sin is death—and don't you forget it. I could barely keep up with the changes occurring in my naive, country, and church-encrusted life. The atmosphere of freedom at Highlander, which placed a premium on respect for young people and respect for privacy, was unlike anything I had experienced before. That summer with Susan gave me the first inkling of what it was like to be grown up and free.

Trips to Nashville that summer began a pattern that was to last through my first period as a SNCC staff member. Between organizing trips and jail stays I always found an excuse to go to Nashville for a few idyllic days with Susan, my first mature love. It helped that Nashville had the most active local movement in the South in those days. Many of the early SNCC stalwarts were still attending college at one of the myriad institutions in the Athens of the South. Susan's sister and her mother seemed to take it on as part of their duty to the movement to patch me up for the next round of action in the deep South. Nashville became a reliable and relatively safe "rear" area, specializing in R&R and spiritual renewal. The colleges and universities of Nashville served the purpose during the early days of the student movement that New Orleans later served when the action moved from the border areas

of the upper South to the Deep South arena of SNCC's middle period—
when Mississippi burned.

THE GREATEST FAVOR SUSAN did for me was to introduce her trench mates—
the black and white brothers and sisters with whom she had shared jail cells
and death-defying freedom rides. Her sister was a student at the University
of Tennessee in Knoxville, where Marion Barry was also a graduate student
in chemistry. At the founding meeting in 1960 of the Student Nonviolent
Coordinating Committee, Marion had been elected temporary chairman.
One weekend during the summer, Susan and I drove from Monteagle to
UT to visit her sister, who suggested that we call Marion. The summer session of the university was almost over and I knew by then that I was going
to work for SNCC in the fall. I was excited about the opportunity to talk
to a SNCCer who had been there from the beginning. Marion Barry and
other black activists had high respect for Susan and her sister who had made
their bones in the struggle while most young white Southerners were either
too timid or too reactionary to even dream of sitting in, much less courting death on a freedom ride to Montgomery, Alabama. Marion, the two
Wilburs, and I found a restaurant near campus where we could talk and
drink coffee. We were so high on freedom that we didn't anticipate what
was about to happen.

The four of us sat in a booth next to the front plate glass window, where
we ordered coffee and doughnuts from a rather sullen waitress. As soon as
she disappeared through swinging doors, an older man approached us and
stated as though it was a clear matter of fact that we would have to leave.
Identifying himself as the manager, he said that it was time to mop up around
the booths as it was near closing time. We had chosen the diner because it
had a sign out front which read, "We Never Close."

While the manager frantically motioned to a younger man who approached with a pail of water and a mop, we quietly but firmly offered to
move to the tables, out of harm's and mops' way. The young man, either
slow or vaguely sympathetic, protested to the manager that, "We never mop
before midnight . . ." The manager's face flooded red, shouting that we were
conducting an illegal sit-in (I wondered if there was any other kind). He
promised to have us all arrested. Susan put her face in his and said through

clenched teeth that we had not intended to have a demonstration. She told him, further, that we only wanted coffee but he had now embarrassed us and everybody else in the restaurant.

"You've made it an issue so now we don't intend to leave. Besides," she said, "we thought you were already integrated, that's why we came here."

All this time Marion Barry was trying to calm Susan and her sister. Thoroughly up in arms now with the bit in their teeth, the two of them were threatening to organize a twenty-four hour picket around the diner.

"Be cool, be cool. There's no real need to get arrested over this—let's just leave now and we'll deal with this backwardness later."

While Marion was trying to calm everyone, the unexpected happened. A man wearing a brown tweed jacket slowly rose from his seat and reached for the shoulder of the manager. We were moving towards the door when the manager slapped the stranger's hand away and shouted to the cooks and waitresses, all of whom were peering from between the swinging doors, to call the police. "This man has assaulted me and I intend to see that he is taken to jail."

At first I thought he was talking about Marion, but I soon realized that Barry was trying to control this tweed-jacketed man who was trying to grasp the lapels of the manager's rumpled suit.

"I most certainly did not assault you, sir, but I consider it an outrage the way you are treating this black man and his friends. I will not stand by and let you insult them in this manner."

It made Marion nervous for white people to be arguing; he gave me a pleading look as if to say, what should we do now? I must have looked pretty useless but I managed to whisper that whatever we were going to do we should do it quickly. I nodded towards four policemen leaping from their cars, heading our way. We wound up following the police down to central lockup to arrange bail for our protector who, it turned out, was a new professor at UT and unused to blatant racism. We told him that he would soon get used to it, or he could look forward to spending a lot of time in jail. The professor laughed and said he'd never done anything like this before. "Something snapped," he said. "I've been under a lot of pressure lately. I just took my PhD exams today."

We gave statements that the teacher had not assaulted the restaurant manager, but they charged him anyway. Years later, when Marion was mayor of Washington, D.C., I asked him if he remembered the stranger who got so upset when we were thrown out of the restaurant in Knoxville. Marion mused, "That happened in 1961, I wonder whatever happened to that guy?"

HIGHLANDER WAS ALSO THE scene of my first face-to-face meeting with Anne Braden. I had only talked to her on the phone up to then, and I don't know exactly what I expected. I remember being mildly surprised at her easy Southern manners. Anne was passionate and intense without being overpowering. My little group at Huntingdon had become accustomed to feeling at total odds with "the Southern way of life." It was comforting to recognize Mrs. Braden as being truly Southern (from Alabama) while holding such apparent non-Southern beliefs and opinions.

When Anne had first called us at college (and I did consider it "us" and not just me), we were titillated with the idea that these "communists" we had so forcefully been warned against, would, of course, hold unorthodox views. Now here she was all soft Southern comfort, with a somewhat old-fashioned beauty that might grace an ad for the Clairol look.

She played a role for generations of young Southerners that made us comfortable in opposing segregation and racial hatred. She did, in person, what Professor C. Vann Woodward, in *The Strange Career of Jim Crow*, did in print. They held that one could be both a good white Southerner *and* an active opponent of segregation.

If Rosa Parks and Martin Luther King Jr. had convinced me to join the struggle, it was Anne Braden who showed me how to do it. In retrospect, Anne, more than any other person, can claim credit or accept blame for guiding me into the century's most titanic clash.

In the meantime, I had been accepted as one of the eighteen Southern participants in a program called the Southern Student Human Relations Seminar. It was sponsored by the U.S. National Student Association, and held on the campus of the University of Wisconsin for three weeks in August. The director was Constance Curry, and the advisor was the Reverend Will D. Campbell. Connie and Will built on the foundation already put in place for me by Myles Horton, Anne Braden, Clifford and Virginia Durr, Rosa Parks, Dr. King, and the students. The seminar provided much education on

Southern history, movement issues, and I carefully read C. Vann Woodward's book, wishing I had read it for sociology at Huntingdon.

The human relations seminar was a watershed event for me, even though Connie told me later that she and Will were concerned that I might be "too advanced" for the other participants. This might seem strange since this was very early in my human relations "career." About the only things I had done up to this time was the student activism at Huntingdon, observing the freedom ride in Montgomery, and working for the summer at Highlander. The idea that I might be too movement-savvy for the seminar, then, says more about the level of most of the participants than about me. The NSA, the YWCA, and the various church organizations were doing a fairly good job of providing entry-level experiences to young grassroots white and black Southerners. In my opinion the seminars run by Connie and Will were the best of these efforts.

Having successfully scared all of us into reading the required materials and books, Connie and Will had the perfect opening for the seminar. We were all familiar with ice-breakers, but the Curry/Campbell dog-and-pony show was nothing short of a glacier-breaker. While Will plucked his guitar and sang along, Connie led out with a lusty version of the country classic made famous by Burl Ives, "Little bitty tear let me down, spoiled my act as a clown, had it made up not to make a frown but a little bitty tear let me down . . ."

After that performance we had nothing to worry about. We could not say or think of anything more hokey. If we had worried about making fools of ourselves, it was now clear sailing. Will would shift his chew of tobacco from one cheek to the other and start another verse. Soon we were all singing along with the two of them like we had grown up together, which I suppose was the point. Will was always laid back with a mysterious air like he knew all about the night of the hunter. His black slouch hat and the old black preacher suit he wore spoke volumes about his attitude toward life, race, and everything else.

Connie and Will were obviously having the time of their lives at the seminar, mentoring us youngsters and it was clear that they delighted in introducing us to the curriculum subjects and the writers, historians and others we met that late summer in Wisconsin. Madison itself was a major player

in our education, many of us having never been out of the Deep South. I
remember eating in the university dining hall. The food was exquisite. I had
never had vegetables that still looked like their fresh selves. The peas were
still green and the carrots still yellow, and even though they were cooked,
they still had a snap and a crunch. At first I thought they were a mistake.
Maybe the fire went out and the cook did not notice.

During our down times when not in seminar, Will and Connie were
nowhere to be found, so we explored the campus and the surrounding area
on our own. I remember a Sunday afternoon when a group of us strolled the
length of a long peninsula far out in one of the beautiful lakes surrounding
Madison.

Families and their friends were gathered around endless grills laden with
the most delicious-looking and -smelling sausages. Everybody was turning up glistening cans and bottles of Milwaukee's finest beers. I remember
D'Army Bailey whispering to me not to stare so hard at the people's food.
That admonition was followed by the sotto voce observation that there
were not many black people out on the peninsula that day. "Maybe they
are all still in church," he speculated. Bailey was from Louisiana and would
become a respected judge in his adopted state of Tennessee. Memphis was
more like Mississippi and Louisiana than the rest of the state. I like to think
that Connie's seminar gave him a giant boost up a tall ladder. D'Army may
have learned from me and other white students that not all white Southern
males are gothic throwbacks.

Eventually our seminar group approached the end of the walkway where
we discovered a racially mixed group tending several grills. A few folks, black
and white, with cane poles, stared intently at bobbing corks in the peaceful lake water. As we arrived, an older black women sang out, "I got one,"
hauling in a decent-sized yellow perch.

A black man hollered back, "Hold her, I'll be right there."

Brushing corn meal off his hands, with the red apron around his waist,
the old man reached for the wiggling fish. He took it to a folding table and
began scaling.

We were fascinated and I remember saying to D'Army, "Say, brother,
who's staring now?"

A couple of young black fellows looked at us as if to say, "These old folk will never change." I noticed that the younger men had rods and reels. Using the opening, I asked, "What y'all fishing for?"

"Walleye," he said, "or muskie. You can get a really big one here—if you have the right bait and equipment and know how to use it."

"And what's that?" D'Army asked.

"Live minnows, and this," the other young fisherman answered, pointing to his shiny rod and reel. "Course the bait and the rod does no good if you don't set the drag real light. One of these big ones hits, he can take thirty feet in two seconds. Set her light, let him run, and reel him in slow with your tip way up."

One of the white boys in our group said, "Keep yo' tip up so you don't give him no slack. Cut him any slack and you got no fish."

D'Army displayed his sense of humor when he fake-punched the young white Southerner and whispered for everybody to hear, "Y'all got a lot of experience in not cutting anything no slack."

Our laughing was interrupted by the sound of heaven when the old folks took pity on the six of us. "Y'all had dinner?" It was the older man who was scaling and frying the fresh fish. "Everybody here done ate much as they can hold. Plenty more fish, brats, beer, and potato salad Momma made. Want some?"

A more rhetorical question was never asked. We descended on the table making the old folks happy. The young fishermen stuck their rods in holders and ambled over, intrigued with our obvious Southernness and being together. We described the seminar and they turned out to be university students from the South. They said to check out a meeting that week of the Socialist Club. I almost fell over: "You mean they won't get arrested?

"Not in Madison," one of the students said.

Back at the seminar Monday morning, we learned a little more about our hosts, Will and Connie. Will was born in Amite County, Mississippi, and had experienced a lot more than most coming from a born-again Southern Baptist background. I identified bone-deep. I had no idea where he was going, but I was willing to go with him. I was responding to something in Will that resonated with lots of young white Southerners. In the same way that historian Vann Woodward taught, through the writings we were studying at the seminar, that one could be a good Southerner and still oppose racial oppression and segregation—Campbell taught by example and his presence. I observed later that Will Campbell became a respected mentor of several generations of young Southern churchmen, through his writings, his witness, and his pulpitless ministry. I discovered that he refused to reject Klansmen and their families, pastoring them in sickness and at their times of death, performing their marriages, and baptizing their offspring. He also became a mentor, guru and sage to the Nashville music crowd who lived near where he settled in Mt. Juliet, Tennessee. This, I think, is particularly important because a right-wing, quasi-racist attitude was almost required if one was to succeed as a country music performer. A recent example of dissension which was severely punished by the industry was the treatment of the Dixie Chicks when they criticized President Bush.

Connie, who had grown up in the South but was the daughter of Irish immigrants, seemed like a Southern magnolia at one moment and a stateless, regionless sage the next. She would be enormously important in my future life, already serving, along with Ella Baker and Howard Zinn, as an "adult advisor" to my organization of choice, the Student Nonviolent Coordinating Committee. It didn't occur to us youngsters that Connie was just three or four years older. In the fall of 1961, James Rufus Forman would become the dynamo we called the SNCC executive secretary. Funny that we didn't think of him as an adult, even though he must have been older than Curry.

Being accepted for the seminar gave me a strange sense of peace and at the same time it quickened my pulse. The old saw about graduation throwing one out into the cold cruel world would not apply to me.

WHEN I WAS FIRST talking to Anne Braden in the early spring of 1961, I didn't know she and the Southern Conference Education Fund (SCEF) were on the lookout for someone to work on the SNCC staff. Anne mentioned the "white student project" to me during the first meeting at Highlander and gave me some history of the idea. SCEF people had been excited about the student movement when the first sit-in occurred in Greensboro, North Carolina, on February 1, 1960. Anne started thinking of getting Southern whites to see that civil rights was their fight, too. At the October 1960 SNCC conference in Atlanta, Anne had the chance to meet many of the new young SNCC leaders and realized that the group was firmly under the leadership of young Southern black men and women. The gathering also included over a dozen white Southern students. Anne realized that young black and white Southerners had an opportunity, through joint struggle, to forge more intimate and stronger bonds than any of their elders had ever had through "talk" meetings and socials.

She initially hoped to convince Jane Stembridge, the first white Southerner to serve on the SNCC staff, to take on the job of "campus traveler" to white schools. Stembridge told Anne that she didn't plan to remain on staff. SNCC could afford only one full-time worker and she thought it should be a black person that replaced her.

Jane's decision to leave was also prompted by the shabby treatment afforded veteran organizer Bayard Rustin, who was dis-invited to be the keynote speaker at the October 1960 SNCC meeting in Atlanta following complaints from several foundations threatening to withdraw grants.

Though Bayard was close to Martin Luther King Jr. and had advised King during the Montgomery Bus Boycott, he was a socialist and had once been in the Communist Party. Worst of all, in some minds, Rustin was a homosexual. Looking back, it is strange how communism and homosexuality were given so much power by those who feared them and how they could be raised to taint the work of the civil rights movement.

Anne also learned that debate had, in fact, roiled all summer about SNCC being associated with SCEF because of the "communist question." SNCC decided to have her at the conference as an invited "observer." Braden thought the best way to take the weapon of red-baiting and homophobia away from our enemies was to simply refuse to play the game. If liberals and movement people refused to red-bait themselves, the tactic could not possibly tear the left apart.

Anne continued to look for a white person to be the campus traveler to white campuses, and I was thrilled when I was chosen in the summer of 1961. SCEF agreed to send SNCC a $5,000 grant to pay me a stipend and expenses, and after leaving the NSA Seminar and Congress in August, I returned to Alabama to get ready for a murky future.

8

My September 11th Farewell

September 11, 2001, now called "9-11," will forever be a tragic day in American history, but for me it also signifies the day in 1961 when I joined the freedom movement. The whole family had gathered at the Seven Z's, our vacation cabin in Daphne, Alabama, on Mobile Bay. My father named the cottage after the seven of us Zellners; he thought the name was evocative of far-off seas and exotic places. It was a little summer beach cottage with one great room downstairs, which meant that the kitchen occupied one corner. Dad had built a small bedroom for him and Mom on the south side of the great room. An upstairs loft had lots of beds for the boys. The cabin was never locked, and all of our friends knew it was open to them if they needed a place to stay. The cabin would be Mom and Dad's permanent home when Daddy retired from the Alabama-West Florida Conference of the Methodist Church.

That cool, gray September morning is sharp in my memory. I woke up early. Mom and Dad were asleep downstairs and my brothers were still asleep in the loft. Dad had reminded me to get up early for the trip to Atlanta. I considered waking up my brother Jim, but he was snoring so sweetly, I didn't have the heart. He had driven almost all night from Durham in his little red beat-up old sports car. When he showed up, it hit me that the family was gathering to send me off as our representative to the movement. After taking a good long look at him sleeping there on the old sofa next to the stone fireplace, I slipped out of the house and headed over to the old Phillips place on my way down the hill, or "under the hill," as the people in Daphne call going to the bay.

Daddy had gotten the land for our cabin from our neighbor Henry

Phillips. He and his wife, Bessie, had been life-long members of Daphne's Methodist church, had raised a healthy family, and had acquired some land on their uncertain fishing income. A well-worn road through the pines led to the mooring where Phillips kept his boat and nets.

Walking past their old house and the ice house where the fish were kept cold, I silently thanked old man Henry for making our cabin possible. When the Bishop transferred my father from the church in Daphne to East Brewton, Alabama, Henry and Bessie were distraught. We had grown close to them so Henry gave Dad the lot next to their house, because it would insure that we would be back.

The Phillips land was filled with virgin pines, so we cut down just enough for space for the house, and just those trees from that small area were enough to build the whole house. The logs were hauled off to the saw mill nearby and cut into floor joists and floor boards, rafters, studs, and boards for the outside of the house. The roof was tin, which made wonderful sounds when it rained.

Then Daddy built a large stone fireplace. He had dreamed of this house for years and had collected the stones from all over, and as he mortared the stones, he would say, "Now, I got this rock in North Carolina when I was on a trip to Boston." He knew the story of just about every stone that went into that chimney. The fireplace had a big iron bar that swung out, and you could hang a pot on it. We also had a grill for that fireplace to roast ducks and clams and oysters right out of the bay.

On my way down through the woods, I remembered Jim and I and Mother helping Dad build the cabin when I was eight years old. The board-and-batten siding had since turned an old weather-beaten green. Helping to build that cabin was the beginning of learning the skills of carpentry which would see me through lean periods in my life. Doug, David, and Malcolm were too little to help but they all remember carrying nails or at least beating on something while the work was going on. Those are wonderful memories.

Mobile Bay was a big part of our life in Daphne. Leaving the trees for the sand of the beach, the salty tang of bay water brought images of Jim and me and sometimes Doug sailing our little skiff, with the rigged-up sail, from our house all the way up to the May Day wharf in Daphne and back. In summer, when all the conditions are right, the eastern shore at Mobile Bay has a jubilee. That is when the flounder, eels, crabs, and shrimp just come right up to the shallows at the edge of the water. We would go down and get bushels of them. I remembered one jubilee when Felix Bigby and I tied a line from the boat to our belt and towed it behind us as we waded near the shore and gigged 108 five-pound flounders. We speared so many of the flat fish, while others were scooping up crabs, that the flounders started flopping over the sides of the boat and getting away. We gave away a lot of the little ones and started gigging only the huge ones of door-mat size. We cleaned them and put them in the freezer, feasting on them for months. Those were the days, I thought, and then I remembered I was about to go away to Atlanta. I didn't know what was waiting for me.

I took a long look at the clear water of the bay, making a conscious effort to imprint the way the grass on the shallow sand bars waved slowly, hiding flashes of the startled blue crabs. We would wade in the eel grass in the shallows and pick up the delicacy known as soft-shell crabs. The uninitiated could not tell the difference, but you could always pick out the ones who looked shiny and clean, just up from the gulf. Local Mobile Bay crabs were darker with patches of brown and green moss clinging to their shells. Mr. Phillips and his son Talley had taught me to distinguish between a freshly molted crab with rubbery bright blue and pale yellow skin and one right next to it which could give one a nasty wound with its sharp claws. The soft-shells we picked up in our hands and placed carefully in a white oak basket for Mom to fry later. The hard ones we unceremoniously scooped in the long-handled net and threw into a wash tub.

The sun was barely up when Jim came down the dirt path and joined me on the bay. He had noticed that Henry and Talley had already gone down the hill to the water as well. Later, they would pull and push their old cart, hopefully full of fresh mullet, back up the hill to the ice house next to the road that ran in front of both our houses.

"If they get back in time," Jim said quietly, reading my mind, "we could plank some mullet by the fire, before you go." I told him that would be great but we'd be gone by then. There was not a soul in sight, as Mr. Phillips and Talley had rowed completely out of sight. The September air was brisk here on the cold sand but Jim dragged our old skiff toward the shallow water.

We slowly crow-poled through the thick grass, peering down through the clear fall water. This had always been my favorite time of year—when time stopped and all the fish and animals were fat from summer and not yet hidden from the cold to come.

Jim was in graduate school at Duke, studying theology—for a career in the ministry. Jim had participated in the early sit-ins at Duke the previous spring. He tried to warn me what I was in for. "I hope and I think your personality is suited for this kind of thing. Mine isn't," he said. "I get too angry." He was by that time, pretty full of anger, and I was less full of anger, because my makeup was more optimistic. Jim had always been a little darker, more existential. He said, "It's gonna be really tough, and it's gonna be tough for you to be accepted. You know, you can be a part of it, but it's really their thing."

I don't know if I saw it as a good thing that early on, but I did understand that the leadership of the student civil rights movement belonged to young black Southerners. Whites in the freedom struggle should and would be, as far as leadership is concerned, in a secondary role. But, I told Jim that I was not in this for the black people—if this was just acting on a missionary impulse, I wouldn't survive—that I had to look at it from a different angle. I was involved because I was fighting for my own rights as well. At Huntingdon, I had seen what happened to people when they stood up on the racial issue. My cautious professor had tried to restrain us, but he was nonetheless crucified for his association with us. No, I was joining the movement to establish my own right to fight for what I believed in.

Jim nodded in understanding as we walked back into the house with our catch of a few crabs. Fried soft-shell crabs and crab omelets were our favorite breakfast. We liked them fried with great big bowls of white crabmeat that had been picked out and scrambled with eggs. Mother also made corn muffins, grits, bacon, hot biscuits and fig preserves. Sometimes, we also had pickled herring and pumpernickel bread, which Dad had learned to like while he was in Europe.

While Mom prepared breakfast with some help from Jim and me, the rest of the family descended the stairs to the table. Besides Jim and myself and Mom and Dad, there was my next youngest brother Doug, then David and Malcolm. Jim was 23. I was 21. Doug, 18, David, 17, and the youngest, Malcolm, was 14. I was especially close to Malcolm because we had just spent the summer together at Highlander.

Breakfast was a noisy, boisterous meal. It was an emotional day, and everyone seemed determined to put a jolly face on it. My family would cover up any potentially traumatic or sorrowful event by being very funny, making lots of jokes, and playing tricks on people. My father had gone to boarding school early on, and the culture was to hide any kind of hurt—stiff upper lip at all times. You toughed it out. We had all learned that from him.

My younger brothers, who were kind of wide-eyed about all this, kept saying, "Bob is going to jail. You better enjoy your last breakfast, because you don't get good food in jail." My brothers are a kaleidoscope of images and memories. Baby brother Malcolm never made a secret of his admiration for and approval of what I was doing. Doug, the next down from me, had suffered in silence, following two older brothers' footprints at Huntingdon, then transferring to Rocky Mount College in North Carolina to get away from my notoriety. But he was no doubt resigned to more of the same, as he stoically supported my actions.

David, next to the youngest, was getting away. Drafted into the Air Force (as Malcolm would be in two years), he was slated to help Uncle Sam fight the powerful Vietnamese peasants.

Jim was quiet and withdrawn, even more so than usual. I sensed that this cheerful celebration contained more than a little irony for him. He had tried to become a part of the movement at Duke, and now everyone was making such a fuss over me going to work for SNCC. In Durham, North Carolina, a number of white students had taken part in movement activities; it was, apparently, no big deal. But in Alabama, fewer opportunities existed for whites to participate, so it became a big deal. Jim's quiet personality had probably made it difficult for the black students to relate to him easily.

Mother took no part in the joking. She always remained ethereal on one hand, but strongly spiritual and tough on the other. She had to be, in a family with six males. Also, when we were small and living in the country, Daddy had small country churches and we didn't have much money. She had to work awfully hard just to keep the clothes clean, and she made sure we all learned how to make beds and sweep floors and cook. I am grateful for that to this day. Many times, she had told me that her secret dream had been to be a missionary to Africa, but she had gotten married right out of college, and like many women at that time, she subsumed all of her dreams to her husband's. She became the perfect minister's wife. She also taught school, but that was secondary to Dad's career as the minister.

Looking across the table at her, I saw tears in her eyes. She was afraid for me, but she was too strong and unaccustomed to expressing sentiment to voice it. Still, I knew her wet eyes were sending me a message to be careful. In the South, a young man with prospects, from a good family, was not supposed to go off and join the rabble. I knew, and they knew, my actions would not sit well with the Klan—even those who were family. Mother was struggling between being proud of me for going off to SNCC and the movement but also wanting to protect me from harm. Suddenly, I felt a powerful tug not to leave this nest. I worried about what would happen to her, to them, because of what I was about to do. Indeed, later on when I was in the thick of things with SNCC, all of my brothers caught a lot of flack for being named Zellner. They told me that they made a pact to always say, "Yes, he's my brother, and I'm proud of it," even though it placed them in harm's way.

I felt privileged that my family would give me their support to join the movement. I knew that most of my fellow recent graduates would choose to go on with careers—grad school or jobs. After breakfast, my father and several of his minister friends would drive me to the Butler Street YMCA in Atlanta. I was touched that in some way they saw the Methodist Conference sending me as their stand-in. After dropping me off, they were going on to one of their "core" meetings, as they called their regular gathering of progressive ministers in Lake Junaluska, North Carolina.

We were still eating breakfast when Floyd Enfinger showed up and immediately pitched into the breakfast, gobbling up huge mounds of eggs and crabs and crunching into one of Mom's fried soft-shells. Floyd's church, which had provided my part-time job while I was at Huntingdon, was located in a white working-class community just outside Montgomery. Floyd had a lot of Klansmen in his congregation, but he was still one of the most outspoken ministers against the group. Chisholm was a small community and since Floyd's was the only Methodist church, that's where Methodist Klansmen had to go. In fact, one of the Klansmen in his congregation was related to

Sonny Kyle Livingston, who had made a public vow to kill me and had the confrontation with my roommate Townsend when we were at Huntingdon. The good Reverend Enfinger was committing an act of bravery by coming with us to Atlanta.

Mom may have been thinking at that last breakfast that I was going to make a missionary-like contribution for the good of the people, but she was also worried. She knew how dangerous it was with her own brothers-in-law as vicious Klansmen who would hurt people and maybe even kill. So she was struggling between pride and fear.

Then it was time to go, and we all went outside to pack up our '56 Chrysler with the Dynaflo transmission. I sat in the back seat on the right hand side. Along with all of the family, some of the neighbors came out who probably thought I was going off to graduate school. My brother Jim gave me a big hard hug, and Mom was pretty tearful by that time. The other little boys were running around pretending that they weren't all that concerned about it, but they were worried about it, too. What I was doing was a decidedly weird thing. I remember looking back at them standing in front of the cabin, and I thought back to building the cabin and all the good times we had there I knew there was a chance I would never see it again. The cabin had become almost a character in our family story, because it was between Mobile and Montgomery and not too far from East Brewton. Now, the little crescent of my childhood—Daphne, Brewton, and Montgomery—was being extended up to Atlanta.

BEFORE THE INTERSTATES, ONE route to Atlanta went from Daphne through East Brewton, and on to Montgomery, and from there to Opelika, then West Point, Georgia, and finally on into Atlanta. That used to be a segment of the main route from New York City to New Orleans—most of it was a two-lane road, up the hills, down the hills, with lots of kudzu-covered forest. Up closer to Montgomery, you come out of the piney woods into the Black Belt, just like a prairie, a large alluvial plain that was ocean bottom for eons. It has deep rich soil, good for grazing cattle, and especially good for cotton. Alabama's Black Belt is the heart of the Deep South with a lot of old towns, where the rich planters lived and built their antebellum houses. You could still see many of them from our car, up the straight driveways with the oak trees on both sides—columned houses—some gone to rack and ruin and others bought up by people with new money and refurbished.

Against that was the stark poverty. White Southerners almost never noticed the poverty even though there was always the big house and the little shacks, because for them, that was the way it was. Someone might comment on the little shacks, "Aren't they picturesque?" Did they even see the people—white and black—who lived in the shacks, sitting on the front porch with cotton sacks hanging up on the sides of the house, and maybe a pile of cotton at one end that they have picked and are waiting to take to the gin. Some of these shacks were called "shotgun" houses, meaning you can see from the front door all the way through to the back, and if you shot in the front door, it wouldn't hit anything until it went out the back door. Others were called "dogtrots," because the two parts of the house were separated by an open-air gallery to let breezes blow through against the sweltering summer heat. Another reason was that in summer, when they had to cook on the wood stove on one side, the other side of the house would not be so miserably hot. Sometimes, the shacks wouldn't have window panes, but instead would have shutters that were hinged at the top that were let down at night or in cold weather. Otherwise, they were propped up, with no screens, just open air. If you were inside the shack, you could look down through the floor boards to the ground where the chickens were scratching around under the house, or where some old hound dogs were resting. Most people kept hound dogs for hunting.

There was an outhouse in the back and a pump over on one side, and the barn right down from the house. There might be some mules in the barn for plowing. There might be three or four cars in the yard. Most of them were up on blocks. You'd usually try to get the same model car, so that you could take parts as needed for the running car, and as older ones became skeletons, they could be dragged off into the gully in back of the house. The kids were in short pants, no shoes, ragged shirts.

It was a good ten- to twelve-hour trip, about four hundred miles, to Atlanta. It was really a fascinating car trip for me. The four ministers began to talk and tell stories—some that I had never heard. They were part of a group of progressive ministers who had made a pact that they would not allow themselves to be run out over racial issues. If one preacher was run out, people would then say, "We should be able to get rid of our preacher—he's preaching the same stuff." So these progressive ministers viewed themselves like rocks in a dam: if you moved one, the whole thing could be swept away. They took a pledge—We will not go North; we will not be run out of the conference. We'll teach what we see to be Christianity, and we will stay. The progressive minister knew that the Bishop of the Alabama-West Florida Conference, by church law, was obligated to give the liberal preachers a church to serve each year, unless he could convict them of a formal morals or ecclesiastical charge. My father was one of those ministers, and the pledge also meant that they wouldn't mind being punished and sent to low-paying charges and difficult churches. They weren't going to prosper in their profession. They would never have the "first" church, the big church, the big salary, or the nice car.

Reverend C. C. Garner, one of the older ministers in this group, had mentored a lot of the younger ones. He was a backwoods scholar, almost completely self-taught. As we continued the trip, the ministers all started talking about their mentors, and Garner told the story of Andrew Sledd. Their own little group was named the Andrew Sledd Study Club. Garner said that many of the early twentieth-century churchmen in the Alabama conference were influenced by the Candler School of Theology at Emory. Sledd was a professor of Latin at Emory who had married the daughter of the Reverend Warren A. Candler, the president of Emory. The Atlanta Compromise at the 1895 Cotton States and International Exposition saw Booker T. Washington embrace the tragic failure of Reconstruction, while W. E. B. Du Bois continued to organize the struggle for economic, political, *and* social equality.

By 1902, Andrew Sledd, whose Southerner views had been ameliorated by two years at Harvard, was aghast at the upsurge of lynchings as the new century began. His article opposing lynch law in the *Atlantic Monthly*, "The Negro; Another View," turned out to be far too progressive for turn-of-the-century Atlanta. Even though his father-in-law, one of the most powerful men in Georgia, had become Bishop, there was no protection for Sledd and he was fired. So Dad's secret group of activist ministers took Andrew Sledd as one of their heroes as they vowed never to leave the Alabama–West Florida Conference.

Then they talked about Dan Whitsett and Andrew Turnipseed who were a little bit older than my father, and had led the young ministers into the social gospel, having put some steel into their backbones. The two had spoken out, after the 1954 *Brown v. Board* Supreme Court decision, on the need for churches to support school desegregation. Whitsett and Turnipseed were both learned and popular ministers slated to be bishops. But after their stand, both were forced to leave Alabama. Whitsett went to Epworth Methodist Church at Harvard; Turnipseed to a big Methodist Church in Brooklyn, New York. Both came back to Alabama near the end of their careers. Ministers like them and in the car with me said, "If we're going to let our congregations dictate what we can preach from the pulpit, we've lost the soul of the church." They were a part of the tradition of strong ministers taking strong social stands and developing a social gospel.

The behavior of the four men on the trip was a revelation to me; they were "off stage," and it was fun. Dad was uncharacteristically quiet, but I sensed he was proud of me. Fletcher McLeod and Dad had been comrades in arms during the battles inside the church for integration and a more socially significant ministry. Floyd Enfinger, of the generation between me and Daddy, had chosen the ministry under Dad's preaching of the social gospel. Daddy had baptized young Floyd by totally immersing him in the cold clears waters of Hurricane Creek, which flowed past the Hurricane Methodist Church on its short trip to the Gulf of Mexico. At about the age of nine I gave my soul to the Lord as Daddy dunked me in the same little creek out from Hurricane, Alabama. Being baptized in the same creek by the same minister always made me feel close to Reverend Enfinger.

These men really believed what they preached, and they knew a person could get into trouble acting on those beliefs. The good feeling and banter, as we whizzed along old Highway 31 going north toward Montgomery, centered on the reality that a new generation was going forth to do battle for the cause. They felt both concern and responsibility because I was following in their footsteps, putting their teachings into action. Grown up now, and going forth to make my mark, I was grateful for the presence of Floyd and Fletcher. I knew I needed to speak volumes to my father. I sensed it would be awkward without the others.

Dad told the story of how C. C. had helped wean him from the Klan when he was still a kid preacher. Dad had apparently told Garner that Klansmen sometimes did good things like taking up a collection for farmers about to lose their land to the bank. Garner argued that cooperatives would help the farmers, but the collective efforts needed broad membership to be effective. Dad said C. C. then asked him (Dad was trying to build cooperatives through the CROP program of the Methodist church): "Who do you think is doing the most to weaken those coops and keep them from spreading?"

Then he answered his own question, "The banks are, the people who own things. And who do you think is doing the most to help the bankers keep the coops weak?" he asked my father. "The Klan." Then Garner gave my father The Lesson, paraphrasing from Booker T. Washington's famous aphorism, a lesson Daddy now passed to me through the story. "Look, James Abraham," Garner had said, "If you want to spend your time holding the Negro down, you can do that. You'll be able to hold that dark brother down in the ditch all right, and you'll be on top of him, but you're still down in the ditch with him, and don't forget that the rich man is clean and walking down the middle of the road laughing at both of you in the ditch."

Then C. C. Garner himself told about his first year of retirement. He had just retired to Stockton, which was just up the Mobile River from Daphne. He had always loved that area because he had served a church at Canoe, Alabama, and at Atmore, not too far away, and close to the Indian reservation where he had a lot of friends. He started going to the Stockton Methodist church, and the congregation knew him by reputation as a nigger lover, an integrationist, and a wild radical when it came to the gospel, so they did their best to discourage him from attending their church. They knew he had a bladder condition and had to pee frequently. On the second or third Sunday that he went to church there, they had the bathroom locked with a sign on it, "Out of Order." He inquired about the problem the first Sunday and said he had to go out to the woods and pee and then come back. The next week, somebody told him that there was nothing wrong with the bathroom, that they were trying to discourage him from coming to church. So, he told us "The next Sunday, I conducted a pee-in. I went over to the bathroom door, and sure enough it was locked, so I just walked out to the front of the church and stood on the stoop. I unzipped and let her fly; peed right off the stoop. Everybody was so shocked and mortified, nobody said anything, but the next Sunday the door was open on the bathroom and it was fixed. That direct action really does work."

When we were going by Phenix City, the talk turned to John Patterson, the governor of Alabama, whose father had been a crusading attorney in Phenix City, also called Sin City, USA, because of mob-controlled gambling, prostitution, and drugs that catered to the soldiers stationed at huge Fort Benning, Georgia, just across the river. Patterson's father was assassinated there, and Patterson had become attorney general and then governor, but in addition to the passionate crusading of his father, he became a passionate segregationist. For a while, Patterson had hitched his star to the John F. Kennedy political wagon, but when integration became an issue, he became a flaming bigot and demagogue. When the Freedom Rides came through Alabama, Patterson saw the opportunity of polishing his own image by fighting federal power. He got into a huge fight with Bobby Kennedy and John Kennedy. My father bemoaned the fact that Patterson was another person with a chance to be a leader and make a difference on the side of peace and racial harmony and desegregation, but he refused to do that. Fletcher McLeod called Patterson "sorry-assed" and talked about how his stand had made it difficult on people like them—stirring up a lot of hate in peoples' hearts and making them think that violence was a good thing.

Then the riding preachers tried to top each other on biblical jokes, testing each other. "When was money first mentioned in the Bible?" "That was in Genesis when the dove brought the green back." "When was tennis first mentioned in the Bible?" "Oh, that was when little David served in the courts of Saul." "Who was the smallest man in the Bible?" "Knee-high-miah." The topper was, "Oh, no the smallest man in the Bible was the Roman centurion who went to sleep on his watch."

THUS WENT OUR TRIP to Atlanta. Jim Forman, SNCC's incoming executive secretary, had told me to go to the Butler Street Y and get a room. That Negro YMCA was in the "Sweet Auburn" area of Atlanta—the heart of the black business district. We saw a white guy on Peachtree Street, which was only a couple of blocks away, but when we asked for directions, he just didn't believe that we wanted to go to Auburn Avenue, telling us it was a "nigra" area. Fletcher, who had been not-so-secretly nipping from a pint of bourbon under his seat, said to the gentleman, "Yeah that's the one. We're applying for membership. Do you think we'll pass?"

When we got to the Y, my traveling companions all got out and walked around for a few minutes, and then came in with me. They stood around the lobby and checked out the place while I got my key. It was a little disconcerting, because they had been the ones who had taught me and taken care of me for so long. Then they said they were going to press on to Lake Junaluska in North Carolina for one of their core group meetings. Dad made sure I had enough money. I had twenty-five or thirty dollars from the collection taken up from my friends and family. It cost fifty cents a night at the Y, and you could get a meal for a dollar and a quarter to a dollar and a half. Once Forman got there, I could start getting my salary, so I felt that I had enough.

Dad made me promise to let him know what was going on, thinking that some of his FBI and other contacts might be of help (though years later, he said they were a bunch of nogoodniks, a bunch of criminals). He actually gave me a hug, which was unusual. First we shook hands. Then he said, "Oh, well," and he hugged me. Then all the other preachers came up and shook my hand and gave me a hug—"You're gonna be our guy," Enfinger said. "You know, you're doing something that we would all love to do, but we 're too old. But we're in the same trench with you. And we're gonna be back in Alabama, fighting it out there every day with the people in our churches and boards, and you're gonna be our representative on the front lines." So I always felt that I was representing the whole Alabama-West Florida Conference in the movement.

They got in the car and drove off, and I waved at them from the sidewalk. I was excited. "Here I am in the biggest town I have probably ever been in outside of New York City, and I don't think I know a single person here except the person I just got a key from." I felt completely free, free and light as a feather, and yet very much alone—about to start a whole new life. I was blissfully unaware that in only a few weeks I would possibly be facing my last day on earth.

WHEN I HAD FIRST gone to the Y desk, the man behind the counter asked dubiously if I wanted a room and looked at me a little strangely, especially with all these white men in suits, preacher-looking types. I told him that Jim Forman had sent me and the men were my preacher friends who had delivered me to start working for SNCC.

He immediately warmed up. He told me all the ropes. He said, "You'll be fine as long as you're here. Mr. Forman asked me to tell you two or three places around here where you can eat. They've got a charge account at one of the places." He recommended a wonderful barbecue place. There were a few white places around, but mostly the neighborhood was completely black.

My room at the Y was spare and simple. I hadn't been in jail at that point, but I learned later on that it was a little bit larger than a jail cell, about eight feet by twelve feet, with a three-quarter bed, a little night table, a Gideon Bible, a linoleum floor, and a window that opened onto a little alley, so it was quiet. There was also a sink beneath a small medicine chest. There was a picture of Jesus on the wall. The bathroom and shower were down the hall. The other residents were a little curious. At first, they thought I was a foreigner from Europe. Then they heard me speak in my thick Alabama accent, but when I told them I was working for SNCC, everything was fine.

9

Briefcase and Broom

The next morning, I got to the SNCC office around 7:30 to meet Ed King, who had been filling in as the interim executive secretary pending Jim Forman's assuming the position. The office was in a storefront on Auburn Avenue, around the corner from the YMCA. A door opened from the street into a hallway with a beauty parlor on the left hand side. On the right was a little room, not much bigger than my room at the Y with nothing in it but one big desk, some basically empty bookcases along the wall, one little filing cabinet in a corner and two chairs—one behind the desk and the other in front. Ed King was behind the desk on the phone when I got there, so I waited in the door. When he hung up the phone, he looked up and said, "Who are you?"

"I'm Bob Zellner."

"Oh, I was expecting you. Come in."

The big old desk took up three-quarters of the room. You could barely squeeze around one side of it, and then it was about three or four feet from the front of the desk to the door. The desk was a gray metal, very utilitarian. Ed was in his early twenties with close-cropped curly hair. He was just a little older than me, fashionably dressed like an Ivy Leaguer. He had on a vest and a blue long-sleeved shirt with a tie. On the back of his chair was a striped jacket. He was very pleasant. "I'm glad you're here. You came early. You are going to need to be here by 7:30 every morning and you don't leave before 5:30." He had a slim-line leather briefcase, and a pad he was writing on. He said, "I'm sorry I've got to leave so fast, but I've got to catch a bus."

"When are you coming back?"

"I'm not."

"Who is coming?"

"I don't know. Just take all the phone messages—who's calling, who they're calling for, and what they want."

Then he said, "Here's the briefcase," and he shoved it toward me. I had assumed that it was his briefcase, but he slid it over to my side of the desk and said, "Here's the briefcase, take good care of it. Everything's in there."

"What's in there?"

"Don't worry about it. Just keep it, and when somebody comes, they'll know who to give it to. Keep it with you at all times. Don't leave it here. If you need anything else, Wyatt Tee Walker with SCLC is across the street. Moses has a desk over there."

"Bob Moses? Is he there?"

"No, he's in Mississippi."

"When is he coming back?"

"I don't know, but if you need anything just go over there and talk to Wyatt, and he'll take care of it for you."

Wyatt Walker had succeeded Ella Baker as the acting director of SCLC. I had first heard of Bob Moses at Highlander Folk School. The SNCC people there said this guy had come down from New York and was doing some work at the SCLC office, and then he went to Mississippi to contact some of Ella Baker's cohorts. They said he was going around Mississippi to see about voter registration. I knew just a little bit about the internal politics of SNCC, and I didn't know that the staff was just getting together that fall of 1961. Since the lunch counter sit-ins and the freedom rides had been led by young people, I figured the organization was already a going concern. I didn't realize they had literally been a coordinating committee up to that point—that the staff was just coalescing. That's why there was such a dearth of people in Atlanta. Everybody was out wherever doing whatever they were doing, and the staff was just going to come together that fall.

The office was so tiny that SNCC staff had to meet in the various nearby restaurants which gave us meeting rooms in the back. The main one was B. B. Beamon's Restaurant on Auburn Avenue, but sometimes we would meet at Paschal's, on the other side of town near the Atlanta University complex. Paschal's was high-class; the little places where we ate around the office, we called the greasies. There was a barbecue place with a wood-burning open pit. The interior of the place was black with smoke from the pit, but it was one of the finest restaurants you'd ever want to have a meal in.

Ed King left within forty-five minutes after I got there. I sat down behind the desk. I wanted to look inside the briefcase, but he hadn't told me I could. There was nothing to read, so I walked down the hall and looked into the beauty parlor. Only black people were inside. They all looked at me pretty strangely until I said, "Oh, I'm with SNCC." They immediately said, "Oh, you're with SNCC. Good, come on in." They gave me some magazines to read. I got *Ebony* and *Jet* and other black magazines. I started especially reading *Jet* because you were likely to run into the names and pictures of many SNCC people. *Jet* became my favorite reading material; I used to take it on the bus with me.

I was trying to find some local SNCC people who knew what was going on, and somebody told me how to get to Paschal's. I walked up to Peachtree, and then got to the street to catch the bus to the Atlanta University area. I had *Ebony* in one hand and *Jet* in the other, and I wondered if people thought I was the whitest Negro they had ever seen. Almost no white people were on the bus. I was really trying to soak up black culture during those days. I was reading *The Black Bourgeoisie* by Franklin Frazier. One of the first things I did when I went to lunch that first day was to stock up on newspapers and *Newsweek*, etc. I knew instinctively I could get a lot of reading done in the next two or three days.

The phone started ringing right away. The caller would just say. "Where's Forman?" If I spoke, they'd say, "Is this the SNCC office? Who are you?" I would reply, "I'm Bob Zellner." I guess word had gotten around that they had hired this white guy to do some campus traveling, because at least most of the callers had heard my name. Reggie Robinson called from Baltimore and several people called from New York—"Where's Moses? When's he coming back?"

Everybody wanted Moses or Forman. "When's he coming?"

"I don't know."

"Why don't you know?"

"Nobody told me."

"Who's there?"

"I'm the only one here."

"Well, when is somebody coming?"

"I don't know. You just tell me what you want 'em to know, and I'll write it out and make sure they get the message."

Forman never called in. Nobody ever did, so I just collected this whole stack of pink message slips. I don't think a single person came into the office that first week. After I locked up, I'd go to the barbecue place for a sandwich and eat it there, or take it back to my room at the Y. I was so lonesome in the room, I would find a place in the lobby with a lamp and a chair. Every now and then I would get into a conversation, and I played ping-pong a couple of times with one of the residents.

ONE MORNING WHEN I had been in the office almost a week, I sensed someone's presence, looked up, and standing just outside the door looking in was Forman, although I had no idea who he was at the time. I just said, "Hello, come in. Who are you?"

Without saying who he was, he said, "Who are you?"

"I'm Bob Zellner."

"Of course you are. I expected you would be here. I'm James Forman."

"Oh, Mr. Forman, please come in."

I jumped up from behind the desk and walked around in front and I took the seat in front of the desk. He had a duffel bag and a reel-to-reel tape recorder. He stood there a minute, and I pointed to the chair behind the desk and said, "Why don't you sit over there?"

He said okay, and then he put his bag in the corner and his tape recorder on the desk. He sat down kind of warily. I stood up and pushed the briefcase toward him and said, "Here's the briefcase."

He said, "Oh, the briefcase."

"Yeah, the briefcase."

He looked at it a little bit. Then he said, "What's in the briefcase?"

"I don't know. I thought you would know."

"How would I know?"

"Well, I don't know."

That's when I learned that he was the executive type. He said, "Well, let's see." He was being very brisk and businesslike. He was wearing a dark gray shirt that was open at the collar, no tie, and what was probably once a blue blazer, now almost shapeless, with baggy pants that were shiny at the knees and at the seat, and a pair of shoes that were just about completely worn out. He looked rumpled like a professor. That was the way he always was. He was thirty-two—an older guy—and big, imposing, with a craggy, pockmarked face. Not a bushy Afro, but a fairly substantial curly Afro. You could tell right away that he was intelligent and quick. He was offhandedly friendly, but kind of feeling things out.

He opened the briefcase and said, "Oh, you know what's in this briefcase? This is SNCC. Probably everything about SNCC is right here." There were letters, minutes of the meetings, all the files from a year and a half since the organization was founded on April 14, 1960. The office file cabinet, meanwhile, was totally empty.

Then he said, "How long have you been here?"

I told him I had gotten to Atlanta on the 11th—five days before, and that I was staying at the Butler Street YMCA.

"You getting enough to eat?"

"Yeah."

Then he said, "Well, let's get down to business." Then he reached over and opened up the tape recorder, plugged it in and put the mike up and then cued up the tape. He said, "I want to know everything about you, man, from the time you were born till right now. Don't leave anything out."

"That's a lot of territory."

 "That's right, it covers a lot of territory, 'cause I want to know what makes a white cat like you want to work with a black outfit like this."

I think he taped it because he had a very strong sense of history. He always did. He would say, "Write it down, document it, keep records," and he was also very security-minded. I was just flattered and thought he was interested in my situation, but he was practicing basic security. He needed to find out why I was there—what made me different, and also if I had the fire in my gut as a committed social activist, or was I there on a lark or as a spy.

I spoke with a thick cracker accent in those days. I spoke into the tape for an hour and a half or two hours. That was only the first session. We had several more sessions after that. We took a break for lunch, and then we talked all afternoon. He was pretty inquisitive, especially when I told about my dad being in the Klan and about my granddaddy and his brothers being in the Klan, and also about my experiences in college, and how I had come to the attention of Anne Braden and other people who had recommended me for the job. I think he realized how wrong I thought things were and my disgust for it all and needing to get as far away from it as possible. The only way I could do it was to throw myself into the struggle completely. We probably taped for about six hours in all. When we were finished, he said, "I hope your story holds up." The implication was he was going to be steadily watching. He didn't warm up to me completely until after the McComb demonstrations and arrest in October. That was really how you became a SNCC person—by putting your body on the line.

At one point, I asked Forman, "Can we talk about how I'm going to do my job?"

"One thing you're going to have to do is go to our next staff meeting. If you're going to do this job, you'll have to know what's going on in SNCC so you can describe it and interpret it to people. I don't know exactly when the staff meeting will be. Moses is in Mississippi. He's probably not going to come here, so we'll probably have to go to Moses. Just keep on coming here like you've been doing. I'm gonna be in and out. Keep taking the messages. In the meantime, why don't you get in touch with Anne and set up some kind of itinerary for yourself, starting the middle of October. By then, we ought to have everything pretty well squared away. We've got to get a place big enough for our meeting—here or in Mississippi, and I'm going to be working on that. We've got a lot of people coming—probably over a dozen."

I didn't realize this was going to be the first full staff meeting. The meetings before that were called coordinating committee meetings, and were mostly attended by representatives of the various movements, like Nashville, Montgomery, Atlanta, and others across the South.

Then Forman said, "We all have to do the work. They call it shit work, but there ain't no shit work. Some of it's detail work, and some of it's not, but we all have to do detail work. Anything you need, go down to the beauty parlor." He went down there, got a broom and told me to sweep the floor, and to start in the hallway near them since they were always helping us out. He said, "The other organizing principle is wherever you go, leave it in better shape than where you found it, and you'll always be welcomed back." That meant either sweeping or sleeping, living in peoples' houses and borrowing offices, all of that. *Leave it in better shape than you found it.*

He was a compulsive floor-sweeper himself. Wherever we were, he would find a broom and sweep or he would give it to other people and say, "We have to keep a neat place. Sweep the floor and write everything down." He had made the point—he was the boss, and it was a novel situation: a black man in the Deep South as the boss of the white guy. I'm sure he said to himself, "White people have been handing black people a broom all their lives, so whenever I have a chance I'll hand the broom to a white guy."

IN THE DAYS FOLLOWING my first meeting with Jim, I gave him my ideas and the list of contacts I had, and as the days went on, more people started to come to the office. During the next few weeks, I met many people around Atlanta and saw others like Connie Curry with the Atlanta-based National Student Association. I had first met her at the Human Relations Seminar in Wisconsin in August. Connie was well-connected because of her work with the Southern students who came to her seminar each summer. She and Ella Baker were the two adult advisors on the SNCC executive committee.

I have always had a special relationship with Bob Mants, whom I also met early on when he was a senior at Morehouse and used to come down to the SNCC office. We were similar in that we were both somewhat rustic and rough cut. I admired Bob because he had a very clear idea of who he was and he didn't much care if someone disapproved of him. Bob took his Atlanta movement experience to southwest Georgia to work with Charles Sherrod and later to Lowndes County in Alabama, where he is still working four decades later, as is Sherrod in Albany, Georgia. Sherrod and Mants are among the very few who came from the outside but stayed in a community to continue their movement work. I see Bob from time to time in Alabama and he is still tall and beautiful and very youthful. Bob's courage is well known so it is not surprising that his friendship with H. Rap Brown, who became chair of SNCC and later took the name Jamil Al Amin, remains strong as he works to get Rap freed from the supermax prison in Florence, Colorado.

I was working on a list of colleges and universities to visit where there were contacts who might be interested in SNCC's work and in joining movement activities. Reverend Will Campbell gave me the names of campus ministers at black and white colleges, so I wouldn't have to visit them cold. I did have to do that at times when I didn't know a single soul there, but usually I would find one contact and if you found one liberal or progressive, they knew others. Unfortunately, it was such a small circle. The YWCA was always a good contact point. Many of the strong African American leaders in the South had been affiliated with the YWCA at one time or another. It was a way that they could do organizing and still have staff positions and salaries. Anne Braden and the whole SCEF network gave me contacts in almost every Southern town.

I started following up on some of the contacts I already had. I was also picking the brain of everybody I could think of in my Methodist network. There was a great deal of intrigue and curiosity and a real hunger for knowledge about fellow students from the other race, on both sides, but especially on the side of young progressive white Southerners. I was not totally aware of the intellectual ferment in the South, but one thing happening at the universities was testing the limits in ways that reminded me of what had happened at Huntingdon. Part of it was from reading authors like John Dollard, Gunnar Myrdal, Tom Pettigrew, and C. Vann Woodward. Their writings all pointed out the conflict between the American creed and its practice in the South and helped to convince a whole new generation of white Southerners that they could still be Southern and be against segregation. It showed them that segregation was basically a recent phenomenon in the South and didn't go back to the antebellum period. Part of my thinking during the early period of campus traveling was to work out a modus vivendi and a rationale for the kind of project that we were going to do, and my feeling was that on every campus and in every town there were some progressive students who wanted to figure out their relationship to the battle forming around them. Could my work with white Southern students help them to deepen their involvement and, by example, maybe lead more of their peers to join the freedom movement? What should their contribution be?

VERY EARLY ON AFTER arriving in Atlanta, I met Casey and Tom Hayden. They had met at the National Student Association Congress in 1960 and were married in September 1961. They just sparkled together, because Casey had so many aspects that Tom didn't have. First of all, she was gorgeous. She was very simple and very Southern, but translucent. She was blond, with cornflower blue eyes, a beautiful smooth complexion, a serene disposition, and an iron will. She was from Texas and combined impeccable manners, gentleness, and a fierce understanding of what was right. Casey always had a kind of otherworldly air, much beyond what she would have gotten from her church upbringing. She was concerned about social issues, but she wasn't an intellectual. If you had to characterize Casey's essence, it would be more philosophical, more existential, more spiritual, along with a fine intellect. Funny, warm, just open and loving without being demonstrative, she was just absolutely Casey.

Many of the white Southerners who were involved very early in SNCC had common characteristics and often it seemed that many things did not even need to be said. Most of my movement friends in the beginning were Southerners, black and white with similarities of age, outlook, and optimism. With our common church backgrounds, we had a certain way of dealing with each other in kind of a brotherhood-sisterhood manner. My cohorts were all intelligent and, without exception, very articulate. Our early staff members were compatible in both our religious backgrounds and important things like soul food and music.

I'm certain I had already met Tom Hayden at the NSA Congress in Wisconsin. He was working with Students for a Democratic Society when it was just a fledgling group. He was from Michigan and was preparing a series of SDS reports on the South. I think SDS had seen that the civil rights movement was going to be the most exciting way of mobilizing students all over the country. I was impressed with all of the SDS guys—their erudition, vocabulary, and the fact that they were just wonderful sharp debaters. He went to McComb after we were there in early October, along with Paul Potter of NSA. Tom was dragged out of his car and beaten in the middle of the street. A photograph was taken with him in a crouched position while he was being beaten by Billy Jack Caston, a nephew of the sheriff. Someone was hitting Tom with what Southerners call the jaws of the pocket knife, and he was bloodied up pretty good. Tom says that picture made him famous. His reports were eventually published in a pamphlet called "Revolution in Mississippi."

Right after I met some of the SDS people, they got me involved with

SDS on the national executive committee. I didn't realize at the time that Tom was getting a lot of his inspiration from us, but I was getting as much inspiration from him and Al Haber and others like them in SDS and NSA. They opened up an entirely new world to me. Until then, the only thing I knew about politics was what I had read in *National Review*, and here were these guys and women who were in the center of political discourse about all the things I cared about—debating the issues, including the world situation. They had intellectualized a lot of things I had experienced and was trying to work through in a philosophical or an emotional way.

Tom had, and still has, a distinctive face with a typical Irish, red bulbous nose, even though he wasn't doing drugs very often, or drinking a lot. His intellect was such that you really loved to be around him, and I think he took to me because I was his extreme opposite. He had grown up in a middle-class family and was the editor of the newspaper at a large university. I'm a back-country guy and went to a small college in Alabama, but we became fast friends.

SNCC had a tradition of women in leadership, but it was not so in SDS, even though there were some strong women. To me, it seemed that male chauvinism was worse in SDS than in SNCC. Some of the main early leaders in SNCC were women. Diane Nash was one of the strongest along with Ruby Doris Smith. Diane had hazel eyes, a light beige complexion and she was so sincere and intense but at the same time relaxed. I had seen her in a film, confronting the mayor of Nashville. It was an extremely powerful lesson, and I thought she was very brave. She would sometimes interject into our long discussions, "We're going to do this because it's the right thing to do." She was very interested in the campus traveling because she thought white students would be the most open. I remember talking to her about how the lunch counter movement and the freedom rides had caught the imagination of the white students and a number of them had come on their own to join. She was not a bit flirtatious but all the men were in love with her anyway.

As I mentioned, the first full-time worker in SNCC was a white woman, Jane Stembridge, who came to Atlanta at Ella Baker's request right after the first organizational meeting in Raleigh. SNCC had also voted to have Constance Curry on the executive committee in the spring of 1960—the first white woman in that role. Casey and Betty Garman and a number of SDS women did a lot of work in SNCC. There was always a chauvinism issue, but it is a reverse anachronism to look at those early days in terms of our present consciousness. Even then, SNCC status was measured in terms of "putting your body on the line," and gender didn't matter.

THE MOVEMENT PEOPLE FROM the North impressed me as the most articulate that I'd ever met; I was intrigued and captivated by the sophistication and erudition of the black and white Yankees. For example, Tim Jenkins was national affairs vice president of the National Student Association. I think he was originally from Philadelphia, went to Howard University, came South a good bit, and really got involved in SNCC. He wore glasses and was a natty dresser. In that era, the overall impression most white Southerners had of black people was of servants, workers—largely poorly educated. But blacks in the movement used words and had ideas I'd never heard before. Tim Jenkins convulsed me with his wicked wit, and I've never forgotten his famous confrontation with William F. Buckley at the 1961 Madison, Wisconsin, NSA convention. A group of us were standing in the lobby outside a plenary session that was debating support for the budding student movement in the South. Buckley was saying that the Young Americans for Freedom, a right-wing group, would "out-organize and bury new groups like SNCC and SDS." Buckley claimed the vast majority of Americans would defeat any attempts to change things in the South because, "we like it that way," and "you can't change 'a way of life.'"

When Bill Buckley said that, a remarkable thing happened. Tim Jenkins, without moving a muscle, seemed to add inches to his lean frame, towering over the famous right-winger. "Buckley," Tim spat out, "in the final analysis, in spite of your erudition, your blue-blood background, that statement simply demonstrates your persistent and malignant slave-owning, crypto-Nazi, Klan-minded, ruling-class, elitist, and unreconstructed reactionary mentality as well as your totally inability to exit the nineteenth century!" Tim said all this without taking a breath, without pause, without hesitation, without repeating a single word. Tim today is a black William Buckley on the progressive side. He's tall and handsome and extremely well dressed. I think he's wealthy. He runs magazines, too. He's still erudite with beautiful speech.

He gave a speech at a SNCC reunion in Raleigh in 2000, and it crossed my mind that he was deliberately making it as obtuse as possible, so that we all would continue to recognize that Tim Jenkins has a great brain.

I was exhilarated to see a black man in the face of a powerful white man. In the South such language was practically a capital offense, and it occurred to me that my new friend, Tim, had not used a single obscenity and yet he had as thoroughly cussed Buckley as any mule skinner has ever dealt with his beast. *National Review* was the only political magazine I had ever been exposed to and now someone had expressed what I felt. I could happily die and go on to heaven.

I loved the big words that some of the Yankees used and I was glad they persisted in using them because it helped those of us educated in the South—black and white—to overcome a certain deficit of intellectual stimulation. I remember one meeting when Harvard-educated John Perdue, asked to report on his research of the power structure in southwest Georgia, began his remarks by saying, as he placed a large stack of papers on the podium, "On the power structure, I have compiled a voluminous compendium of information. . ." He was interrupted by groans, hisses, laughter, and shouting, "Hey bro, break that down . . . voluminous compendium . . . what the?!"

"Okay," Perdue said dryly, "I have assembled a large stack of papers on Daugherty Country and environs . . ."

I GRADUALLY CAME TO realize during staff meetings that not only was the campus traveling project under discussion at some of our meetings, but also the whole question of what SNCC was doing and its future. It took a little while for it to dawn on me that I was in on the ground floor. SNCC was in transition that year from a coordinating committee to full-time staff members like Diane Nash, Ruby Doris Smith, Charles Jones, and Charles Sherrod who were willing to give large batches of time to community organizing. I met Julian Bond, a student at Morehouse who, along with Lonnie King, also at Morehouse, had helped launch the Atlanta sit-ins and student movement. Forman convinced Julian in the spring of 1962 to join the SNCC staff as communications director and begin, among other duties, our publication, *The Student Voice.*

All that fall of 1961, we would go to B. B. Beamon's on Auburn Avenue for our meetings. Forman made an agreement with the restaurant that we could run a tab there and eat and meet in the back room. When Jim first introduced me to some other staff members at an early meeting, he looked down at me and said, "And this guy is Robert Zellner and he's really all right. His accent is a little on the peckerwood side, but it's okay because he is supposed to represent us on white campuses, hopefully. I suggested that he come to the staff meeting because if he's going to interpret what we are doing, then he needs to know what we are doing. Anyway, he's not so bad after you get to know him a little. I've already taped him for an hour or so, and I better tell you right now that his granddaddy was a Klansman, and his father for a short while; but I don't think he is." Forman's hand shot out, "Only kidding, of course." And he grinned at me.

Those fall meetings were very long, and people would come in and out, some from out of town, many visitors from northern groups interested in supporting us—it was so open and inclusive—the real meaning of "the beloved community."

Ella Baker, one of our advisors, was always there. Ella had lots of influence, because she had been instrumental in the beginning when she worked for Dr. King and SCLC and had organized the original student demonstrators to come to Shaw University, in Raleigh, North Carolina, on Easter Weekend of 1960. She wanted to make sure that the student movement would be an independent organization, rather than being absorbed as a youth branch of existing civil rights groups such as SCLC or CORE. SCLC had provided eight hundred dollars to get the conference together and its leadership may have hoped to get SNCC as the youth wing of SCLC. Ella, in her quiet way, convinced the students that they needed to have their own organization. Her vision, and indeed ours, was not to have a central charismatic leader, but a series of local leaders in various areas, with a coordinating aspect from leaders and staff who would make some general policies.

During those Atlanta staff meetings, everybody was smoking, and Ella had a bad asthmatic condition. She would sit by the door, and when necessary, she would go out and get fresh air. Ella was usually quiet so that you became aware of her immense influence and wisdom gradually. She always wore a little pillbox hat, like Jackie Kennedy, and a suit. She had sensible, classical clothes, and very few outfits. That was kind of the organizers' way.

We all had one good outfit and then jeans and some shirts. Most of us paid so little attention to our clothes that every six months or so people would say, "You know, this is too raggedy for you to be wearing. You need to get rid of it." People told stories about Forman's shoes. He would wear them until they were just in tatters, and we would connive to steal his shoes and hide them so he would be forced to go get another pair.

I remember Anne Braden saying during the first couple of months of my work when I was visiting her in Louisville, "Do you have any clothes? Do you have a suit?" I had had some suits in college, but not anymore. So she went with me to get a suit and paid for it —$55—and she said they would just take a dollar or so out of my salary until I had repaid it.

Early on in those Atlanta meetings, a continuing theme was emerging. Should we launch seriously into voter registration? Already two distinct wings were forming among SNCC staff. Prior to the fall of 1961 the predominant form of SNCC work was nonviolent direct action. Diane Nash and John Lewis, along with the majority of the Nashville veterans, favored a continued emphasis on direct action. Some saw demonstrations to be more militant than voter registration work and more likely to arouse the Southern grassroots. They were among the frontline troops who had lived through the lunch counter sit-ins and the freedom rides; most of them had been tempered to a brilliant resilience while coming of age in backwoods jails and prisons. They were convinced the Kennedys and their foundation contacts wanted to detour the struggle out of the streets into what was considered more sedate voter registration campaigns. The militants could see the seductiveness of the promise of big money and the hint that, since voting laws were clear, "the federal government can give you more protection." It was like, you young people calm down and we will facilitate funds for you through all these big foundations.

Direct-action SNCC people didn't want voter registration to sap the spirit of the movement. They favored local activity that got underway quickly under the leadership of SNCC staffers like Charles Sherrod in southwest Georgia. They were not against voter registration efforts but felt it should be considered secondary, with the main focus on integrating the lunch counters, theaters, bowling alleys, libraries, and schools, and when appropriate to branch out to white-only beaches and parks—even to pray-ins in white churches.

So, in the early days, the philosophy of SNCC was slowly being hammered out, and the heated and strong feeling on both sides—direct action vs. voter registration—was becoming quite evident. Some wondered if the organization would split into two different groups with some people doing what Bob Moses was doing already—organizing around voter registration in Mississippi. He had made so many good contacts with older activists there, like E. W. Steptoe, Amzie Moore, and Medgar Evers, and they were hungry for help. People were being threatened and killed for attempting to register.

At one of our meetings, Ella Baker listened to all of the arguments and let things play themselves out, and then, in her usual style, when she felt it was time to reach consensus, she said, "Now, we have two apparently different philosophies and directions and thrusts here. Think about voter registration in Mississippi and Bob Moses setting up the mechanism to do it. Large groups of black people going to the courthouse and demanding to register—nothing could be more direct action than that. There's no reason why we can't have two different tasks in the organization—they can go on together and at the same time." The policy that every issue be resolved by consensus was one reason why our meetings lasted so long. We asked if someone still felt unreadiness on an issue, would they still be able to go along with it, in the sense of democratic centralism. In this instance, we decided that it wasn't necessary for the organization to split in two, which would have shortened its life considerably and diminished its impact on the general movement.

The momentum for all activities and building the strength of the local people often happened at mass meetings at local churches, with music, music, music. The use of music to pull everyone together developed very early, and I found it extremely moving. It came to full bloom in the Albany movement in 1962, but whatever your ideological commitment or intellectual involvement, or your fears—the movement's music leveled us all to the same emotional and spiritual plane. None of us have ever forgotten those songs, and in the shock-troop days, in dangerous situations, the music gave the people strength and courage—soul force. It also gave quite a bit of pause to the posses, state troopers, and police. For some people who were going to break up the demonstrations and do possible violence, they had to steel themselves to attack people while they were singing and while they were praying. A lot of the police would say, "Well, you know, I'm just doing my job," and the demonstrators would confront them, "Are you a Christian? Do you think this is a Christian thing to do? Why are you mistreating us?"

I was quiet during the SNCC staff meetings. I would talk to people during breaks and have conversations with people, but mostly I saw my role as getting as much information and understanding as possible, because they were the experienced ones, the veterans who had been through arrests, beatings, and prison. Sometimes there were a few other white people at the meetings—Connie Curry and Howard Zinn, who was then teaching at Atlanta's Spelman College. And Casey and Tom Hayden might be in and out, and later Dorothy Burlage, who came to work with Connie in the NSA office.

In the meantime, Jim Forman was keeping an eye on me—keeping me close to observe me and to prevent my doing anything foolish. I don't think he trusted me until after McComb, Mississippi.

10

Murder and Mayhem in McComb

I don't remember exactly where I was when I heard that <u>Herbert Lee</u> had been murdered at the cotton gin in the town of Liberty in Amite County, Mississippi, on September 25, 1961. Lee had been working with Bob Moses on voter registration. But right after that news, Forman made the decision that we would have a SNCC staff meeting in McComb on October 4. McComb, Mississippi—that had to be the first time I had ever heard of the place. I had been working on my campus travel schedule for two weeks, but before I could leave on the tour I needed to know a lot more about SNCC. Forman said the best way to learn was to go to the staff meeting in Mississippi. Since Mississippi seemed to play such a large role in SNCC's current activity, I figured I better start there, so I did some quick research in the Atlanta public library—starting with McComb. I felt guilty going into a segregated library, but we needed the information.

McComb is in Pike County, located in the piney woods of south central Mississippi. Though I grew up in deepest darkest rural Alabama, I was afraid of Mississippi. My childhood was filled with blood-chilling stories of lynchings like that of Mack Parker, hung from a bridge in southern Mississippi, and Emmett Till, a fourteen-year-old Chicago child murdered in cold blood by supposedly grown Christian white men in Money, Mississippi, in 1955.

McComb, from its founding in 1872, always was a working-class and agricultural town. The town took its name from Henry Simpson McComb, magnate of the New Orleans, Jackson and Northern Railroad, which had its terminus in McComb. The new town was formed while south Mississippi was still in the potentially revolutionary grip of Reconstruction. About sixty-one years before I first laid eyes on McComb, a Southern white man arrived who would do the most to shape McComb and the surrounding piney woods. His name was Captain J. J. White, and he had just been released from the Federal War Prison. Though most would not speak of it, it was assumed that White had been convicted of war crimes committed during what became known (or mostly unknown in American history) as the Fort Pillow massacre. The slaughter occurred when rebel troops commanded by General Nathan Bedford Forrest (later to lead the Ku Klux Klan) overran the fort, which was defended mostly by uniformed black Union soldiers. When the African American troops surrendered to overwhelming force and numbers, they were summarily executed.

It was not reassuring to me to find that Captain White, a war criminal convicted of murdering black soldiers, was the one who built the sawmill south of town and the McComb Cotton Mills. Captain White's mills, along with the maintenance shops of the Illinois Central Railroad (successor to the New Orleans, Jackson and Northern) and the McColgan Brothers ice house, were the foundation of McComb's economy.

The decision to meet in McComb set a precedent for SNCC to go to wherever the hotspot of activity might be. There was no meeting in a safe reliable space in the rear—you held them on the front lines, and the meeting became part of the front-line activity. When we heard about Lee's murder, it confirmed what everybody had been thinking, that Mississippi was going to be a bloody affair—whites there weren't going to allow voter registration without people forfeiting their lives. Forman told us, "Staff needs to gear up, get to Jackson on the evening of the third, get a few hours sleep and go into McComb before daylight." With Lee's murder, the police and Klan vigilantes would be on the watch for our coming in, so we figured the best time to go in would be three or four o'clock in the morning. Forman said for safety cars would caravan together from Atlanta to Jackson. At the time, we had no new cars. Everyone had raggedy cars. I had already gotten myself a used car for the student traveler project. Anne Braden helped me, and it cost $700. It was a green 1953 Chevrolet—raggedy, but a good fast car, with protective coloration.

The point of the McComb meeting was to have the whole coordinating committee ratify what the core staff was suggesting—yes, we can do voter registration, and yes, we can do direct action at the same time. Staff members were becoming policy makers, determining the direction of SNCC's work. They would then bring it to the coordinating committee for discussion, opinions, and a final decision. Events moved so fast that important decisions were being made in the field by the active staff, to be ratified later. The immediate decision was whether Moses and the others doing voter registration would do it as part of SNCC, and the answer was yes.

Nobody dreamed what that day in McComb would become.

OCTOBER 4, 1961, BEGAN for me when the Atlanta people drove from Tougaloo down to McComb. I was the only white person. Before daylight I could sit up, but by sun-up I had to be hidden, and I lay on the floorboard of the car. Every time we stopped for gas I'd be covered up completely. Once when I complained about the heavy, hot blankets—that we should have brought sheets, the others laughed and teased me about being a white cat feeling more comfortable in sheets.

Driving to Mississippi, I remembered my recent trip to Atlanta from Alabama and found I was having an emotional reaction to the big houses we passed. I hadn't seen those houses when growing up, They were the seats of powerful people, and I felt the same way about those houses that the average black Southerner did—they were totally alien, symbols of illegitimate power that I viscerally opposed. And they exercised that power over not only black people, but also poor white people. I had already developed a strong sense of populism—of being in favor of the little guy, and I realized I was off to do battle against the "big house."

On the way into Mississippi, I was also feeling the difference between my home state and Mississippi. In Alabama you would be wary and somewhat on guard, but that didn't compare to everybody's apprehension and tension the closer we got to Mississippi. The welcome sign at the state line depicted big magnolia blossoms, and it said, "Welcome to Mississippi, the Magnolia State." The magnolias are redolent of the antebellum South and the big plantations. We also saw the signs on the edge of small towns—for Rotary and Civitan clubs, and there was one of a saw blade with a man on a horse, saying, "The KKK welcomes you to . . ."

Whenever SNCC people went into Mississippi, there was a good bit of gallows humor. On this first time, I remember the feeling of quietness and the kind of tightening up. It was like girding for battle, then pulling within yourself so you wouldn't be so exposed—putting on some psychological armor. In the car, it would manifest itself when an experienced veteran would say, "We have to be careful here. Watch the rearview mirror. Definitely do not exceed the speed limit, and don't go obviously too slow." Someone would joke, "Yeah, you know what a Mississippi liberal is? . . . It's a man who will hang you from a low limb." Then someone said, "Listen, if we really cared about living, we wouldn't be in this situation to begin with." There was always that kind of camaraderie. We were all in it together.

From Atlanta to Jackson took us around eight hours. We left Atlanta in late morning and got into Jackson by dark. We went straight to Tougaloo College, an all-black college that became a favorite place for movement people to stay. It wasn't exactly free territory, but it was relatively free—like sanctuary. There were three cars in our group, another couple that had gone on earlier, and another couple that were joining us later. In all, there were six or seven cars. We were pretty worn out by the time we got to Tougaloo. We met in the cafeteria for a little while, and then we all went to bed.

It was an hour and a half to two hours to McComb. To get there by five, we must have left about 2:20 in the morning. The instructions were for the cars not to all go in one line but to always have two cars together. It was pretty quiet all the way into McComb, because people were continuing their sleep. I slept in a corner of the back seat so I could slip down on the floorboard very easily if need be. I put my head back, and it seemed that five minutes later we were coming into McComb. I remember wanting to see what it looked like, but the others put me under the blanket even though it was still somewhat dark. Looking out occasionally, I could see we were in a black section called Burgland, on a gravel road. There were shallow ditches on both sides of the street and little picket fences, and there was a little store with pool tables on the first floor of the Masonic Lodge where SNCC had reserved the upstairs meeting room. I was anxious to get to our room, so I zipped out of the car and up the outside steps into the room which was about thirty by sixteen feet. It had four windows on the long side and no windows on the other side and one each at either end. The spare, austere room was furnished with several folding chairs and a couple of tables in one corner, an American flag and a Masonic flag, and several small cabinets.

Somebody brought in some breakfast. I had no idea it was going to be one of the longest and most terrifying days of my life.

PEOPLE STARTED COMING IN and gathering in little knots to say hello. "Oh, I haven't seen you since Highlander." "What's this about so and so?" "What's happening in Albany?" "Where's Cordell?" "What's Reggie doing?" "He's on the way?" There was a lot of catching up. The few who I remembered meeting at various times, I went over to and greeted. They responded in such a way that I could tell they had heard a fair amount of discussion of me. Someone asked if I really thought I would be able to talk to white students about the movement. One comment really set up what happened later in the day. "You're gonna have to be cool. You're gonna have to stay out of things if you're ever going to get anything done." Bernard Lafayette always had a wry sense of humor. He said, "The white people are going to string you up, boy. They're gonna be on your ass like white on rice. You better lay low or you're never even gonna get to a white campus."

It was obvious that they all loved each other—these were the veterans who had already spent time in jail together, and I remember thinking, they are not at all full of themselves—just going about their business, completely open and doing what has to be done. This was the core of the movement, and I was a part of it. I had gotten some idea of their bravery in Montgomery where I had visited Jim Zwerg in St. Jude hospital. I remember saying to him, "Your freedom ride is over." And he said, "Oh, no, as soon as I am able to get back on my feet, I'll go back to the bus."

That was an incredible memory for me. If a soldier gets wounded, sometimes he or she will say, "Okay, I did my duty, I'm gonna go to the rear now."

SNCC life for me really started at that staff meeting on October 4, 1961, in McComb. I already knew that Jim Forman was going to be very important in my life, but I didn't know what to make of Robert Moses at first. All I knew was the immense mystique that surrounded him (and that grew ever larger with the years). That day in McComb when I first came face-to-face with him. I was what? Enchanted, mesmerized, astounded? Yes. He was quiet. He was roaringly quiet. Here he was standing stolidly, equal weight on both feet, peering intently into my eyes. His eyes were deep brown and clear white, hooded slightly behind round gold-rim glasses. He had on a short-sleeved plaid shirt and was built a little like a boxer. He looked me directly in the eye and said simply, "I'm glad you came. Thanks for taking my messages."

People were coming into the room in ten- or fifteen-minute intervals. Bob said, "We may not have much time so we'd better get started. Everybody here doesn't know each other," and he started introductions. "We all know Chuck McDew, our SNCC chairman. Charles Jones, Reggie Robinson, Marion Barry . . ." and so on around the room.

Moses then gave a quick rundown of the local situation. Herbert Lee, a farmer who had been helping Moses organize in the black community in Amite County, had been shot to death on September 25 by E. H. Hurst, a white Mississippi state legislator from Amite County. Hurst, Lee's next door neighbor, had followed Lee to the cotton gin near Liberty. After parking behind Lee, Hurst got out of his pickup truck, walked up to Lee's truck and threatened him with a gun, telling him, "Get out of that pickup, nigger."

Lee said he wouldn't get out of the truck until Hurst put the gun away. Hurst refused to leave or put the gun away so Lee got out of his truck on the opposite side to leave. Hurst walked around the front of Lee's truck and shot him in the head. The body lay in the dust at the cotton gin for over three hours. A quickly-assembled coroner's jury found no cause of action against Hurst. Two black witnesses to the murder were forced to testify that Lee attacked Hurst with a tire iron. After Moses convinced them to tell the true story to the FBI and to John Doar of the U.S. Justice Department, the information was passed to the local police and the sheriff broke the jaw of one of the witnesses. (The other witness, Lewis Allen, was later shotgunned to death in December 1963 as he locked his front gate on his way out of the state.) That was more or less the report from the voter registration wing of the SNCC staff in McComb.

McDew stood up to make the report of the direct action project. "Hollis [Watkins], Curtis [Hayes], Brenda Travis and the others have just been released from over a month in jail for trying to use the white waiting room at the Greyhound bus station in McComb," McDew reported matter-of-factly. "Brenda," he continued, "returned to school yesterday and was refused admittance by the principal. Hollis Watkins and Curtis Hayes are going over there today with her to try to get her reinstated. If that Tom principal don't let her back in, the kids are going to walk out on that handkerchief head."

I thought later how much like a movie it was when Chuck suddenly stopped talking, and everyone in the room held their breath because of an eerie sound. I didn't know what it was at first because I was not that familiar with the civil rights anthem, but soon the words were unmistakable. I was listening to young voices lustily singing "We shall overcome." The singing got louder and someone in the room said quietly, "Holy Jesus!" Then the students, who were from McComb's Burgland High School, noisily tramped up the stairs. Without hesitating the students flooded into the small meeting room and, in my memory, they immediately sprawled on the floor. Poster boards and magic markers materialized, and they started making picket signs.

Their plan was to march from McComb to Magnolia, the county seat, to protest the murder of Herbert Lee, the August arrests of the McComb students, and the expulsion of Brenda Travis. This was six miles through hostile countryside! Actually, I felt fairly calm, considering the circumstances. I didn't realize at first that this march would be the first of its kind in Mississippi since Reconstruction a hundred years before. At that time, marches in Jackson were black marches of jubilation celebrating the 1870 election of Hiram R. Revels, the first black United States Senator. I remember thinking that Mississippi in 1866 refused to ratify the Thirteenth and Fourteenth amendments to the Constitution, yet a mere four years later enough change had occurred that Mississippi was readmitted to the union and sent a black man to the Senate.

Returning to what was going on under my nose in McComb, I felt I was only minimally involved. After all, my job was to visit white campuses, and if I got mixed up in something like this march it would be highly unlikely that I would ever be able to set foot on a single white Southern campus. Besides, I told myself, I can't go on this demonstration because my father will lose his church and my mother will lose her teaching job. Also, I said to myself, I can't go (not that anyone's asking me, of course) because I'll be the only white person in the march and that might cause more violence than usual. "More violence than usual," I thought to myself. "How much violence is 'usual' in these cases?"

During this long colloquy with myself the students finished their signs and began filing down the steps to form a line of march outside. This caused me to start talking to myself again. "I'm lucky," I thought to myself, "I know what I'm going to do—or in this case, what I'm not going to do. I'm definitely not going to go on that march."

For a fleeting moment I wondered how the other SNCC people decided who was going to go and who was going to stay behind to mind the store. Suddenly it hit me, "What the hell am I talking about . . . what about these kids . . . what's going to happen to them . . . and what about their parents . . . and what about their jobs? This is Mississippi, for Christ's sake . . . in 1961 . . . these kids are going to be massacred."

About half the kids and some of the SNCC staff people had filed out when I slipped into the line and headed down the stairs. Nobody said anything to me and I learned later that this was the SNCC way. Nobody ever suggested that such and such a person be part of any particular direct action. Each person made up his mind each time. There were no orders.

LEAVING THE GLOOM OF the Masonic Hall I was suddenly blinded by the sun of a glorious, brilliant October day. The black people of the Burgland community in McComb, Mississippi, were sky high, right up there with that sun. Smiling, laughing black faces lined the unpaved streets or hung over their front fences and whooped with joy to see this spectacle in deepest, darkest Mississippi. There was banter between the townspeople and the young marchers. We were the old guys, McDew, Moses, and I. I was all of twenty-one, and maybe McDew and Moses, a little older.

As we approached the railroad tracks things began to get quieter until you could hear only the shuffle of feet on dusty gravel. Even the weather, it seemed, began to change as we crossed from "nigger town" to the sidewalks of white McComb. The sky seemed darker and the footfalls were quieter until this nervous quiet was shattered by a shout,

"Zellner, I'll kill you . . . you dirty bastard. I'll kill you!" At first I thought I was hearing things. Nobody here knew me. I'd never been to Mississippi before and even these kids, I was sure, didn't know my name. They knew I was one evermore standout eyesore of a white man in that all-black march, but they didn't know my name. I kept looking for the source of that scream, "Zellner, I'll kill you." The scream seemed to get louder and louder until I finally located a red-faced, bald-headed white man leaning halfway out of a pickup truck.

"Doc," I thought, "good ole Doc from Huntingdon College, captain of the basketball team, my nemesis from school, the man who hated me most, the Klansman who always talked like my first two names were 'nigger lover' as in 'nigger lover' Bob Zellner."

"What luck," I thought, "I never knew where the son-of-a-bitch lived and now by the greatest good luck I've found out."

As I stared dumbfounded at Doc it occurred to me that the whole town, maybe even the whole state, was rapidly mobilizing to annihilate us. Chains and pipes materialized from nowhere. A speeding car cracked through our line trying to run someone down. Students scattered in unison like a school of fish in the presence of a shark, then immediately come back together when the clear and present danger was past. One man ran his old truck into a telephone pole trying to hit some students, then leaped out with a pipe wrench, swinging it wildly over his head like a club. Our people were beginning to be hit.

When the line approached the City Hall in McComb, it was clear that our intention to pause briefly and then proceed to Magnolia was not going to work. Not only was it too late in the day to risk the open country but our progress was blocked by a huge mob of white people that had formed in the street just beyond the City Hall.

What happened then, as I learned later, was typical of SNCC. When in doubt, pray. Hollis Watkins, who I could see from my place in line, stood up on the stoop of the City Hall, raised his left hand, bowed his head and began to pray. I remembered that he was one of the ones who had just gotten out of jail. In a quavery voice Hollis said, "Oh Lord . . ."

Just then a beefy red-faced policeman reached for him and said loudly, "You're under arrest!" Hollis raised both hands over his head and shouted, regretfully, I thought, "Oh Lord!" It was as if he was saying, "Oh Lord, here we go again . . . how much jail time do I get this time?"

It wasn't funny at the time but every time I tell this story I think of the incident with great merriment. Humor and religion: sometimes I don't know which sustained us the most. As other marchers attempted to lead the group in prayer, the same thing happened as with Hollis. Then a small mob of white men began to gather around me. Without seeing him I could sense that my old friend Doc was in this group somewhere. They'd reach over and shove me or lightly poke at me and then look at the police who were by now standing around waiting their turn to arrest a praying marcher. Each time a member of this small mob would hit me the cops would wink or look away and their body language said very clearly, "He's fair game, get him and get him good." I clutched the Bible that Charles Jones had given me earlier. I was standing quietly, determined not to show them any fear. Martial arts training was coming in handy now because I was able, without showing much effort, to minimize the effects of these blows by imperceptibly moving at the very last second, slipping a punch here, rolling with a punch there. At this point I had not even raised my arms to cushion the blows.

As the licks came faster and heavier now I became aware that Bob Moses and Chuck McDew had quietly moved to my side to absorb some of these punches. One stood in front of me and one in back and they faced the attackers without attempting to fight back. They were both stocky and solidly built and they seemed to have absolutely no fear. I would remember this moment as a time of a brotherly male bonding as fierce, I suppose, as any welded in war. When those two—McDew, a dark, superbly trained and conditioned football player, and Moses, light-skinned with the raw power of a boxer, came to my aid I experienced a wild moment of exhilarating insanity.

"We can," I thought, "whip all these lowlifes."

Then, with some disappointment, I remembered we were supposed to be nonviolent. This nonviolence was certainly new to me because I was Southern born and bred and a pretty fair street fighter, as well as being trained in boxing, wrestling, and fencing. The Zellner boys had had to fight their way into every little Southern town their Methodist preacher dad had ever been assigned to.

That moment with me, Moses, and McDew against the mob was fleeting, however. I was in the throes of a most pleasant feeling of security, serenity, and absolute joy to find such brave stalwarts for companions when the cops came over and grabbed the two of them. To this day I remember the sound of the billy clubs and blackjacks the cops used as they thudded into the heads of Moses and McDew. I was thinking, "How can one human do this to another human being—especially with everyone watching?"

Then I thought, "If they act like this in public what will they do to a person in their jail?" At this point I became aware of a strange feeling of detachment. I was being beaten while I watched my new-found friends being brutally gashed and bloodied and yet I felt at peace. I had a sense of standing above myself—of being an observer—of actually watching myself being harried by a small knot of men at the edge of a much larger mob in the street. My senses seemed—and now I am convinced they were—heightened to almost super proportions. Then, with Bob's head bleeding profusely, they dragged him and McDew off. At that point, they could easily have arrested me, but the police obviously didn't want to arrest me, nor did they want to stop the mob from beating me. I watched in great fascination as the larger mob armed itself. They already had pipes and bats and wrenches and now they were methodically tearing down a brick wall in order to fill their hands with missiles. I heard their screams now as the large mob—the one in the middle of the street—was pleading with the small mob around me, about twelve or fifteen men, to drag me out into the middle of the street.

Next thing I knew, they marched our whole crew into the town hall. I believe I was the only person left outside, and it seemed clear that the police didn't intend to protect me or keep the little mob around me from taking me out to the bigger mob. It would have had a different outcome when they first started pummeling me, if the police had come and said, "Out of here," and they could have arrested me very easily. It was like they wanted me to be beaten to death and could say, "There was nothing we could do, there were four hundred people beating this guy to death. Do you expect us to risk our lives for this guy?"

"Bring him here," the larger mob screamed, "We'll kill him. Bring him here." Their banshee screaming sounded like grief—a moan, then a shrill trilling like you hear sometimes in middle Eastern countries during a time of mourning. Then dutifully my little mob began to pick me up and move me bodily toward the street. Up to that point I had been rather passive. I held my Bible close.

Suddenly a thought popped into my head. I heard very clearly in my father's preaching voice, "God helps those who help themselves." "Yes," I thought, "if they take me into that street there is no force on this earth that can save me. They will definitely kill me."

Left: My father, Reverend James Zellner, top row, third from left, with missionary colleagues somewhere in Europe in the early 1930s; standing next to him is Dr. Bob Jones. (Zellner family collection)

Below: Dad (right foreground, wearing glasses), with Dr. Bob Jones (holding hat) in a Polish crowd during the same trip. (ZFC)

Left: "The old Klansman with a stick," Granddaddy J. O. Zellner, in Birmingham. Date unknown. (ZFC)

Below: My parents—James Abraham Zellner and Ruby Rachael Hardy—in their wedding picture, 1935, Fort Deposit, Alabama. (ZFC)

Above: The Zellner family in Newton, Alabama, about 1943. Little soldiers, Jim and me, standing with Doug. David in Mom's arms. On the porch are Uncle Harvey's oldest daughters, Ruth and Madline.

Above: Me on the waterfront in Mobile while living with Uncle Doug and Aunt Peg.

Left: The Seven Zs, cabin, before Daddy built the big fireplace and chimney.

(All photos this page courtesy Zellner family collection)

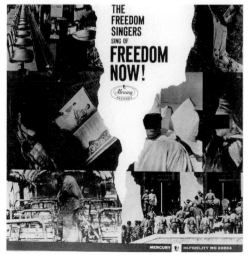

Top: Nashville SNCC meeting, 1961. Susan Wilbur is second from the left in the second row (Bob Zellner collection; photographer unknown). Middle left: My mug shot after being charged with criminal anarchy in Baton Rouge, February 1962 (BZ, courtesy of sheriff). Middle right: A fundraiser in New York City following the Baton Rouge arrest. From left, Anne Braden, Charles McDew, and me (photo courtesy of the Anne Braden Institute for Social Justice Research at the University of Louisville). Right: Cover of one of the SNCC Freedom Singers albums.

Julian Bond and members of the Student Non-Violent Coordinating Committee, Atlanta, Georgia, March 23, 1963. Dottie Zellner is next to me behind Julian. Susan Wilbur is in the next row over my shoulder. (Photograph: Richard Avedon.)

Bob conducting nonviolent workshop with students one night in Talladega, 1962. Joan Browning is to my right. (Wisconsin Historical Society)

Dottie and me in Atlanta, 1963, before our wedding. (Photo by Danny Lyon/ Magnum Photos)

Bob taking pictures at a demonstration at City Hall in Danville, Virginia, 1963. (Wisconsin Historical Society)

Top: Jean Wheeler addresses SNCC staff at Waveland, Mississippi, November 1964. Left: SNCC workers Dorie Ladner, Sam Shirah, Donna Moses, Doris Derby, and others. Bottom: Bob and Dottie take a break during Freedom Summer, Greenwood, 1964. (Photos by Danny Lyon/Magnum Photos)

Above: Jim Forman and Marion Barry in Greenwood, Mississippi, 1964 (Danny Lyon/ Magnum Photos). Left: Bob in the Zellners' apartment in fall 1963 while attending Brandeis (Wisconsin Historical Society). Below: Signs from Mississippi Freedom Summer, 1964 (BZ).

Above: Cordell and Bernice Reagon and Willie Peacock, three of the original Freedom Singers, lead an audience that includes Chuck McDew and Jim Forman, June Johnson, Bob Zellner, McArthur Cotton, Avon Rollins, Ben Grinidge, Joy Reagon, Hollis Watkins, and William Porter. Date and exact location uncertain (Photo by Danny Lyon/Magnum Photos). Below: SNCC and CORE staffers hand out press releases to and are interviewed by national media during the 1963 William Moore march. Bob, Sam Shirah, and Richard Haley are among those interviewed (© 1963 Charles Moore/Black Star).

Top: Me during Freedom Summer, Greenwood, Mississippi, 1964 (Photo by Danny Lyon/Magnum Photos). Below: Bob, Dottie, and Jack Minnis conducting GROW workshop in New Orleans, 1968 (Wisconsin Historical Society).

*With daughters Maggie, left, and Katie, in New Orleans during the
GROW period. (Zellner family collection)*

*Dangerous Communist
Zellner, arrested during
Masonite strike in
Laurel, Mississippi,
1971. Prisoner
Double-O-9.*

With Connecticut Republican Congressman Chris Shay and his wife, Selma, 2000. (Bob Zellner collection)

Right: Telling my story to students, trying to keep hope alive.

Left: With Congressman Michael Forbes and Melissa Bishop, Southampton Town Democratic Chair at the MLK monument in front of Brown Chapel in Selma, 2000. (Bob Zellner collection)

Above: The Reverend Doug Tanner and staff carry John Lewis's banner over the Edmund Pettus Bridge in Selma, Alabama, 2000. Right: Same occasion, Bob with Bernard Lafayette and his wife, Kate (Bob Zellner collection). Below: SNCC reunion in Washington, D.C., 2000. Left to right, Larry Rubin, Matthew Jones, Bob, Marshall Jones, and Harriet Tanzman. The Jones brothers are SNCC Freedom Singers. I am holding Jim Forman's book (Wisconsin Historical Society).

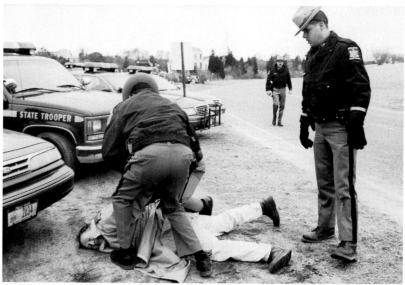

My days of being arrested for civil rights are not quite over. In 2003, I was manhandled by police during a demonstration over the Shinnecock Indian Reservation near where Linda and I live in Southhampton, New York. I recently won a lawsuit against the state troopers over my injuries. (Courtesy Dana Shaw of the Southampton Press*)*

Above: Our Zellner family in front of the fireplace at the Seven Zs, 1963. Mom and Dad seated. The five brothers are, from youngest to oldest, left to right, Malcolm, David, Douglas, Bob, and Jim.

Above: Mom and Dad on their fiftieth wedding anniversary, Daphne, Alabama. Right: My former college roommate, the late Townsend Ellis, sang at Linda's and my wedding. (All photos from the Zellner Family Collection)

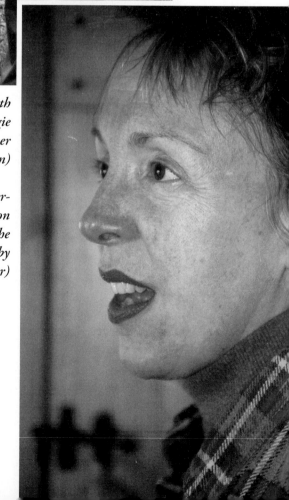

Above: Bob with daughters Maggie and Katie. (Zellner family collection)

Right: Linda Miller-Zellner at home on Towd Point in the Hamptons. (Photo by Bob Zellner)

With this thought in mind I very deliberately placed the Bible on the steps of City Hall and with both hands took hold of the railing pipe that ran down the center of the City Hall steps. It occurred to me that this railing was placed there to help old men and ladies ascend and descend the three tiers of steps to the City Hall.

"I'll try to ascend," I thought quixotically.

Then it became a contest. When I showed this first bit of resistance, the mob, which I thought could not get any louder or more frenzied, exploded. My mind returned very rationally to the contest at hand. If I can hold on here, I have a chance to survive. If they pull me loose, I die. I don't know what held them back but the large mob in the street continued to rely on the small group of men around me.

"This is the vanguard," I thought. "These are the militant Klansmen." Their mettle was being tested now so they set about with grim determination to detach me from my railing. Several grabbed my belt while others took hold of my legs, stretching me out horizontally from the pipe, which I clutched in both hands. There were, I estimated, two or three men holding each of my legs. Others attempted to pry my fingers loose from the somewhat rusty pipe. I was glad it was rusty because, I reasoned, the friction would improve my grip. I calmly noted that my strength was incredible. How could this many men not pull me loose instantly? I was actually in pretty fair condition going into this fight, having just come off years of ballet dancing with the Montgomery Civic Ballet, exhibition diving, and the aforementioned boxing, wrestling and fencing.

"So," I thought, "this is a good contest. I certainly have good motivation at any rate."

It didn't seem odd to me at the time that I would be having these rather detached, meandering thoughts, all the while trying to dodge the blows aimed at my hands now by a lead-filled pipe and the odd baseball bat and wrench. Things were happening fast but my thinking and my physical actions seemed to happen even faster. With lightning speed I would watch the pipe or the wrench descend toward my hands and then at the last possible millisecond I'd release the grip of the endangered hand and grab the rail in a different place. This would give me also a dry, blood-free grip on the rail, which would hopefully enable me to move further up the steps. My mind seemed to be keeping up with many things at one time. The men pulling on my body fell into a rhythm. They'd pull hard and then let up momentarily to gather for another pull. When they leaned back, I'd move up the pipe and hold on for their next pull. It kept coming into my mind, "This is a great contest and I think I'm winning."

This moment of hubris was short-lived, however, as one man behind me became suddenly more hysterical and went for my eyes. I felt particularly vulnerable there because my hands were fully occupied holding onto the rail. This man slipped his hands over my head from behind and began probing into my eyes with his fingers. He seemed to have a purpose in mind beyond just putting his fingers into my eye sockets, and then I realized he was trying to get hold of my eyeball. "Will he really be able to get a grip on my eyeball?" My sociology training came into play at this point as I thought, "This is what they mean when they say 'eye gouging'—this is mayhem."

Once again I decided to help myself if I could without letting go of the rail. I'd wait until he just about got the eye where he wanted it, between his thumb and finger, and then I'd jerk my head in such a way to make the eye slip from between his fingers.

The hysteria of the men around me seemed to reach a peak and they all started climbing on top of me. I supposed they reasoned if they could not pull me loose from that hand rail then they could weigh me down enough to break me loose. So they played how many grown men can we pile on top of Zellner. While they were piling on I realized I had reached the top of the flight of stairs. The last thing I remember was that my head was sticking out of the pile and rested on the top step. I literally could not move. I could do nothing to stop the big brown boot that crashed into my head again and again. Just before I passed out, I thought, "So this is the way I die—like a football being kicked in a scrimmage."

The next thing I was aware of was a man's face in my face saying over and over again, "I shoulda let them kill you, I shoulda let them kill you!" I later learned that it was the police chief, George Guy, saying, "I shoulda let them take you."

Even before I realized I was in the police chief's office I said in my calmest voice with as much authority as I could muster, "I'd like to make a phone call."

There was a whoop of laughter but I recall one voice that said, "For goodness sake let the man make a telephone call. Nobody knows where he's at." Then, I noticed for the first time that the mob had filled the corridors of City Hall. The open door to the office was filled with rough characters holding every known weapon. Both sides of the door were lined, it seemed, from top to bottom with squeezed red faces peering at me. One great joker kept hollering, "You think I can hit him between the eyes from here with this here wrench?" Then he'd shake his Stillson wrench at me and grin like he was a great friend of mine.

When my eyes cleared up a little I repeated I'd like to make a call. We'd been trained to insist on a call and to never leave a jail willingly without first letting someone know where we were and where we were going. The chief said, "Why, you're not under arrest. You're free to go. Go on, get out of here."

He motioned toward the door and the crowd in the door parted leaving only the sweating faces stacked along the door jamb. I could tell the terror was about to begin again and I didn't want to show fear so I said rather loudly, "I do not choose to leave and I insist on making a phone call."

"You insist, do you?" the chief said in a rage. He grabbed me by what was left of my shirt front and hurled me toward the door.

"Get out of my office you dirty nigger-loving son-of-a-bitch. I only brought you in here cause you looked like a good nigger lover—a God-damned dead nigger lover."

He shoved me into the hallway and I was swept down the hall and out the front door. I was thrown unceremoniously into a beat-up car which filled up quickly with men from the mob. They all had on white shirts—two in the front and two in the back with me. The leader was the driver, although he never said anything, and I don't know to this day if any were law officers. The two in front were pretty old and beefy with big pot bellies and real red faces. To me, they seemed hard-core Klan guys. In the back were a couple of younger guys who were supposed to be in fighting trim—the very active Klan guys. I wasn't tied up and wasn't handcuffed either, because it might have signified that the police had some jurisdiction over me. They could easily say, "Well, he was in the courthouse, and he was mouthing off, and these people dragged him off, and there was nothing we could do." This was a lynching in process as far as I was concerned, and I was the lynchee. They had a noose. They never put the rope around the neck. They just brandished it in front of me.

Other cars and some pickups nearby roared to a start like everybody was going to drive the Indianapolis 500. Off we went into the countryside. My eye was really hurting now but I immediately asked where we were going. Someone in the car said, "If you're lucky you might make it to the jail in Magnolia."

I HAD NEVER BEEN to Magnolia and had no idea where it was until we got to the edge of town and a sign pointing to the left said "Magnolia" six miles. The car I was in and the long caravan of pickups sped past the sign. Instead of turning left toward Magnolia we continued straight on out into the country. I became convinced I would not survive the day. Once again now, just like during the beating, a sense of peace descended on me and I marveled at the contradiction. When it seemed there was a chance I'd survive I'd become frantic and nervous with an overpowering sense of dread. When it looked certain that I would die I would become calm. These people had been try-ing to kill me all afternoon, and now there didn't seem to be anything to stop them. At this point, however, I sensed some indecision on their part. Before it had been "Just let me at him. I'll rip him limb-from-limb." Now they didn't seem to know exactly what to do.

Somebody said, "Everybody saw us leave town with him."

"Yeah," someone else said, "but ain't nobody goin' to do nothing to us for doin' anything to him."

"That's true," another said, "but we can get some of the boys from Amite County to take him off our hands. We'll say we put up a fight but they got him away from us anyway." Another man from the front seat turned around and said with some glee, "Yeah, we can even black one another's eyes."

Every time I'd try to say something they'd say, "Shut up, nigger lover."

A man who looked like my uncle Harvey called me a nigger-loving motherfucking Jew communist queer Goddamn Yankee from New York City. That was too much for me. "Look, friend," I said, "Five out of six is not bad but I'm not from New York. I'm from further south than you are. I'm from East Brewton, Alabama."

That seemed to really piss them off but it did get their attention. I figured that they must know that I wasn't a Yankee because Doc had been in the mob before and he must know these yahoos. He's probably back there in one of those pickups, I thought.

I don't know why it seemed so important to me for them to know I wasn't a Yankee; maybe it was because I was still convinced they intended to kill me. So I took the opportunity to look each of them in the eye and ask, "Do you think you are capable of killing me by yourself or do you have to do it like cowards in a bunch?"

I was playing with their heads, because I was convinced that they were going to kill me, and I wanted them to know that it was a cowardly thing to do. This was not Southern justice. I was getting more and more Southern as I went along so I speculated out loud that there was not a man among them that could whip me in a fair fight.

They started arguing among themselves, and the CB radios were working, and I knew they were in contact with somebody somewhere. "Well, we can't just string him up. Everybody saw us leave with him. Is anything going to happen to us? They have us hanging him, and I ain't gonna do it. Let's turn him over to those boys down in Amite County. None of them were in McComb." This was the Klan way; they could call on an action squad that would come from somewhere else.

They stopped the car, and, after removing some rails at a cattle gap, proceeded to the back of a cow pasture near some trees. Stopping under a field pine, a man from another vehicle, a rickety old flatbed wood truck, ostentatiously removed a rope with an elaborately tied hangman's knot. For the second or third time that day I heard myself saying under my breath, "These people are overreacting. They've got to be overreacting. This is after all, for Christ's sake, my first demonstration."

WHEN THEY STARTED ARGUING again among themselves I thought I had a chance. The few men and vehicles around me in the woods were outnumbered by the cars and pickups just beyond the ridge of the field back up on the road. Every pickup truck, it seemed, was equipped with gun rack and a long whip antenna. Then they loaded me back into one of the pickups and off we went again. This time they did take me to the jail in Magnolia. It was a low, squat little brick building standing out in a yard under a huge live oak tree. It didn't look big enough to be a jail, but then it occurred to me I had never been in a jail before. Just because it looked like a jail you'd have in a photographer's studio to take joke pictures of Cousin Jane and Uncle Henry in prison stripes, didn't necessarily mean it wasn't a jail. Anyway, it would have to do because it was the only one offered to me. By the time the caravan reached the jail I realized that most of the entourage had quietly slipped away. I remember feeling some ambivalence toward the uniformed police who came forward to escort me to the cell. I thought, "Are they protectors or not? Is this part of an elaborate charade leading still to my undoing?"

The next thing that happened was a trusty, a black prisoner, came by and proceeded to put about five or six mattresses in my cell, saying, "You might need these."

I realized he was trying to tell me something. But I said, "I think one is enough."

And he said, no, take them. He said there was talk about them coming into the jail for me that night. He said, "If they come with gasoline or anything like that, you get in the corner and put those mattresses over you and hold out as long as you can."

I realized I was still not safe. I was very touched that he was so concerned. I mean, he didn't ask me who I was or what. But he knew what was going on. So then I had to sweat that out.

I didn't have long to collect myself and my thoughts in my cell before another uniform came to take me out. I had been trying to find a shiny surface to use as a mirror so I could assess the damage to my face and my body. The guard caused me to jump when he shouted,

"Okay, let's go!"

I really didn't want to leave that cell. My sense of time was totally screwed up. I didn't know if I had been in there ten minutes or two hours. The guard opened a door to the outside and the daylight streamed in. I immediately went limp and fell to the floor. I did not intend to leave that building without maximum resistance, no matter how nonviolent I was supposed to be. The uniformed guard suddenly laughed and said, "It's all right. The Feds want to talk to you."

Disbelief, fear, anger, relief, everything flooded over me at once and I realized my system was finally overloaded. I felt like a package, highly prized, and at the same time despised as something unclean. I felt that for hours since those moments on the City Hall steps I had simply been carried along by the tide, tossed here and there willy-nilly wherever the force would take me. Now I finally put my foot down.

"No," I shouted with determination, "I will not leave this building. I have not been allowed a phone call to a lawyer. If it is the FBI, as you say, then they can come here to see me."

"Okay," the guard said with a grin and stepped out the door. In a conversational tone of voice he said to someone outside, "Here he is but you'll have to come get him."

At that four crisply dressed look-alike white men with white shirts and ties peered in at me on the floor and said pleasantly, "We need the sun so we can take pictures."

They lined me up against the outside wall of the jail and asked me to face the low sun in the west. When they began taking pictures of my wounds I stood there rather numbed and thought to myself, "All this because I had the audacity to march with some Mississippi black young people."

The sheriff and assorted deputies and a few remnants of the mob were standing a short distance away when one of the FBI agents sidled up to me and whispered, "It was pretty rough out there on the City Hall steps, wasn't it?"

"Yes," I said, "It was nip and tuck there for a while."

"Well," said the agent, "we didn't want you to think you were all alone out there. We got it all down. We took real good notes. We wrote it all down."

Suddenly I realized that the FBI had stood there through the whole thing and had taken notes. First they were gonna watch me being made into a greasy spot in the street by this mob and then they were gonna watch me being taken into the car, being taken off for my last ride. And I realized that they had recorded a lynching which for no reasons of their own hadn't happened. And I was so mad I didn't want to speak to them anymore. I never ever had any illusions about the FBI or the federal government from that point. That taught me more about politics in this country and about the Feds than anything I ever learned after that. I realized they had recorded my death and they had gotten a description of everybody. They were going to be ready to testify or whatever, but it wasn't going to make a difference about my poor, damned body. So I went back in the cell.

Years later when the FBI refrain, "We can't protect. We can only investigate" had become a grim joke with us in SNCC, I thought back to that afternoon and realized the many times the cops could have stopped violence in its tracks with very little effort. The mob in McComb had constantly looked to the police for approval of their violence. The cops gave their approval and the federal officers did nothing to stop the violence. When that little FBI agent whispered in my ear I learned a valuable lesson. Never depend on the federal government. Especially never count on an agency headed by J. Edgar Hoover. I didn't really want to talk to them after that. I'd take my chances with my Southern haters. I knew where they stood.

THE NEXT PERSON I saw was Jack Young, one of the few black lawyers at that time in all of Mississippi. He came down from Jackson. I didn't realize it until later, but he was almost paralyzed with fear. He looked cool to me then, talking to me in jail. He asked, "How are you doing?"

I said, "Fine, but I'm going to need a toothbrush, and a few supplies, some books and stuff like that. You know, whenever you get a chance."

He said, "What are you talking about?"

I said, "Well, I guess I'm going to be in here a few days, right?"

I knew there was a SNCC policy of "Jail, no bail." If you got arrested you just stayed. We didn't want to tie up a whole lot of money in bail. You stayed until you could work it out somehow. He said, "Bob, if you make it through the night, you're going to be lucky. This whole state is mobilizing to get your ass. I don't mean to unduly alarm you, but you have got to get out of here. We're trying to get you bail right this minute."

So I said, "Well, okay, whatever Forman says, whatever you guys work out."

That's my last clear memory of that day. I believe Jack Young got me out because I left the jail with him. I remember coming out with him and seeing his car, a new blue Cadillac. Someone had taken a glass cutter and carved "KKK" into all his windows.

I spent that night at Momma Cotton's house in McComb with Reggie

Robinson, Diane Nash, Marion Barry, and Charles Jones. Most everyone else had been arrested. We left town before daylight and reached Jackson just as the sun was rising, rested up, and drove the next night back to Atlanta. It was a demoralizing experience for us. We viewed our return to Atlanta as a retreat. For me, it was my first demonstration and my first time in jail. Some of the others had been in sit-ins and on freedom rides. They'd been arrested before. But it was like nobody had been around the murderous atmosphere and mayhem of McComb. It had been very brutal.

Ella Baker was instrumental in rallying the troops. We continued our staff meeting in Atlanta. We met for a number of days. We began to evaluate what had happened. And Miss Baker said, "It's going to be rough now, you know. We just have to stick it out. We can't leave. We've got to go back to McComb." That was the last thing anybody wanted to do, but eventually SNCC staff did go back both for the trials and for continuing voter registration.

CHUCK McDEW, SNCC's CHAIRPERSON, Bob Moses, the leader of the Mississippi voter registration, and I were the only "adults" arrested during the march and prayer service on October 4. We were charged with contributing to the delinquency of a minor. Brenda Travis was sixteen at the time, and over a hundred students from Burgland High School walked out when Brenda was expelled for being arrested in the sit-in at the Greyhound bus station. I felt like telling the judge that it was Brenda Travis who contributed to my delinquency. She was a much more experienced freedom fighter than me; this was my first arrest, her third.

My father and I had decided to test the criminal defense system in Mississippi by trying to get a white lawyer to represent me. Attorneys Jess Brown and Young were among the few black lawyers admitted to practice by the state courts. William Higgs in Jackson was the only white lawyer in the state willing to defend civil rights workers and he was being banished from the state on a drummed-up morals charge.

Dad and I discussed our plan with Jim Forman and my present lawyer, Jack Young. At my arraignment in city court I would inform the judge that I had fired Attorney Young due to the large case load he carried. I would explain to the court that the difficulty arose from the fact that no white attorneys would represent civil rights workers. Young and Brown represented most freedom defendants in the state and the burden was too great to allow an adequate defense for the hundreds in jail.

The first date for our trial was in mid-November. Judge Brumfield began by lecturing us on race relations.

"Before you came here, Bob [Moses], the races here in McComb got along fine. Now you outside agitators have spread discord and caused the community to separate. We had good relations between the races but you are leading these children like lambs to the slaughter, and if you persist, then they will be slaughtered."

Then Judge Brumfield said something that stuck in Bob Moses's craw. "Isn't it true, Bob"—always the first name, never "Bob Moses," and certainly never "Mr. Moses"—that before you came to our town, several of our fine colored citizens had been allowed to register to vote? Isn't it a fact that that happened right here in Pike County?"

When I was called to stand and face the bench, the judge read the charges: disorderly conduct, breach of the peace, resisting arrest, and contributing to the delinquency of a minor. When he asked how I pleaded, I answered in a strong voice that I was not guilty.

Brumfield looked up then and, seeing that I was standing alone, asked, "Are you represented by counsel, Mr. . . . . Zellner?" I explained that I could not get a single Mississippi lawyer to plead my case.

"What's wrong with Jack here? Wasn't he representing you?"

"Yes, sir," I answered, "'Jack, here,' as you refer to attorney Jack Young, no longer represents me."

"Why not? Isn't Jack good enough?" Brumfield inquired.

"Mr. Jack Young is an extremely good lawyer, Your Honor," I replied, "But he and his associate, attorney Jess Brown, are handling almost all the civil rights cases in the state of Mississippi. Over a hundred of his clients are involved in this case alone. Mr. Young and Mr. Brown need some help. As you know, sir, these two men are incredibly hard-working and skilled at what they do. They are among the few Negroes admitted to practice in the state of Mississippi, but I am confident they are not the only attorneys competent to practice constitutional law."

Judge Brumfield looked more and more uncomfortable as I spoke to the court and the audience. The entire black community seemed to be present. "Young man," the judge interrupted, "have you made any effort to obtain counsel or is this just your speculation?"

Exactly the question I was waiting for—I pounced on it. Talking fast, I told him Dad and I had left no stone unturned to find a lawyer in Mississippi. I pointed to Dad who was sitting on the front row holding a folder documenting our contacts with John C. Satterfield, a white Mississippi lawyer who happened to be the current president of the American Bar Association. Brumfield sputtered and seemed to be looking around for help. While he was thus speechless, I took the opportunity to quote from Satterfield's letter to me: "Attorney Satterfield's letter reads in part, 'Mr. Zellner you are a disgrace to your race. If you want to be a Negro, why don't you just turn black? I wouldn't represent you under any circumstances and I doubt that any white lawyer in the great state of Mississippi would either."

I went on that Daddy and I had written, phoned, and telegraphed more than a hundred Mississippi lawyers whose answers were substantially the same as Satterfield's.

Brumfield rallied in an effort to regain control over his courtroom. "Why don't you just continue with Jack . . .," since I had put him on the spot for not granting attorney Young the courtesy title of "Attorney," the judge fumbled for words. ". . . your lawyer, the lawyer of record, you know what I mean?"

"I know what you mean, Judge, but even you have to admit that this attorney is completely overworked. That's why I fired him and I guess you will have to allow me to represent myself, unless you have a suggestion as to where I can find a good Mississippi lawyer willing to represent me in this important case."

"Me find you a lawyer . . .? This case is continued until the next term of court, and you, Mr. Zellner, better come with your lawyer!" The gavel went BANG!

The judge didn't want to hear from Daddy because he had written letters to the judge, the sheriff and Governor Ross Barnett demanding that I be protected when I showed up in court. Reverend James Abraham Zellner had done the whole Christian thing by telling each level of law enforcement that some advisors had recommended that I not even show up for court and forfeit the bond because it was too dangerous to appear. I had never given any thought to that option but Dad explained that we felt honor-bound to return for trial because that's what we promised when I was bonded out of jail.

Daddy had told them all, "I know you fine Southern gentlemen will guarantee the safety of my son. He has undertaken an obligation to return and you are sworn to protect him and his fellow defendants."

From then on, each time I showed up for a trial date and the judge found that I had been unable to get a lawyer; he continued the case until the next term of court. They never got around to trying me. I hope the bond money was returned to SCEF.

11

WORKING ON THE CHAIN GANG

I came into the SNCC office early on a quiet Sunday morning on December 10, 1961. I was in Atlanta for a few days and eager to finish the plans for my next road trip to Southern campuses. Sometimes I approached a campus cold, with no contacts, but work was slow that way. A contact on campus or in the community saved a day of sitting around a coffee shop ferreting out the odd "liberal" or "concerned" student or faculty. Two names constituted a veritable network.

I didn't expect anyone to be in the SNCC office but there was James Forman—sweeping again, the executive secretary of our organization, pushing a broom. He looked up as I entered the cramped office. He usually wore a suit—always the same one; the cliché "rumpled" would have been a compliment to Jim's suit. Having grown up in a Southern Methodist minister's house, one of five boys, with a schoolteacher mother, I was acquainted with the look of a suit of clothes that could barely keep up appearances.

With a gleam in his dark brown eyes, Forman extended the broom toward me. I accepted it, familiar now with his routine. "You may be a hero to the New York literati," he laughed, "but here in Atlanta this morning, you ain't nothing but a poor-ass SNCC field secretary. Everybody got to do his time on the broom. Keeps us humble. And since you're white, you need to sweep a lot." It was exactly like the first time we met a few months earlier.

"Ain't no 'shit work' in SNCC, it's all just work," Forman repeated one of his favorite sayings, sat down in front of the typewriter, and adjusted a stencil. His eyes betrayed, as usual, a generally amused expression. I remained so aware of his qualities—intelligent, opinionated, and prone to argue strongly for his position, he also possessed an acerbic wit and a disarming sense of humor.

And as I had learned, he was endowed with immense physical courage and coolness under fire—a steady resolve that saved lives on occasion.

I pondered again what my recent college mates would think of me now, being handed a broom by a black man to sweep a cluttered office full of broken furniture. I wondered what would amaze them more—the part about me sweeping or having a black boss? How many Huntingdon College magna cum laude graduates, I thought, took jobs wielding a broom at the behest of a Negro superior?

As Forman began banging on the typewriter, he asked casually, "What you doing today?"

I told Forman I was making some calls and lining up some contacts before heading toward Texas. When he didn't say anything, I continued, "I thought I'd hit Alabama, northern Mississippi, and maybe stop at the University of Arkansas in Fayetteville on the way over. Anne Braden's got a couple of names for me there."

"How about going down to Albany?"—he pronounced it *All-benny* like they did in southwest Georgia—"They've been having a hard time getting started but now things are going to happen and Charles Sherrod and Cordell Reagon need help. We are going to have a little freedom ride."

I must have looked like I'd been hit with an ax handle. Jim looked me dead in the eye. "I know you need to go on the road and that you have to get to those campuses sooner or later, since that's what the five thousand dollars is for, but . . ."

"Sooner or later?" I said, thinking of the grant that the Southern Conference Education Fund had made to SNCC for my campus traveling. My job was to contact white Southerners and introduce them to the movement and try to explain what was happening. I had marched in McComb a few months before, where I was beaten, nearly lynched, and then thrown in jail, in order to become a part of what I was reporting. How could I explain the sit-ins and freedom rides without being a part of the action? In SNCC, one's commitment was sometimes measured by the extent to which one's body was on the line in the toughest places.

"Several people are going, man, and I just thought you might want to go along. You know that Interstate Commerce Commission ruling was supposed to take effect last month. Look, I would not tell you to go. . . but we do need you. We want to make it pretty close to half black and half white. You remember that Sherrod came to McComb to help us out the day you and Moses and the rest were tried in front of Judge Brumfield? Now we need to help him out—we've been working on it about a week and we are going today."

"Today?"

"I already got the tickets. We're going down this afternoon on the Illinois Central and we're going to integrate the train and Chief Laurie Pritchett's white waiting room."

"Who's we?"

"Besides you and me, there's Tom Hayden; Joan Browning, one of our white volunteers; Lenora Taitt from Spelman; Norma Collins, our office manager; and Wyatt Walker not only advanced me the money for the tickets, but also said Bernard Lee—'little MLK' himself—can go along to represent SCLC. Oh yes, we'll have international coverage on this freedom ride; Per Laursen is riding with us. And Casey Hayden will be going along as our designated observer."

Per was a Danish journalist writing a book on the civil rights movement in the American South to be called *Grace and Grits*. Laursen filed stories from time to time with various European news outlets.

"Europe," Jim was saying, "is more interested in us than these so-called newspapers down here, or in this country, for that matter. If we can blow the lid off Albany, we'll get attention. We may have gotten our asses kicked in Mississippi. Hell, Herbert Lee was killed in McComb and that got six inches in the *New York Times*. But if we do this right, Zellner, we can kick ass in southwest Georgia. Okay?" I was still skeptical.

"You really should do it. I've called in our plans to the SNCC folk in Albany—when we're arriving and so forth. Sherrod and them will have a crowd at the train station, and when Chief Pritchett orders us to leave the waiting room, we'll just leave. There's nothing he can do, and we will have proved our point that the government is not enforcing the ICC ruling for integrating transportation facilities. You'll be back here in a couple of days ready to go back on the road. Nobody is supposed to get arrested. Try thinking of yourself as our secret weapon, a Southern white cat with stories of how SNCC is destroying segregation in the South. Run around the block, pack light, hurry back and be ready to go. Go! Here they come."

I ran past Tom, Casey, and Per Laursen as they entered the office.

Tom and Per looked like they were going on safari. They were obviously ready to be arrested if necessary. Their knapsacks, no doubt, contained the regulation toothbrush, toothpaste, Kleenex, and a book to read. Casey was dressed in style, as always since, as Jim said, she was to be the "observer." Observers were not supposed to attract attention; they avoided arrest so as to report to the press and headquarters.

I was still housed in the Negro Butler Street YMCA, around the block from the Auburn Avenue SNCC office; I paid fifty cents a night. Rent was cheap because I didn't spend many nights in Atlanta. I threw some things together—enough for a few days. I had already picked up the SNCC habit of keeping a toothbrush and a good paperback with me at all times, never knowing when jail might come, and a benevolent jailer would let you keep one or the other, or sometimes both.

Back at the office the mood was festive. Everybody acted as though making an integrated foray into enemy territory was the jolliest occasion imaginable. Lunches were packed and everybody checked to see if their "jail clothes"— khakis, jeans and work shirts—were in order. We weren't supposed to be arrested, but everybody remembered trips with James Forman that ended in the hoosegow.

THE TRAIN CREW SCOWLED at our integrated group, and the conductor asked us to move. When we refused, they let it pass. Most sane people were competent to segregate themselves, they seemed to think. Leave this crazy group alone and when they are gone, life in the South will revert to its quietly segregated correctness. It will be okay as long as the other passengers don't get the idea that they can henceforth sit where they please. Most of our group slept or read, and some gazed at the Georgia countryside as it drifted by. I sat on the right side next to the window cradling a stack of student newspapers from around the South. I planned to scan them for evidence of any stirring of enlightenment on Southern campuses. I was pessimistic.

Per Laursen relieved me of this duty by taking the aisle seat, whipping out his reporter's notebook and asking me to fill him in on Albany. I suggested he talk to Forman since I knew very little except what I'd heard about the place. But Forman was dozing so Per asked me why SNCC was putting all of its staff into Albany. I filled him in as best I could. The staff had been together for only a short while, I explained, though most were experienced jail veterans seasoned in the sit-ins of 1960 and the freedom rides earlier in the year. The group had jelled when fifteen of the most experienced freedom fighters decided over the summer to become full-time organizers.

Brenda Travis, age sixteen, Hollis Watkins, nineteen, and Curtis Hayes, age eighteen, had helped with Bob Moses's voter registration campaign. This led to Herbert Lee's murder in Liberty, Mississippi, and was followed by the Klan and police terror in McComb, which had welded SNCC together, hardening everyone's resolve to become professional revolutionaries.

Sherrod and Reagon, now patiently building the Albany movement, had both been involved during the summer in Mississippi. Our main "adult" advisor, Ella Baker, had counseled us to return to McComb as soon as we could rest a bit and lick our wounds and bruises. In all our discussions concerning the work in the Albany area, we had constantly reminded each other of the importance of digging in for the long haul. If the bad guys got the idea that a few days of violence and brutality could rid their area of those "Snickers and Slickers," we would never be able to organize in the rural South, the location of the vast majority of black people. We did not intend to be run out of southwest Georgia the way the Klan thought they had chased us from southwest Mississippi.

I reminded Per that all the SNCC people were not involved in Albany. Moses, SNCC Chairman Chuck McDew, and the others were still in jail in McComb. James Bevel and Diane Nash had just gotten married and were continuing the SNCC project, Move On Mississippi (MOM). Marion Barry, John Lewis, Julian Bond, and others were carrying on their duties. We were headed toward Albany because Forman thought our organizers in southwest Georgia deserved a shot at their dream—the total mobilization of a Deep South community to end all forms of segregation. And they had been successful so far, not just in mobilizing the young people but in building a community-wide movement. The kids took the lead in going to jail; now the adults were stirring. When children get involved, many parents tend to follow. I ended my monologue saying I was particularly interested in the work because Charles Sherrod was determined to prove that white organizers could function in even the riskiest field work. Albany was an example of our commitment to organize in a way that was consistent with our goal of the "beloved community."

I began stuffing papers in my bag. Per said, "Wait, I've got more questions." The train slowed and he looked outside.

"Okay, later," I said.

THE TRAIN PULLED INTO Albany's Union Railway Terminal. Casey Hayden gently shook Forman awake and he was delighted to see his idea of the freedom ride working. He was often surprised when plans worked the way they were supposed to. After waking Jim, Casey discreetly exited from a different train door. Nobody in the terminal building looked like passengers. They looked like cops and there were lots of them, and they had allowed in only two SNCC people, Charles Jones and Bertha Gober, along with A. C. Searles from a local black newspaper.

Seeing our SNCC comrades made the occasion feel like a homecoming. I remembered Charles Jones from McComb, his gorgeous bass voice singing, "Woke up this morning with my mind stayed on freedom." Bertha Gober, an undergraduate from Albany State, wrote one of our freedom songs, "We'll Never Turn Back." During the march in McComb we had sung her haunting, aching melody ". . . we have hung our heads and cried, cried for those like Lee who've died . . ." She and another Albany State student, Blanton Hall, had helped spark the Albany movement by being arrested in the white waiting room of the Trailways bus station at the beginning of the Thanksgiving holiday.

Police occupied the white areas in the terminal, and Albany Police Chief Laurie Pritchett, dressed in a starched white shirt and sharply creased blue pants, came over to us and asked us to leave the station.

Forman asked, "Does that mean that this facility is segregated?"

"It means," the chief's voice rose sharply, "I'm ordering you to move on or be arrested."

We moved quickly, Bertha Gober and Jones steering us toward the white exit into bright December sunshine where we were soon surrounded by cheering people from the Albany movement who had been waiting for us in front of the terminal. They shouted approval of our test of Southern hospitality on Georgia's trains. Pritchett reacted like a cat when the mouse is getting away. He had not counted on us leaving when he barked his order. About to board the cars and vans waiting in front of the terminal, our integrated group was becoming too much of an affront to the tightly segregated Albany society.

Had we managed to get into the various cars and leave for the Shiloh Baptist Church where we were to attend a mass meeting, our plan would have worked. Just as it looked like we would get away, Pritchett's temper got the best of him. He shouted, "Officers, move out!" and, to us, "Don't move! You're under arrest."

They grabbed and stuffed us into police paddy wagons and eleven of us broke into song, waving like we'd just won a big election. Along with eight of us from Atlanta, they arrested Charles Jones, Bertha Gober, and Willie Mae Jones, another Albany State student. The civil disobedience phase of the Albany movement was underway with a bang and a song. On the way to the Albany jail Bertha and Charles led off with a deafening chorus of "Ain't gonna let nobody turn me around." The metal walls of the paddy wagon reverberated with a new verse, "Ain't gonna let Chief Pritchett turn me around . . . . "

There was a mass meeting at Shiloh Church that evening, and an estimated two hundred people attended—some who had witnessed our arrest, and relatives and friends. The songs were reportedly incredible and we realized later that the Shiloh meeting was part of the recognition of Albany as a lasting monument of freedom music and singing. We missed it all, because we were downtown being fingerprinted and charged with disorderly conduct, obstructing the flow of traffic, and failure to obey an officer, before being processed into Pritchett's jail. I would become well-acquainted with a variety of Albany detention facilities over the next few months.

We had not been disorderly, we had not obstructed the flow of traffic, and we had not failed to obey an officer. We used an interstate transportation facility as the Interstate Commerce Commission ruling intended—in a nondiscriminatory manner. The grudging new ruling had been purchased in Birmingham and Montgomery with a lot of blood and suffering amid burned buses and broken heads. The federal order integrating interstate facilities, ironically, had to be wrung from a reluctant John F. Kennedy and his supposedly tough attorney general brother Bobby. JFK had been elected because large numbers of black voters, mostly in the North, had left the party of Lincoln for the Democrats in the 1960 election. We in SNCC were willing to concede that his little brother might be tough on aging communists and certain labor leaders, but he was not tough on Southern racists. To the Kennedy administration, the recently promulgated ICC rules of the road were for international consumption only; they were tools in the cold war, not weapons for the fight for democracy in the Old South.

President Kennedy had protected his Democratic hindquarters in the South by appointing known racists as federal judges. His first appointment was one of the more egregious examples, that of Harold Cox, former college roommate of Mississippi Senator James Eastland, chairman of the Judiciary Committee. Eastland had told Bobby Kennedy that if JFK would give Cox a federal judgeship, then Kennedy could have Eastland's vote to confirm Thurgood Marshall's nomination to the U.S. Supreme Court. On the bench, Cox was a disaster. He once referred to some black witnesses as a "bunch of chimpanzees," and he routinely said "nigger" in open court. His rulings, unsurprisingly, often failed to enforce civil rights and Constitutional protections.

Police Chief Laurie Pritchett and those who ruled Albany, Georgia, and environs, did not intend to charge us with violating their segregation laws, just their Southern sense of order. Segregation laws could be challenged with the nominal support of the U.S. Justice Department. Maintaining law and order, however, was a local matter, allowing President Kennedy to congratulate his friend James Gray, owner of the *Albany Herald*, on the fine job of law enforcement being done in southwest Georgia. Gray was a racist carpetbagger from Massachusetts, who had married into Southern money and power.

THE THREADS CONNECTING PAST, present, and future were becoming apparent. The freedom rides of the spring, (where I had observed the aftermath of the Montgomery massacre with the Durrs, writer Jessica Mitford, and my Huntingdon college mates) had resulted in the ICC ruling that the Albany students, and now, we, were testing. The ruling had taken effect on November 1. In Albany our organizers had managed, in only two months, to construct a movement powerful enough to capture the imagination of the nation and the world; these SNCC operatives were veterans of the bloody freedom rides. The Albany movement would become the model for later upheavals in the South such as Birmingham and Danville, Virginia. Another thread connecting Albany to the past was the similarity to the federal reaction in the freedom rides.

The bargain that the Kennedy brothers struck with the governor of Mississippi was that the freedom riders would not be killed (as they expected to be) when they got off the bus in Jackson. This would avoid the black eyes that America, the land of the free, the home of the brave, was sustaining throughout the "un-free" world. How could the United States lead the free world with apartheid so visible in the American South?

In exchange, then, for sparing the lives of the integrated interstate travelers, the state of Mississippi could quietly arrest the freedom riders, trucking them directly to Parchman Prison farm in notorious Sunflower County, home of James Eastland, where they could be punished out of sight of the world press. Never mind that the state was enforcing unconstitutional segregation laws.

The deal that covered Albany was made during the 1960 presidential campaign when Governor Ernest "No, Not One" Vandiver gave his support to Kennedy in exchange for a promise that Kennedy would never send federal forces to enforce desegregation. As long as Chief Pritchett and his law didn't "brutalize" the demonstrators, at least not in public, he could do violence to citizens' democratic rights to his heart's content. The federal government would not interfere. At the end of the first phase of the movement in Albany when Martin King bailed out of jail—and bailed out of Albany contrary to his pledge to share Christmas dinner with the hundreds of movement prisoners—Mayor Asa Kelly announced that Attorney General Robert Kennedy had called within the hour of that afternoon's truce to congratulate the city "for preventing an outbreak of violence."

While being fingerprinted and mug-shot for Mayor Kelly's jail house rogue's gallery, I thought about the propensity Southerners have for displaying sweetness in the daylight while creating hell in the cell. What would we find in the jails that were being prepared to receive us? The fat little cop who took my prints smirked while praising me for knowing the fingerprinting procedure. "You've done this before, ain't you? I sure appreciate the way you roll that finger for me. People who ain't done it before will oftentimes smudge the paper." He grinned like a mule eating briars, "You done it right the first time."

I didn't say anything. At this point I didn't have a lot of jail experience, but I remembered from our training workshops the danger of being too friendly with police. They often played variations of the good cop/bad cop routine to see what they could learn. The lawmen in Mississippi, I recalled, had alternated between threats and being just a good ol' boy curious about how a nice Southern gentleman like myself got mixed up in "all this." Another ploy I learned in McComb—a cop would whisper that another was a "bad ass," telling me to come to him if there was trouble.

All jails are different. Now it was comforting to be with friends. In Mississippi I had been the only white person arrested and it was my first time in jail. I had been terrified in Mississippi, especially when my own lawyer said he was worried that I would not make it through the night. Here in Albany I had a chance to be the experienced one, telling Tom Hayden and Per Laursen what to expect. This happy state didn't last, however; Tom bailed out to fulfill a speaking engagement for Students for a Democratic Society. Forman thought it was a good idea because Tom would spread the word about Albany the way he had with the campaign in Mississippi when he wrote a pamphlet called "Revolution in Mississippi."

I supported Tom's leaving because I had recently been asked to serve on the SDS national executive committee and I wanted closer ties between the organizations. SDS could help focus national attention on our work in the deep South, and SNCC could continue to inspire northern students to revolt and organize. Publicity would help us raise much-needed money.

Per stayed in long enough to see how it was so he could write about Southern jails, and he and Joan Browning were bailed out late Monday in time to attend a mass meeting. I decided to honor SNCC's policy of jail, no bail. If I believed in the principle of noncooperation with evil, it didn't make sense to court arrest and then get out on bail as soon as possible. Besides, if the ruling class of Albany and its hired hands, the police, cooperated, it would be possible to organize the first mass jail-in of the rural South. I would remain in jail for a while.

AFTER ARRAIGNMENT I WAS placed in a large cell block with the general white prison population. One of the first things you learn about jails is that they are run by the inmates, not the authorities. Another thing that seems more or less constant is that there is usually one prisoner who is the leader or boss of the jail—not always the strongest or toughest one, either. Usually it is a man who is intelligent, serving a long sentence or sentences for a nonviolent crime.

In the Albany jail the leader was a slender man named Shug. He reminded me of a cross between Popeye and Art Carney playing Norton on "The Honeymooners." He talked out of the left side of his mouth and had a disconcerting habit of looking slightly past your head as he talked, like he was watching someone behind you. A three-time loser, the man was a safe-cracker and proud of the fact that he made his living with his brain, not his brawn.

Shug took to me right away. I had expected hostility from the white inmates, most of them Southern. Surprisingly there was not much recognizable anger directed towards me. I found out that Mr. Shug—that's what all newcomers were told to call him—had interceded in my behalf. Mr. Shug had been pointed out to us while Tom and Per were still in with me. Not long after they left, Shug eased over toward me holding out a cigarette—a high compliment from anybody in jail, where the two most common drugs, alcohol and tobacco, are worth more than money.

This particular Lucky Strike was even more of an honor, coming from the Man himself. Shug wanted to know how much money I was making in my line of work. He had always been confident, he told me in a whisper, that he was the smartest guy in the jail. Incarcerated for years, he knew the men inside out, especially the long-timers. Now he claimed he was not so sure he was the most intelligent man in that jail. Listening to me talk, he said he could tell two things. One, I was educated, and two, he was pretty sure I was a Southerner. That was what made him ask about my salary.

"You must make an awful lot of money."

"No, not really."

"Well," Shug said, "what do you call not a lot? It may sound like an awful lot to us poor sons of bitches in here."

I told Shug it would not sound like a lot to him or anybody else in the jail.

People are often surprised, I said, to find out how little we can get by on.

"I bet," Shug said. "Look, I'm a safe-cracker, and pretty good at it. That's how come I run things around here. Guys in here could tear my head off, but they're not as smart as me. That's why they let me be in charge."

I could see he was desperate to clear up a puzzle for himself. To change the subject and also because I was curious, I asked him about an old man who walked about the cell block all day in a shuffle, always the same rate of walk, never taking a step longer than six inches. Shug said you could always tell a man who had spent a lot of time on the old chain gangs. "That man was on the chain for more than thirty-five years, he went in as a teenager for murder and he'll never take another step in any other way than that, six inches at a time. That man was shackled day and night for almost forty years. He's still shackled to that chain, only now you can't see it."

Now he tried another tack. "I know it doesn't look like I'm any good at robbing safes, what with me being in here and all, but you would be surprised if I told you how much money I've handled in my life—the times I'm not in here, you know. Like I say, I've been very successful at different times, but I bet I've never even dreamed of the money you are making, doing what you are doing. Am I right?"

When I told him again that I barely made enough to get by on, he seemed to get exasperated. "Look, Bob, is it okay if I call you that . . .? You don't have to tell everyone else in here. Just tell me in confidence. I won't tell nobody. This is one professional to another. Now how much is it, if you don't mind? You got to be making millions. No person in his right mind would do what I've heard you are doing if they weren't making millions."

It looked like I had to tell him, so I said that I made exactly what every other SNCC field secretary makes, ten dollars a week.

"I understand," Shug whispered, "that you have to put out that cock-and-bull story for mass consumption, Bob. But this is Shug you are taking to. You don't expect me to buy such a story. You got to be making more than me, that's what's driving me crazy. How much is it worth to do what you are doing? It don't make sense. You could get killed. These guys in here would beat the shit out of you except I've told them you are making a kill-ing. Hell, now they are not even mad at you. But I got to know how much you are making. I don't even have to know where it is coming from. If it is

Moscow gold, that's your business, but don't hand me this ten-dollars-a-week business. Bob, don't insult my intelligence, please!"

I assured Shug that I was a member of SNCC out of conviction and I believed that segregation was bad for people. Black people and white people.

"You can get convicted," Shug said, "and I'm not going to let you off the hook. I'll just keep trying till I find out how much money you're making. Then I'll know whether or not it'll be worthwhile changing my line of work.

In the following days and weeks Shug kept talking to me. He said he was still trying to figure out if he was the smartest one in that jail. The more I professed to make ten dollars a week, the more Shug figured I was making millions.

On the first Saturday night in the joint a controversy broke out about whether I should get an allotted share of the hooch that was brewed weekly in our cell block. The prisoner cooks, trustys, would "steal" corn meal and raisins from the pantry, add a little sugar and copious amounts of warm water, and let it ferment into a reasonable facsimile of beer. A five-gallon bucket served as a vat. All week each prisoner would listen to its gurgle and fizz while the aroma promised a Saturday night break in the deadly monotony. One glass of that green, warm homebrew and no inmate need worry about irregularity. It would go through you, Shug grinned, "like grease through a goose."

Shug settled any argument by explaining that everybody got his share as long as he obeys his rules. "Bob here, obeys my rules like everybody else, so he gets his share. Anybody don't like it, take it up with me."

December days were passing, and I heard that Dr. King was leading a prayer march on the 16th. He was arrested along with 250 demonstrators, and I thought—not bad to spend Christmas in jail with Martin Luther King Jr. But he was released on bail as part of a settlement with Albany officials, and I spent a sad holiday, enhanced by missing a big New Year's Eve celebration.

I was supposed to go to New York for a party at Harry Belafonte's house, and the great singer Lena Horne was going to be there. I was to talk about Albany and McComb, and I was very excited about it all. I had been to New York only once, when I graduated from high school. In SNCC, we never knew when fame might be burnished by missing events because of untimely arrests. People at Belafonte's party could have talked about the fact that Zellner "was missing in action."

AFTER THE FIRST GO-ROUND in Albany, in February 1962 I got a taste of prison Louisiana-style. Chuck McDew and I were charged with criminal anarchy and stayed in jail there until early March. I then came back to Albany for trial in city court. Charles Sherrod was sitting in the white section with Tom and Casey Hayden and me. The deputies smacked him across the face and dragged him to the back of the courtroom to the colored section, so naturally the Haydens and I and a couple of the other white defendants got up and joined Sherrod in the black section. Then we were all dragged out of the courtroom and slammed roughly into an elevator where the bailiffs and the cops proceeded to kick our asses good. My jail life changed dramatically after that because we were all convicted. Most of the freedom riders bailed out to await the appeals process, especially since we were sentenced to hard labor. It was March by now and starting to heat up, so working on a Georgia road gang did not appeal to anyone. I had never served time on a chain gang before so I decided to begin serving my sentence. There would be time later to bail out so my conviction could be appealed.

I learned that jail conditions, not very accommodating before, deteriorated dramatically after conviction. Before, we were "technically" innocent. Now that I was definitely guilty of violating the sacred laws of Georgia, I was remanded to the custody of the High Sheriff for punishment. This consisted of being thrown into a dark cell with a dirt floor where the only light filtered under the large wooden door or down from a naked light bulb twenty feet off the ground. The "cell" measured no more than about eight feet by ten feet and housed between twelve and fifteen men. This seemingly impossible feat was accomplished by stacking the beds against opposite walls, six bunks high. The high-status criminals occupied the top-most bunks because it was quieter way up there, and the only way to get to one's bunk was to use the lower bunks as a ladder. The single electrical cord in the top of the cramped cell also served as a way to heat up a cup of instant coffee, tea or soup. Inmate electricians rigged a tin Prince Albert tobacco can as a heating element. The can was split in two and held apart by rubber cut from an inner tube. The pieces of metal were hooked to the bare copper wires of the light cord. When lowered into a mug of water, electricity arced between the halves, bringing the liquid to a boil. Add instant coffee, tea, or split pea soup, and voila!—it's what's for dinner. When cooking was going on, our cubicle was dark except for an occasional match lighting a cigarette or sparks from the cooker. At night, after a hard day on the road it was easy to see who ranked at the bottom of the pecking order: me. I reached the electrode last; if I could stay awake that long.

Soon, however, my status changed. Lucky for me, my jailers thought that the height of punishment would be to assign me to an all-black chain gang. "If he wants integration so bad, he'll get integration all right. That son-of-a-bitch will have to work his time and his ass off on a nigger road gang." When I heard this I felt like Br'er Rabbit: "Please, Mr. White Man, don't make me face the humiliation of riding around this town and county on the back of a state truck on an all-Negro chain gang."

The only whites on my gang were me and the captain. The black prisoners welcomed me like a lost brother. They told me quietly that they had been instructed not to say a word to me but we found ways to communicate. The best thing that happened was that word got out in the black community that I was on the road gang. The movement people found a way to get advance information of where we would be working on a particular day and they would come by and wave, lifting my morale and that of the black prisoners. Suddenly our bunch was the most popular chain gang in Georgia history. Each car that came by would surreptitiously drop goodies for us—candy, toothpaste, toothbrushes, soap, cotton handkerchiefs and bandanas, all highly prized items for men doing hard time on the gang. Smiling black faces would give us the thumbs-up after dropping our favorite cigarettes, chewing tobacco, and snuff. Soon our black gang had so much stuff that I started sneaking some of it back to the white cell block where I was still housed. That's when I became a VIP in our little white hovel. The white guys started placing orders, "Can you get me a plug of Old Pork Twist chewing tobacco, I ain't had none of that since I been in this hole, fourteen years. . . If you cain't, try to get me some Black Maria plug. If you can do that then I can die happy."

Even my "Cap'n" loosened up eventually. One day my black gang was loading red dirt on a big dump truck way out in the middle of a field. The truck's sides were so high that we were exhausted trying to throw the red clay high enough so that at least some of it would wind up in the truck. The wind was high along toward the end of March, and suddenly a skyscraper of a thunder cloud loomed up out of what had seemed like a blue sky. Before we could move, lightning was popping all around us. Knowing something about lightning in the middle of a huge field, we and the captain realized at the same time that we were in big trouble, us and the truck being the highest things for miles around. The first thing Cap'n did was lower his shotgun from its customary place sticking in the air over his slumped shoulder. He looked once at the truck, then shook his head as he turned and started trotting toward the highway across the open field. I looked ahead in the direction he was running and could barely make out the low profile of a lone cinder block building way over on the highway. I remembered passing it before, a flyblown redneck tavern. We looked at each other, dropped our shovels, and jogged off after the fat white man running with his head down and a death grip on the twelve-gauge shotgun in his right fist.

We overtook the captain in short order and the younger black men of the gang strung out in a long file running for the protection of the building. I let my pace keep me at the back of the pack, closest to the guard, who was, by this time, thoroughly winded and wheezing loudly. He was not in work shape like us. As we neared the building I saw my black fellow prisoners disappear through a back door clearly marked, "colored." It was raining in sheets now. Rain, thunder, and the lightning made it difficult for me to think. I wondered if I was supposed to follow the crew into the Negro section, or wait and see if the captain wanted me to go up front with the rest of the white people. I looked back to see if he would give me any indication of what he wanted me to do, but it was clear that he was still too far away to appreciate my delicate dilemma of Southern etiquette. So I said to myself, "They are the ones that put me here, so let them figure it out." I ducked into the back with the rest of the Negroes.

The moment I entered, I decided to play a trick on the captain. Sticking my head through the opening in the wall I said, very matter of factly, "Two six packs of Bud, please." Without blinking the bartender hoisted two six packs up to the window, just as the captain puffed through the front door. "Zellner," he bellowed, "get your ass out of that window and come up here with your own kind." To the black prisoners he said, "Don't y'all touch them beers." When I reached the front of the road house, he was muttering about losing his state job, "Niggers drinking beer on a god-damned chain gang." The story had a happy ending, though. Grateful to be alive, and not lightning-struck, Cap'n relented and gave each prisoner a cold one.

I was on the chain gang about a month before I bailed out.

12

CRIMINAL ANARCHY IN BATON ROUGE

I n February 1962, in East Baton Rouge Parish, Louisiana, I had my
first experience with police torture, Southern American style. SNCC
Chairman Chuck McDew and I had been at our trial in McComb,
Mississippi, and decided to take a bus to New Orleans with a stop in Baton
Rouge. Dion Diamond, one of our SNCC field workers had been arrested
and imprisoned there during student demonstrations at Southern University.
Dion had left Howard University, had organized in Virginia and Maryland,
had been a freedom rider, and had been arrested while working with black
students in Baton Rouge. We planned to visit him, talk about his bond, and
then head for New Orleans.

Both Chuck and I had good contacts and friends in the Big Easy. Oretha Castle and her sister were leaders of the movement (Oretha would later
marry my friend Richard Haley, who worked for CORE and who proved
to be so steady and strong on the William Moore march in 1963). Dave
Dennis, who in 1964 would organize for CORE in Mississippi, was from
Louisiana and worked in New Orleans. He would make the impassioned
speech at James Chaney's funeral in Meridian following the murders that
summer of the three civil rights workers in Philadelphia. Tom Dent, the
son of the Dillard University president, was one of our supporters and later
wrote a great book about his travels to movement hot spots.

We never made it to see our friends and eat and party in New Orleans.
When our wheezy old bus smoked into Baton Rouge, Chuck and I took
in the early evening scene. Even though it was still February the street were
warm and swarming with people. As the driver wheeled us through the
Negro district of town, we could see revelers inside the various night spots

beginning their Saturday evening—glad to have made it through another week. Student demonstrations had roiled the local black campus. Chuck and I wondered aloud if the police wouldn't take out their frustrations on some black skulls tonight.

"Naw," Chuck did his best imitation of the local boys in uniform, "these cracker cops hope these black dudes will drink up their anger and be ready for work Monday morning back at Mister Charlie's plantation house."

I asked McDew not to call them that, "I am a cracker, too," I said.

"Shut up, Nigger," Chuck snapped, "here's the station, watch yo' ass now."

That ended the discussion of calling white people names. We tried to inconspicuously check our bags in a couple of lockers. We didn't know how long we could visit Dion, and we would need them handy for the last leg of the trip to New Orleans.

As WE LEFT THE Baton Rouge bus station, McDew hailed the first black person we saw and asked directions to the Parish Prison. Pulling his hat down over his eyes, the man said softly, "What business you got down there, man—you don't want to be nosing around that particular area."

Chuck explained that we were going to see a friend about his bail, got the directions, and we set out. Along the way we talked about the fact that we didn't have great news for Dion. We couldn't raise his $7,000 bail, and he would have to sit tight until we did. We soon reached a stucco brick wall about twenty feet high, topped with sparkling concertina razor wire. The wall was washed in a searing white light. At the entrance to the prison, a small knot of police eyed us up and down while Chuck asked directions to the visiting area.

"Ain't no visitin' area, boy. But you could ask the night duty officer over there," one officer said pleasantly. Another offered, "Turn left and go the end of the hall. He's on the right down there." Chuck thanked them, and as we headed down the hall I heard one of the cops say in a stage whisper, "What ever happened to 'Sir'?"

Now Chuck is a dark Negro and powerfully built—he was a star football player. So going down the hall I whispered a plea that he not let himself get provoked.

The desk sergeant looked at us like we had descended from Mars, "You boys wants to visit who? If I ain't mistaken that nigger is a stone trouble maker and besides, colored day is Thursday. Where y'all from anyway?"

McDew introduced himself as chairman of the Student Nonviolent Coordinating Committee. "Mr. Diamond works for us and I would like to discuss his bond."

The sergeant smiled an unfriendly smile, "And do you have the bond for *Mister* Diamond?"

"No, I don't. That's what I need to talk to him about."

"Well, you can't see him, I already explained that Colored day is Thursday and seeing as how tonight is Saturday, you ain't going to see him."

While the desk man busied himself with papers I noticed the other policemen had moved from outside and were now slouching against the far wall taking everything in. Chuck asked if we could leave a message for Dion and would it be possible to leave him some supplies. The sergeant shoved a paper across the desk and said you can get these things but hurry up, this desk closes at nine o'clock."

We hurried to the nearest drug store where we got some paperbacks and toiletries. Walking back we saw a lot of patrol cars around the prison entrance and others with flashing lights converging from different streets.

"What's up?" Chuck wondered aloud. "I guess Saturday night in ol' Baton Rouge must be heating up." Thinking we'd soon be enjoying red beans and rice at Dookie Chase's in New Orleans, we agreed that we felt especially sorry for Dion being locked up, facing unknown horrors.

"We brought these back for Mr. Diamond—" Chuck had begun to say, when several cops the size of Green Bay linebackers descended upon us. One slung McDew into the brick wall and hissed in his face, "MISTER Diamond! Who you callin' Mister, boy? You like Mister Diamond so much, you won't mind going on in there with him and enjoying what he's been enjoying."

They took McDew down the hall; I wouldn't see him for about two weeks. Then they turned to me while the one holding me tried his best to break bones. "Put the cuffs on this nigger lover while I hold him real tight, you hear?" This was the beginning of a nightmare of brutality and torture. While they squeezed the cuffs on my wrist, cutting off all blood flow, I remembered our training and demanded to know what the charges were.

Vagrancy, I was told. Knowing that pleading my case would mean nothing, I nonetheless mentioned, while being hustled down the corridor, that we had money and a bus ticket to New Orleans, and I wanted to make a phone call to my attorney.

The no-neck cop who put the cuffs on so tight laughed and said to the other one, "We got ourselves a regular comedian here."

ALL SATURDAY NIGHT I was just one of the boys among the fifty or sixty inmates in the large cell block. When the bulls threw me into the lockup they had, mercifully, not said anything except here's another vagrant. One of the guys commiserated with me. Looking at my crumpled suit and tie and my once-white shirt, he said in a midwest accent, "These local yokels will arrest anybody on the way through, charge them with vagrancy, and dare them to fight the charge. They know that nobody is going to appeal the eleven-day sentence. We just suck it up and remind ourselves to never, ever, darken the door of Baton Rouge again."

I liked the guy and the others in this small group. They didn't seem to be Deep Southerners, or maybe they were a little higher class than the average robber or killer. I told them about getting off the bus and being arrested for vagrancy.

A well-dressed man in a tweed jacket told me he had stopped to get a burger, walked to the edge of the street to check a route sign to be sure he was headed west on Highway 90 to Houston, and was grabbed by two cops, cuffed and brought to the lockup.

When he protested that he had just left his car for a leg stretch and a burger, the officers said, "Yeah, yeah, we'll send a wrecker for it. The storage, though, will cost you some money."

The well-dressed man said 90 percent of the people were in for vagrancy or loitering. "We have to stay eleven days while the sheriff spends twenty-five cents a day to feed us and pockets five dollars a day per man. Pretty good money."

They gave me some advice. "The heavy hitters here are housed in the back cells. They pretty much run things and we short-timers try to stay out of their way. Remember, don't go back there; there's no percentage in it."

As the newest man I was relegated to a smelly, stained, very thin and lumpy blue-tick mattress on the cold cement floor of the day room. Even so, being exhausted and emotionally wrung out, I slept soundly until a horrible battering woke me up. Two fat deputy jailers came down the prison corridor banging empty tin cups against the iron bars. Behind them in the bedlam trudged two black trustys pulling the food carts. Haggard, unshaven men emerged from the double row of cells behind the day room, lining up with their backs against the wall. In a high falsetto one of the jailers screamed, "Ain't this your lucky day. Here's your usual delicious breakfast soufflé—etouffé a la baloney, *and*," he lingered over the word, "a special treat for you highly educated gentlemen, who can read, brand new hot-off-the-press newspapers!"

He tossed in a stack as men began grabbing them. A buzz enveloped the day room as prisoners grabbed baloney sandwiches and lukewarm tin cups of coffee, staring at the fat Sunday paper. I could see the headline in World War II-sized type. Across the top of the front page were the words "CRIMINAL ANARCHY CHARGED." Under it, the subhead read, "Two held attempting government overthrow."

The falsetto-voiced jailer, having given a moment for things to sink in, sang out, "Seems we have an important visitor amongst us. A sho-nuff dangerous commie," glancing teasingly in my direction. "He's a real criminal anarchist, whatever the hell that means, and something I do understand—a real live Yankee nigger lover. Read it and weep, gentlemen. I think you all know what to do, and welcome to it."

The jailers spun around together and clicked their heels before stomping off down the hall with the carts and the trustys in tow. I understood what was taking place and went quickly into survival mode, moving into the corner of the day room as far as possible from the back cells and closest to the disappearing cops. I was covered on two sides, and I would play it by ear to be as nonviolent as I could but to give up my life as dearly as possible. At the same time I was in need of seeing the whole article so I would know what the inmates were reacting to. I got some encouragement when the man from the night before, with a stricken face, quietly slid one of the papers over to my corner, whispering, "Better stay in that corner."

Before long a little dude with broken and badly blackened teeth sidled over and got in my face. Past martial arts training kicked in and I couldn't resist shifting my weight slightly and backing one foot, hands hanging lightly by my sides. These shifts were not lost on the little street fighter and he actually backed up a half a step.

Recall of what had happened in McComb slowly impinged on my consciousness—at least the detached feeling of observing things from a slight distance. I was calm but acutely aware of the struggle between my fighting history and the relatively new training in nonviolence. I wondered if Gandhi, King, and John Lewis expected us to be completely nonviolent even in prison.

I had quickly read enough of the front page to know that my cellmates would be challenged to defend "the Southern way of life." But as luck would have it, the hyperbole of the article might give me a degree of protection from the hoods, most of whom are cowards at heart. The indictment quoted in the paper said something like, "on or about the 19th day of February, 1962, SNCC members Charles McDew and John Robert Zellner, did with force of arms attempt to overthrow the government of East Baton Rouge Parish, the State of Louisiana, and the United States of America."

My fellow inmates could be forgiven if they found themselves unable to decide if I was a pacifist or one tough dude—"force of arms," and all that. I was soon surrounded by men demanding to know if I was the nigger-lover. I stood my ground in my corner, not having much choice. The little guy with the bad teeth, thinking he had mass support now did everything he could to get me to lift my hands. Not taking his bait, I survived the initial onslaught without being beaten.

A couple of guys from our conversation the night before, which now seemed to be an age ago, brought another mattress to my corner. There, I held the mob at bay through the power of Zen. My tormentors often sat on the floor at a distance and described in vivid terms the castration that was in store for me if I so much as dozed in my corner. Displaying their cell-made shivs, the short guy shaved most of his arms and legs to show how sharp their weapons were.

"This here," he grinned, "will peel out yo' nuts as slick as a whistle," flourishing his blade in a quick circle. "Same as castrating a calf," he chuckled.

When I could no longer stay awake twenty-four hours a day, I began to allow myself to doze during the day so as to be wakeful at night, the most dangerous time. The inmate terrorists then, possibly with the advice of the jailers, began to douse me, in the face if they aimed well, with cold water. Sleep deprivation is an effective form of torture because the subject of the brutality, though showing no injuries, begins slowly to lose his mental faculties. The other method was to whack the bottoms of my feet with a broom handle that the jailer had conveniently left inside after the morning sweeping—in case I stretched out and dozed at the same time.

Threats of castration, water torture, and sleep deprivation were the order of the days for me for about two weeks. Jim Dombrowski of SCEF in New Orleans found us a lawyer and I told him right away, "They're not letting me sleep. I can't take this for very long. I gotta get somewhere."

So they put me in one of the cells in the general cell block. It had a wall on one side and three sides were bars from ceiling to floor. I might be away from them so they couldn't kill me, but they would still throw water on me, or they would take shifts and poke me with a broom handle through the bars. So the psychological torture continued.

I saw the lawyer one more time and told him I could not hold out much longer. After he left I didn't know if my plea had done any good until a couple of jailers showed up and said to get my things, I was being transferred. I smiled at the notion of "gathering up my things." I had a single item. Except the clothes I had worn for over two weeks, I possessed a tattered cowboy novel I'd been given by one of the good guys in the cell. I cherished that book, having read it several times.

Trudging down the gray prison hallway with the guards, one in front the other behind, I was still somewhat apprehensive. Any change from the tortuous conditions I had endured for two weeks was certainly welcomed, but I was suspicious that the "authorities" had any intention of making life more bearable. The risk, I decided—no matter what, was worth it.

I THOUGHT I HAD died and gone to heaven when, rounding a corner into a short corridor just off the main guard desk, I spied the hand of my dear friend Charles McDew protruding from a tiny opening in a solid steel door. Passing by I heard him whisper, "My brother, thank you, God!"

Afraid to speak, for fear of jeopardizing a chance to be close to my brother and friend, I was glad when the guards shoved me into the next tiny cell, slammed the door and disappeared. Listening for their retreating footsteps, I heard a whisper from the next cell, "Zellner, I thought you were dead!"

"I'm okay," I lied, about to break into tears. "A little worse for wear, for sure, but still here. How you doing?"

"Hot!" Chuck hissed. "You'll see soon."

"What do you mean, and why are we whispering?

"Never mind that now," McDew replied, "but look across this little hall. See that fire extinguisher hanging on the wall?"

"Yeah, I see it, why?"

"Well, if you give me a minute, I'm gonna tell you. We got plenty of time, don'cha think? See that shiny silver plaque on the side of the extinguisher facing us?"

"Yes."

"Well, you hillbilly, if you look close you can see my face reflected in its shininess."

"It's hard to see," I said.

"Wait, I'll stick my hand out this little slit. Maybe you'll see the movement?"

"I see it," I shouted, "I can see you, Chuck!"

"Shuuuush, if you keep hollerin, they"ll come back and take you back where you been. But first they gonna whip yo' ass till it won't hold shucks. They whipped the last one in that cell something pitiful when all he did was speak to me, and he was white, too."

McDew was doing that white accent thing he does.

"By the way, where you been?" he asked.

"In holy hell," I said. "I been staying with the white people . . . I'll tell you about it later. Hey, Chuck, can you see me in the fire extinguisher?"

"Of course, I can see your face, ofay. You can see mine, and I can see yours—but yours is so ugly I can't remember why I wanted to see it in the first place." He was clearly delighted.

"If you keep talking in that fake Southern accent, they going to come back, and it won't be me they be whippin'," I said. In addition to bantering with him, I spontaneously burst into song. I was so happy to be here next to Chuckie. Happiness didn't last long, however.

"Is your cell getting hotter?" I asked Chuck.

"Getting? What you talking about? My cell ain't getting hotter, it's been hot."

I touched his wall and involuntarily jerked my hand back, "It feels like an oven," I gasped.

"Feels like? It IS an oven. Don't you realize that yo' poor ignorant peckerwood ass has been thrown in the sweat box?"

"The what, Chuck? I can't take much more of this, man. How long you been in there?"

"I been in here ever since the night me and you were captured by these Nazis, how long do you think I been in this hole?"

I tried to cheer him up. "Let's talk about something else and take our minds off of it. You got anything to read?" I asked.

"*To read!*" Chuck whispered in a soft scream, "Bob, you really know how to hurt a guy. I have a candy wrapper. If I read the bleeping wrapper one more time, I promise you I will go stark raving, homicidally mad!"

"Oh," I said.

"And you?" Chuck asked in his best sarcasm, "What's in your library today? What did you check out?"

"Well, I have a book," I said.

"You have a WHAT!!"

"I have a book."

I told him that an inmate had slipped it to me when I was in an isolation cell in the center of the cell block. I kept it hidden as much as possible and the guards had not seemed to notice when they brought me down here. I told McDew that I had practiced a lot of magic in my short life and I had a way of hiding something in plain view. "Obviously, you didn't notice the book either, when I came in."

"Zellner, could you spare me the magic and the hiding and just hand it over to me."

"And how am I going to do that, genius? Maybe yo' magic is stronger than my magic."

Silence. "Don't rush me, I'm thinking." McDew said.

"Take your time. Like you said we got plenty of time. And see, like I said, talking about the book took our minds off the heat. Right?"

He then suggested that while he was thinking, I could tell him about the book. "Tell me everything from the very beginning. What's the book about anyway? Is it fiction, what?"

I explained that it was fiction and not a book I would normally read but that it had been a godsend and I considered it to be very valuable in the circumstances . . .

I told him the title was *Riders of the Sawtooth Range.*

"Cowboys? Great, just what I need, cowboys!"

"I told you it wasn't something that I would . . ."

"Okay, okay, go ahead . . ."

"Well it's about these two cowboys way out on the . . ."

"Sawtooth range . . ."

" . . . Sawtooth range herding cows and they have to make expense reports before they can get any more money for grub, etc."

I told Chuck that the whole point of the story, it seemed, was that neither of them could read or write or at least they couldn't spell. McDew opined that they were a lot like me. I asked how he knew about my spelling and he reminded me that he was the chairman of the organization and who did I think had been reading my reports.

"Oh, never mind," I said.

I went on to explain that one of the cowboys, Clyde, the smart one, had suggested that they copy some of the words off the stuff they already had like the can for kerosene, which of course said, "kerosene." Another that they were able to lift was chewing tobacco because that's what it said on the tobacco pouch. The only other one they managed was on the note the boss had left them with which clearly stated "be sure to itemize each item you list in the 'Miscellaneous' category." The funny part was the weekly expense account they had to leave at the trading post for the boss.

"That's the funny part?" Chuck asked helplessly. "Okay, but don't give away the ending. I'll save that till I get my hands on the book itself."

"Have you figured that out yet?" I asked hopefully. "How I get this treasure over to you?"

"No, now that you had to go and ask . . . But go on."

"Well there's not that much more," I said. "But it sure takes one's mind off this goddamned heat," watching more sweat drip on the *The Riders of the Sawtooth Range.*

Chuck was suddenly very serious, "Z, are you drinking a lot of water?"

"No, why?"

"Man, you're more ignorant than dirt! Doncha know you got to drink water like you never ever drank it before, if you expect to get out of that hot box over there alive and in your right mind?"

"Why?" I asked, suddenly aware of a powerful thirst.

"Because, by the time you feel thirsty, it's too late, you will never be able to catch up. I take a sip of this hot spit they call water, running out of my drinking fountain-slash-wash basin, once a minute whether I want it or not. Ain't you ever been in a sweat box before?"

"McDew," I said, "how am I supposed to know about these things? This is only the second time in my life I have been in jail, as you know, if you have been reading my reports as you say you have," I finished lamely. Now I was drinking water like my life depended on it.

"Okay," I said, "I'm drinking."

"See that you keep it up," Chuck advised. "The best thing these fascists can hope for is for you to pass out from the heat and they will find yo ass too late—so sad. By the way there's a trusty here, a Louisiana brother, who has tried to be friendly. I don't exactly trust him as far as I can throw him, but he is bringing me some salt and—"

"He's bringing you some salt?" I replied, trying to sound interested. I was suddenly deathly tired and I noticed I had stopped sweating. I was drinking water now like there was no tomorrow, but I could not quench my thirst. I saw a blurred vision on the black wall of a tall glass with fog on the outside, ice cubes floating on cool spring water with a sprig of green mint. I felt somewhat faint and Chuck's voice was slowly receding but I could still hear him talking . . . something about salt.

"—and next time he brings me some salt, I will ask him to give you some and you can hand him the book and he will pass it over to me."

"What has salt got to do with anything?" I managed to whisper. We were still crouched at the tiny slits in our cells, clinging to the first genuinely friendly contact either of us had had for weeks.

"Salt, you crazy cracker, is what's kept me breathin' for two weeks and will keep you alive. You can't sweat like this and live without salt; yo' brain can't take it."

I vaguely heard McDew giving me a lecture on electrolytes and how African Americans had adapted over the years to hard labor in hot climates and that's why it was so important for me to be sure to take my salt and drink plenty of water because poor-ass white boys like me could not take this heat like black men, blah blah blah . . .

I remember the last thing I tried to say to McDew was not to get his hopes up about the book, especially the ending, because there were several pages missing in the back and it was hard to tell how many.

"Man, you had to tell me that. Why didn't you just wait for me to find out?"

"I didn't want to disappoint you," I mumbled. "And, besides, you can have fun making up your own endings. I made up a whole bunch."

"Swell," Chuck mimicked my accent, "Just spare me your endings and let me make up some of my own—WHEN I GET THE BOOK! Okay?"

"Okay," I said before slipping to the floor.

After a while I realized I was lying on the floor which was slightly cooler than the air above. I could hear Chuck's faint voice calling my name, telling me to put my face at the bottom of the door and breathe the air from the corridor. He kept asking if I was all right but I could not muster the energy to answer. A while later I heard McDew hissing loudly, "Here they come, can you believe this?"

Loud banging began on what seemed to be the door of his cell and a harsh male voice said, "Wake up in there, nigga, you got visitors, now you watch yo mouth and be nice to these little girls. This here, ladies, is our black communist Jew, and in a minute you'll see our white communist."

I heard giggles. Big Voice bragged, "You might say we have with us today a black Red and a white Red, I don't know which one smells the worst, don't you get too close now, you hear?

In the hall I heard a girl's voice demanding, "Hey, say something in communist."

"Always willin' to oblige, ma'am," Chuck replied in his best fake Uncle Tom voice.

"No, I'm serious say something in communist—you must speak the language."

"Okay, how's this? Kish mir ein tuckus!"

Throughout this interchange I was beginning to breathe again so I lifted myself back up to the slit in my door and peered out. I didn't speak Yiddish but I was pretty certain that my friend Chuck had just told the little white girl to kiss his ass. It did seem to satisfy everyone. As they turned to my cell the little girls in school uniforms were laughing, "He said something in communist! Yeah, I heard him, "Kish mi . . . something. I never heard communist before."

"One of his names is 'Zellna,'" lectured Big Voice, "sounds communist to me, and one of the commies tryin' to raise both their bonds calls himself 'Mister Dombrowski.' I don't know 'bout that black one, maybe his real name is McDooski."

The children were losing interest so Big Voice directed them on down the hall saying that the crazy people were even more interesting than the communists.

In the cell right across from us, I learned, they kept mental patients, and they were naked, with excrement all over the place. We were on the psycho ward and the punishment block.

Chuck was telling me about the poor souls across the hall, often on the way to or from some mental institution, for overnight or a week. I was still woozy from my introduction to the hot box. Chuck promised me I would "get used to it." I did not think so. I lay on the bare steel of the bunk for a while and finally gave up and transferred to the concrete floor, the first I had ever felt that was hot.

Late in the afternoon, as far as I could tell because here in the hole there was no daylight to be seen, Chuck hissed another warning, "Somebody's coming, Z, get the book ready."

I soon heard a hurried whispered conversation. The new voice was unmistakably Creole, a real Louisiana sound. A light-skinned Negro looked through my slot and pushed in a small golf-ball-sized cloth bag, tied at the top with brown string, and whispered, "My man ova heah axed me to give you this. He still got some. You got sumthin fo me?"

"Oh yes, I almost forgot, and thanks for the salt." I shoved the book through the slot. In my haste, and because the slot was tight, the front cover ripped off. The back one was missing already so I hoped it wouldn't make much difference. I passed the cover through after the man had taken the body of the book. I breathed a prayer that Chuck would get it all right; it meant so much to him.

When he left I heard nothing, Chuck was so absorbed in the book. After a long while I ventured a whispered question to McDew.

"How you like it? I asked.

"Like what?"

"The book," I said hopefully, "how you liking the book?"

"Don't play with me, what the hell you mean 'how I like the book?'" Trouble and concern mounted in his voice. "You didn't . . . Ain't no book showed up over here . . . Is the book gone?" He wailed.

"I gave it to the man like you said, didn't you tell me to get the book ready? I was ready—the man gave me the salt, and I gave him the book. He didn't give it to you?"

"Nooo," Chuck moaned, "I knew he was no good. Why did I ever trust that no-count. Bob," he said, "never trust a trusty!"

EVERY TIME I REALIZED that Chuck was in the cubicle next to me, I was so happy, I began to cry. Sometimes, we would sing freedom songs, and it drove the guards crazy—at one point I swear they turned up the heat to the point we could not raise our heads from the bunk. Soon, I was beginning to break under the pressure of the heat while Mc Dew begged me to hold on. He thought I was killed in McComb. Now he was afraid I would never make it out of Parish Prison. After a while, I told Chuck, "I can't take it anymore. I'm gonna start screaming."

"See if you can take it a little longer, because otherwise they're gonna really hurt you."

"At this point, I don't really care if they kill me."

"What about me? Those Visigoths might kill me, too."

"Too bad." I said taking a deep breath.

"Wait up just a minute, you never told me about the book. If you insist on getting yourself killed, you might as well tell me the story of the book. It might take your mind off the heat and besides you lost the book when I told you to be careful."

"You told me?" I sputtered. "Exactly whose genius idea was it to give it to the trusty in the first place?"

"Will you just tell me the bleedin' story and then go kill yourself?" McDew pleaded.

"Okay," I said, the teacher in me coming out, "Let's review."

"Review hell. We don't need no review, just get on with it. The two ignorant cowboys can't make out an expense account—like you. You make up the worst expense accounts I have ever read . . . but never mind, tell the story."

I told Chuck that the book was divided into twelve chapters, one for each week the cowboys spent on the range and each chapter ended with a copy of the expense account they left at the trading post for the boss at the end of the week. The expense account for the first week said: 1. chewing tobacco 25 cent; 2. kerosene 75 cent; 3. miscellaneous 770 cent.

The second week, I said, I think I remember they shot a coyote. That box of shot pushed the miscellaneous category up so the expense report read: 1. chewing tobacco 25 cent; 2. kerosene 75 cent; 3. miscellaneous 870 cent. The next week there was no unusual activity so the expense report read . . .

"The same," Chuck guessed."

"The next week . . ."

"Nothing much happened."

"Right," I said.

"Zellner, does anything ever happen in the godforsaken book, if you can call it that?"

"No," I replied, "It's just that kind of book."

"Who would ever write such a book and what fool would ever read such a messed-up book?"

"You were very interested in reading it." I reminded him.

"Screw you, Zellner."

"Oh wait, I left out the good part where the smart one has sex with an Indian girl." McDew perked up. I now had his undivided attention.

"Why didn't you tell me that part, asshole?"

"Wait," I said, "Maybe it was the dumb one. The book said he was really good looking, blond, blue-eyed, that sort of stuff . . ."

"I don't care which one it was, just tell me about it. What about the girl, what did she look like? At this rate, I might as well go back to my candy wrapper. I still got it, you know."

"You better hold on to it," I said. "I was lying about the Indian maiden."

"There's no girl! Zellner, screw you."

I felt bad about holding out hope for Chuck when there was none, but the back and forth about *The Riders of the Sawtooth Range* had kept me from screaming for another hour or two.

Eventually I did start screaming until they came. They just said, "No, your time is not up yet. Then I would scream some more. Finally, they opened the door and pulled their guns. "We're gonna kill you," the two ugly guards yelled.

I said, "That'll be a relief to me. You gotta kill me or let me out of here—both of us, because as long as I can scream, I will scream."

Finally, they let us go take a shower, but even that was part of the torture. They said, "We understand you've had enough. You don't have to go back in there. We'll put you in a regular cell. You get to take a shower every day. Everything is going to be different." They brought us to the shower, and when they took us back they put us in the sweat box again. The heat was turned up even higher, it seemed.

WE WERE IN THE sweat box for the rest of the time. We were in jail about thirty-five days before SCEF raised bail for Chuck and me, but we had to leave Dion behind. McDew and I were indeed tortured, but Dion suffered a worse fate. He was repeatedly brutalized during the fifty-nine days of his original sixty-day sentence. SNCC then bailed him out just before his sentence was up, because if you serve your entire sentence, there is no appeal. His case was appealed over a couple of years, all the way to the U.S. Supreme Court, which refused to review it. This was unusual, because we usually won once we got into federal court. So Dion's conviction in Louisiana was upheld, and the state agreed that if he would turn himself in to the Baton Rouge court, he would get credit for time served, they would suspend the remainder of his sentence, and he wouldn't have to go back to jail. Instead, when his lawyers brought him back, the Baton Rouge authorities captured him and put him in the same torture cell for sixty more days.

Some of us think that these folks who did things to us are like war criminals, and many of them are still alive. A few are being brought to justice now in high-profile cases. I used to think that maybe they led miserable lives themselves, but I really don't think they ever drew an uncomfortable breath. Like Medgar Evers's murderer Byron de la Beckwith later said, "Shooting that nigger was no more painful than my wife having labor pains."

Much later, at the bus station in Mobile, I ran into one of my fellow prisoners—the nice man in the tweed jacket. Our seats were back to back and he turned to me and said, "How'd you like the East Baton Rouge Parish Jail?"

We shared stories and I learned the secret of how I survived Baton Rouge. It turned out he was one of my angels. First of all, he reminded me of their bringing me mattresses and telling me to make sure to stay in a corner near the front. He said that there were two or three people who were determined to watch my back and try to minimize attempts to hurt me, and they did it the whole time I was there. Then he said, "I am curious about one thing, though. You remember that first little guy who came up to you—with those blackened teeth? You wouldn't have had a moment's trouble if you had just knocked the daylights out of that little son of a bitch. We all knew you could have."

I had to explain to him that I was doing my best to be nonviolent in the tradition of SNCC, the group I worked with.

13

Organizing in Talladega

Talladega, Alabama, was my first community organizing project for SNCC. They didn't directly give the Talladega assignment to me—it was a stop-gap measure. I was in the Atlanta office between campus trips in the spring of 1962. Jim Forman abhorred any vacuum in work schedules, even if you said you needed a few days to write letters or do some research or rest.

He said, "Well, go write letters or research or rest in Talladega, because I've been promising them that somebody would come over there. The students at Talladega College want to do some workshops because they are eager to integrate the lunch counters in that little town and they have some folks that are ready to go. I don't have anybody to send over there."

"Don't you think it would be better to send a black staff person?"

"Yes, and I will, but since you have time, I want you to go over there. They want to have a speaker this Sunday at the convocation, and I want you to go and talk about McComb and your campus traveling. Just tell them about what SNCC is doing."

He gave me the name of a young woman, Dorothy Vails, who was student body president and head of the campus Social Action Committee. I went to Talladega on March 5, 1962, and spoke at the convocation. Dorothy introduced me, and I talked about SNCC. This was an all-black college. I got a really good response, and we all met afterwards and went to dinner at the dining hall. All the activist students came over and said, "When do the workshops start?" They asked if I knew how to do them, and I told them I had been in them and could get them started until SNCC sent somebody else from Atlanta. That Monday, I got wrangled into teaching the workshop.

I found out later that they all thought I was a light-skinned Negro.

One young woman came up to me at one of the workshops and said, "Bob, when Dorothy introduced you to speak at the convocation, I thought you were a white guy."

"What made you think that?"

"Well, you look as white as anybody I've ever seen."

"People have said that. How did you know that I wasn't white?"

"The way you talk, and you're a SNCC guy. And when you smiled, I saw your dimples. White people don't have dimples."

It was touching when she came to me later on and said, "Bob, you are white."

"What do you mean?"

"I found out you're white."

"Does it make any difference?"

"I don't know, but you're white, right?"

"Well, I was raised white, but I don't really consider it a big difference."

"I've never met a white person I could actually talk to."

"You can talk to me."

"Can I ask you some questions? Can I smell your hair?"

"Sure."

I leaned over, and she smelled my hair, and she said, "That doesn't smell like chicken feathers."

"No, I hope not."

"I thought all white people's hair smelled like chicken feathers."

"Not to my knowledge."

"When you take a shower and it gets wet, does it smell like chicken feathers then?"

"No, I don't think so."

"My God. Can I feel it?"

She felt my hair, and then she said, "That feels just like silk."

Her dad was a high school principal, and she was raised in a middle-class family. But she said, "We just have all these ideas about white people, and I'm finding out that almost none of them are true."

She said she originally thought we put on something to make ourselves lighter. "I know now it doesn't rub off, but for a long time I thought it did."

I said, "White Southerners are raised with just as many misapprehensions about black people, and none of them are true. In the end, we're just people—that's all we are."

I WENT BACK TO Atlanta for a week or so and then returned to Talladega on March 17 with Joan Browning, one of the Albany Freedom Riders—also white. We did some workshops on the philosophical basis for nonviolence. We talked about satyagraha, Gandhi's method of action which was based on courage, nonviolence, and truth. We pointed out that it took more courage to be nonviolent than to fight back in traditional ways. We discussed Tolstoy and Walden Pond and Emerson's coming to see Thoreau when he was in jail for not paying taxes, and how when Emerson asked Thoreau what he was doing in there, Thoreau responded, "What are you doing out there?" Joan participated in some of the demonstrations, and after a brick was thrown through the plate glass window of the Greyhound bus station, where we were sitting, she said, "If I keep hanging out with you, Zellner, I'm going to wind up being killed."

As it turned out, I was the main SNCC person in Talladega for what seemed like months on end. Brenda Travis came to live on the Talladega campus while I was there. She had been expelled the day of the bloody McComb march, back in October of '61, and then sent to reform school. She was released on condition that she leave Mississippi and go into a foster care home. A white professor at Talladega, Hermann Einsemann, kind of adopted her, and she came to live on the Talladega campus during this period.

In some of the workshops, we role-played as many of the situations as we thought people would get into, starting with sit-ins. The role-playing was quite elaborate. We had all the cast of characters that would be at an actual sit-in—the sit-inners, the people running the lunch counters, the manager, news people, police, hoodlums, and observers. We set up the lunch counter, the stools and chairs, and then everybody would go through the scenario several times, so each person could play different roles, and sometimes it was so realistic that people would really get into it. A lot of times, you saw they loved to play cops, and they loved to play hoodlums. They made really good hoodlums. They knew all the words and actions. As a result, they were quite well-prepared for the violence to come.

People would go on the sit-in depending on how they did in the workshop. The sit-inners were the high-status people. One young man, Edward White, was a firebrand, and he had always been in fights. That's a good person to work with, but you have to go through a lot of training to get real discipline there. Everyone told him, "You can't go because you're gonna fight." He said, "No, I want to be a sit-inner."

We'd go through the role playing, and he would take it for a long time, and then he would start fighting. It was so real. He'd get furious and go tackle somebody. Once the real action started, nobody would ever let him go. There were other jobs for him. On one of the sit-ins, he was acting as an observer. He was standing on the corner so he could see where the people were sitting in. He had all the telephone numbers to call to report what was happening—without being discovered. We observed that his cover had been blown, and the hoodlums realized he was connected, so they came over to confront him. Everybody was just holding their breath. The main hoodlum hit him so hard it knocked him through a plate glass window in a store. Later, the storekeeper charged Edward with "breaking and entering." The guy who hit him then jumped through the shattered window and pounced on him, but Edward went into a perfect fetal position with his hands over his head, exactly as taught in the workshop. This gave time for other people to come and nonviolently get between Edward and his attacker. There was glass and blood all over the place, but he never fought back. He was the biggest hero that night at the mass meeting. We told him, "You did it. You are nonviolent. You can get through in the crunch." After that they would let him go in the sit-ins.

THE TALLADEGA STUDENTS SAT-IN at all the local lunch counters. Talladega is a small town, and the college was its main economic support—even so, there was just egregious segregation. Students were needed as customers, but they couldn't sit down at the lunch counter. There were continuing demonstrations, and lunch counters were later desegregated, but there was too much resistance while I was there. The whites mobilized the fire department, and deputized a lot of people, used fire hoses and dogs. It was an irresistible force meeting an immovable object. The power and strength of the movement were still building; much of it was happening in these little towns, but there wasn't a lot of news coverage.

On one particular April march to the downtown, we were going to see if we could march around the courthouse, have a short rally, and then march back to the campus. We were stopped as we got to the town square, and the authorities brought up the fire trucks. Sometimes you would make a decision on a demonstration based on the atmosphere or the temper of the crowd. Some of our people hadn't been to the workshops, so it would be a short test march, and we wouldn't challenge an order to turn around. When we were stopped, we had a brief prayer, but the police came and attacked folks at the head of the march. We decided that everyone who had been through the workshops should join hands in kind of a human chain. There were a lot of little children and community people. We would put them in the middle and walk back to campus that way.

We began to walk, with the cops right behind us. The one behind me kept prodding me with his nightstick, and there was something so sharp touching me. He had taken a razor and attached it to the stick; it was ripping my shirt apart and tearing my back up. I didn't want to cause anybody any alarm, so I just gritted my teeth and decided, as long as he doesn't kill me, I'll be all right. We walked a quarter to a half mile back to campus, and they pushed us through the main gate, and as soon as they did, everybody who had been on the outside, including the girls, started pulling their shirts up, and it turned out every cop had taken a pocket knife blade and sharpened it like a razor and embedded it into their nightsticks. They were cutting everybody's backs to ribbons. That's the kind of sadistic things the Alabama racists would do.

That was one time when nonviolence came close to breaking down, because all the guys who had not been in the march were so infuriated, they challenged the cops to come on the campus. That was a real confrontation.

There were some sympathetic reporters in Alabama, and occasionally events would draw national reporters, especially if violence was involved. If there was violence and it wasn't covered, it was like it didn't happen. They would put it in the local paper, and sometimes in the Birmingham, Mobile, or Montgomery papers. I also came to realize that I had become a lightning rod in Alabama and if a story involved me, it would make the papers.

An interesting example was a day in 1962 when former Governor Big Jim Folsom had a political rally at the Talladega courthouse. Alabama in those days had a law that a governor could not succeed himself. Folsom had been out for a term and was seeking to return to the governor's mansion; his major opponent was George Wallace. Folsom, as a progressive, populist Alabama politician, had a lot of support in the black community. We had a march planned the same day as the Folsom rally, and we didn't want it to appear that our march was directed at Folsom. We decided that if asked we would say our march was not against Folsom but at segregation here in Talladega. So Folsom's people moved his rally inside the courthouse. Per Laursen, the Danish reporter who had been arrested with us in Albany, was in Talladega. He was inside the courthouse and had an interview with Big Jim Folsom. He said to Folsom, "What do you think of the civil rights demonstration today?"

Folsom said, "Well, I believe the people have a right to protest and have a right to petition the government for redress, but they do seem to be raising an awful lot of hell here, and I think it's all on account of that Ralph Zellmer." Julian Bond was speaking at the mass meeting that night. He heard about Folsom's remark and thought it was the funniest thing. For years when he saw me he would say, "Here's Ralph Zellmer."

DURING THE TALLADEGA CAMPAIGN, I was arrested for conspiracy against the State of Alabama. The arresting officers were state investigators. I was walking across campus, and all of a sudden the whole campus was inundated by state police cars. Troopers leaped out of the cars, screaming, "There he is, get him." I didn't want to actually run, so I kind of hurried off in the other direction. Students started skirmishing with the police, but they got me and dragged me down to a squad car. I had just gotten a letter from the U.S. Justice Department and hadn't even opened it yet. It turned out to be about Eleanor Roosevelt who was conducting hearings in the Deep South with the Civil Rights Commission, inviting me to testify on state and local efforts to keep black people from voting. When they put me in the car, I still had the letter in my hand. Luckily the back window was open so I threw it for the students to pick up. It fluttered and went under the police car but one of the students dove under the vehicle, grabbed the letter and ran off.

The former First Lady wrote about my eventual testimony in her last book, *Tomorrow Is Now* (1963). These days when my students find out that Mrs. Roosevelt wrote about me, they smile and ask if I also met her uncle Teddy. This is a quote from her book, "We must know what we think and speak out, even at the risk of unpopularity. In the final analysis, a democratic government represents the sum total of the courage and the integrity of its individuals. It cannot be better than they are . . . In the long run there is no more exhilarating experience than to determine one's position, state it bravely and then act boldly."

I don't know when the State of Alabama decided to move against me in Talladega. I think I was arrested so the authorities could justify banishing me from my home state. This was my first Alabama arrest, but I already had police records in McComb, Mississippi; Baton Rouge, Louisiana; and Albany, Georgia.

Alabama lawmen and politicians were embarrassed that I was from Alabama. They'd show the other states how to deal with agitators, inside or out. They planned to use my activities in Mississippi and Georgia to show a pattern of misbehavior justifying banishment.

Politics aside, when a request for an injunction against our activities was filed in the Talladega circuit court, Alabama authorities were confident of getting a favorable ruling from a local judge. What they didn't count on was that their legal maneuvers constituted such a gross violation of our constitutional rights that the National Lawyers Guild gladly offered us excellent pro bono representation. Many Guild members were radicals and libertarians who understood that civil liberties were always trampled in times of turmoil and struggle and must be protected.

SNCC, I remember, had zero money for bail and operating expenses, much less for high-powered legal defense lawyers. Thus it surprised the authorities when Lawyers Guild president Victor Rabinowitz, a renowned constitutional lawyer and partner of Leonard Boudin, defender of Castro and other revolutionary causes, came to little Talladega. Victor was accompanied by his partner, Joanne Grant, correspondent for the *National Guardian*, a leftist New York newspaper. Earlier, Joanne had accompanied

Dorothy Miller to Moscow against the ban of the U.S. State Department; Joanne had continued on to Peking, China, a real no-no!

In some embarrassing ways the freedom movement had held the Guild, the *Guardian,* and people like the Bradens and Dombrowski of SCEF at arms-length. This tendency of the liberal left to red-bait those more radical than themselve was counterproductive. It became clear after the sit-in movement began in Greensboro, North Carolina, on February 1, 1960, and the freedom rides in the spring of 1961, that young people had the bit between their teeth. We were running away with the movement and had no time to look under beds for communists. If we found some, we were more likely to charge them rent or put them to work doing something useful in the Deep South. We had also observed who came through in the crunch— Dombrowski, the Bradens, and now the Lawyers Guild. Thus we cheered when Victor and Joanne showed up in Talladega.

The everyday slog and the relentless work load could get us down, so spirits always soared when outside help arrived to reinforce what we already knew—that what we were doing was important and that the word was getting out up North. The joy was even greater when the help came from a progressive Southern lawyer, who by definition had to be both courageous and slightly crazy to get involved in civil rights cases. One such lawyer was the outspoken Charles Morgan Jr. from rough-tough Birmingham. Victor was already comfortable with our legal standing, assuring us that the Bill of Rights applied even in the primitive backwoods courts of darkest Alabama. What Big Chuck brought was joie de vivre and utter fearlessness. Chuck was not bashful about letting the courthouse thugs and hangers-on know that he was onto their game. He'd been to enough rural courtrooms in Alabama to know that the "Courthouse Gang" was there to prop up the powers that be by hanging around to whittle sticks, spit tobacco, and glare menacingly—we called it "the hate stare"—at outsiders or anybody else the sheriff and the judge didn't like.

Morgan went about his work in Talladega with such gusto that we felt less stressed. After court we gathered around him in his tiny motel room as he spun hilarious yarns of past exploits. "The other day," Chuck said, "I had to go down to Greene County—that's in the Black Belt—where I'm defending a poor black man. I told Camille, my wife, I might not make it back if the rednecks down there know about me ranting up here in Birmingham against Bull Connor. When she asked if I really had to go, I told her yes, if this man is to escape spending the rest of his natural life in jail for just trying to register. 'What'd they charge him with?' my wife asked. I told her it was carnal knowledge of a chicken, a tough charge to defend against."

From the center of his sagging bed Morgan would lean over and put down his sweating glass of iced bourbon and branch water. He'd grab the phone and call the respected journalist Claude Sitton at the *New York Times*. "Claude, I got a report from the front." Pause. "What do you mean what front? It's the only front that matters right now—Morgan defending Zellner, the Bradens, and now Rabinowitz and Madame Grant—nothing but me standing betwixt them and the benighted lawlessness of the Great State of Alabama! My favorite kind of story, Mr. Sitton." Another pause. "Sir, it certainly is news that's fit to print. You ought to be down here to see it for yourself, but since you ain't, let me tell you about it in living color." Sitton was an Atlantan and the *NYT*'s chief Southern correspondent. He reported widely on civil rights from 1958–64. Morgan's bantering with him was partly for our entertainment and also to make sure that our activities would stay in the national focus, thus bringing additional support and some measure of protection.

Rabinowitz and Grant had been added to the injunction when they showed up for my hearing. By the second or third day of the hearing, Morgan and Rabinowitz, with help from another volunteer attorney, Arthur Kinoy (later a co-founder of the Center for Constitutional Rights), had prepared a countersuit against the state of Alabama, Talladega County, et al. That morning our group, led by Morgan, had woven our way through the usual crowd of whittlers and spitters outside the courthouse. Inside, Chuck motioned for me to follow him down the stairs. We marched into the basement where many county employees worked, and he announced loudly with a big smile, "Mr. Zellner and I have just accused all of y'all of being white."

Most of the time things in SNCC were so hectic and our lawyers were so busy trying to keep us out of jail or getting us out of jail that there was no time for preparing proactive suits. In Talladega, however, we were lucky to have these feisty attorneys working for us. So when Morgan impishly accused all the county employees of being white, he was deadly serious.

Our counter-injunction asked the federal government to ban segregated courtrooms, all-white juries, and all-white judges and sheriffs. Morgan and Rabinowitz asked that all proceedings against civil rights workers and black voter registration aspirants be removed to federal courts.

The very next morning our entry into the courthouse changed dramatically. As Chuck and I approached the front steps and the waiting courthouse gang, he simply pushed his seersucker jacket aside just enough to reveal a huge gun snugly nestled in a beautiful brown leather shoulder holster. The gang parted like the Red Sea for Moses, and we sailed peacefully into the courthouse. As it turned out, Chuck was friends with the sheriff and had cleared this ploy in advance, but at the time his only comment was, "Zellner, maybe you know how to be nonviolent and survive. My mama told me, 'Son, walk loudly and carry a big piece.'"

We were sworn to nonviolence in all our public affairs, but . . . we were kicking ass in the courtroom and it seemed that Charles Morgan Jr., Esquire, of Birmingham, was prepared to kick it on the courthouse lawn if push came to shove.

While I was in jail in Talladega, my brother, Jim, who was in theology school at Duke, came down to visit me, and of course, they wouldn't let him see me. He said, "Can I at least give him a note that I was here?" The note said, "These damn sons of bitches won't let me see you." He was so naive, he didn't realize they would read what he had written, and so they immediately confronted him with it. They said, "We should put you in jail for using profanity."

After I left Talladega, in spite of the banishment, I would go back occasionally and speak to the students. Talladega proved to be a very good campaign with continued sit-ins and boycotts by the black community. By 1963, a year before the 1964 Civil Rights Act guaranteed equal access to public accommodations, a local agreement had been worked out to integrate the lunch counters. We found that white customers also stayed away in such situations because they didn't understand what was going on, and the merchants saw their businesses just drying up. Sometimes, a merchant might want to integrate but was afraid to be the first. So the merchants would get together and say, hey, let's all do it at the same time.

14

George Wallace and Me

My relationship, if you can call it that, with George Corley Wallace of Barbour County, Alabama, was a strange one. Alabamians of all colors were entwined with George and his wife Lurleen for years, no matter what side or sides one took on the "Wallace Question." He was a bundle of contradictions and peoples' opinions and support or opposition to him changed with the seasons.

I have sometimes felt exasperated with the black people in my state and their actions and attitudes toward Governor Wallace. If any group ever had reason to hate a person, Southern blacks had it for him. When George had his last "change of mind," right before meeting his God, the black citizens of Alabama, at least many of the older ones, welcomed him back into the fold like the long-lost lamb, the prodigal returned. They heartily forgave him, seemingly unmindful of the irony of being able to vote for one who had denied them the vote and basic citizenship for so long.

Virginia Durr and I often lamented that the largeness of heart of many of our black friends caused them to overlook or minimize the fact that our George had the real blood of real people on his hands. We felt that true forgiveness could only come after genuine contrition and a clear understanding of one's wrongdoing, followed by a detailed confession and the sincere asking for forgiveness.

My position on Wallace's "death bed conversion" was that the man had switched sides so often that he himself didn't know where he actually stood. Before he died, when he was seeing Jesse Jackson and others, I thought of going to see him, but I couldn't muster a large degree of forgiveness. He hadn't shown me that he was honestly contrite. If I had seen him, I would

have asked him if it was worth the bloodshed and mayhem that he encouraged and probably increased in order to have the political power that he had
enjoyed for so long in Alabama—an unprecedented four terms as governor
for himself; one for his stand-in wife. I would have asked if he had ever appreciated the contradiction of his "being for the little people" and then setting one group of them against the other, often using the power of the state
against the group that was black. There's a kind of justice in the universe,
and he certainly did suffer after that guy shot him in Baltimore, but I didn't
really feel sorry for George. I think Wallace made the ultimate pact with the
devil—"I'm gonna go against my own principles." If I thought that he had
been a dedicated racist forever and ever amen, it would have been a totally
different thing, but he was not. He knew better, and that, to me, made his
race-mongering twice as bad.

The younger George Wallace was an active Methodist layman and was
considered somewhat progressive on both economic and racial issues. I
often mused on the irony that Wallace was a member of the Reverend Sam
Shirah's Methodist congregation in Clayton, Alabama, and was the Sunday
School teacher for Shirah's son, Sam, who became a hero of the Southern
freedom movement.

Wallace began his political life as a disciple of James E. "Big Jim" Folsom,
the much-loved populist governor, and many of the progressives in Alabama
wonder why George never picked up Big Jim's common touch that would
have enabled him to sidestep the "racial issue" as Big Jim had. Folsom, elected
governor in 1946 and 1954, once entertained black New York Congressman
Adam Clayton Powell at the Governor's Mansion in Montgomery. When
complaints were made about Folsom drinking Scotch over there at the
mansion with Powell, Big Jim said the charge was an untruth spread by his
political opponents. "Everyone in Alabama knows what a damn lie that is,"
Folsom is reported to have said. "They know I only drink Bourbon."

SO WALLACE, FOLLOWING FOLSOM'S lead, started out in Alabama politics
as a racial moderate. Smart alecks, of course, say that being moderate in
Alabama in those years only meant that you didn't believe in slavery. All
in all, Alabama was/is a strange place. One peculiar thing about the state
was that for some years during the early modern civil rights movement,

the NAACP was banned in Alabama. After the NAACP was banned, Fred Shuttlesworth and his Alabama Christian Movement for Human Rights emerged in Birmingham, and of course the Montgomery Improvement Association was carrying on. So protest activities continued, and Reverend Shuttlesworth was one of the great militants of all time—full of physical courage and an eloquent speaker.

Wallace lost his first run for governor in 1958, against John Patterson—the attorney general responsible for the NAACP ban. In that first campaign, Wallace adopted the moderate platform of his mentor, Big Jim Folsom, emphasizing farm-to-market rural roads, money and books for public school education, and he de-emphasized race even as the White Citizens Councils were rising in the wake of the 1954 *Brown* decision. Wallace came by his populism honestly, having once occupied temporary housing with his young wife and their first child in a renovated chicken coop.

Patterson, meanwhile, ran a typical Southern campaign of waving the bloody shirt and re-fighting the Civil War. It may sound strange to the modern ear, but that is how I grew up in south Alabama. My granddaddy, who lived much closer to the "War Between the States" than I ever realized, was fond of saying, "Why we could have whipped those Yankees with corn stalks . . . only they wouldn't fight that way." My history teacher at Huntingdon College in Montgomery, Dr. Chancellor, taught all his classes the same way—he re-fought the Civil War, which he insisted on calling "The War of Northern Aggression."

Yelling "Nigger, Nigger, Nigger" was enough to give Patterson the keys to the governor's mansion in Montgomery. After his defeat in 1958, George issued his famous pledge that he would never "be out-niggered again!" Thus began the segregation phase of Wallace's political career, which would make his name known in every American household. Four years later he rode white supremacist fervor to victory, and in his January 1963 inaugural speech he famously declared, ". . . I draw the line in the dust and toss the gauntlet before the feet of tyranny, and I say . . . segregation today, segregation tomorrow, segregation forever!"

I AM SURE THAT Wallace was well aware of my activism as a student at Huntingdon, my meetings with Dr. King and Ralph Abernathy, Dad's and

my visit to Alabama Attorney General MacDonald Gallion, my visits with
Virginia Durr, my time at Highlander, and on and on. One of Wallace's
first moves after being elected governor was to order Willie B. Painter, a
state investigator, to follow me and arrest me when possible. To make sure
Willie followed orders, George often sent his newly appointed chief of the
Alabama troopers, Al Lingo, to make sure I was arrested. Lingo was a well-
known Ku Klux Klansman who had worked in Wallace's campaign, and he
arrested me personally at least twice.

I was arrested by Lingo and Painter in January 1963, four days before
George Wallace's inauguration. At the time of my arrest, John Hill and
Sam Shirah were both students at Huntingdon. John Hill had come back
to Huntingdon and was trying to finish his education. Sam was an activist
Methodist, and his minister father and mine were colleagues in the Alabama-
West Florida Conference of the Methodist Church. Sam had been active in
Birmingham along with others in this church network. He had been invited
not to return to Birmingham-Southern College. He eventually became a
SNCC staffer and a full-time organizer in the South.

The main legal problem with that arrest was the minor fact that it occurred four days before citizen George Wallace would become Governor
George Wallace. After my arrest, Wallace became apoplectic when the federal
government began an investigation. He did his best to intimidate local FBI
officials and force them to drop the inquiry.

On January 8, 1963, I had been on SNCC staff a year and a half. I had
been arrested in McComb, Albany, Baton Rouge, and Talladega. These
arrests and the movement work they represented were adventurous and
exciting and important, but I was still emotionally involved in Montgomery
and was working with the students at Huntingdon College. Montgomery
and Huntingdon were the spiritual heart of my commitment to a life of
struggle and service.

I was committed to continuing the work I had started at Huntingdon—
wanting the powers at my college to admit that students had the right to be
involved in political and social issues of the day. In the fall of 1961 when
the administration threatened to expel any student attending a Methodist
youth conference at Lake Junaluska Methodist Center in North Carolina,
I had arranged with the Methodist Student Movement president, Wayne

Proudfoot, to go to Huntingdon to report to the students who were forbidden to go.

Wayne, a Native American, told the students that Huntingdon could not keep them from attending a national Methodist meeting simply because the gatherings would be racially integrated. The progressive group of ministers around my father encouraged us to keep the pressure on Dr. Hubert Searcy to show a little backbone and stand up to the segregationists on the Huntingdon board. They would pressure the college from the inside while we applied outside pressure from the civil rights movement and the national Methodist network.

I continued this campaign by visiting the campus each time I found myself near Montgomery. I confess that I had no idea how far the school and the state would go to protect the tender ears of Huntingdon students from the historic battle for human justice raging around them. On the evening of the eighth I went from the Durrs' house on Felder Avenue over to meet some students at the Tea Room, a café for students in the brand new college gym where the Huntingdon Hawks played basketball. I liked it there because I had been a strong supporter of the Hawks the year before, the first season on their new court.

The early evening was beautiful and balmy for a January night. There were lots of students about and even though Sam Shirah and John Hill and I were trying to keep a low profile, a low buzz began to develop. There was nothing overt, but I got the sense that a whisper was circulating and it was focused on our booth in the café. I had nodded to a couple of acquaintances, jocks from the team. They knew about my politics because Doc, the former team captain, had helped to beat me in McComb.

Now it seemed they might want to complete Doc's work. John tried to reassure me, "You have every right to be here. You are an honors graduate and just because they don't like your movement work, they are not going to hurt you. This is America for Christ's sake and Huntingdon calls itself a school for ladies and gentlemen."

I laughed and complimented John, who hardly ever said more than two words at a time, on his speech. I reminded him of the incident when a security guard had shot into mine and Townsend's room. Sam said, "Just stay in here and you will be all right."

Just then, one of the friendly acquaintances came by and said in a low voice, "Zellner, don't go outside."

"That does it," I said to Sam and John, "I'm heading out; I did not mean to get you guys in trouble. Stay in here."

To their credit John and Sam walked out of the Tea Room with me. I told them I would try to see them later and I headed toward Fairview Avenue, the main entrance to the college where I could get a bus back to the Durrs'.

I didn't get very far because the courtyard outside the café looked like a set from the OK Corral. A group of jocks and townies blocked my way and behind them, lurking behind trees and bushes, I thought I spotted Dean Owens, the crazy ex-Marine who toted a pistol around campus and threatened everyone who was politically left of Eisenhower.

Two or three of the larger jocks took a couple of steps toward me so I slowly took my good jacket off. The largest guy asked me in a fake-friendly voice what I was doing on campus. "You trying to start some more of your crap here, Z?" another asked. A voice from the back hollered, "Bob, you going to be nonviolent when we kick yo' ass?"

We traded a few insults until the big one, Henry, stepped forward like he was going to start in on me. "Okay, Henry," I said like I was talking to only him. "You always wanted a piece of me when I was here, and now you think you can finally do it with little risk. But I tell you what, since it'll be just you and me, I'll give you your chance even though I have taken a commitment to nonviolence. Tonight, just for you, Henry, I will put aside my vow to nonviolence and mix it up like you want to."

"Now Bob . . .," Henry started to say, but I interrupted.

I looked at the others and said, "I know we are all gentlemen here and we know it would be unfair for me to have to whip a bunch of you at the same time, so, if you don't mind, I'll take you one at a time. Who's first? You, Henry?"

I caught a glimpse of the silver-haired Dean Turner in the background. I wondered if he and Dean Owens had quietly instigated this little reception for me in an attempt to break my habit of returning to Huntingdon.

Henry had not shown any particular interest in continuing the confrontation since I used my Huntingdon-taught psychology to reduce the gathering from a mob to a collection of individuals.

I continued to concentrate on the big one. "Well, Henry, what'll it be? You game or should we put this off to another time more convenient for you?"

I wondered if Henry was remembering that I had never been defeated in hand-to-hand combat on campus in spite of some tough plow boys who had come very close—closer than I wanted any of these yahoos to know.

"Look, Bob, you got that martial arts and everything and besides we was just funning you . . ."

Meanwhile, the crowd was visibly thinning and I could tell that the deans had remembered urgent business back at the office. John and Sam were still behind me so I turned my back on Henry and the rest and said, "Sam, John, buy you a cup of tea?" We strolled back to the Tea Room.

Then things got serious. The three of us apparently remained in the café long enough for the deans to get hold of the police. We didn't have much enthusiasm for long conversation so I gave them a quick report of SNCC activities and an update on the efforts of national Methodists to put pressure on Huntingdon to change its policies. I included information on movement efforts involving SNCC, CORE, NAACP, and SCLC to increase black voter registration. John and Sam made it clear they thought it would take a federal army to force the Black Belt counties to register blacks.

Leaving the Tea Room the second time, I noticed that the courtyard and the parking lot were practically deserted. As soon as I saw the white state-looking car near the curb, I knew what was happening. The first thing I thought of was whether I had addresses, phone numbers, or notes in my wallet that might compromise any of my contacts. I slipped the wallet out of my back pocket and tried to give it to Sam.

"See that car over there," I nodded in its direction. "It's a state police car and I am about to be arrested; take my billfold and keep it for me."

"Bob, you always dramatize everything," John said. "You haven't done anything—why would anyone arrest you?"

"I'm serious, you fool. Take the damn wallet," I hissed.

Sam looked confused as a man suddenly emerged from the other side of the white car and headed in our direction.

"Bob, could we talk to you for a minute?" I recognized Willie B. Painter, the state investigator who almost always followed me while in Alabama.

"Who's we?" I asked, trying to shield my efforts to get Sam or John to take my wallet.

"Me and Mr. . . ." I didn't get the name that Painter mumbled.

"I have nothing to talk to you about, Mr. Painter. Good evening." And I continued down the sidewalk.

"Maybe you'll talk to me, Mr. Zellner," the other man said menacingly, getting out of the passenger's seat.

By this time I suppose John and Sam were in shock. The strange man told me that I would talk to him one way or the other. When I asked the meaning of the threat he explained that he could arrest me. When I asked on what authority, the man shouted, "Okay that does it, you are under arrest; come with me." Holding my arm, he headed to the car.

"You are arresting me on what charge?" I asked, offering no resistance. The strange man stopped and looked at Painter, who stared back with a pained expression. I suddenly thought that these two are not exactly on the same page.

"Conspiracy against the State of Alabama," he stammered. "That's it— conspiracy." Looking to Painter, he got nothing in return.

"Conspiracy to do what?" I asked.

"That's enough out of you Mr. Zellner, get in the car," he said, shoving me into the backseat.

John and Sam were standing just outside the car staring in amazement at me in the backseat. While Willie B. ran around to the driver's seat, I quickly rolled the window down and tossed my wallet onto the grass next to the curb right at Sam's feet. I was sure that he could see it but I wanted to be sure. I leaned my arm out and pointed to the wallet and back to him. We drove off in a squeal of tires and left John and Sam standing there open-mouthed.

No sooner did we leave than the car radio came on and a familiar voice— that of Floyd Mann, head of the Alabama Highway Patrol—commanded, "Willie B., don't you have anything to do with arresting Bob Zellner."

"Uh oh!" I said loudly, "Does that mean you are in trouble, Willie?" We actually were on a first name basis—Willie B. had followed me for so long.

"Please be quiet, Bob," Painter pleaded miserably.

"Well, if you can't answer that question," I replied, "How about telling me who this gentleman is?' I nodded toward the man in the front passenger's seat. Just then the radio squawked again and it was Floyd Mann, "Are you there, Willie? Do you hear me and did you hear me about Bob Zellner?"

"I did, Chief," Painter turned a paler shade of pink. "I heard what you said about Zellner, ahh . . ., but we're on the way down to the county jail with him now."

On the other end came a "Damn!" and then silence. I could not resist saying quietly, "Hot dog, Willie, are you in big trouble?"

As it turned out, the other man was Al Lingo. It was still four days before Wallace took office, and Lingo wasn't head of the highway patrol—yet. He was a Klansman, straight terrorist Klan, a mean, mean guy, on the way to that powerful position.

The wallet left lying in the grass played an important role. Dean Charles Turner found it, or perhaps somebody found it and gave it to him, but he took it straight down to the police and of course they went through it.

WHEN WE GOT TO the county jail I was surprised to find that the county prosecutor was there, and I thought I heard the agitated voice of Floyd Mann coming from a room just off the booking area. I heard snatches of conversation. "What's he charged with? The complaint is signed by . . .?" I heard a number of times the names Painter and Lingo.

I noticed that Willie B. had disappeared and I was being ignored in the booking room, so I adopted the position that as long as my opponents are arguing among themselves, it was best to leave them alone. I thought I heard Mann say, "I'm not in this and I have directed Willie B. to keep hands off."

Suddenly somebody noticed me and hollered, "Get him out of here!"

Somebody replied, "But he ain't been charged."

So they picked some poor schmo who didn't know anything about it to swear out the complaint. Along with vagrancy, they charged me with conspiracy against the State of Alabama. Of course, there was no evidence at all that I was doing anything. Even if I was, I wouldn't be "conspiring"—it would be totally protected behavior. They were convinced I was in Montgomery to organize demonstrations at Wallace's inauguration, which I wasn't. I wasn't even consciously aware that he was about to be inaugurated, even though I had seen workers setting up bleachers for the inaugural parade—which turned out to be a big anti-civil rights Klan affair. I was only doing my SNCC job of campus visitation and talking to the students, but to the authorities that was the most dangerous thing I could be doing. They probably thought I was organizing against Wallace, as well. But sure enough, they were in trouble because I later sued them for a quarter of a million dollars—Willie B. and Al Lingo and George Wallace, because Wallace was still John Q. Citizen, hadn't been sworn in as governor, and had ordered my arrest illegally.

My good friend Clifford Durr was my attorney and soon after he arranged bail, I was charged with another felony, false pretenses. This arose because Dean Turner turned my wallet over to the police, who found in it a receipt for a camera I had bought at a local store. Forman wanted us all to have cameras, but they didn't last very long because cops either confiscated them or broke them if you took the wrong picture. They would take the camera and smash it. I had just written an $85 check for a new one, a Retinal Reflex. I liked to have good cameras, and I liked to take good pictures. The police took the receipt for the camera from my wallet and went to the camera shop and picked up my check, which the shop had not deposited at the bank.

Wallace and his prosecutors were delighted with the prospect of trying me on something other than the political charge of conspiracy. Conspiring to do what? They had no evidence of plans to demonstrate at Wallace's inaugural. So their Plan B was to convict Zellner on a bad check charge and send him to the penitentiary for ten years. Maybe he wouldn't survive the Alabama prison system!

Chuck Morgan assisted Clifford Durr at my trial. Clifford in frail health and was exhausted, and Morgan was always spoiling for a civil rights legal fight. I remember at one point coming out of the courtroom and I had a cigarette in my hand and my hands were cuffed in front of me, and the photographer was there, and I didn't expect the photographer, so I smiled and he took the picture. Chuck told me later, "No matter if you are acquitted or convicted or there's a hung jury, never smile when you come out of the courtroom, because you weren't supposed to be arrested to begin with."

When they took me to the jail, I guess it was the same jail Rosa Parks had been in, and Martin Luther King, and even Hank Williams a time or two. One of my classmates from Huntingdon was the brand new jailer. The newsmen interviewed him, and they asked how it felt to lock up his old classmate, Bob Zellner. I wasn't treated badly at all.

Cliff and Chuck had a good defense for the all-white, mostly male Montgomery jury. The prosecution said that I had purchased a camera for $85 from the pawn shop on Friday afternoon. Because I traveled so much, my SNCC paycheck was automatically deposited in Atlanta each week. The police wouldn't let Mr. Erlich, the shop owner, deposit my check. Instead, the cops called the bank in Atlanta to see what my checking account balance was and were told that at the moment there was less than $85. But they were also told that the bank knew the account and knew that a deposit was made each Friday. The bank said the check would be honored. Nevertheless, that was the state's case against me.

"The check," Mr. Durr argued, "could not be evidence of false pretenses since it was never presented for payment, nor was it ever returned for insufficient funds." The prosecutors could not have it both ways. In closing arguments, Morgan marched his ample frame up and down in front of the hometown jury, waxing homespun as he asked each juror, "How many times have you, or your spouse, bought groceries on Friday based on the family paycheck that was to be deposited that afternoon?"

Then in summation, Clifford Durr, as courtly a Southern gentleman as anyone ever saw, rail thin in his crisp seersucker suit and bending slightly forward because of his bad back, delivered the final blow. He asked the jurors, "How would you feel if the Governor or the police were mad at you and took the check out of your grocer's hand, called your bank and then tried to put you in jail for ten years because someone at the bank said you didn't have enough money?"

However, long before Cliff drove these last nails into the coffin of Wallace's case against me, Chuck had done something in open court that determined the outcome of the trial. It is rare that the opening shot is the one that decides the battle, but that is what happened. We had spent weeks asking the progressive ministers of the conference and their wives to attend my trial in support of a fellow Methodist in trouble because of an issue of conscience. We had asked them to be prepared to be called as character witnesses.

Mrs. Francis McLeod, the grande dame of Alabama Methodists and the mother of a brood of charismatic and successful preachers in our conference, agreed to lead the charge against the state for trying to imprison me for ten years. This famous Methodist momma was the mother of Dad's best friend, Reverend Fletcher McLeod. Another son, Powers McLeod, was everybody's pick to be bishop someday.

Chuck's simple but brilliant maneuver, as the judge gaveled the crowded court session to order, caught everybody off guard. He stood and addressed the judge, "Your Honor, there are several preachers here with their wives who are character witnesses for my client, Mr. Bob Zellner. Mr. Durr and I have not had the opportunity to interview all of them. In the interest of saving the time of the court, if it please your honor, would you ask for them to stand so we may identify Mr. Zellner's character witnesses? I don't know how many of them are here."

Before the prosecutor could object and before the judge realized he was being poleaxed in his own courtroom, the judge asked the character witnesses to stand. Almost the entire audience stood up. Case closed.

After that, the best the prosecutor could do was to get the jury to agree to disagree. The resulting hung jury turned Wallace the bull into a steer. Wallace declared, through his prosecuting attorney, that the state would try me over and over until they found a jury that would convict. To avoid this, they demanded that I plead guilty to anything as long as it was on the law books.

I refused the deal and was prepared to go to trial again, but Clifford, to clear the books, agreed that I would enter a plea of nolo contendre. This helped the state save a little face, so the prosecutors selected "trespassing on the Huntingdon campus," my own dear alma mater. Pleading no contest was a downside of this arrangement, but the fact that it helped prepare the way for my later suit against Governor Wallace and his enforcer, Al Lingo, was good.

I am told that the subsequent lawsuit, *Zellner v. Lingo*, is cited in law schools as a historic case, remarkable for what is not formally apparent from the official papers. Progressive and informed Alabamians were intrigued with the lineup of sides fighting the lawsuit: Wallace and his handpicked Klan top cop Lingo, along with the hapless state investigator, Willie B. Painter, on the defensive; fending off the attack from my side. Of prime importance was the federal judge who would be hearing my civil lawsuit over the denial

of my civil rights—Frank M. Johnson Jr., the nemesis of Governor Wallace
and already a certified hero of the freedom movement. No movie script could
create a more dramatic confrontation. The second ace we had in the hole
was outgoing Governor John Patterson, who had no more use than Judge
Johnson for Little George. Patterson, certainly no friend of the movement,
liked us beating up on his bantam rooster opponent. It was a great plan.

Patterson would testify that he played no part in my arrest and might
confirm that he had specifically ordered his top cop, Floyd Mann, not to
arrest me. Mann himself, one of the bravest and most honorable civil servants produced by my state, was another ace in our metaphorical hand. As
the then-head of the Alabama Highway Patrol, Mann would swear that he
specifically ordered his investigator, Painter, "not to arrest Bob Zellner."

This lineup made our case in the simplest terms: Wallace and Lingo,
both private citizens at the time of my arrest, had usurped the machinery
of the State to carry out a private political vendetta. We should have sailed
to a happy conclusion. Victory would have helped to clip the wings of the
bantam rooster, and might even have helped to save my state the reign of
terror which Wallace and his Klan helper subsequently unleashed in Birmingham, Selma, and other places.

The press would have had a feeding frenzy off a courtroom clash between
so many rivals. What a spectacle it would have been to see one famous
segregationist, John Patterson, testify on behalf of an infamous civil rights
trouble maker, just to skewer another segregationist, George Wallace! It
would have been exhilarating to observe the tussle between the very decent
lawman, Floyd Mann, and the embarrassingly odious Klansman, Al Lingo,
who was succeeding Mann.

Alas, all good dreams must end. My case was dismissed with prejudice
by Judge Johnson before the trial began. My attorney, Ben Smith of New
Orleans, filed some papers late. The judge, because of his history with Wallace,
no doubt, felt he must follow every particular of the law. The technicality
saved Wallace.

Zellner v. Lingo was the first of three lawsuits I have filed for redress of
violations of my civil rights. The first two were in the heat of the battle, this
one in Alabama in 1963 and another in Boston in 1965. Our lawyers then
were trying to keep us out of jail or get us out of jail. The third was related

to a run-in with state police over the Shinnecock reservation skirmish in Southampton, New York, in 2000, which I will discuss later.

WHENEVER I WAS IN Alabama during this period I was accompanied by surveillance cars, twenty-four hours a day. Perhaps the most bizarre incident was in the spring of 1962 when they followed me from Montgomery, where I was staying at the Durrs', down to Mobile where my grandmother was on her deathbed. My shadows sat out in front of my aunt's house the night my grandmother died and then they followed us to Loxley, Alabama, a tiny town in Baldwin County, and terrorized everybody at the funeral. A lot of my relatives were George Wallace supporters, but they abandoned him after that. They said, "No matter what Bob did . . ."

My mother and father and all these relatives went to the police that were parked around my aunt's house—of course causing a huge uproar in this tiny town—to track this dangerous criminal Bob Zellner at his grandmother's funeral. Mom and Dad told the police that if they would get out of the yard, they would bring me to them after the service. Of course, the police didn't move, and we left right after the funeral and they followed us all the way to Pensacola, way across the Florida line.

IN THE FALL OF 1962, I had a brief respite from Alabama violence and courts. Anne Braden asked me to go to the University of Mississippi, where James Meredith was attempting to enroll as its first black student. I had no contact with students in Oxford, but I did know the Episcopal chaplain, Duncan Gray. He put me in touch with Dr. James Silver, the historian who later wrote *Mississippi: The Closed Society*. My other contact there was the William Faulkner family. I stayed with Faulkner's sister, and she told me the rules. I was not to talk about anything that I was doing in Oxford, and I was not to talk about William Faulkner. I did some work on campus and recruited a small group of students who were aware of Meredith's pending enrollment. They later went and sat supportively with him in the cafeteria. I was on campus the day after the riots and shooting surrounding his enrollment; remnants of tear gas were still in the air and the ground was strewn with debris.

IN THE SPRING OF 1963 it was back to another major confrontation for

Alabama, George Wallace, and me. The William Moore March took place immediately before the SCLC Birmingham campaign. The march will remain clear for me forever. William Moore, a U.S. postman from Baltimore, Maryland, had decided as a matter of conscience that during his vacation he would walk from Chattanooga, Tennessee, to Jackson, Mississippi, to deliver a letter to Mississippi Governor Ross Barnett. Moore didn't agree with segregation, and he wanted to make a personal freedom walk. As he walked along he wore a sandwich board. The front said, "Eat at Joes"; the back said, "Both black and white." He was shot and killed near Anniston, Alabama, where the Freedom Riders were brutally attacked in the early summer of 1961.

Moore's letter to Barnett spoke of brotherhood and reconciliation. There was a slight lull in SNCC activities at the time, and we decided that a group from CORE and SNCC, which had been the two main organizations in the Freedom Rides, would take up William Moore's march. We would start over in Chattanooga and try to complete the march to Jackson. We had a press conference in Chattanooga to kick things off, and away we went. We were all young and in shape. I'm not sure we even knew where we would camp or sleep each night, but we each had little backpacks. The whole distance was about four hundred miles. People came out to give us encouragement. One day, we stopped for a break and people brought us food. We had a two- or three-car support caravan with sandwiches and food. On one of those stops, a big black limousine pulled up, and a figure in a black suit got out and started coming around shaking everybody's hands. We had no idea who he was until he came over and said, "Hi, I'm Billie Sol Estes. I want to wish you luck. I support your cause." Apparently, he was a member of a biracial Pentecostal church.

I think there were five or six people from SNCC and five or six from CORE. One of the marchers was Sam Shirah, my old friend from Alabama, and he was chosen to lead us the day we were to cross into Alabama, because George Wallace had been Sam's Sunday school teacher. Thus it was Wallace who would be directing Al Lingo as he met us at the state line. They had already made it clear that we wouldn't be able to walk in peace across Alabama. We marched okay in Tennessee and Georgia, although we did have some opposition—no snipers, no serious injuries, but a lot of bottles, a lot of rocks. We just considered that par for the course.

We probably had two nights on the road before we got to the Alabama border. Sam Shirah put on the sign that Bill Moore had worn, and when we got to the Alabama line, the road was a little hilly and then it went into a little bit of a valley. There were hills on both sides of the road, and behind the fences, were huge crowds of people. They weren't supporters. Most were Klansmen, rednecks—all hecklers. Al Lingo said, "You can't come into the state of Alabama. If you do, you will be arrested." Several of us decided that we were going to be noncooperative at this time. When we were arrested, we weren't going to walk away or resist. We would go limp, and we wouldn't cooperate with the trials or any other procedures. So Sam and myself and Eric Weinberger and one or two other people were in jail for about thirty-five days. The charges against us were inciting a riot and disturbing the public peace.

The rationale the authorities gave for our arrest was that if we had been allowed to walk, we would have all been killed. It was a "protective arrest," which should not have carried a charge of a crime or punishment. Also, the ones of us who were noncooperative and went limp were shocked with cattle prods, which have a high-energy charge and burn you and cause you to go into spasms. When the police used the electrical charge on us, the crowd just went into a frenzy. They thought it was the greatest thing on earth.

It felt like being hit by lightning. It feels like your heart is gonna run away with you. It's one of the worst pains you can imagine. But we weren't going to cooperate. Our determination was stronger than the cattle prods, so they eventually dragged us into the paddy wagons.

We were housed in the Fort Payne jail. I remember the jailer's wife, who seemed to be sympathetic, brought us corn bread, a big slice of raw onion, and buttermilk. That was our supper for practically every meal. I liked all three foods, so I had plenty to eat, but Eric announced that he was going to go on a fast, and he said he would not eat at all while he was in prison. I told him I would do my best to fast while I was with him, but every seventh day I would eat. I knew we were in their clutches, and they would like nothing better than for us to starve ourselves to death. He said, "It's a point of principle for me." He would have fasted to death. Eventually, they took him to the prison hospital and fed him intravenously. He was very close to death when they finally started feeding him. He wouldn't drink much water, either.

A group of ministers came to get Sam and me out of jail to go and confront Governor George Wallace who was scheduled to speak at the annual Methodist conference at Huntingdon. So we left a few days before we were scheduled to get on bail. We must have looked like shipwrecked sailors, because Sam and I had not cooperated through the whole thing, and we had no clothes except the tattered ones we had worn from the beginning. We had no toiletries, and some of us had lost a tremendous amount of weight. I had actually eaten only five meals or so in a little over a month.

At Huntingdon, Sam's mother asked Wallace, "Why did you arrest Bob and Sam?"

He said, "If I hadn't they would have been killed."

"Then, why didn't you arrest the people who would have killed them?"

He smiled and said, "That wouldn't have happened."

Both Sam's mother and father were good friends of Wallace, and some others in the conference attendees confronting him were former Wallace supporters, good solid Methodist folks from Alabama. We shamed him so much and so many people jumped on him about it that even though he was scheduled to make the major speech at the Methodist conference, he left the campus without speaking.

Years later, Mom told me a story about the clothes I wore to Huntingdon at that Methodist conference. She said she kept them for years in Dad's old Klan trunk, the one he had made from a large hollow log. It was a beautiful piece of furniture where Dad kept his old Klan robes, his ceremonial Klan sword with the ivory handle, and the oath books with all the Klan secret rituals.

Mother told me that she often thought about those old tattered clothes I had at Huntingdon and how they symbolized, for her, the torture and degradation we had suffered at the hands of various Alabama Christian gentlemen. She took out the tattered old once-yellow corduroy pants and the raggedy shirt occasionally, wondering what to do with them. Every time she saw them she cried, so she said, "I finally took them out to the back yard and burned them. I felt better after that."

15

JOHN BROWN: LIVE LIKE HIM

S NCC was called to Danville, Virginia, in 1963 because the community wanted to integrate the library and the lunch counters. It was a segregated mill town. Reverend Hildreth McGhee and another young Pentecostal minister wanted to take on segregation. There were also some activists in the union, and they were interested in changes in the town as well. We started having workshops on nonviolence in one of the local churches. Avon Rollins, a SNCC staffer from Knoxville, and I were on the ground in Danville. We didn't demand a lot from the movement people who joined us from time to time, other than the ability to be nonviolent when called for. We ran workshops training local people in nonviolence so they could join the sit-ins, marches, and other demonstrations. Other SNCC staffers spent varying amounts of time in Danville. Mary King came to work on communications; Ivanhoe Donaldson and Cordell Reagon helped with workshops; Dottie Miller and Jim Forman came in periodically to help with strategy and communication and as liaisons with legal people; most of the SNCC Freedom Singers came through at various times, including Bertha Gober, Matthew Jones, Bernice Johnson Reagon, and others.

The opposition in Danville was violent and often brutal. When the sit-ins and marches started, the cops deputized what seemed to be most of the adult white male population and supplied them with makeshift clubs. During a march, they would surround us with fire trucks and beat us. We had a lot of night marches, because people were in jail, and the whole black working-class community would become mobilized at a night mass meeting and then march to the jail.

Of 123 people in a march on June 10, 1963, ninety were hospitalized.

The press was there but if the press took any pictures, the police and the deputized thugs beat the reporters and took their equipment. I had my camera, was not marching and was standing over with the press. Reverend McGhee and his wife were leading the march, and Dottie was in the march. They got to the jail and knelt down to pray. The police chief called in the table leg deputies, while fire trucks surrounded our group and blocked them in the alley. I knew they were about to beat everybody. All the reporters were standing there, but nobody raised a camera or took out a pad. I asked why no one was going to take pictures of the slaughter about to occur.

"Because they're gonna break our equipment."

Police Chief E. G. McCain was about to give the order, and the firemen were all standing there, so I thought I would just provide an example of what to do when you are a newsperson. I walked up real close and took a picture. The police chief said, "Okay, Zellner, you don't value that camera very much." He walked over and took the camera from around my neck. Holding the camera by the leather strap, Chief McCain smashed it on the ground three times. Each time, the crunch of it hitting the pavement gave me new pain. It had been an awfully good camera. Then he opened the busted back, took out the film and said, "Now, anybody else want to take pictures? No?" Then he arrested me, and he arrested Reverend McGhee, and they took us not inside the jail, but to the back of the jail and said, "Watch." That's when they turned on the fire hoses and started beating people.

Preparation for this kind of treatment helps when you meet it, and part of that was to be ready for whatever might happen, including getting killed. I particularly remember the fire hoses. When the water hits it's disorienting because it's more powerful than you expect. It just knocks you all over the place. It slides you along and skins you up, and it's cold, and the force is so hard, it can break your bones. It can wash you into a brick wall or a pole or metal cans. You try to get into a group and hang onto each other. The main thing is to try to run from the area because you just can't stand up under it. We learned to make a strategic retreat. I remember Forman prevented an assault one night on the steps of the city hall in Danville. Authorities had quietly let the deputies into City Hall even though it was closed and locked, fire trucks were in front of the steps, the sanitation workers were there with their table legs, and Forman went up the chief of police and said, "You can't do this. There are women and children here, and enough people have been injured." The chief gave us three minutes to leave and we left.

In a nonviolent situation, you objectify a lot by removing yourself psychically from the situation. More than once, I observed the effect on my own body and what was happening around me. I remember splintering glass from the fire hoses, because the water would knock the windows out, and I thought how stupid it was to be using the fire hoses against the people but to be destroying property and stores as well.

So, the cops stood there with their guns drawn on us and one said, "McGhee, your wife is out there, what kind of man are you? Aren't you going to help her? Zellner, your girlfriend is out there. Aren't you going to help her?" They literally washed Dottie under a car. Then, when she started to climb out, a cop hit her in the head with his stick. In the hospital that night were people with their breasts split completely open, noses split, eyes knocked out, ears ripped off. A local guy had a movie camera and took film at the hospital of staff sewing up person after person.

They charged Avon Rollins and me under a law known as the "John Brown statute"—inciting the black population into acts of war and violence against the white population. They also charged Dottie, Jim Forman, SNCC photographer Danny Lyon, and several other people who had been in and out during the summer. At an emergency meeting, we decided that all nonessential staffers under indictment should try to escape from Danville. We couldn't afford the high bonds. Dottie, Forman, Mary King, and Danny Lyon were to leave. But somebody had to stay. SNCC wanted to leave what they called "a salt and pepper team," so Avon and I decided to stay. We made our way to the church up on the hill and took sanctuary inside, because we reasoned that the cops wouldn't come in immediately and arrest us on this John Brown felony charge.

Avon and I huddled in the darkened Baptist church, surrounded by some of the bravest local deacons. The others were spirited out of town. Like Albany, Georgia, Danville's black community was mobilized from the preachers and teachers on down the line to the cab drivers and factory workers. The cab drivers arranged the escape by dividing the SNCC fugitives among a number of taxis, heading in different directions. When out of sight of the ever-present cops, Dottie, Jim, and the others would sneak into various civilian cars to be delivered into the countryside where a SNCC getaway car was stashed behind a country church. From there they sped toward Atlanta.

Two nights later, community people brought the film from the massacre to the church. Avon and I were going to try to escape from the church in the dark of night and make our way through a gully to a nearby store. A cab would take us to a car out in the country. Then we could take the film to Washington so the world could see what was happening in Danville.

About two or three o'clock in the morning, Avon and I crept out the back of the church. We were about to go down a deep ravine into the gully. The cops were waiting; they turned the spotlights on us and just started shooting.

In a lot of situations, one looks back and remembers the funny part, and we don't think back that we are out there in the middle of the night and the police are firing at us. I remember thinking, they couldn't actually be shooting at us. You always think they are shooting in the air or something, and then you look and see the fire coming out of the gun barrels, and it's all leveled directly at you. Also, you can feel the bullets whizzing around you. We didn't know whether to run forward or go through the woods, because we were afraid that they would really hunt us down and kill us. So we decided to run around to the front of the church, hoping that someone would let us back in. The police were running behind us shooting at us, and not being familiar with the grounds outside the church, around one corner, we ran into a huge pile of cinders where they had emptied the pot-bellied stove. We both fell into the cinders, got up still running, and someone timed it just right and opened the front door of the church. We zipped inside, and they bolted the doors again. The police didn't break in that night, and we felt that we were okay for a while.

In the years since, when I've shared the speaker's platform with Avon and we tell about the escape from the church, he tells the story differently. He claims he hit the mountain of cinders first and fell down and that I left tracks all over his back—leaving him in the dust. I told Avon that might be so, but it only goes to show that he was leaving me behind until he hit the cinder pile.

To be safe, we gave the film to an amply endowed woman in the church, and she put it in her bosom and took it away. The next morning the police broke the door down. We figured they would do that, and they captured us and took us off to jail. The John Brown charge was a serious felony charge and called for a high bond. The charge itself would no doubt be declared unconstitutional. It's like sedition laws against labor people. They would arrest people on it, but they would almost never try people on it because they knew it would be thrown out. Police wanted to keep anarchy and sedition charges on the books in order to intimidate freedom fighters.

I found it ironic that they charged us with acts of war and violence against the white population, because the exact opposite was true. They had tanks. They shot tear gas and aimed the fire hoses. Any time we had a gathering, they were likely to surround us and beat people and tear gas us and shoot at us. The police had a habit of attacking whenever and wherever we gathered.

To RELIEVE STRESS AND keep everybody's spirits together, the community held a series of small fund-raisers in the heart of the black community. Usually, nobody's house was big enough, so the gathering would be in the back yard. Everybody would chip in and bring food and beer, and lanterns would be hung, and somebody would bring a little record player so people would be able to dance. A collection would be taken up. If the police found out where we were, they would mass a large force, try and surround the place, and try to catch everybody. The idea was to catch all the SNCC people and put them in jail. If you ran, they would shoot at you. One night, they surrounded a party and surprised us out of the blue. All of a sudden, they attacked, shooting in all directions. The amazing thing was that people weren't killed. Everybody ran. I ran two or three houses down, and went into a house, and everybody jumped into closets and climbed under beds, but the woman of the house, seeing me, was terrified and said, "Oh no, you can't stay here. Everybody else can be passed off as a relative from the neighborhood. I hate to do this, but you've gotta go. "

I said, "Okay, but the police are in the backyard. Can you let me out the front?"

She took me out the front door. The house was high up on stilts, and there was a hill, so one end of the porch was real low, and the other end was very high off the ground. When I went out the door, she slammed the door behind me, and the cops turned the spotlight on the porch and started shooting at me right away. It was like shooting fish in a barrel. I was there on the porch with this big spotlight, and the bullets were flying all over the place, so I ran down to the end of the porch. The low end of the porch was where the police were, so I had to take a chance at the other end. I ran down to the high end and just leaped into the darkness. When I hit, I rolled, and then jumped up and sprinted behind the house where there was a little outbuilding. On the left-hand side of the building, out of sight from where the police would be coming was a huge pile of brambles—bushes, briar stickers, and God knows what else was in there, snakes, broken glass, rusty nails. I thought my only chance was to dive into there. I was very athletic at the time, so I jumped as high as I could and turned a flip so I landed on my back in this huge pile of mess and immediately relaxed so I would sink as far as possible. I knew there would be a lot of settling noise. So I tried to get everything quiet before they were able to get around to me. They were shouting and shooting, shining the spotlights, but by the time they came near me I was settled in. They searched the whole back of the house, and some ran into the woods behind the house. It seemed like I was in there an hour or so. Then, after everything got completely dark and they were all gone, I was still afraid to move.

Then, I heard a tiny voice, "Psst, hey mister, hey mister. Mr. Bob, they're all gone. Come follow me." So I climbed out and this little kid took me through the woods to somebody else's house that he knew, and they called somebody to come and retrieve me.

I have no idea how they missed me in the bramble patch. I was never hit by a bullet. Glass was breaking, wood was splintering everywhere from bullets, but I was a criminal trying to escape. When you're in the thick of it, it's like a soldier's training. We were so well-trained and so disciplined in nonviolence. Actually, we had conditioned our souls to the point where we wouldn't feel anger.

OVER THE COURSE OF that summer we were arrested five or six times, and on a lot of different charges. They would bring us up on disorderly conduct or disturbing the peace, or rioting. They would convict us, and they'd take us off to jail, and we'd have to make bail. Usually, we would serve some of our sentence, and before the end of the sentence, we would get bailed out so that the charges wouldn't be moot, and we could still appeal. After one arrest, several of us were convicted and sent to the work farm near the town. By then, I was shell-shocked. I knew that I was exhausted, but didn't know the depths of it.

One time, I was in jail with Danny Foss, a young PhD candidate from the Brandeis University sociology department. A fan of SNCC, he had come to Danville on his own when he heard about the summer's activities. Every time I got arrested, Danny was arrested with me or he soon followed me to the cells. He had a disconcerting habit of antagonizing police in the jail. Generally, if we were in the jail, we would avoid this. But the cops would come in the cell and beat Danny and I would have to go over and try to nonviolently protect him. I wound up getting beaten myself. After one of these episodes, I told Danny, "I don't mean to offend you, but we're in jail. There are no news people around, no cameras, and these people want to beat the hell out of you anyway, so why antagonize them to the point where they do it? And unless you haven't noticed, every time you get beaten, I do too. I'm pretty exhausted with all this crap."

Danny, who had every neurosis imaginable, pinched his face in the most horrible way and said, "Bob, unless I'm in imminent danger of death, I sink into a deathly lethargy."

I said, "Okay, that's it. If you can't work out whatever personal problems you have about this, I'd rather you have narcolepsy than continue on this path."

Danny Foss got me to go to Brandeis University that fall. One day we were talking in the cell—at least Danny was somebody to talk to. He commented that I looked tired.

I hadn't thought that much about it but I suddenly realized how I felt. I had joined the SNCC staff in the fall of 1961 and now I was coming up on two years of practically nonstop action.

I had been arrested in Mississippi, Alabama, Louisiana, Georgia, and Virginia and charged with everything from criminal anarchy in Louisiana to committing acts of war and violence in Virginia. I had been beaten, nearly lynched, and shot at. Was it possible to take a break?

Danny asked, "Do you think you can be serious about going to grad school for a while? Brandeis is a great university with a great sociology department."

I had told him I majored in sociology and psychology at Huntingdon, and he reminded me that my good friend and jail buddy, Chuck McDew, had studied at Brandeis the year before. I told Foss that it would be a great dream but I couldn't do it for a number of reasons. I still owed a lot of money for my undergraduate degree, I was planning to get married to Dottie Miller and, besides, it was July already and nobody would take me as a graduate student on such short notice. Danny's pockmarked face was framed in a ray of late afternoon sun. The dark slashes the bars made across the high cell window bounced off his face, pulling the dark black hair of his big head down across his bemused expression. Danny was a New Yorker, a big momma's boy, and the most intelligent student ever to grace any Brandeis graduate school.

When he told me the university was in Boston, or in Waltham, a suburb, I remembered a beautiful old Waltham watch I had at some point, and I must admit that the idea of studying in Boston, the city of "higher learning," had a certain romantic flare. I realized later that smart Danny was letting me have time to talk myself into going. I told him how my Dad had always talked about the time he spent in Boston as if it was a fantasy, magical. Daddy had sailed for Europe from Boston and later he returned as a young churchman to help defend Methodist Bishop Oxnam against charges of communism. Besides, I said to myself, here I was a poor preacher's boy from deepest, darkest, backward Alabama, not exactly a hotbed of free thinking or real education, about to marry a beautiful, sexy, sophisticated, New Yorker. Maybe, I thought, Dottie, an honors graduate of Queens College, will be impressed if I land a spot at Brandeis. I had not thought much past us getting married. The fall after Danville might be a good time to change gears. I had not inquired about the SCEF grant to SNCC, under which I had technically worked the last two years. I might continue, but I sensed that Anne Braden and Jim Dombrowski already had some questions about my approach to the job. They thought I should spend more time on the road and less time in jail or heading up local campaigns like the current one in Danville. Forman, being my immediate boss, as SCEF and SNCC had both wanted it, was usually more persuasive than Anne, who was further away.

I woke from my reverie, thinking if this Brandeis thing works out, which it probably won't (who ever heard of somebody applying in July for graduate school beginning in a few weeks?), Dottie and I could get a leave of absence or something. I knew neither of us had any intention of leaving SNCC. It had become, literally, for the both of us, our lives.

When Danny and I got out of jail in late July I told him that I did not plan to go to jail any more that summer because Dottie and I were getting married. I had already missed a couple of wedding dates from being indisposed behind bars. Miss Miller had let me know in no uncertain terms during my last call from jail to tell her that I was detained by the law, that under no circumstances was I to be arrested again. "By God, we are getting married. Get yourself to Atlanta. It's all set up. Stay out of jail, at least until we are married." I said something lame like she should tell Chief McCain that "under no circumstances was I to be arrested anymore."

I HAD FIRST MET Dottie Miller on one of my times back in Atlanta. She was volunteering for SNCC in the evenings and working during the day in the research department of the Southern Regional Council, and we met when I was at SRC investigating some funding for SNCC. She was volunteering in the evenings in the much-needed communications program in the SNCC office. Dottie and her sister were the children of Barney and Sara Miller and had been raised near Gramercy Park in Manhattan. In early April 1962, I went to New York with Dottie and Bill Hanson, also of SNCC. Bill had his jaw broken in Albany and Dottie had arranged for her dentist father to work on Bill's jaw and teeth. Dr. Miller was my future father-in-law. Barney, a white-haired distinguished-looking Englishman, raised in Leeds, still said "Cheerio" to all his dental patients and friends. Although Dottie's parents met in Canada, they married in New York in 1934, but only after Barney, a qualified dentist, spend three unemployed and hungry years. Dottie was what was called a "red diaper baby," a child of parents who were radicals or communists during the period from the 1930s to the 1950s. They were typically smart, efficient, and outspoken. She had first come South in 1960 for training in nonviolent resistance sponsored by the Congress for Racial Equality—CORE. She was arrested in a demonstration and served time in jail in a cell with other white women, segregated from her fellow activists, the rest of whom were black.

The South and the movement were always in Dottie's heart. She returned to Atlanta in June 1961 to do research for the SRC, hoping to work eventually for SNCC, and she did become a SNCC staffer in June 1962. Of course, by the time we started courting, she was quite familiar, from doing research and writing for SNCC, with my work in McComb and Albany and on campuses all over the place.

WHEN I GOT OUT of the Danville jail, I went to the lady's house where I was staying in the black community, I took a long shower to wash the jail off, ate a delicious meal she had prepared for me and two ministers, and then slept for about fourteen hours. The next day I saw Danny being beaten as practice in one of our nonviolent training workshops in the basement of McGhee's church. I reminded Cordell Reagon not to let anybody hit Foss too hard—that he had just gotten out of jail where he had been whipped pretty good. "I know that, Bob," Cordell sang out, "but these sessions got to be realistic if these kids are gonna be cool while they are sitting down or going limp. "

"I know what you mean, Steve McQueen, but the boy has got bad eyes; he's a scholar but he don't holler. Brandeis can't do without him, I hear, and we don't want to return him with a detached retina to go along with black eyes and Coke-bottle eyeglasses, you know what I mean? Go easy or get in there and let them beat on you—you Freedom Singer, you."

I pulled Danny up from the concrete floor and told him to go take a break. The only thing he said was, "Zellner, did you call Brandeis yet?" I walked away from the workshop with Danny. "No, I did not call yet. You are serious about this, right?"

Danny had been very patient and I realized that I had told him all my thoughts on the subject. He steered me to the battered old pay phone in the church basement and took charge. He had a pocket full of quarters and first he dialed the sociology department and had me talk to Dr. Maurice Stein. We had a good talk and Stein said time was short but he wanted me and I could still get in. Stein told me to call President Abraham Sacher. Danny dialed his number, too, and eventually he came on the line. When he figured out who I was, that I was with Danny Foss, and that I was applying late because I'd been demonstrating all summer and in jail much of the time, he assured me that the details were being worked out.

And they were. My tuition was to be paid and I was even going to receive a stipend for my living expenses. When I told him there were just a couple of details to work out—a SNCC leave of absence and getting married—he laughed and said that was fine, I had until September 23rd when classes started. "Welcome to Brandeis," he concluded.

My head spun as Danny gave me a crushing bear hug with his puny, white arms.

The weeks following that phone call went by in a blur. I wrapped up duties in Danville, dodging the police as much as possible. My last act was to be a distant observer of a mass march to the police station, jail, and City Hall. It was to be a send-off to the hundreds of young people and adults of all walks of life who had endured our strenuous training workshops. I couldn't afford to get arrested because I had a ticket the next day for Atlanta to get married to the brilliant and lovely Dorothy Miller. Needless to say, the police, using field glasses, spotted me on the hill near the staging church. They scooped me up and headed for the jail. I learned that they were tapping our phones and knew I was leaving to get married. The cops knew about Dottie and her part in the demonstrations earlier that summer; they had beaten her in the head. They all had a big laugh and asked how "Dottie" is doing. I'm sure they enjoyed my one phone call, which I placed to my fiancée in Atlanta. When I told her I would miss another wedding date because I had "accidentally" been arrested she said, "You better get your ass out of jail, make your bail and be here, because we're getting married." That was one time when I did get bailed out the same night, and I flew to Atlanta and married Dottie on August 9.

Julian Bond rounded up the minister by midnight that Saturday night, while all the SNCC people in town had a gala party. By wedding time many were drunk. Casey Hayden and Julian stood with us during the ceremony, James Bond, Julian's brother, and Jane Bond, his sister and Dottie's roommate, took over duties as hosts. Others in the wedding party included Tom Hayden and Connie Curry.

While all this was going on, thieves were outside stealing my clothes from the old green Chevy I had used for two years. We had planned to leave on the honeymoon immediately after the ceremony. We drove to Alabama to see my folks, then to New Orleans to see friends, then to California for fund-raising speeches, then to Corning, New York, for a speech at a conference, then to DC for the March on Washington, then back to Atlanta to finish up reports, collect a few remaining belongings, and close Dottie's apartment. Then we drove to Brandeis for classes which started September 23, 1963.

While I was at Brandeis, Dottie was running the New England SNCC office in the basement of the Harvard Epworth Methodist Church, near the Harvard campus. Dorothy Burlage had opened an office there for the Northern student movement to raise money and awareness of SNCC. Dottie and I did fund-raising, recruited students, and supported SNCC while we were in the North for four semesters, but we returned South for the summer of 1964 and other major events.

IN RETROSPECT, DANVILLE WAS an interesting campaign. The opposition would mobilize strongly as long as the movement people were mobilizing. Afterwards, there would be some accommodation to our demands, then a little backsliding and then more demands from us. At least by then, they knew what was possible for the community to do, and that there were a lot of very courageous and dedicated people in the black working community. The unions at the mills changed some of their behavior. They were also under pressure from different federal regulations and union rules, so seniority lists were integrated, and work fountains and work areas and lockers were integrated. The library and theaters and bowling alleys were nominally integrated, so a little progress was made.

But when I think back about Danville, I am still stunned by the amount of violence, pain, and suffering that confronted the movement. In Danville, the powers that be would do absolutely horrendous things and make sure no news got out, so the terrible events and injuries occurred as if we were in a vacuum. As always in the movement, "If it didn't make the news it didn't happen." To me, Danville was one of the most consistently bloody confrontations of all the campaigns that I was in.

16

"This Is Not a Social Call"

In the spring of 1964 while still in Boston, Dottie and I began screening people for SNCC's Mississippi Summer Project, also known as Freedom Summer. We recruited and interviewed all over New England. The project began with an orientation in Oxford, Ohio, for the large group of young people who were going to Mississippi. I went through the first week in Oxford, as a trainer in workshops on nonviolence.

The Freedom Summer Project was controversial from the beginning. Bob Moses and a few others were absolutely insistent on our doing it, and while there was indeed opposition, at that point nobody had more moral authority than Moses. He had been in Mississippi so long. Discussion of the summer project began in the fall of 1963, and SNCC's rationale sometimes has been portrayed as rather cynical. Actually, it was very political because we knew that if black people were brutalized and arrested, neither the country nor the government was going to care. But if the son of white lawyer so-and-so or the daughter of white senator such-and-such got beaten or arrested—or God forbid, killed—people would pay attention and demand that the government do something about it. It's hard to believe that this would still have to be in our thoughts as late as 1964, after the Freedom Rides of 1961, McComb and Albany in '62, and Birmingham and Danville in '63. After all of that brutal history and accompanying worldwide news coverage, we still had to pressure the government to do something to protect the people in their right to vote—the simplest and most basic right of a democracy.

By 1964, we could count how many people had already been killed, and only one of them, William Moore, had been white. We needed to home in on the closed society and the bastion of segregation—Mississippi. We would have to pull out all the stops. A thousand volunteers from middle-class families, black and white, from all over the United States would converge on Mississippi. That would get attention and possibly protection for people attempting to register and vote. Some of the critics inside SNCC felt that bringing in volunteers would in some ways interfere with the kind of grassroots organizing that had been the essence of our work for three years—the effort to build up the people in the community and develop resources from within.

In any case, plans for the summer project came together. As the volunteers gathered for the orientation program on the campus of Oxford's Western College for Women, most seemed aware of the fierce opposition they would be facing. Some veteran staff members were concerned that the new recruits weren't fearful enough; we wanted to make absolutely sure they knew what they were getting into. We didn't have to exaggerate. If any of the summer volunteers thought at first that we were overdoing the fear factor, by the end of the first week when the three civil rights workers disappeared in Neshoba County, they realized we were deadly serious. Still, though the volunteers knew it was a life-and-death situation, very few who had signed up to go to Mississippi backed out after the orientation.

WHEN IT WAS APPARENT that James Chaney, Michael Schwerner, and Andy Goodman were indeed missing, our first order of business at staff meeting was to designate someone to go to Neshoba with Rita Schwerner, Mickey's wife. It was immediately problematic. A black person wouldn't be able to go with Rita and do the things she was going to have to do, because the local white authorities wouldn't deal with a black person. It needed to be a white person. It should be a Southerner, and it should be somebody who had experience. There weren't a lot of choices: It was me, and I never gave that a second thought. James Chaney was a young black worker from Meridian. I had never met him. I knew both Andy and Mickey. I may have met Andy in New York, and I saw him during that first week of orientation in Ohio—one among many, but he seemed more sophisticated and knowledgeable; he seemed to be an exceptional person. Mickey had worked with the Congress of Racial Equality and was already the leader in the Meridian office. I had some close relationships with CORE staff from visiting New Orleans, which was kind of a CORE town, and because of the William Moore march which was a joint SNCC/CORE operation.

The Jackson COFO (Council of Federated Organizations) office knew there was trouble when Schwerner failed to call in from Neshoba County. We had established rules that when you went into the field, you had to call in regularly, and if you didn't, our security machinery would go into full alert. It was a Sunday, and we already knew the three were probably missing by the time they would have been jailed in Philadelphia, the Neshoba County seat. However, the timing is somewhat complicated here, since COFO did not sound an alarm until after the young men were released from jail and taken by the mob.

In retrospect, if the FBI or Justice Department had called the jail before the three were released, their lives might have been saved. The local law/Klan would have known they were under scrutiny, and some of us might have gotten to the three workers on Sunday night before they were taken off to be murdered. Neither the Justice Department nor the FBI would make the call. They told us that the three would have to be missing twenty-four hours before the FBI could assume that anything bad had happened to them. We kept telling John Doar in the Justice Department about our ironclad security mechanism. People's lives depended on it: if somebody didn't call in at the proper time it meant they couldn't—they were in a place where they couldn't make a call.

We realized that even if we got the FBI or Justice Department to go in, the black community probably wouldn't talk to them. They'd had too many experiences of talking to the Justice Department or the FBI who immediately gave the information to the local police, which was practically the same as giving the information to the Klan. Early on, I think we all knew in our bones that our three workers were dead.

But traveling with Rita, I held out hope that we could find out otherwise—maybe they had been kidnapped, and we might find information that could lead to where they were being held. But then officials "found" the burned-out car the three had driven when they left the jail. We asked to see it but were told it was none of our business. Of course, the sheriff and his deputy were both in on the murders. Rita would look the authorities right in the eye, and say, "My husband is missing, and our two workers are missing, and they disappeared here, and they disappeared in the car you have found, and we insist on seeing it." The locals' attitude was halfway civil because the news people were everywhere, and Rita had a lawyer. They took us to see the car. We spoke briefly to the press and told them we were gong to Jackson to see the governor. One of the sheriff's men then said, "I will take you to the city limits and kiss your ass goodbye, and you are strictly on your own." It was part of the terror tactic.

AT ONE POINT DURING our search, I thought it odd and symbolic that Rita Schwerner and I, accompanied at different times by a varying number of people, had gone all the way from the local and county "authorities" in Neshoba County and Philadelphia, Mississippi, to the president of the United States. This journey took us from the threatening glare of Sheriff Rainey and Deputy Price, both complicit in the murders, to the "helpless" hand of the FBI local operatives—supposedly pulling out all the stops to find the missing boys—to the state capitol building and the governor's mansion in Jackson. There, Rita and I encountered Governor Paul Johnson in the company of my old friend, Alabama Governor George Corley Wallace.

Seeing Governor Wallace in Jackson was bizarre. We had just escaped the wilds of Neshoba County where neither the local law nor the federal law was willing to offer protection. In order to say we had touched all bases, Rita and the CORE, SNCC, and COFO leadership decided we should go to Jackson and demand a meeting with Governor Johnson. SNCC Chairman John Lewis and other leaders had flown into Meridian and, like Rita and me, had gone up to Klan country to find out what they could. The feeling, as they fanned out through the woods and swamps near the area where the burned car had been found, was that we had to do something. Braving gators, mosquitoes, and poisonous snakes—reptile and human—during the search was the least of everyone's concerns.

Demanding a meeting suddenly became moot when Rita and I, accompanied by Reverend Ed King, got out of our car in front of the governor's mansion in downtown Jackson. I noticed a gaggle of uniformed state troopers, cameramen, and reporters with notebooks hurrying down the sidewalk past us, surrounding two men in suits. With considerable amazement, I realized it was George Wallace and the Mississippi governor. Motioning to Rita and Ed to follow, I blended in with the reporters, moving up close to Johnson while being careful to keep out of Wallace's line of sight; Little George knew me but Governor Johnson did not. What could be better, I thought, to get some action than to have Rita confront the governor of the terrorist state of Mississippi? Paul Johnson was as responsible for the Klan action against our workers as the actual murderers.

Johnson was in a jovial mood with the press corps. We could hear the tail end of what he was saying, obviously in response to a question about the missing civil rights workers, "George Wallace and I are the only ones who know where they are, and we are not saying!"

"Is Governor Wallace here to offer you advice in the current situation?" one of the reporters asked.

I was afraid to wait any longer so, smiling broadly, I stuck out my hand to Governor Johnson. Counting on the inability of any politician to resist grabbing an extended hand, I was not disappointed.

Johnson clasped my hand. I took his in both of mine, clamping down with a death grip. Still smiling, I turned to the press people and said loudly so everyone could hear, "Governor Johnson, I'm Bob Zellner and this is Rita Schwerner, the wife of one of the men you are talking about. Is it true, as you just said, that you and Governor Wallace here," nodding my head toward Wallace, "know where the missing civil rights workers are?"

Bedlam ensued. A reporter blurted, "He was kidding, right?"

They shouted questions while the troopers, incredibly slow to move, finally pounced on me. Johnson was trying to yank himself free of my grip, but I was holding on with both hands like life depended on it, I bought time while the troopers tried to break my hold.

Through it all, we had been approaching the front door to the mansion. I kept my eye on Wallace. George had run up the steps and darted inside and was now peering at the melee through the front door glass. Johnson shouted at his trooper bodyguards, "Get me loose from this madman, you fools!"

I continued to yell to the press. "If these governors can joke about this tragedy, how serious do you think they are about finding our men?"

A reporter I knew tried to say something, "They didn't know you were listening, Zellner."

"They knew *you* were listening . . . Are you going to report this?" I replied. "Look at Governor Wallace hiding in the house," I shouted. "He and Johnson don't have the nerve to speak to Mrs. Schwerner!"

At last the state police separated me from the governor. He ran into the house to join his fellow governor of the great state of Alabama. Following our "meeting" with the governors, we walked over to the Federal Building where we were ushered into the presence of former CIA head Allen Dulles, who was President Johnson's personal representative sent to oversee the search. Gaining no satisfaction there, James Forman booked flights for us to Washington, D.C., where we linked up with New York Congressman William Fitz Ryan. We went to the White House and had a long visit with Pierre Salinger, LBJ's press secretary, who suggested we speak to Nicholas Katzenbach, the acting U.S. Attorney General, while waiting for the President to be available. The highlight of the meeting with Katzenbach was his reply to Rita's concern that not enough was being done by the federal government to find her husband and James Chaney and Andy Goodman, nor was our government doing anything meaningful to protect voter workers from further terrorism. Ignoring completely the second part of Rita's concern, and the growing likelihood that our comrades would never be found alive, Katzenbach's cool retort was to ask Rita what qualifications she had to direct a search of this magnitude.

Her reply was classic movement style, "The main qualification I have, unlike you and apparently the President, is that I cannot be bought off."

Sitting in the Attorney General's office, in addition to Rita and me, were Congressman Ryan and SNCC Executive Secretary James Forman. We were taken aback by the belligerence in Katzenbach's voice. Forman cut to the chase and asked the top law enforcement officer of the United States if he would personally guarantee the safety of Buford Posey, a white Mississippian who had given helpful information to the Justice Department concerning relatives who were potential suspects in the kidnappings and possible murders of the civil rights workers. Forman explained to Katzenbach that as we were speaking, the government's witness was sitting in his house in Neshoba County with a shotgun across his lap, hoping to get out of his native state alive. Forman told of others, going back to Herbert Lee, who had died as the result of federal officials "sharing" information with Mississippi officials—the same as turning the names and information over to the Klan. "Can you assure me, and the people in this room, that Buford Posey will make it out of Mississippi alive?"

The Attorney General fixed Jim with a cold stare and said in a monotone, "We've lost witnesses before."

The meeting with the President was no less shocking. LBJ came into the sitting room where we waited, walked over to Rita and took her small hand in both of his, leaned over her slightly and said, "I'm so pleased to meet you."

Rita smiled tightly and replied, "I'm pleased to meet you too, Mr. President, but this is not a social call."

When Rita told the President essentially what she had said to the Attorney General, that she did not think enough was being done to find the missing SNCC workers or to protect voter registration workers in Mississippi, the President gave her a look like a hurt puppy and said, "I'm sorry you feel that way but I have an important meeting of the National Security Council that I have to get to."

President Johnson turned on his heel and disappeared as suddenly as he had come. It was like he had not been aware what the meeting was about and was disappointed that Rita was not just another happy constituent to pat on the back. As we left, Pierre Salinger scolded Rita, saying, "You don't talk to the President that way." She had not been deferential enough.

The absolutely amazing thing about the whole episode was that while meeting with everyone from the county sheriff to the president of the United States—with almost every meeting witnessed and covered by the press—not a single person, including the Attorney General and the President, gave any indication that they even cared about doing a public relations job, much less showed genuine concern. This was the summer of 1964. The world had already been treated to images of burned buses, bloody Freedom Riders, armed attempts to overthrow the government when Meredith enrolled at Ole Miss, and assassinated government witnesses. Now a terrorist Klan was running amok with the active encouragement of Southern state governments and law officials.

17

How Gladly They Stood

I spent most of the summer of 1964 in Greenwood, Mississippi, in Leflore County. The county and town are named for Greenwood LeFlore, a slave-owning Choctaw chieftain who lived in Greenwood and raised a family that was both Native American and African American. Greenwood is a strange little place in the heart of the Mississippi Delta. It isn't a river town like Vicksburg or Greenville, with their ameliorating patina of cosmopolitanism. The bluffs along the Mississippi River are where many of the plantation owners had their homes, while their cotton plantations were in the interior of the Delta. Some of those owners were international travelers and realized there was another way of life besides sharecropping and neo-slavery.

Greenwood was a tough town. It was the hometown of Byron de la Beckwith, who had murdered Medgar Evers in 1963. Beckwith was famous for driving around town in his car with seat covers made of Confederate flags and with a gun rack. Beckwith was a local hero. The pick-up with the gun rack over the back window was a redneck status symbol; usually they also sported a CB radio whip antenna. When we saw these trucks, we knew we were being tracked by organized Klan, heavily armed and with the latest in communications equipment.

I went to Greenwood because Dottie was working in the communications department—an extremely important job for the well-being and the safety of everybody in the summer project as well as for public relations. She worked as deputy to communications director Julian Bond. Greenwood seemed pretty vicious to me, and a lot of blood was shed there, but strangely enough it was considered a relatively safe area in the summer of '64. SNCC had been there so long, and it was where the national headquarters was located for Freedom

Summer. Even though a lot was happening in Greenwood, it was a whole lot safer than Tallahatchie County or some of those other outlying areas. Stokely Carmichael was project director at the beginning of the summer in Greenwood but was being called to other areas to start things up or to be available when violence was occurring. Sometimes we were up all night listening to hair-raising car chases in Tallahatchie County or other backwoods locations. Peter Orris no doubt saved many lives by working all spring setting up a CB base station for the SNCC headquarters in Greenwood. By '64 we had enough money to buy new basic Plymouths for staff, equipped with better radios than the Klan. SNCC cars were fast and maneuverable, but Forman had saved money by getting the white ones so the Klan targeted all new white Plymouths in the state. Our drivers got them as dirty as possible as quickly as possible so they would be less noticeable. Eventually, Stokely was gone almost all the time, so Forman asked me to coordinate the volunteers and the freedom schools. I became project director by default. Local leader Silas McGhee, who was shot by the law that summer, came back in the fall to become project director.

I remember trying to make sure that local people remained in the forefront and being embarrassed that *Motive* magazine, a Methodist publication, was doing a feature article on my work at that time. They followed me around with a camera; I was self-conscious, but I understood that they were trying to get the word out to Methodist youth.

Very few white people in the Greenwood community, or in the whole state, had anything to do with civil rights workers. Some would try to stay inside the society and be of service there. Some might boldly come to the office, but usually if we were going to meet with them, we did so in secret. Another choice for a moderate or slightly progressive person was to be a member of the Mississippi Human Relations Council, made up of white and black Mississippians. Even the terrorists had to draw distinctions between the inside moderates and the real "outside agitators" and "civil rights workers." It seems that someone was always "listening." If a white person said the wrong thing in a diner over a cup of coffee, someone would correct them right away, and if they maintained their silence or admitted error, it was okay, but they would remain a suspect. A white person who got involved or took any action would be punished—you could suffer an economic boycott by the White Citizens Council, your house might be shot into, the traditional cross might be burned on your lawn, you could receive threatening telephone calls. Then your choices often were to stay and fight, or to flee. I do remember Lady Montgomery. Her first name really was "Lady." She started by calling up the Greenwood SNCC office and wanting to talk to people. We met and she became a sympathetic white person. She was one of the few. She was obviously from the upper crust, and she had connections and could give us information. There were also the Barones, who lived in Greenwood, and there was a small Catholic underground. There weren't a lot of Catholics or Jews in the Delta, so consequently those who were there may have felt somewhat under siege themselves. Some among the Chinese population were also sympathetic. They had come to build levees or railroads generations before and had stayed. They sometimes ran grocery stores in the black community.

Though SNCC was the initiator, the Council of Federated Organizations (COFO) had been formed to sponsor the summer project and to help pull in national, state, and local support. COFO included SNCC, CORE, SCLC, and the NAACP. Working in Greenwood, we tried to balance voter registration work and Mississippi Freedom Democratic Party (MFDP) organizing, along with the Freedom Schools effort, but the need for voting just cried out. The Delta rural population was majority black with Greenwood and other towns being around fifty-fifty white and black. But practically no blacks were registered to vote. Maybe a few school teachers, undertakers, or business people had been "permitted to register," but even then often they did not actually vote, because that might be pressing the issue. We're talking about maybe fifteen black voters out of a county population of ten thousand. The few blacks who were "allowed" to vote lived in town; black people out in "the rural" were not registered.

The Mississippi Freedom Democratic Party was a strong part of our focus that summer. It was easier to organize with that as our specific goal rather than work around the abstract idea of "the right to vote." The formation of a political party began in the spring of 1963 when Al Lowenstein from Stanford, and others had sent some volunteers down to Hattiesburg, Mississippi. They ran a political campaign with some candidates from the black community; a dress rehearsal for Freedom Summer '64. The MFDP grew out of that mock election held in 1963. The election was our answer to white Southerners who were fond of saying "Niggers don't want to vote. They're incapable of it. They're not interested in it." The growing excitement and enthusiasm for the MFDP revealed a tremendous hunger for political inclusion. Aaron Henry and Ed King ran for governor and lieutenant governor. Since blacks weren't allowed to go to the county caucuses, and they weren't allowed to register or vote, they set up their own procedures, paralleling the regular Democrats' official processes. Everybody who signed up for the mock election, registered, and when the election came, they had their own polling places. Black Mississippians cast thousands and thousands of votes across the state. It gave concrete evidence that the grassroots were not only organized, they were ready and eager to move. This strategy also gave the black people training in holding local meetings and nominating candidates, preparing campaign literature, dealing with the press, and a host of other activities. We in SNCC and the MFDP were educating future generations of political leaders for Mississippi, which in a remarkably few years would have more elected black public officials than any other state.

THE OTHER MAIN ASPECT of our work in Mississippi that summer was the Freedom Schools—a fantastic idea. The concept was born in McComb in 1961 because one of the first things that faced us was the expulsion of scores of kids from high school. They had demonstrated at the library and the bus station where they were arrested. Over a hundred students arrested with Bob Moses, Chuck McDew, and me in McComb on October 4, 1961, were expelled. The early SNCC kids—Hollis Watkins, Curtis Hayes, and others—were leaders on their high school campuses. A Freedom School was set up for them in Jackson. Sometimes the classes were taught by SNCC staff who were appalled at what they discovered. The books being used for black schools in Mississippi in the early 1960s were from the 1920s. Many textbooks referred not to the Civil War, but to the War Between the States or even the War of Northern Aggression. Charlie Cobb and some of the SNCC people developed the idea of the Freedom School, and it came to full flower in 1964; Staughton Lynd was chosen to be the coordinator. There were traditional subjects but also debates and discussions—violence versus nonviolence, black leaders, and black history. Volunteers with particular expertise would be commandeered to go to the Freedom Schools and share their knowledge.

Most of the time, the schools met in churches, or they would simply meet outside. A lot of times, the Freedom School would be out in the yard of the local Freedom House, and if a church became available, the school would move. From the beginning, because of the voter registration meetings and mass meetings, churches became targets for bombings and arson. Many were burned down because Freedom Schools were meeting there. In Philadelphia, Mississippi, a church was burned because it was being used for the freedom activities. Local whites were so sure we would rush to support the church people that they laid in ambush for us; it later led to the murders of Schwerner, Chaney, and Goodman. A few times, if a church wasn't available, volunteers built community centers, as in Holmes County where Hartman Turnbow was one of the leaders. Those centers were used for a long time, and now some of them are in ruins.

The community in Greenwood was so thoroughly mobilized, I don't think that many black ministers could resist. Sometimes it was the minister who took the lead and came forward to give the church space, even if some of the deacons might be a little reluctant or fearful of fires being set. But in the majority of cases, the minister's congregation got organized by SNCC or COFO or the local movement. Then they came forward and donated their church. So in movement history the role played by ministers and by the churches is indeed important.

Local young people wanted to do their own thing in testing public accommodations. The McGhees of Greenwood are an example of a really strong family with young boys. There were three brothers, Clarence, whose last name wasn't McGhee, but he, Jake, and Silas were all Mrs. McGhee's children. Growing up in Greenwood, they had their own piece of land, so they were very independent-minded and brave. Their mother, Mrs. Laura McGhee, was as fierce as they come. Clarence, an Army Ranger of the Big Red One Division, was as lean as a piece of leather, the toughest man I ever met. He and I would debate violence and nonviolence in the Freedom Schools. He believed in violence for self-defense. I said that I had the highest respect for him, and he said he did for me, even if I was nonviolent. Clarence told me and the Freedom School class that as a dark-skinned black man in uniform, he never knew when someone might try him. He showed us some of the self-defense things he had learned.

Silas and Jake insisted on testing the public accommodations act that passed Congress on July 2, 1964. They said that now that they had the legal right to go to the theater and the bowling alley, they were going.

We discouraged them because SNCC was concentrating on organizing MFDP and feared getting bogged down in sit-ins. Silas and Jake said they were going to do it anyway, and that we couldn't keep them from doing it.

The two of them would go to the theater and buy tickets, and they would see the movie, maybe, if they weren't mobbed before the movie. Then when it was time to leave there would be a mob outside that was going to beat them up, so they would call the SNCC office. The police cooperated with the thugs, letting them beat Jake and Silas whenever the opportunity arose. So I would organize a caravan of two or three cars—one car couldn't do it, but if you had two or three, you could get in there and get them out of the theater into the cars and get back okay.

One time they did arrest Jake, and he called and said, "I'm in jail. I need a lawyer. Will you go get my mother and bring her down."

The Lawyers Guild always tried to help us, and they would send lawyers down for a week or ten days at a stretch; sometimes we had some young lawyers who might not understand the South. But I picked one up and got Mrs. McGhee. I told the lawyer, "We want to go down and find out what the charges are, what the bail is, and we want to arrange for bail and get Jake out of jail. The main thing you want to remember is whatever discussion you have with the police or the police chief, Mrs. McGhee must be there. She is the one looking after Jake's safety. This is important, because they're gonna try to talk to you, and not her."

Sure enough, when we got to the police station, the police chief verified who the lawyer was and took him into his office and closed the door. So Mrs. McGhee walked over and put her hand on the doorknob, and one of the local cops says, "You can't go in there."

She says, "Oh, yes I can, they're talking about my son Jake. I've come to get him out of jail." Then the policeman stepped between her and the door, knocking her hand off the doorknob. Before he could blink, Mrs. McGhee hit him right over the eye so fast, it knocked him out. As he was sliding down the door he reflexively reached for his revolver. I said, "Oh, my God. He's gonna pull his gun and shoot in all directions." Mrs. McGhee hit him again. Every time she hit him, his head hit the door. So, I tackled the guy and held his gun before he got it all the way out of the holster. Meanwhile, the police chief and the lawyer, hearing the commotion, tried to come out of the office, hitting the poor guy in the back of the head with the door. Finally the chief says, "Zellner, what's happening out there."

"Ralph is trying to shoot Mrs. McGhee," I said, "and I'm not going to let him."

"Are you against the door?"

"Yes, Ralph is leaning against the door."

"Well, let us out."

"If you make Ralph promise not to shoot Mrs. McGhee."

So the chief says, "Ralph, do you promise not to shoot Mrs. McGhee?" Of course, he was unconscious so I gingerly dragged him out of the way. His face was swollen where Mrs. McGhee had hit him. I thought, "Now we are really in for it."

Ralph starts to come around a bit, and the chief tells me to let him go and told Ralph to take his hand away from his gun. I thought they were going to arrest Mrs. McGhee for sure, but they didn't, and the lawyer explained to me later that they would not want to embarrass Ralph or the Greenwood police department by saying that Mrs. McGhee was arrested for knocking him out.

Silas McGhee was young and not afraid of anything. One night the Klan captured Silas. I think he went by himself to the theater, not even with Jake, so they just grabbed him when he came out. They took him to a barn outside of Greenwood, where they probably planned to kill him. They tied him to a chair and an overhead beam and left him there for a little while. They had beaten him badly, but he was able to get loose and get out of there.

About three weeks after the barn escape, they did shoot Silas. Those Mississippi rednecks, who thought they were the toughest of the tough, must have thought Silas was one of the toughest individuals they had ever seen; they had captured and beaten the guy, and he still would not stop. This time, he was in his car and the bullet came through the window and hit him in the cheekbone, glanced downward, and lodged in his throat. He was falling out of the car with blood gushing from a gaping wound in his head when I caught him.

Silas had driven me, Dottie, Forman, and some of the other people from SNCC headquarters to a local eating place in the black community. It was raining and Silas said he was tired and would stay and watch the car. A half hour later we heard the gunshot. I knew before I got to the door that something bad had happened to my friend. I plunged across the rain-shiny street in time to see a car a lot like Byron de la Beckwith's speeding down the block. Silas opened the driver's side door and slipped slowly head first toward the puddled surface of the road. A neat hole the size of a half dollar was centered in the window glass, now spidery with cracks. Blood spurted from another hole in the center of the left side of Silas's head. Against my will the words formed in my brain, "He's done for." That was chased away with the next thought which was that only a miracle could save him now; followed closely with, "Let's make that happen."

I cradled Silas's head before it touched the street. While sitting cross-legged on the muddy street. I whipped off my white shirt and T-shirt. Balling up the undershirt, I quickly tied the white shirt around the tee shirt and Silas's head, using the sleeves and shirt tails to tie a tight pressure bandage directly on the swelling wound. The blood stopped.

Someone had positioned a white SNCC Plymouth for a quick getaway. I was glad to see George Green in the driver's seat, the best wheel man in the organization, and he knew the fastest route to the hospital. Forman shouted that the black doctor was being called to meet us at the hospital.

I don't remember much about the ride to the hospital but I do remember talking to the unconscious Silas encouraging him to breathe. All I could hear was a gurgling sound in his throat. I turned him on his side so the blood and water would not collect in his throat and kept a constant pressure on the bandages plugging the wound.

The emergency entrance to the hospital and the immediate area was crowded with cop cars. It was raining hard now and my window was down to give Silas as much air as possible. I heard a woman's voice above the rain and the noise, "They finally got that Silas nigger!"

Our guys had jumped out immediately to get emergency help for Silas.

They came right back and said the medics would not bring a gurney; they were waiting for the colored doctor. I told them to keep pressure on the side of Silas's head. I walked into the emergency entrance and grabbed the first rolling gurney I saw and took it to the car. We gingerly lifted Silas up and rolled him inside.

"This man needs help," I announced, and not a person moved. Looking at each of the medical staffers like they were a whole new form of poisonous life, I asked if someone would help this man who had been shot in the head.

Finally one said, like it was a perfectly sensible explanation, "I'm sorry but we cannot wait on him, it is not allowed, we always call the colored doctor and I'm sure he'll be on the way."

Cops slouched against the walls of the ER. Now two of them came up and said, "We're sorry but you are going to have to leave."

I'm sure we looked at them like they had taken leave of their senses. I could see a number of SNCC people in the hallway, so I didn't take the cops seriously. George Green, like me, had taken a position next to Silas and I knew an atomic bomb could not move him.

I replied in my best Southern manner that we wouldn't be leaving until Silas received the medical treatment every human deserved under the Hippocratic oath each of the medical staff had taken, adding that they had made me ashamed to call myself a Southerner.

"The hypocritical oath aside, if you refuse to leave, Mr. Zellner," a little fat cop said, "we'll have to place you under arrest."

Incredibly, he wanted to arrest me for "indecent exposure" because I was undressed from the waist up. "This is my shirt," I said pointing to the bloody bandage wrapped tightly around Silas's head. I asked the little cop if, since I certainly was not going to leave, he insisted that I unwrap this man's head and put my bloody shirt back on.

Well, finally that was too much even for Greenwood's finest, and the cops stood back and waited with us for the "colored doctor."

Greenwood's only black doctor finally arrived and acquitted himself admirably. First he ordered us to wheel Silas out to a waiting ambulance, which we did posthaste. I heard him tell the cowards in the ER, "If this man does not make it to Jackson alive, I hope it will be on your consciences for the rest of your natural lives."

The doctor climbed in the back with Silas and off they drove into a deepening flood. As the ambulance surged slowly toward the main road I wondered if we would ever see Silas alive again.

However, at the end of that summer of 1964, Silas returned to Greenwood and became the first locally born and raised SNCC project director. The .38 caliber bullet, fired at point-blank range, had luckily gone through the window which may have slowed it somewhat and flattened the slug considerably. Also, thanks to providence, the Klan bullet that was intended to end Silas's life struck him a fraction of an inch below the jaw bone, not above it. The missile glanced downward into Silas's throat, not upward into his brain, sparing his life.

I GOT ALONG FINE with Stokely Carmichael, and was glad to work with him in Greenwood. We first met in 1961, became good friends, and had a close relationship, even up to just before he died in November 1998. I think I was the only white speaker at his memorial service in Washington, D.C., and I think I was followed to the podium by Louis Farrakhan. Stokely was always independent-minded. He and Abbie Hoffman did some work in Greenwood—they had some personality similarities. They were both born stars, charismatic, personally appealing and funny and had an absolute knack for focusing attention on themselves while getting a job done.

I was in Atlanta before Stokely came on the SNCC staff and maybe helped him get his sea legs in the Deep South, suggesting some ways to operate without getting himself killed right away. He said once that knowing me helped him understand white Southerners better. Stokely wasn't as committed to nonviolence as some of the other staff and was always more political than religious, but he certainly understood the tactical uses of nonviolence. If we had not used it the summer of 1964, the events would have been a war. In a way, it was a war, but the other side was waging it, and we had the moral weight and our side won. Stokely did something else as well. Because he was not philosophically committed to nonviolence he would press the issue to a closer edge with the bad guys.

Some of his comments and actions might have gotten him killed in certain situations, but Stokely knew where the fine line was and was willing to go right to it. In demonstrations, he would sometimes confront white racist law officers, calling them out to their faces, calculating that The Man would not kill him in such a public place. If he miscalculated, he was willing to pay the price. With his great grin and his fearlessness, he was de-legitimizing law enforcement as a source of terror—taking away the weapon of fear and saying, "We're not scared of you, and these people are not afraid of you." If he had to risk a revolutionary suicide to accomplish his aim, he figured it was worth it.

Local people couldn't believe him. He operated this way in Lowndes County, Alabama, in 1965, and in other areas where he organized, and they kept telling him he would not survive if he kept tearing the law people down. He would say, "Maybe I won't survive, but tear 'em down we will." Then they would see him the next day on the *Today Show*, grinning his grin, doing his thing, and people would day, "Well, Stokely's still kicking. I guess it's possible to do and say what he does."

It is difficult to assess the impact of the SNCC kids on Mississippi from 1960 on. Amzie Moore, himself a longtime civil rights leader, was from Cleveland, Mississippi, in the Delta. As a U.S. postal worker (no relation to William Moore, the postal worker gunned down in Alabama), he was somewhat insulated from the pressure of the White Citizens Council and the Klan and the organized white community. He talked about how fearless the young people seemed as they tried to register voters. In an interview, Moore described Bob Moses and the SNCC staff people that came to stay with him and start projects: "When an individual stood at a courthouse like the one in Greenwood and in Greenville and watched tiny figures [of the SNCC workers] standing against a huge column . . . [against white] triggermen and drivers and lookout men riding in automobiles with automatic guns . . . how they stood . . . how gladly they got in the front of that line, those leaders and went to jail! It didn't seem to bother 'em. It was an awakening for me . . ."

People like Amzie Moore, Fannie Lou Hamer, E. W. Steptoe, and Aaron Henry had fought lonely battles in their communities for many years. We could understand their reluctance about the young new workers. Sometimes, like Amzie, they had a special economic niche or they might be bootleggers, beauticians, morticians, small store owners, federal employees, independent farmers owning their own land, or union workers. Many were war veterans like Medgar Evers, Amzie Moore, and Aaron Henry, who said, "I fought for this country and I'll continue my fight in this country against the enemy—now my fellow Americans." They were determined to vote and welcomed our emphasis on voter education and registration in black communities. Local people, at great risk to themselves, welcomed the volunteers during Freedom Summer.

Long before that summer, the techniques, tactics, and strategies of nonviolent direct action began to be applied to voter registration. Voter registration in most cases is kind of mind-numbing, water dripping on the rock, staying at it, sticking to it. In registering black people to vote in Mississippi you had all of that plus the theatrics and mental elements of nonviolent direct action; you had to do a number of things at one time. You began with a tremendous organizing effort to put out canvassers to talk to people at the grassroots—on their front doorsteps, in churches, at schools, in the playgrounds or the pool hall—wherever you found them. Then you went with them to register to vote, and you stood with them while they took the voter registration literacy test at the office of the voter registrar. Many of the people you are taking down to register are to some degree semi-literate or illiterate. So at the same time you had to be setting up an educational system to teach basic reading and writing, maybe to teach people for the first time to sign their own names instead of an X. Both Highlander Folk School and SCLC's citizenship schools helped tremendously in training people to meet these huge literacy hurdles that were put in place by white state and local officials to keep blacks from voting. If poor schools and high rates of illiteracy did not do the trick, intimidation would.

The infamous questions were to interpret certain sections of the Mississippi Constitution to the satisfaction of the registrars, who might have only a ninth-grade education themselves. Semi-literate people were thus asked to interpret to a ninth-grade Southern racist, to his satisfaction, an article of the state constitution. People who taught constitutional law could fail the registration test. Other questions often asked included how many bubbles are in a bar of soap, or how many angels can dance on the head of a pin, or how many windows are there in this courthouse?

Still, we spent hours teaching people how to take the tests. The side benefit was that people learned to read and write. When you applied nonviolent, direct action techniques to voter registration, you also had to have a massive propaganda campaign going on nationally and internationally, putting pressure on the federal government to force local officials to provide at least a modicum of protection. Sometimes, the amount of protection you got was based on the media coverage, public opinion and world opinion, or the federal government. It was progress if the local police would simply be neutral—there had been cases when a person trying to register was actually beaten by cops, or thugs and bullies would get the nod from the cops to start their beatings. That fear had to be overcome.

We would go to people's homes, canvassing, getting them signed up, getting them organized in groups, getting transportation for them, a place to park, some food. People stood for days and days on line, sometimes hundreds of people. And as lines built, we adopted the idea of viewing the effort as a demonstration. You have five hundred people waiting, and they would take three applicants in a day. It's incredible the amount of effort that had to be expended to break through in Mississippi and to get black people registered to vote.

We all kept careful records—who applied to register, how many times a person applied—because each registrar would have rules about when you could come back if you were turned down, like in thirty days, or ninety days. In many cases, people simply didn't get registered. In other cases, what would start as a trickle would become a flood.

IN SPITE OF THE often brutal responses in Greenwood, sometimes things could be funny, and I often think of how laughter and humor, along with music, were part of our sustenance. Sometimes we turned redneck humor back on them. Hilarity is a potent weapon. On a sweltering day, a huge gathering of Greenwood black citizens waited in the sun for an opportunity to be turned down as potential voters. A speeding pickup truck drove up to the line, skidding to a stop inches from an elderly black woman. Two country-looking white men leaped out of the cab and reached into the truck bed for something. Many in the line thought the white men were reaching for weapons, but the black people moved only a short distance, determined to hold the form of the line. I was on observer duty that day. It was difficult to stand with a clipboard in my hand watching a potentially violent episode unfold. I had to admire the courage of the local folk and gave silent thanks for the hours spent in mass meetings and nonviolent workshops. I was watching true nonviolent direct action in practice—Greenwood's black citizens standing silently, in the direct presence of danger, demanding the most basic right enjoyed in all democracies. Voting, we knew was a right, not a privilege.

Suddenly the men jerked a dark object from the back of the truck and placed it on the ground next to the long line waiting to register. Gasps of surprise and relief rippled up and down the line, as the two slowly walked toward the courthouse leading a wrinkled up old monkey wearing a cotton smock and a sun bonnet. A rope was tied around the animal's neck and a hand-printed sign hung down the monkey's front and back reading, "I Want To Vote Too!"

Some in the line tried to stifle giggles and laughs. Others spoke angrily, "That is an insult."

"Hey, no breaking in line, we been here all morning," a young black man yelled.

Muttering swept the line of sweating people. How can anybody insult us by using that monkey. A large, vocal black woman, a leader in one of the strongest Greenwood neighborhoods, on first seeing the small ape, shouted, "Get that sorry monkey out of here!"

Then the dozens started.

"That's no monkey," someone called out, "that, folks, is an eighty-year-old white woman, and she has a right to vote, too!"

"That's right, you got that right, and if anybody thinks that old white lady there on that rope can't vote, then you got to deal with me. She's got as much right as we do."

Some men and a few of the women in the long line, known to participate in a game of chance every now and then, started slapping down dollar bills on the sidewalk leading to the courthouse steps. "Dollar get you ten, my man, if that thing ain't a full-grown wrinkled up old white lady!"

During all this, the white men slowed to a stop. The line had imperceptibly turned their backs to the two men, while the monkey was seemingly engrossed in the side-betting and the dozens and the remarks sweeping up and down the line. At one point a very large black man—I think he ran the pool hall downtown—looked over his shoulder at the two men and asked in a loud voice, "Say, brother, are you sure that's a white woman?"

The two men briefly and quietly consulted one another and then led the monkey back to the truck. As they were driving away the great citizens of Greenwood quietly picked up their money, gave a few restrained high fives and rubbed palms before resuming their place in line.

A LASTING GIFT FROM GREENWOOD was getting to know movement people like Sam Block and Wazir Peacock, whose early work in Mississippi was so vital to the success of that brutal summer of 1964. Lawrence Guyot was another who was quite a revelation. As a Southern white man I was quite taken with his manner. Guyot, which is the name used universally, let you know right away that he was not trying to be as good or as bright as a white man, he was already better and smarter. And it was true! Guyot was a large, light-skinned black man who did not take anything from anyone. Having him as a boss during the summer of '64 was great. He was a good movement leader, and what better way to forget the terror around us and the total frustration of trying to light a fire in the middle of an iceberg, than having a good poker game every time Guyot rode into town. He would get me and any other players to the table and my enthusiasm for the game and the relaxation it afforded me, blinded me for a time to how good Guyot really was.

18

SEEING STARS

During the early sixties, a lot of singers and actors began coming South to visit SNCC projects and perform at fund-raisers. Since some of these celebrities were white, it was safer for them to travel with me and Dottie. Many of the big stars had adopted movement people as their heroes. We were just as intrigued with them because we could not really imagine being idolized by people like Marlon Brando, Sidney Poitier, and Lena Horne. The extended "rat pack" of socially conscious show people also did events and performances for SNCC and SCLC in New York and on the West Coast.

Harry Belafonte's help to the movement was absolutely essential to our work. He and Sidney Poitier brought cash from New York to Greenwood in 1964 and were followed by the Klan after landing in a field in a little Piper Cub and being picked up by SNCC workers. In Greenwood, they stayed with Dottie and me and in later years Harry would reminisce about the time he slept in our bed in Greenwood, Mississippi.

The full extent of Harry's fight for freedom and justice world-wide may never be known. In March 2008 he spoke at length to a conference of Mississippi civil rights veterans and never missed a beat and had us all laughing and crying.

I remember helping to organize a fund-raiser at Miles College, a black school in Birmingham. At the concert, I met and hung around with Ray Charles and Johnny Mathis. The damnedest thing happened at the concert. Ray Charles raised so much hell on the homemade stage that all the supports fell off. It did not help that every Negro in Birmingham tried to make his or her way onto the tiny platform while Ray pounded the keys. In the next act Johnny Mathis strode to center stage, opened his mouth to sing "September Song"—"It's a long, long time . . ."—and the stage collapsed in a cloud of dust and bodies.

Every event SNCC organized was supervised by specially trained "observers" or "marshals." Jim Lawson of the Nashville movement had taught us to do this. Several SNCC marshals joked that they stopped a sprinting Johnny Mathis a half-mile from the college. Mathis was a track star in college, and they swore they would never have caught him if he had not gotten out of shape since his competitive days. They had a hell of a time convincing Mathis that it was rickety construction that made the stage collapse and not the KKK.

Another funny thing happened when I was driving Marlon Brando to an event in, I think, Gadsden, Alabama. Forman and I met Brando at a small airport and Forman said that since we had no FBI protection—even with such a distinguished visitor—that it would be safer if Mr. Brando and I drove in one car to the mass meeting. Forman put it this way, "Zellner, you drive Marlon, and the two of you try to act like ordinary white people."

"I can do that," I told Forman, "I don't know if Mr. Brando can."

Forman looked at me like I had taken leave of all my senses. "What are you talking about, man? Marlon is an actor."

Mr. Brando and I dashed to my old green Chevy and we took off. Brando had not said much in regard to the initial question of protection for us. "Bob," he mumbled to me, "where the Christ is the FBI?" although Forman had explained for the umpteenth time that we had no protection. Apparently, the big star had never believed that we were like wild rabbits loose in Alabama and Mississippi—"It's open season on civil rights workers at all times and Uncle Sam doesn't care and Mr. Charlie likes it like that."

Now Brando sat quietly in the front passenger seat while we drove through the Southern night. Suddenly he turned toward me and mumbled, "Man, I got to piss. Forman hustled us out of the airport so fast, I didn't have a chance to pee." "Okay," I said, and he kept on talking. "The little crop duster you guys had me on didn't even have a bed pan, and I have got to pee, Zellner." "Okay," I tried again, "We'll be there in a few minutes. "I can't wait a few minutes, Bob." I was surprised he knew my first name. "Is there a bathroom near here?"

"There's a truck stop up here a ways—we can make a speedy stop there, Mr. Brando."

"Don't Mr. Brando me, Zellner. Call me Marlon or hey you, but don't call me mister."

"Okay, Marlon," I agreed.

He was quiet for a minute, but then he got agitated again. "What kind of bathroom they got at the truck stop?"

I told him it was a normal bathroom for truck drivers and travelers. "Yes," he said, "but do they have stalls or just a line of urinals, and it's okay, too if they have dividers between the urinals."

He was quiet for a minute, and I had to pursue it, "Why dividers between the urinals?"

"It's just terrible," he replied, "you have no idea. If there's just a line of urinals along the wall, and I'm standing there taking a whiz, some guy next to me doing the same thing all of a sudden will say, while turning quickly towards me, pecker in hand, 'Ohmigod, you're Marlon Brando.' It's ruined many a good pair of shoes for me."

All this time, he was setting me up, baiting the hook and then reeling me in, so he could tell his urinal story.

WHILE I WAS ORGANIZING nonviolent workshops in Alabama at Talladega College and preparing students for lunch counter sit-ins and marches, Jim Forman persuaded Pete Seeger to make a series of appearances in the South to raise money and support our work.

In preparation, I talked by phone with Pete and his wife Toshi, who did all his scheduling. I told Pete that I couldn't wait to bring him to somnambulant little Talladega. I described the town square with its antebellum courthouse and the ubiquitous Confederate soldier standing atop his obelisk facing ever Northward.

Dottie and I traveled with Seeger to most of his Alabama appearances including Stillman College in Tuscaloosa, and Miles College in Birmingham, both private church-related black institutions. Before driving down to Talladega, Pete asked me to find him a large log and a sharp double-bladed ax and to place them center stage for the event in Talladega. The audience was humming with anticipation in the packed auditorium when I introduced the famous political figure, musician, and American icon.

"Pete Seeger has come to us tonight to demonstrate the love and support that the American people have for what you young people are doing here in the heart of Dixie. Pete has not been a stranger to sacrifice and controversy and I know that he has a lot of respect for our movement and the difficulties of sometimes going against the wishes of your parents and other elders. But we must be free! Here he is . . . Pete Seeger. Pete, say hello to a whole bunch of freedom fighters here tonight."

If we thought he was getting a little old, we were in for a shock. Seeger ran from the wings hollering, "Zellner, give me that axe!"

I was as amazed as the audience as he grabbed the huge axe and swung it fiercely at the log. WHACK!

"Bring me a little water Sylvie, huh!" He'd chop that log. " Bring me a little water, now" . . . Whack! Pete sang that whole work song whacking that log. Then he grabbed a banjo and picked while talking about slavery and working and protest songs and freedom songs. He would sing "Abiyoyo" or pick up the twelve-string and sing a protest song from the days of the Lincoln Brigade. When he got to present-day freedom songs he would talk about the SNCC Freedom Singers and motion for me to come sing with him. This was always the signal to call people from the audience to join us on stage and rattle the roof with our fight songs. Even after the last song, "We Shall Overcome," with everyone crossing arms right over left and swaying to the music, the crowd would linger while people lifted up song after song, adding new verses about the march that day. Pete would smile and tap his foot at the end of his long leg and pick until we were tired out or it was time to hit the road for the next gig.

That was the spring of 1962, more than forty-five years ago, and Pete and Toshi Seeger are still going today. I still get to sing with Pete on occasion. I believe he will last forever.

On one leg of the trip with Seeger we were deep in conversation about singers and performers. Pete thanked Dottie for setting up the concerts and me for singing with him. He said that the Southern black freedom struggle was like fresh water to all manner of artists. "That's why we, they, come down here to be with you. It is not just that they want to help. There is something here for them that they don't get in their work and in their careers."

By the way, Pete said, there's a guy down here now who is going to be a star. "He will take the country by storm," Pete declared.

We were excited and curious because we knew that Pete did not engage in puffery or hyperbole. Dottie guessed that it might be one of the Freedom Singers. They had already been a hit at the Newport Folk Festival. Our singing group consisted of seasoned organizers who shunned personal promotion, but we always thought the public might anoint one or more of them a star.

"Not many people have heard of this singer, but he is a great poet and artist from way up the Mississippi River in Minnesota." Some other SNCC folk were with Dottie and me and Pete in the car, and several of us asked in unison who it was. "Anybody we ever heard of?"

"I don't think so," Pete smiled, "Unless you have seen or heard of Bob Dylan."

"Bob Dylan," we hollered. We jokingly told Pete we all knew Dylan "and he will never amount to anything—you can't understand a word he sings!"

We told Pete that Dylan wanted to sing at all our events in Mississippi and the local people were always asking us what he's saying and we can't tell them because we can't understand him either.

Pete had been black-listed for years because of his progressive politics, but the man was right up to date. By early 1962, Dylan was beginning to make a name for himself in folk music clubs in New York and elsewhere. He had recently released his first album though few had heard it yet. But Pete knew Dylan would be massive, a true poet of the American and human condition. Soon we learned Seeger was right, and Bob Dylan joined our stable of stars.

Seeger, Belafonte, and others organized benefit concerts at Carnegie Hall, Town Hall, the Village Gate and other venues for SNCC, SCLC, and SCEF. Often we were called from "the field" to the city to speak or generally help out at these events. The stars, Forman explained, wanted to see and hang out with the movement "stars."

One time in New York, I was assigned to accompany Dylan backstage and make sure he got to the cocktail party following the concert on time. That was where the heavy hitters with the big bucks were and they naturally wanted to see the stars like Bob Dylan, Belafonte, Poitier, Joan Collins, Ray

Charles, Johnny Mathis, Tony Bennett, Marlon Brando, Lena Horne, Paul Newman, Nina Simone, and Joan Baez, to name a few who performed for us at various times. Donors also wanted to see the SNCC kids: Diane Nash, John Lewis, Chuck McDew, Ruby Doris Smith, and that white boy, what's his name?

We got through Dylan's set all right but the audience kept demanding more and Bobby kept pouring it on. I motioned to him several times from the wings, pointing to my watch and making a drinking motion with one hand. He'd shake his head "No" as if to say, "You fool, this is the really important thing tonight." Meanwhile, I felt terrible letting the organizers down.

Finally, with sweat pouring off him, Dylan came into the wings for the last time. I said we really had to get down there to the party. "Money is important, too."

"I know, Zellner; I got to see a couple people first. Won't be a minute." Dylan wiped his face with a dry towel and opened the door to reveal a long line of people peering expectantly at the new star. This was the height of Dylan's early white-hot fame; folks didn't want to let him go. Bob Dylan didn't want to let them go either. He spoke to each person until there were just two people left.

I tugged at his arm, "Man, we really got to go. There ain't going to be anybody left over there at the party."

Just another couple of minutes, I thought. Maybe we will be all right. Then it happened. The next to the last person in the line took out a ragged envelope and handed it to Dylan with a pencil, "Write me a song," he demanded.

Bob Dylan, the new big star on the American scene, stood without uttering a word for twenty minutes, writing on that sorry envelope. Needless to say we missed the entire cocktail party where he was to be the main attraction.

Bobby handed the paper wordlessly to the geek, shook the hand of the very last person, and turned to me ready to go. I must have looked sad because, in an unusual show of feeling, he grabbed my arm and said, "Don't worry, Z, I know where they're going to be."

On the way in the cab, I found myself wondering what he wrote on the envelope. "What'd you write on it?" I asked.

"Write on what?" he asked. He was sprawled out, his boots taking up half the back seat. It was like he had not the slightest idea what I was talking about.

"The envelope. What did you write on the envelope?"

"Oh, hey, I didn't write nothing for the geek. I'm playing around with something on the war. It's nothing."

"For a half an hour? Nothing?"

"Twenty minutes," he stated, as if it was the end of this particular conversation. Soon we were in the Village and sure enough, everybody, including the heavy hitters, was still there at a room off the Village Gate.

19

SEED POD EXPLOSION

I n the summer of 1964, the concentration on voter registration and the
Mississippi Freedom Democratic Party was part of a political strategy
aimed toward the Democratic National Convention in Atlantic City
in August. I didn't go to the Convention. I wanted to, but the decision had
been made not to flood the place with SNCC people, and I had been present at so many major events over a three-year period.

Black citizens were barred from the Mississippi regular Democratic
Party activities, and there was very little Republican structure in Mississippi. As we built parallel political procedures within MFDP, there were a
lot more candidates than had been in the mock election of 1963 and a lot
more interest in the black community. The idea was to duplicate as much
as possible the procedure of the established Democrats in Mississippi so
the MFDP could go to Atlantic City and challenge the credentials of the
"regulars." Our people would be true Democrats, in supporting both the
presidential candidate and the platform—not true of the segregated regular
Mississippi Democrats.

Lyndon Johnson was fighting for support of the regulars, but it didn't
make sense—most white Mississippians, regardless of party, were going for
Barry Goldwater. Johnson could have had an historic conversion, but he
was too much into the old politics to see what an opportunity was before
him. He didn't want to alienate the South, and he opposed our challenge
on narrow political grounds just to be reelected. He sold his soul for a mess
of pottage, as the Bible says, and it is one of the historic crimes of this past
century that as a supposed protégé of Franklin Delano Roosevelt, Johnson
was unable to support the MFDP challenge. He'd come out of the political

milieu in the South where other people had helped prepare the foundation for the civil rights movement. So here's this idiot who has a chance to be one of the great political figures of American history and says, "Oh, no, I need to be a politician rather than a statesman."

At the convention, we had congresswomen and men along with some senators supporting our challenge. The MFDP enjoyed tremendous grass-roots support in the Deep South demonstrating clearly that we could organize a new Democratic Party in the region. Lyndon Johnson put Hubert Humphrey in charge of destroying our MFDP challenge and in facilitating a compromise—that the DNC would seat two of our delegates, but they didn't even leave it up to the MFDP to choose which two. Great pressure was brought to bear on attorney Joe Rauh Jr., Representative Edith Green, and all the labor people who supported the challenge. The DNC just pulled out all the stops to intimidate our supporters. The SNCC and grassroots leaders said, "You have to make up your own mind." Fannie Lou Hamer and the local leaders said, "We didn't come here for no two seats."

The compromise offered little at the time, but the challenge insured that in the future Mississippi would no longer be able to send a segregated delegation. These stirrings finally broke the back of the Dixiecrats; after that there was a major political realignment, the South becoming a Republican voting bloc as white Southerners left the Democratic Party. In 1968, further efforts to challenge the Mississippi delegation ultimately led to rules changes. But the national Democrats were not adept at doing the grassroots organizing they could have done on the basis of those rules changes—they missed the implications possible in those changes. Rather than alienate Hard Hat Joe and returned Vietnam war veterans, they could have made common cause with them and tried to do what we did later on with the GROW Project. We said working people, black and white, need to get together now. The upper-class Democrats, the McGovernites, and others misinterpreted what working-class support for the civil rights movement could have meant for the party. National Democrats didn't have a united-front class strategy, which laid the groundwork for getting the hell beat out of them for years and years by the Reagan-Bush strategists. Republicans were able to convince working-class white people that they had their interests at heart and built a Republican structure on the basis of a backlash to the civil rights movement.

George Wallace was actually the architect of the present-day Republican Party. Also, by then, identity politics and black nationalism were entrenched, leaving little hope for a grassroots effort of black and whites uniting on a progressive strategy.

In some sense, our Atlantic City challenge had a negative impact. By 1964, people had already been on the front lines for two, three, or four years. They had been beaten and battered. There were a lot of deaths and much trauma. Also, we didn't understand battle fatigue at that time, so a great deal of cynicism began to set in after the summer of '64; we harbored anger because the nation's response to the murders of Chaney, Schwerner and Goodman was strong only because two of them were white Northerners. If it had been three black workers it would just have been adding three more to the list of martyrs that had gone before.

But in the great scheme of things, Atlantic City was a tremendous success. It broke the back of massive resistance in the South. Mississippi was still resisting school desegregation and black voter registration. Bringing hundreds of mostly white middle-class students from across the country, then challenging the seating of the regular Mississippi Democrats at the Convention, captured the imagination of progressives all over the world, similar to the results of the Freedom Rides in 1961, when young and old came from all over to be imprisoned in the notorious Parchman Penitentiary. Afterwards, they went home or joined the SNCC staff, arousing a lot of national attention. So after the summer of '64 there was a tremendous seed-pod explosion of people who had had searing experiences in Mississippi. Steeling them as organizers, it gave them a lifelong Holy Grail of social action and involvement. People like Mario Savio went back to Berkeley to start the Free Speech Movement because of his work with COFO in the summer of '64. SDS was of course much affected by SNCC all along, and the Southern Student Organizing Committee (SSOC), mobilizing white students, was given a tremendous boost by Freedom Summer. Some of the students went back to help Cesar Chavez organize farmworkers. Marshall Ganz dropped out of Harvard for the SNCC staff and went on to work with Chavez, later returning to Harvard a well-educated man.

SNCC pushed Martin King to take a strong stand on the war, while Julian Bond's Georgia Senate struggle helped launch the antiwar campaign.

The women's liberation movement was reinvigorated, to say the least, by the civil rights movement. It is unfortunate that some scholars have made careers on characterizing SNCC as a bastion of male chauvinism. Many early abolitionists made horribly racist statements, so much so that scholars today would read them out of the movement. Much of the sixties movement was progressive on "the woman question," especially SNCC. To apply today's consciousness to the words of progressive men and women who were organizing fifty years ago is not good scholarship. Stokely's rap about the position of women in the organization being prone has been knowingly misinterpreted, while Casey Hayden's answer is not nearly so famous. She responded to the widespread belief that SNCC women were expected to clean up the freedom house by saying, "Don't be ridiculous, *nobody* cleaned up the freedom house.

A strange and contradictory thing about the women's movement and SNCC was who did what and why and when. I did more cooking than most women did, and I don't remember women bringing me coffee or doing a lot of cleaning. Some complaints might be valid but some are based on the notion that, relatively speaking, SNCC men were supposed to be more conscious and aware than other men. They were and are often held to a different standard. But just look at some of the strong women—Fannie Lou Hamer, Modjeska Simpkins, Diane Nash, Anne Braden, Joanne Grant, Ruby Doris Smith Robinson—who were active in the movement and were unquestioned leaders in whatever organizations they affiliated with. Ruby Doris was our boss and ruled with an iron fist.

I was present at the Waveland staff meeting in the fall of 1964 when Stokely made his infamous statement. He was doing one of his traditional raps, one line after another, and the question came up about the women's memo on their role, and he said, "Well, everyone knows that the women's position in SNCC is prone." It was meant as a humorous statement, and we all laughed. Academicians now ask how we could joke about something like that. Well, we joked about death, we used the word "nigger," we joked about everything. Then you have wits like Chuck McDew, who says that Stokely's comment shows his basic conservatism, because there are many more positions than prone. We were having meetings for days and Stokely just said something that popped into his head, and then we went on to other issues. If you talk to someone with absolutely no sense of humor and no understanding of the situation, you can't explain it to them, because the more you try, the worse it gets.

Every male in 1964 and 1965 was a chauvinist and they may still be. I am a male chauvinist because I grew up in this paternalistic, male-chauvinist society. I've struggled with my male chauvinism for years, and as a feminist, I consider myself slightly more progressive than the average American male. Certainly, Stokely Carmichael in 1964 was a male chauvinist, as were all of the men in SNCC, but the women in SNCC were uncommonly free to exercise leadership and did. I found in SNCC, you didn't do leadership based on your official position—you were a leader on the basis of what you did. Women were often more powerful than the men, especially in local communities.

I sometimes have difficulty explaining to middle-class white people, especially women, that we had a lot of strong women leaders in the local grassroots movements who were constantly reaching back, bringing men forward saying, "You need some leadership." I try to explain the totally different situation in black male society back then. One must understand the historical emasculation of black males and the threat of lynching to grasp the widespread female black leadership, particularly in Southern rural areas. Another example is my theory about white men, racism, and sexism. A man in this society who is not a racist or sexist is rare indeed, being steeped as we are in paternalism and one of the most virulent forms of white supremacy in the history of man's inhumanity. When Imus protests that there is not a racist bone in his body it is a big mistake. It's much easier to say I am a racist and a sexist struggling to overcome my afflictions.

I am a racist, because I grew up in this racist society. I have struggled with my racism for more than fifty years, but I'm still a racist.

20

TRAIN WRECK

After Freedom Summer, Dottie and I went back to Boston and Brandeis in the fall of 1964. It was incredible, but we soon ran into none other than Willie B. Painter. We were walking home from a SNCC party and passed a dark doorway, and I saw Willie B. standing there. I said to Dottie, "Don't look now, but Willie B. Painter is standing in the door back there." She said, "Bob, you have lost your mind, this is Boston, he is in Alabama." Then we heard footsteps coming up from behind, and Willie B. caught up with us.

He said, "Bob, what are you doing in Boston?"

I said, "Willie B., I have a strange sense that you know what I am doing in Boston."

Unbeknownst to me, George Wallace was speaking at Harvard Law School the next night. He had campaigned in 1964 for the Democratic presidential nomination. He had already lost, but he loved the spotlight and was still traveling around speaking whenever he had the chance.

Willie B. said, "I guess I'll see you tomorrow night." I wasn't aware that Wallace was going to speak at Harvard, so I just said, "Well, you may see me, you may not." I wouldn't give him any information—period. Then when I found out about the speech and realized that Willie B. was concerned about me showing up at Harvard, I didn't want to disappoint him.

I decided to do a little organizing. Some SNCC-connected Harvard students told me that the law professor who was moderating Wallace's appearance would bend over sideways to protect a guest from hostile questions or verbal attacks. Demonstrations were outlawed. But the SNCC students arranged a place for me to sit near the area where the microphone would be set up to take questions from the floor. A large student would get to the mike first and I could hide behind him to avoid the possibility of Wallace recognizing me and refusing my question.

Wallace gave his usual spiel—pugnaciously "sending a message to the pin-head bureaucrats" in Washington. He said the American people were fed up with being bused and punished with affirmative action. He bellowed that if he were president, he would bring the nation back to a true respect for the God-given right of the various states to shake off the tyranny of the federal government. The governor claimed race relations were fine in Alabama because everybody liked it as it was—where everyone knows his place. As for all this talk about violence and voting—why everybody who wants to, in peace-loving Alabama, can vote.

At the end of his tirade the first student asked a softball question. Wallace answered and the boy stepped aside. I looked up and said, "Governor Wallace . . ."

Before I could continue, he spun around and sprinted toward the back of the stage. Moving slightly to my right, I looked past the lectern to see what George was doing back there. I saw him dart down some steps to huddle with a uniformed Alabama trooper on one arm and Special Investigator Willie B. Painter on the other. The instant Wallace bolted, the moderator began pounding the gavel, shouting, "I rule that question out of order."

I shouted back along with half the audience that no question had been asked. "I don't care," the professor screamed, looking for the disappearing governor, "I rule that question out of order, now sit down!" I stood my ground and the audience began chanting, "He didn't ask a question." Others shouted, "How you can rule a question out of order that was not asked?" After all, they were law students.

The professor finally allowed me to go ahead with my question. I said, "Where's Governor Wallace? I saw him disappear down the stairs. Maybe he doesn't want to be asked a question by me. I'm Bob Zellner with the Student Nonviolent Coordinating Committee. I'm from Alabama."

Then the students started chanting, "Make him answer. Make him answer."

As this was going on, Wallace was being led slowly back to the podium. It probably didn't look good for the Fightin' Judge to run from someone totally unknown to the audience. George peered at me over the lectern and the professor told me to go ahead. So I asked a rather convoluted question, but it made the point. I said, "Governor Wallace, in your talk, you said there's good race relations in Alabama and there's no persecution of black people and black people can register to vote in Alabama. In light of that, how can you explain . . ." and I mentioned a number of cases like the Birmingham church bombing for which he bore almost direct responsibility. I mentioned all the martyrs in Alabama, the times people were arrested around the rights of black people or attempts to register to vote. "How can you explain all that if there are good race relations in Alabama?"

He said, "Bob Zellner, I don't have to answer any of your questions." Then to the students he said, "This man has been in practically every jail in Alabama." Suddenly there was thunderous applause, not for Wallace, but for me. It wasn't so much for me, as it was against Wallace. Immediately, I thought, "Oh, Jesus God, now the papers are going to say that Wallace got a standing ovation from the students at Harvard." There were Alabama reporters and the state troopers traveling with him.

Afterward, I called Virginia Durr in Montgomery and told her to get the papers the next day because they were going to say that George Wallace got a standing ovation from the students. She said, "They're that crazy?"

I told her the story, and repeated, "I guarantee you the reporting will be a standing ovation for George Wallace at Harvard University."

To this day people ask me if in my confrontation with Wallace, the students gave Wallace a standing ovation. In fact, one of the headlines of the Montgomery paper was, "Zellner loses in bout with Wallace." That's how familiar they had gotten with the small rivalry between George Wallace and me.

Wallace had reason not to want me at his speeches. Every time he ran for president, I organized a truth squad, and wherever he went, we would go there. I had organized events at his rallies before, and I was always popping up at unexpected places right in his face.

While we were in Boston, the police sent regular reports on me and Dottie to police in Alabama. This is recorded in the files of the Alabama Sovereignty Commission. Willie B. Painter bragged that he knew everything there was to know about me. When he emerged out of the doorway that day on the Boston street, he introduced himself to Dottie and said he hadn't had the pleasure of meeting her before, but he did know where her parents lived in New York.

I STAYED IN BOSTON for the fall semester and the spring semester. I was arrested and beaten during the Selma March activities in 1965, but I was in Boston at the time. Although SNCC had been organizing for a few years in Selma, the big campaign came in 1965. The main organizing that spring was by SCLC, but John Lewis and others from SNCC were among those beaten so badly on Bloody Sunday on March 7, 1965. The violence was so stark that people mobilized around the country. We headed up the organizing in Boston for the response to Bloody Sunday. We had been sending truckloads of food, books, and clothes from Boston to Alabama and Mississippi, but after Selma, we began to organize politically by having demonstrations at the Federal Building. We were seeking federal intervention in Selma and the creation of a national climate for protection of the marchers and passage of a voting rights bill.

Boston was a good place to organize, because there was a tremendous infrastructure of supportive students and professors as well as long-time liberals and progressives. We had strong groups at Harvard, Radcliffe, Boston University—all the major colleges and universities. The outrage over Selma was palpable. We organized an informational picket and then upped the ante by springing civil disobedience on the Boston federal offices. We did workshops and training as if we were conducting sit-ins, including ACLU-trained observers and legal aid in reserve. We began by blocking the doors of the federal building. If they weren't going to allow black people to vote or protect marchers down South, we would shut the building down. Our group sat in the revolving doors and on the sidewalk in front of the doors. Of course, the police tried to clear us out, but at my door, we linked arms and legs. Our mass entanglement was tremendously strong, and the cops got frustrated. It took a lot of them to break it, and they picked me out as one of the instigators.

When the cops tried to break me loose, one did his best to break my finger and my wrist. We had a lot of observers, and so I said to one of them, "This policeman is breaking my finger and wrist." He immediately stopped, but when they were carrying us to the police vehicle, we all went limp. That really made them mad. Even though there were TV lights and cameras going and radio people everywhere, this cop raised his fist back and hit me in the face as hard as he could. Bam! I was so nonviolently mad, but all I did was keep him in focus so I could read his badge number when my eyes cleared up. I then called out to the observer, "1859 is the badge number of the person who just hit me." The cop then shoved me into the vehicle, and four or five more cops climbed in and started beating me like a punching bag. I was seeing stars and passing in and out of consciousness. Noel Day, one of our black civil rights workers who pastored a church in Roxbury, came piling in like a football player, knocking cops in all directions. He put his body over my body. Then they started beating him. When they got me to the jail, they did their best to clean me up a little. They called the jail doctor, and I was so beaten up, I couldn't speak and I couldn't see, but I could hear. The doctor said, "This man is seriously injured. You have to take him to the hospital. I will not have the responsibility."

"Well, we can't take him to the hospital like that. How are we going to explain it?"

I guess they didn't think I could hear, but I did and the doctor said, "I don't care how you explain it, but you have to take him to the hospital." They took me to the hospital and wheeled me in on a gurney, and I heard the people in the ER say, "My God, what happened to him?" and the police said, "We don't know, put it down as a routine automobile accident."

This was Boston, Massachusetts, in 1965. This was another case where we sued. We had all the witnesses, and the badge number and the names of the cops. It never went anywhere. I don't even know whether complaints were filed against the cops. We were so concerned about keeping the movement going that I don't even think we pursued it, and our lawyers didn't go forward with it.

After Danville and Boston, I believe I began to question nonviolence. By the summer of 1964, a degree of disillusionment was setting in among some long-time workers. The murders of Schwerner, Chaney, and Goodman in Neshoba County fanned the flames. We had faced such unrelenting brutality for a number of years, as well as the basic indifference of the federal government. The Feds would do something only when absolutely forced to do so. It was hard to take the hypocrisy of the government, still putting themselves up as the leader of the free world, the bastion of democracy. We got along better with the Klan and the killers and the terrorists, because they made no bones about what they were doing.

Very few politicians, Southern or national, had the courage and willingness to stand up and take the cost. They apparently didn't believe or see that they could have gotten a tremendous boost from such activities. Even the little tiny bit that they did has already put JFK and RFK into the pantheon of greats, but what could they have done if early on they had said, "Look, there's laws against killing people for wanting to register to vote. I'm gonna put you in jail, George Wallace, we're not gonna pussyfoot around with you, we're gonna put you in jail if you stand in the school house door against a court order, and then we'll have court, we'll let a judge decide whether or not you're to be punished."

But instead the killers and the bad guys got off more or less. Can you name a single Southern official, except the small fry, who was ever charged with a civil rights-related crime, much less tried and convicted?

In '64, I remember that there were debates in the Freedom Schools about violence versus nonviolence. I was one of the few people in SNCC that continued to defend the nonviolent position, but mostly as a tactic or strategy. I wasn't so sure of it as a philosophy of living, any longer. I still believed in dedication and selflessness and giving your life up for the cause, but I was becoming in a sense a little more revolutionary, because almost every nonviolent guru or philosopher has said that the only thing worse than not being nonviolent in the struggle is not struggling.

I remember specifically testing the waters on nonviolent strategy in '64. Because I had been so closely involved investigating the murders of the civil rights workers, at the funeral for Chaney and in the days following, I went around and polled people—if you want to consider going to kill Rainey and Price, talk to me. Nobody seriously considered it. I probably was motivated by grief and anger and a certain degree of cynicism, and it probably wouldn't have been a good thing, although I often wonder what those murderers and killers and terrorists would have done if some of them had suddenly started showing up dead.

IN THE SUMMER OF 1965, after the birth of our daughter Margaret Rachel
on July 20, Dottie and I came back to Atlanta to full-time SNCC duty.
Dottie worked in the communications department with Julian Bond while
I joined Jack Minnis in the research department. Jack was a brilliant and
creative strategist. We were researching voter registration laws and the laws
on independent political parties growing out of the problems we were having
in Mississippi, and attempts to form a political party in Lowndes County,
Alabama, where Stokely and others were working. The Alabama Democratic
Party was symbolized by a white rooster and the slogan, "White Supremacy,
For the Right." A black panther was chosen as the symbol for our Lowndes
County Freedom Organization (because it can eat a white chicken). It later
became the symbol for the more militant national Black Panther Party. At
some point, Stokely brought a drawing of a black panther to Dottie. He
asked her to "fix it up" a little because it was a big scraggly line drawing. So
Dottie evened out the lines, made the whiskers a bit more upstanding and
inked in the body, so that it was entirely black. We were quite surprised
to see that panther drawing appear on television some weeks later, and of
course, one still sees it in many contexts.

The summer and fall of '65 were some of the toughest times to be in
Atlanta, because we were old hands and the tension between whites and
blacks was getting worse. There was a big influx of former volunteers coming on staff and working on projects. I felt bad about it because everybody
would go out of their way to say to Dottie and me, "You know, when we're
talking about white people, we're not talking about you." I would have to
say, "Well, I'm white people, so you are talking about me."

It was confusing. I thought back to when I first joined the staff in 1961,
and Forman and some others found my race useful because many of the young
people working with them in the rural areas had never met a sympathetic
white person. Most of the SNCC staff had been in colleges and universities,
so they had met a few whites and saw we weren't all peckerwoods, a term
sometimes used by blacks to describe whites. A peckerwood in the pantheon
of shibboleths or epithets in black terminology is about the lowest form of
white humanity. It beats white trash and cracker. All those folktales and the
great superstructure of the racist ideas were peeling away during the movement
until you finally came to say, "We're people." A truly great feeling is a flash

of genuine color-blindness. I don't know if you forget or if color becomes so totally irrelevant because you're simply relating to each other as human beings. When I talked about SNCC brothers and sisters, people would sometimes ask what color a particular person was. I found myself sometimes pausing to remember, color not being uppermost in my mind. Maybe my presence was useful. In addition to working to recruit white Southerners, it might be useful for SNCC to point out in the black community that Zellner was on the staff. "He's white and Southern, too."

The rising anti-white sentiments in 1965 didn't anger me so much as challenge me. I had never had the relationship with black staff that some of the northern volunteers had. I carried very little guilt on my sleeve; sometimes a guilty conscience could be a troublesome by-product of liberalism, a crude description of which might be, "beat me for I have sinned." I had long since done away with my "liberalism," and I didn't recognize any particular feelings of guilt. I was doing everything I could do. My closeness to black friends was person-to-person. Black people easily spotted white guilt. Some would take a whack at it. In Danville in '63, Ivanhoe Donaldson slugged my friend Daniel Foss. Danny was a bumbling Brandeis intellectual, but he had detached retinas. He had already been beaten by the cops and for Ivanhoe to lose control enough to slug this guy was like slapping a baby or something. I told Ivanhoe if he ever laid another hand on Daniel Foss I would put down my nonviolence long enough to break his neck. Ivanhoe was okay about it—that is how we were. If somebody said something insulting to me personally, I would just say, "You don't treat me like that. Don't treat me as a category. I am not a category. I am a person."

But by 1965, there was a kind of exceptionalism growing, the nationalism was growing, the anti-white feeling was growing, but they kept saying it applied to white people, but not to Dottie and me. Also, the struggle was on between people wanting more structure in the organization and the so-called "freedom high" group. There were gender divisions, class divisions, and philosophical divisions—how free to be and how organized to be. Then, of course, there was Vietnam, and SNCC took an early position against the war. When Julian Bond was elected in 1965 to the Georgia House, the other representatives refused to seat him on the basis of his SNCC activities and opposition to the war. Jim Forman and I accompanied Julian to the well of the Georgia House of Representatives when he was denied his seat. Of course, he was ordered seated by the U.S. Supreme Court the following year.

I BELIEVE THAT INFORMERS or government agents, black and white, had been in our SNCC meetings and activities since the beginning. Sometimes the white informers would be the more radical voices. Jim Forman had trained us so well at the start that we almost always could tell who the informers were. In 1964, we did a lot of screening for summer project recruits. Dottie did a careful job in vetting people who might be informers in New England. We would discreetly tell each other that we suspected certain people. I remember Jack and Jill Schaefer in New Orleans who were part of a group, the Red Collective, and they turned out to be agents. They had an airplane and a newspaper, and all kinds of funding with no visible means of support. When Wounded Knee happened in 1973, they went up to join the most militant group of American Indian Movement folk. They were police agents.

The Mississippi Sovereignty Commission formed in 1956 to spy on integrationists and civil rights activists. When its files were finally opened to the public in 1998 they revealed that some of the informers among us were employed by the Commission itself. One of my really good friends was identified as a police agent by a fairly reliable person, and I don't really know whether I'll ever know the truth and how to treat it.

We became increasingly aware of agent infiltration as our problems and issues increased after the summer of 1964. COINTELPRO certainly coordinated their agent provocateurs in SNCC. COINTELPRO is an acronym for "Counter Intelligence Program," an illegal FBI operation to investigate and disrupt "dissident political organizations" in the U.S. Covert operation have been used throughout FBI history, but formal COINTELPRO operations of 1956–71 were broadly targeted against organizations that were considered to have politically radical elements. In the FBI's view, this included Dr. King's SCLC, certainly SNCC, and supposedly white supremacist groups like the Klan. The founding document of COINTELPRO directed FBI agents to "expose, disrupt, misdirect, discredit, or otherwise neutralize" the activities of these dissident movements and their leaders. Never mind that this was unconstitutional.

When Dottie and I returned South in 1965, the agents in and around the Atlanta SNCC office seemed to encourage divisiveness and confrontation on the black/white and other issues. Sometimes you would know who the agents were, but it could also tear the organizations apart trying to guess about people. Another COINTELPRO tool was misinformation. They would use informers or anonymous calls or send anonymous letters to make accusations against certain leaders and those accusations would appear to be coming from another leader. They would also interfere with the marriages and domestic situations of individuals. One example was during Stokely's marriage to Miriam Makeba, the famous singer from South Africa; they would send letters to Stokely saying that Miriam was having an affair with one or another African leader. The letters suggested that he commit suicide. Time and time again they would either expose an affair that someone was having or they would make it up whole cloth. In one situation, a national Black Panther Party member supposedly put a gun in Forman's mouth—probably instigated by government agents. In some cases, the government agents would go into a volatile situation and urge people to go further in their actions so they would cross the line into illegality. We assumed our office phones were tapped and we know for sure our home phone was tapped after we moved to New Orleans. The telephone person actually came to the house and told us the phone was being tapped from downtown and had requested that it be monitored. We found tacks in the driveway or there could be snakes in your mailbox or car, or sugar in your gas tank. A lot of COINTELPRO moves were so skillful that I'm sure they have never seen the light of day.

Part of the tactics included the use of drugs where they would induce a temporary psychotic state in people. Forman once was stuck in a psychotic state for a long time. I didn't use any drugs because I was convinced that with so many arrests, if they ever arrested me for use or possession of drugs, I would never see the light of day. But I did drink. I once attended a conference in Connecticut and had some kind of episode that lasted two or three days. I don't remember drinking anything more powerful than beer, but I was so out of it that I sensed somebody had given me some LSD or something.

IN FEBRUARY OF 1966 Dottie, Margaret, and I moved to New Haven where I worked as the campaign manager for congressional candidate Robert Cook, a Yale sociology professor. The offer came as a blessed relief. We could remain on the SNCC staff and manage the campaign for Cook. He was an early peace candidate, and we had support from Harry Belafonte, Dr. Benjamin Spock, William Sloane Coffin, and Senator Wayne Morse.

Forman thought the move was a good idea, as a way of keeping the Northern communications going and continuing my work with students. I wound up organizing a good number of students to go South on various projects. Robert Cook didn't win. His emphasis on peace was too early to get traction, and he was challenging an entrenched incumbent, Robert Gaiamo; we only got about six percent of the vote. But we did form AIM, the American Independent Movement, to run Cook's campaign and did a lot of good organizing. AIM remained as a force for a long time around New Haven.

While directing Cook's campaign, Dottie and I began developing a plan for organizing poor and working-class black and white people in the Deep South. The project eventually became GROW, or Grass Roots Organizing Work, and it lasted for a dozen years organizing black and white woodcutters (Gulfcoast Pulpwood Association), factory workers (Masonite in Laurel, Mississippi), and poultry workers. Informally, we also called it Get Rid of Wallace. Originally we wanted GROW to be a SNCC project, feeling that it was time to move into the white community of the Deep South. Great power, expertise, and experience had been generated by the civil rights movement, spearheaded by SNCC, but by the end of 1967 the organization was in the process of pulling out of Mississippi and voting to become an all-black group. As the first white Southern field secretary for SNCC, I was to become the last to leave.

I never felt any personal animosity from Stokely or any of the old hands. I did feel it from some of the newer people that I didn't know very well, especially the people concentrated in the Atlanta office. In fact, Forman told me later that if we had hung on just a bit longer, things might have been different. It was ironic, because the Atlanta project reflected some of the most virulent anti-white feelings and many of the staff there were fired shortly after I left. Forman felt that if we had stuck it out, we would have been able to weather the storm altogether. I don't think so. I think it was a historical shift.

The general staff meeting at Kingston Springs, near Nashville, in May 1966 was the first since our meeting at Waveland in November 1964. I believe it was the first time that the subject of the position of whites in SNCC came up as a specific agenda item. I was not at that meeting. Stokely replaced John Lewis as chair, and it marked a huge shift in the organization. It was a strange story. At first, John was reelected unopposed. Then, later on when there was a much smaller group present, Worth Long proposed that they reopen the question of SNCC chairperson. Worth was not on the staff at that time, but he was a close friend of SNCC.

It is a comment on the informal nature of SNCC that some non-staff person could ask for the reconsideration of something as important as who would be chairperson. In any case, it was reconsidered and Stokely was elected. The changeover was quite dramatic, because it meant different philosophies and methodologies for the organization. John Lewis had played a key role in so many battles for so long, had good relations with Dr. King and SCLC, and had many white friends. John Lewis lived by the SNCC dictum that the individual was not to be the leader, the individual was not to be the star, but you represented the group, and you were the spokesperson for the group. Any searching for personal charisma, personal stardom was anathema to the old-line SNCC folk.

Some jokingly called Stokely "Starmichael" during Freedom Summer and again after he became chair. He had a different way of doing things. It may have been what was called for, because at that point there were a lot of changes going on. We had a huge Atlanta office and infrastructure and printing presses and a fair amount of income. It was the changing of the guard from the old religious orientation to the new political. Nobody at that point could envision what the new political direction was going to be, except that we could feel the undercurrents of white-black tension. History, in my opinion, has not dealt adequately with this schism in SNCC, because a lot of people who argued that it was a good thing for SNCC to be all-black based their stand on the possible takeover of SNCC by white people. That is an argument on which someone would have to try hard to convince me. Maybe the new breed of white people in SNCC, who were mainly SNCC volunteers from '63 and the summer of '64 coming in and showing a fair amount of arrogance and lack of deference, could have planted the seeds of that fear of takeover. But my view was that even up to 1965 and 1966, SNCC leadership was firmly in black hands and properly so. Any white person in the organization who ever had any influence at all, knew who led SNCC. A few whites had been in positions of leadership in some of the field offices, but very few.

I think John Lewis's ouster was another evidence of the organization becoming more political and more Northern. Stokely was a respected organizer. He had a lot of the SNCC attributes—impeccable physical courage, great showmanship, great creativity in terms of organizing and tenacity to go in and get the job done. He also was articulate and sometimes glib in a way that John Lewis never was.

Kerhonkson, New York, in December 1966 was the last full staff meeting that any white staff persons attended. The Kerhonkson meeting was held at the Peg Leg Bates Hotel. Forman had arranged with Peg, as his friends called him, for us to meet there cheaply in the off-season. Peg's country club, which he started in 1951, was the first black-owned resort in that area—at an old turkey farm in the Catskills near New Paltz. I was there. It was the dead of winter. The meeting unfolded like Greek tragedy. Everyone played their parts and the outcome seemed inevitable, which is one reason, maybe, that it turned out the way it did. Dottie did not go to the meeting. I drove up with Ella Baker and Joanne Grant. I must have felt pretty numb on the drive up, because I kept thinking that Joanne and Ella were treating me almost like I was sick and only they could bring me comfort. Probably I didn't fully understand that the die had already been cast and SNCC would become all-black. This is somewhat understandable because many in the movement had shielded Dottie and me from the harshest of the anti-white attitudes which had been growing in our organization. Perhaps they wanted to make an exception in our cases because we had been with the movement so long.

Driving north to Kerhonkson, I felt the oppressiveness of the cold dreary day. Old snow lay on the ground and along the roadways it had picked up the black tinge of car exhaust and burnt tire rubber. Conversation inevitably turned to what we could expect to happen at the staff meeting. Ella asked, in a roundabout way, if Dottie and I had been treated all right. I told her everything was okay with us but I had heard other stories of poor treatment of whites.

I told them, "I'm probably not going to hear a lot personally, not only because everybody wants to spare us, but I let it be known a long time ago that I don't play liberal. I didn't come South to help black people, I was already here, and I got involved to free myself. Old SNCC buddies know I don't take shit, I can get that from white folks I grew up with; I don't have to take crap from black folks, too."

Joanne was slightly exasperated, "We know that Bob, but what have you heard about others?"

"It's only hearsay," I said, "But after the experience we had in Mississippi in '64 and this recent stuff, some of the staff vowed never to speak to a white person again. That is understandable in a way. I never did figure out how black people found the grace to put up with the treatment this country has dealt out without going crazy or killing somebody."

Just before the vote was taken to end white involvement in the SNCC staff, some veterans expressed sadness over our departure. One leader was heard to say that he felt bad because Bob and Dottie had been in the thick of the fight long before many of the people voting to dismiss them had been in the organization. I thought that was a shuck and jive and tried to keep the focus off us personally and concentrate on the principles involved. It was clear to most that I understood concerns that SNCC was becoming too white following the summer of 1964 when many white Mississippi Freedom Summer Volunteers came on staff. What I did not agree with was the fear that our organization might be "taken over by white people."

My experience was that white staff exercised influence in the organization only to the extent that they appreciated and abided by the principle of black leadership. Old hands were clear that this was proper leadership for a primarily black organization working on mainly a black agenda. When white volunteers displayed arrogance and a take-over attitude, they didn't last long in SNCC. What, then, was the driving fear? How, exactly, could white people "take over" a black-led organization?

To me, the fear (felt primarily by newer staff but also by some old hands) had to do with SNCC's image in the national black political, activist community. The fear was that nationalists would see SNCC as a white-dominated organization. It is ironic, however, that at the same time our group was moving toward a more exclusivist position, Malcolm X, after a trip to Mecca where he saw blue-eyed Muslims, was moving away from a simplistic black-white dichotomy to a more revolutionary and inclusive stance. That meant that Malcolm, having split from Elijah Muhammad, was willing to work with all who were going his way regardless of color. It is instructive also that the Black Panthers, the " baddest dudes" on the block, made it clear that they intended to work with all revolutionaries, regardless of color.

With the clarity of hindsight, it seems now that we made a mistake. By 1966 and 1967 SNCC was being battered from all directions. The federal government, through COINTELPRO, played a role, but the fears and distrust it created may have been little more than nudging SNCC to go ahead and do what it was already inclined to do.

In the introduction to one edition of his book, *SNCC: In Struggle*, Clayborne Carson asks a probing question which I think has never been adequately addressed by movement folk. He posits that the civil rights movement, and SNCC in particular, had made brilliant use of three tools that helped to bring about revolutionary change in the Deep South: 1. nonviolent direct action; 2. long term grassroots work in local communities; and 3. an interracial staff. Carson's question to the movement was, when these potent weapons were largely discarded in the late sixties, by SNCC and other nationalists, what did they offer in terms of strategy and tactics to take their place?

Another part of the puzzle that led up to the decision at Kerhonkson is the background on two key organizational decisions made before the one on white exclusion. I should make it clear that I agreed and still agree with both prior decisions—even as I disagreed with the final one at Kerhonkson.

First, SNCC was the first major national civil rights group to formally oppose the war in Vietnam. Many people, even some who personally opposed the war, thought it was a mistake for SNCC to take on the war issue because it might distract from our concentration on ending segregation. The second wound SNCC inflicted on itself, in the opinion of some, was its policy position affirming the right of Palestinian self-determination. There had always been a strong alliance between Jews and African Americans because of the Jewish tradition of upholding justice and the practical view that if black people are not safe in the country, then Jews can't be far behind in the persecution sweepstakes. The Palestinian decision may have been a turning point affecting that long alliance.

Some see the series of three ground-breaking decisions as nails in the SNCC coffin. Others think that the first two could have been survived, had not the agreement to become an all-black staff given SNCC's disaffected supporters an easy way out. Most observers and participants do agree that the three steps taken together spelled the eventual doom of the organization. Maybe many of our supporters were already looking for the exit and the nationalist turn simply greased the skids.

SOME PEOPLE FROM THE Weather Underground were in the general area of the Kerhonkson meeting. There was a lot of drinking going on—for some of us probably to numb our hurt. The main issue was the black-white question, and almost all of the white people who were there felt handcuffed in a way. We wanted to make our position clear, but we didn't want to "fight" for it. We felt if we lobbied and organized and cajoled and maneuvered against the vote to become all-black, our work in the movement would be rather meaningless. So we said that we would participate in the debate very carefully and mildly. It was still painful. My basic position was that SNCC shouldn't be an all-black organization—that we should continue to struggle with the issue inside the organization. For me, the work was always against black and white separation. Also, on the argument of fear of white people taking over the organization, my question was, what white people? I was one of the most influential whites within the organization, but I wasn't going to take over anything, wasn't interested in taking over anything. Dottie wasn't either. We were always clear about where the leadership in the organization rightfully belonged.

Some bizarre stories followed the Kerhonkson meeting—that there were certain restrictions on staff relating to white people and that some black staffers vowed to no longer speak to white people. A white woman friend told me that while she was traveling home from the meeting in a car with some old and close SNCC friends, a black woman in the car passed her a written message rather than speak to her.

Some accounts say the white people left SNCC soon after that meeting, but Dottie and I remained on staff for a while. We were still living in New Haven and had already developed the GROW proposal. We proposed to do the project as a SNCC project, and I attended my last SNCC meeting in

Atlanta in May 1967 to discuss this. Rap Brown had been elected chair to succeed Stokely, but I never felt any personal animosity from him. I always considered him, like his brother Ed, a wonderful, beautiful, gentle person. I also knew Willie Ricks, one of the most vocal of the black power advocates, who changed his name to Mukasa and also refused to speak to white people. Here again, it was strange, because I had a good personal relationship with Willie, Rap, and Stokely. Later on when we had the GROW project going, Rap was in jail in New Orleans, because they said he had carried a rifle on an airplane. I was based there, so I would go visit him at Parish Prison. At one time, he chuckled and said, "Zellner, it's kind of ironic that we kicked your ass out of SNCC and now you're the only one who will come and see me." Some of those who adapted the strong nationalist position also said that it was not personal and that it didn't mean that they couldn't be friends with white people. In fact, the Panthers had a pretty good attitude. White people couldn't be Panthers, but the Panthers would work with white revolutionaries.

I PRESENTED OUR PROPOSAL for the GROW project in Atlanta in May, 1967, saying we would like to do it under SNCC. The negotiating went on with me in one room and the SNCC Central Committee in another room. Some people complained that I had made it into an emotional issue. Both the Kingston Springs and the Kerhonkson meetings suggested that white people in SNCC should organize in the white community. We agreed with that, and I wondered why I and others hadn't moved to that position earlier, but it was more complicated than it sounds. I had been reluctant in 1964 and 1965 to develop a white organizing project because first of all the thought was terrifying on the face of it. For those of us who had been in SNCC organizing in the black community for so long, were we now to go to the very people we had been ducking and dodging and who had been shooting at us and beating us all the years and say, "We're gonna organize white folks now"? How could you work with white people without them stringing you up?

SNCC, however, by 1967 was mesmerized by the image of being all-black, and lots of influence came from relative newcomers who didn't know us very well. Admittedly, I came rather belatedly to SNCC with this plan for the GROW project which we had been working on for quite some time. We had been developing it with people in SCEF and the people we were working with in New Haven and other advisors and people around the country. It was a well thought-out project to target poor and working-class white Southerners and help them think about changes to improve their lives, and the need to link up with the expertise and the experience and drive that existed in the black community; perhaps they might even try to reach their goals together.

I presented these ideas to SNCC. I said it was arguable that black people can be organized as black people without it being a negative formation, but anybody would agree you can't organize most Southern white people as white people and have anything but a racist group. So white people had to be organized in conjunction with blacks in order to combat their racism and so they could see what they had to do to destroy the superstructure of oppression and privilege and segregation. We told them it needed to be done by SNCC because we now had the expertise and the contacts in communities to demonstrate the power developed in the black community—the same power to offer to poor working class white people, so that both groups could go forward together.

Our proposal was in the face of the pell-mell rush toward black nationalism. Even though we had the example of Malcolm X, the great prince of black separatism and black nationalism, moving toward a more inclusive position, SNCC, having started as integrated, was moving in the opposite direction. That was the train wreck that we had.

Dottie's and my long history with the group gave us the temerity to make our proposal. The debate then came down to whether we could do the project in some special staff status where they could still say that SNCC was all-black. It was not a very open debate and some people opposed to being all-black were fairly quiet. It boiled down to wanting to make an exception for "Bob and Dottie," and the GROW project. I wasn't willing to do it. Dottie wasn't willing to do it on the basis of principle. What they proposed was that we remain on staff but not come to meetings. We found this unacceptable. First, SNCC had never demanded that anyone accept second-class status. Why should we? The next proposal was to come to the meetings but not vote. Our answer was the same. They were trying to avoid telling us that we were off the staff. I said to Forman, "You're my leader, what do you think we should do," and he said he couldn't recommend anything. I later told him that if he had laid out any strategy or tactics that had an end game we both agreed on, I could have absolutely gone along with him. If he had said, "Let's just temporize on this for a certain time. There are forces that we are dealing with, and afterwards we can go on," I would have been willing to wait, but he always said that I forced the issue and lost. Bill Ware was one of the main people who was agitating for programs and staff to be all-black. He is one of the people who has been identified in various ways as an agent provocateur.

From the beginning of the discussion Dottie and I had made it clear that we were going ahead with the project. The only question SNCC had to answer was whether we would do it with or without them. When my comrades said no, I realized it was my last day in SNCC. It was huge for me, because I had been on the staff since 1961. SNCC was our life. It was our existence. It was our total identity. We didn't realize the extent that our souls had belonged to SNCC—that we were road warriors. I was only twenty-seven, but with a tremendous amount of experience crammed into five or six years. With the GROW project, we were looking at more years of intense organizing and at the end of that . . . who knew; we had no sense of what it would be like to live in a normal workaday world, no concept of working at something that didn't require total dedication. It was like being cast into outer darkness, because SNCC was our family in a very strong sense.

We were lucky in moving from the SNCC staff to a welcoming SCEF staff, where we had an autonomous project and could raise our own money and establish our own policies. But it was never the same again. It was like the end of the most important years of our lives, but we realized that there's no way to be twenty-seven and have the best years of our lives behind us.

Forman and some others kept in close contact with us after we left and did some work with our project. We always had an integrated staff at GROW, and all of our community projects were integrated. As time passed, I grew more supportive and had a greater understanding of Black Power. Even as the black nationalism tide rose, I realized that it was a political position. There were positive and negative things about it, but I probably accentuated the positives. For one thing, I wasn't going to second-guess any of the black people in SNCC. They were intelligent, autonomous people. It was hard to realize that the whole thing was in the process of falling apart not only over nationalism, but on a lot of other fronts. One of the things that is unique about my story is my longevity on the SNCC staff. From early fall 1961 until I left in 1967, the last white staffer to go, there had been only the four semesters of respite at Brandeis, and even then I was speaking on SNCC's behalf at least three times a week. Because of this variation of places and assignments, I participated in possibly more and more varied campaigns than anybody else except Forman, who was involved in almost everything. Six years is a long time to be so consumed with such a variety of campaigns in such a variety of locations, while always focused on survival, especially after I was told that specific people were supposed to kill me. Richmond Flowers, a relatively decent attorney general of Alabama, told me once that he didn't know how I survived so long.

Over the years, I have felt some estrangement from a few individuals from early SNCC days. But now, when we all get together, no matter what the feeling was back then or during the changes, we are still intensely together. The years and months fall aside, and we are SNCC again, and some people kind of stand back and marvel at the phenomenon of our still being so close. Some now are very outspoken that it was wrong of SNCC to eject us, but generally it's the people who felt it was wrong even at the time. Nobody who felt it was right at the time has now come and said, "I was wrong about that." I still have to intellectualize it at times, because it was so personal and so painful.

I also mulled over, when I had some distance, the arguments over whether SNCC should be more structured or less structured. In the early days of SNCC, I would think back to Myles Horton's admonition that no organization should last longer than twenty-five years; SNCC lasted about ten (ironically, Highlander recently observed its seventy-fifth anniversary). Those last years were painful times for many of us, and people dealt with it in different ways. Some people went to Vermont and got naked, others drank a lot—some did both. We went South and organized.

21

GOODBYE AND GROW

T he end of SNCC could have been devastating for us, as it was for some, but we had work to do. So we took the advice of Joe Hill, who said, just before the State of Utah murdered him by firing squad in 1915, "Don't mourn, organize!" Dottie, Margaret, and I moved to New Orleans in 1967 to get the GROW Project underway. James Dombrowski, Ben Smith, Virginia and Walter Collins who also lived there, and the vast SCEF/SNCC network helped purchase and build a residential workshop center to support our field organizing. We had seed money from SCEF and raised other monies mainly from foundations, because we founded a group called Deep South Education and Research Associates. We bought a beautiful three-story house on Napoleon Avenue with banana trees in the yard and a cabana in the back. It was about four blocks from the Mississippi River, in the heart of the Crescent City. It cost $28,500. Prices were depressed because everybody thought a bridge was to be built across the river and would blight the beautiful neighborhood. We outfitted it with thirty-eight bunk beds, a large library meeting room, and a restaurant-sized kitchen.

We picked New Orleans because it was close to Mississippi and Alabama and was a relatively safe area. We didn't want to spend time and energy on security that might be necessary in a rural area.

Our daughter Cathrin Ruby (Katie) was born in New Orleans on November 18, 1968, making us an organizing family of four. We lived on $600 a month which was more than our SNCC salaries had been.

The staff grew as the work grew, bit by bit. In the early days we were five. We had begun the project with the idea that SNCC- and SCEF-related folks in the New Orleans area would work with us and come on staff as funds permitted. Jack Minnis lived in New Orleans with his wife, Earlene Gidrey, a school teacher from Cajun Louisiana, and their two young sons, Jacque and Pierre. Like many movement spouses, Earlene brought home the bacon while her mate saved the world. Minnis had served as the highly respected SNCC research director. Jack had, like Dottie and me, stuck with SNCC until the end. When GROW began getting off the ground, he was delighted and threw himself into the work with his usual brio and creativity.

The general idea for GROW was to use the Highlander model for our center and to begin organizing work, starting with any contacts that we had, which would be basically in the black community. We would then branch out and try to find receptive and sympathetic white people. Then we would network from that. New recruits would win others to the cause and the freedom fire would spread. Our very first effort failed to catch fire. Starting with Fannie Lou Hamer in Ruleville, Mississippi, who was familiar with some poor white people from the Delta who either worked in Head Start centers or had their kids in them, we found people who had crossed the racial barrier and thrown their lot in with the black community. It turned out they were so poor and so desperate their involvement was mostly a dead end, but we did meet some interesting people.

Ike Traxler, for example, lived on a bayou between Ruleville and Rosedale. He said he paid "a lot" of rent for his house, $5 a year, but it was worth it, because the water was full of gar which he could catch and eat so even when he didn't have a penny, his family could survive. Ike eventually was stabbed to death in a barroom fight, but we met a lot of his relatives, who worked raising chickens. They were receptive, and we learned that poor white people often accepted help or friendship from wherever it came. They were all so poor. We stayed with them during the winter in houses so ramshackle the wind blew straight through. Some of our staff were Northerners, so that was a tremendous education for them. One of Traxler's nephews went barefoot even when the ground was frozen, and he had no toes on either foot. Our photographer took this guy's picture and asked him, "Ralph, what happened to your toes?"

Ralph said, "I chopped them off cutting kindling."

"You mean all at the same time?"

"No, at different times."

Their stoves were usually a thirty-gallon oil drum and the fuel used was motor oil. This was why so many of those houses burned up. The can was in the corner of the room. They would start a little wood fire in the bottom of the drum, and then they'd drip the oil on the fire. Soon there was no wood left—just the oil dripping in.

But we didn't have much success organizing these poorest of the poor, and we came to the conclusion that as receptive as they might be, especially in the Mississippi Delta, their greatest need was for a good social work system. GROW couldn't provide that. Instead, we were already looking for factory situations or unions or strike situations that would bring us in contact with the white working class. One day a guy came through who was on the boycott circuit. He was boycotting a particular make of pants and said he had been to a union hall in Laurel, Mississippi, where the workers were on strike at a Masonite plant. He said 20 to 30 percent of the people in the hall were black, and the rest white. He said it was a wildcat strike and the strikers weren't getting a lot of support from their union. They had a picket line set up, and scabs were coming across the line. We decided to get involved, and that's where we made our organizational breakthrough.

A lot of white people, including Bob Analavage and Jack Minnis, came on the staff. We went up to Laurel in a little old VW bug, so here we were crammed in, and accompanied by a big black German Shepherd named Deacon (after the Deacons for Defense). On the way we talked about our plans and decided not to tell them right off who we were, but if we went to a second meeting we would have to tell them, because the FBI would be there and would blow our cover anyway. When we drove up, we were told to find the main gate of the plant and the union hall would be right across from the gate. Then we realized that we had Louisiana tags, and the union people would think we were scabs. In fact, they started throwing stuff and hollering at us, so I immediately jumped out of the car and acted friendly. "We're not scabs, we came up here to talk to you guys."

They showed us where to park and introduced us to one of the union guys, Orange Harrington. We said we heard about the strike and that we just wanted to come up, wish them good luck, and see if there was anything we could do to help. They couldn't think of anything, but they were very glad that we had come and that we weren't scabs. They added that it would help if we could do anything about the scabs coming in from New Orleans. We asked who the president of the union was. His name was J. D. Jolly and they said we could meet him the next weekend—to set up a meeting with him.

We went back home and started researching the plant and decided to go up to Jackson to meet with Claude Ramsay who was head of the AFL-CIO in Mississippi. He told us more about the strike and the issues. Litton Industries planned to open an automated shipyard in Pascagoula, so they needed to break the contracts of all the craft unions on the Mississippi coast, a powerful but splintered group of organized working people, black and white. Craft unions were weak because each looked after only their narrow craft interest. The union at Masonite was different. It was a strong CIO industrial union, originally organized by the Wobblies. So this was to be the opening gun in a unified attack on all unions in Mississippi. He said the guys in Laurel needed all the help they could get.

We asked if Ramsay thought they'd be receptive to us when the found out we were former SNCC people and affiliated with SCEF; we felt we needed to tell them up front. He agreed and gave us the name of their lawyer, who turned out to be the lawyer who argued the case for the regular Mississippi Democratic party in 1964, who would recognize who we were. Then he picked up the phone and called the guy. "I got Bob Zellner and Jack Minnis here, and they're interested in helping you all out. They want to know if there's anything they can do." The guy said to send us down.

It was a really messy situation because it was a wildcat strike and no support was coming from the International Woodworkers of America. It appeared that the national union might get into bed with the company, and they were Klan-baiting a lot of the local union people. Ramsay told us that evidently there were some real bad Klan guys in the union—compatriots of Sam Bowers, the head of the White Knights of the KKK, one of the most violent of all the Klan groups operating in the 1960s. Bowers had started the White Knights because he felt the other KKK groups were too moderate; he was one of the murderers of Chaney, Schwerner, and Goodman in 1964 and of Vernon Dahmer in 1966. Ramsay told us to be careful about a guy named Herbert Ishey, that he was one of the executioners for the Klan and very active in the union.

We went to Laurel and met with the lawyer. We said we wanted every-body to know who we were and that we felt black people and white people needed to get together. He said, "I know, but the people over in the union hall need help, and I've called them and they are waiting for you now. Go talk to them and be sure to talk to a guy named Herbert Ishey."

We debated going to the hall but finally concluded that if we were going to do this work we had to go. If we were afraid of the Klan or a simple thing like dying, we would not be in this particular line of work. We went to the hall, and a lot of union guys were standing out in front. They were very quiet and very white. Orange Harrington was standing there, and I greeted him. He said, "Hi, how are you doing? They're waiting for you in the back."

They took us into a room, where about twenty white guys were sitting around a big oval table. He introduced us to Mr. Jolly, the union president. I introduced us by name, then explained that we now worked for SCEF after spending years on the staff of SNCC. "Mr. Jolly, we've all been jailed, charged with everything from trying to overthrow the government to being communists. We want you to know who we are and where we're coming from. Our organizing project is called GROW, which stands for Grass Roots Organizing Work, and I might as well tell you, because the FBI will, that we also call it Get Rid of Wallace. We work with black and white people who believe they are stronger working with each other rather than against each other. If we can help you, we want to."

He introduced us to the people at the table, and the last guy was Herbert Ishey, a great big guy with a cigar box in front of him, and as he kept flipping the lid, I saw something thing very heavy and blue and metallic in there. Ishey raised his fist and hit the table and he said, "Goddammit, I don't care who you are. We need help from wherever we can get it. You think you're the only ones who have trouble with the FBI. They call us Kluxers. We don't care, commies or Kluxers, we need to get together."

So that was the way we started out in Laurel.

I stayed with Herbert Ishey probably more than anyone else in Laurel. Two years later, he wound up running for office in Laurel on the same ticket as Susan Ruffin, who was the leader of the civil rights office in Laurel. When we started organizing with the Masonite workers and later on with the pulp-wood workers, there were red-baiting stories in all the major newspapers.

Later we had working class rallies with as many as two thousand black and white people out in a cow pasture—old Mississippi rednecks with the whip antennas and Wallace stickers on their trucks, standing next to black folks, all of them talking about how the power structure was holding them down.

THERE WAS A PULPWOOD strike at Masonite about a year or so after we started, and we opened an organizing center in Laurel called the Working-man's Committee House. One night about 2:30 A.M. we were striking at Masonite and trying to keep the pulpwood from being brought in. The train crews were union and wouldn't take the pulpwood in as long as there was a picket line, so we had to keep the picket line up twenty-four hours a day. I was taking coffee down to the picket line, and three big burly wood cutters said, "Come here, Bob, we want to talk to you about something." I walked over where they were.

"We want to talk to you about this communist thing. Come with us." They started walking down this dirt road. I knew that a Wackenhut guard had been killed down that road about two weeks before. Every now and then you ran into a situation like that, where you'd love to beg off, but I took the walk with them. We stopped and were smoking cigarettes and chewing tobacco, and I said, "What about this communist thing?"

I knew it was bugging them. They told me that they had looked it up and as far as they could tell they were communists, because it said people should share and share alike and that everybody was equal. We had been saying to them, "No matter if you are a communist or a Klansman, your behavior is what counts. If you're going to have a strong union, you must have black and white in there. You know you don't want black people crossing the picket lines, and you can't have segregated drinking fountains and bathrooms and lockers, the way you had before. You can't have segregated seniority lists. You have to do more than you ever expected to do, but when you do that, then you have strength and they can't beat you."

The GROW Project was successful. We had seen it all along as a pilot project to discover what techniques would work, and we proved that it could be done. We knew from the beginning that it had to be done on a material basis. We were studying Marxism, and we knew that an idealistic approach alone would not work. Any kind of appeal to conscience, brotherhood, or

Christianity had to be superseded with a practical, down-to-earth, material approach—you lose money from segregation, both white and black have poorer schools, poorer work conditions, play, health care, housing. When you get together you win. You believe that if your behavior changes your ideas will change, because you will see that there's no difference and that people are equal. That was in fact what began to happen.

One of my duties as co-director of GROW (Dottie was the other director) was to shepherd our supporters "to the field" whenever they chose to visit the project. Supporters included people like John Heyman, head of a New York foundation, or individual donors. Jim Dombrowski had impressed upon me the importance of updating supporters on developments, advances or defeats. He had introduced me to Ethel Clyde, from New York City, the heir to the Clyde Steamship Company, who was an avid supporter of the Southern Conference Educational Fund. She had come to New Orleans in 1954 when Virginia Durr was hauled before the Eastland Committee on suspicion of being a communist. Ethel picked up the tab for Cliff and Virginia's hotel room and all the restaurant bills she could reach and even the expenses of Virginia's lawyer from Montgomery.

When Virginia had told me the story of that sojourn in New Orleans, she said it was impossible to enjoy the city because of the stress of the trial, her concern about Clifford's health, and her fear of what Mrs. Clyde might say to her very conservative Montgomery lawyer. At one dinner she swore she heard Ethel say to the lawyer, "Are you a communist? I hope so because I owe my great health and long life to it. I've enjoyed it immensely my whole life." Virginia said she later found out, after making discreet inquiries, that what Mrs. Clyde had actually asked the attorney was, "Are you a nudist?"

Mrs. Clyde was elderly when I met her and she kept saying to Dombrowski, "I'm too old for any new friends." Jim assured her that he would come personally "when GROW needs money, but you will be excited about what Bob and his young people are doing in Mississippi."

Anne Braden had introduced me to Corliss Lamont and his wife, Margaret. Corliss LaMont's father was a partner of J. P. Morgan. The library at Harvard is named after Lamont. Anne also introduced me to John and Sylvia Crane, whose name was famous for appearing in the toilet bowls of America. They were heirs to the Crane plumbing fixture fortune. Other supporters taking a special interest in our work with poor and working class white and black Southerners included the Rockefeller Brothers fund, the Haymarket fund, writers Bert and Katchia Gilden, and many others who had been supporters of SNCC. I am sure that some funders turned to GROW because of disappointment with SNCC's decision to become all-black, but even so they were justifiably excited about our well-planned attack on racism at its roots. We were taking on the Klan in its own bailiwick, the poor and working class from the Deep South outback.

Two great supporters who were with us from the beginning were Sue and Richard Cummings, owners of a fancy fabric company in Los Angeles. They donated all the fabric we needed to dress the windows, doors and seating of our great big house in New Orleans. Once we were settled in and field work got under way, our reports to SCEF, broadcast to the movement and the nation, spurred Sue and Richard to pay us a visit. They arrived in their new Cadillac Eldorado convertible and we squired them around New Orleans, retiring about 10 P.M. while they continued prowling Bourbon Street. Bright and early next morning, a Sunday, they were up and raring to go to Laurel, site of our most active project with the Masonite workers. On the two-hour drive to Laurel, I told them the details of the project. I reminded them that many of the people we were working with now had recently been Klansmen and some were still making up their minds. Others were attending both meetings, ours and theirs. I cautioned Sue and Dick to look at what people were doing, not what they said because "the last thing that changes with white Southerners who are used to racist terms and casual discrimination is their rhetoric—the way they express things. Some of the people you will meet today have been or still are Klansmen. Be cool. You've never met anyone like the folks you will meet today."

What I did not say was that I was equally sure the folks in Laurel had never met anyone like their guests today. I had told the union committee leadership that I would be bringing visitors from California. The union committee that was running the strike at Masonite—since the International had removed their officers, confiscated their treasury, and dismissed their officers—was made up of black and white rank-and-file members. Each time visitors were expected, the committee selected one of their number to be a special host, accompanying the guests throughout the day's activities.

I had briefed the Cummings on the agenda for the day. Sub-committees would have been meeting since 7 A.M., (Southern working people, black and white, start early to beat the heat). At nine o'clock the entire union committee and guests would gather at the committee house (a freedom house we had obtained in Laurel) for reports. One would be on the legal situation; we had provided lawyers to challenge the trusteeship. Another would be from the political committee. White and black unionists were running on a "working man's ticket," along with Susan Ruffin, a black leader in Laurel, who was running for mayor. So there was Herbert Ishey, a former Klan enforcer, running for Water Commissioner and Road Supervisor on the ticket with the black civil rights leader. Mississippi had never seen anything like this, I told our guests.

M. O. McCarty, our designated host, met us in the yard of the committee house. The nine o'clock plenary session was just beginning. I introduced the Cummings to Mr. McCarty and he took them around to meet everybody. The first meeting we had attended of the union had been all white men; now the committee was made up of white and black women and the old male leadership, white and black. I took pride in introducing our guests to the women members, most of whom were militant, natural leaders. While the meeting unfolded a group of union members and community activists put the noon meal together in the large kitchen. I noted with pride that union men were helping the women in the kitchen.

The plenary was followed by a country feast, the likes of which only an aroused working class, black and white, can put on in Mississippi. Sue and Richard had to try three kinds of potato salad and as many different kinds of fried chicken. A good time was had as everybody arranged themselves around the large tables, covered a short time ago by reports, legal briefs, and the committee news sheet, *The Rights of Man*, which Jack Minnis helped the union people to publish each week.

After dinner, we all took to our cars and pickups to drive out to Jasper County for the weekly mass meeting in a cow pasture. The sheriff of Jones County was not sympathetic to the union strikers (his bread no doubt being buttered by Masonite), so to avoid harassment from the law, the union held its rallies next door in Jasper County. The former Klan guys had adapted some of their favorite activities to the new interracial grassroots work: the car caravan, outdoor rallies in somebody's cow pasture, and handing out literature. Now instead of hooded night riders caravanning through the black community to intimidate, the black and white unionists and their supporters would make a big show of driving through Laurel before heading out to the country for their meeting. Sunlight now illuminated the speakers on the back of the flatbed truck, whereas before it may have been a burning cross. Instead of stuffing hate literature into mailboxes in the dead of night, the new tactic was for salt-and-pepper teams to fan out into the community and pass out a new kind of literature, touting racial cooperation and understanding.

On our way to the cow pasture, M. O. and I rode in splendor and luxury in the back of the Cummings' Eldorado. The dust of Mississippi might have be clinging to its exterior, but the big Cadillac had a great air conditioner. My seatmate looked only slightly out of place in the big car with the fancy couple from California. McCarty reminded me a little of my uncle Harvey, a life-long poor sharecropper. M. O. had the huge cal-loused hands of a working man and a leathery, perpetually crimson neck. Like Uncle Harvey, he had moved from the hard life of a dirt farmer to the relatively easier factory life. Well, Harvey had moved from the farm outside Dothan, Alabama, to Mobile, where he worked on the construction crew of his son-in-law, my cousin, Charles Jordan. Harvey always hungered for novelty and excitement—a good attitude to have if you are a self-educated country man, recently arrived in the city.

Since leaving Laurel's outskirts, we had ridden in silence. Maybe Richard and Susan were contemplating what awaited them in Jasper county, an even more rural and out of the way place than tiny Laurel. Maybe to break the silence, Susan suddenly spun in her seat and asked, "Tell me Mr. McCarty, what do you think of the Negroes?"

Without skipping a beat M. O. gave the standard Southerner's answer to a Yankee's question, "Well, I get along with them just fine, I just don't want one marrying my daughter and I don't want to have to eat with them." Well, that was a conversational nonstarter.

When we got there, other members of the union committee stood next to an open gate leading into the pasture. Hundreds of cars and pickups were arrayed in semi-circles around a long, high flatbed truck, conveniently located under a huge oak tree. Speakers were already gathering on the truck bed which served as a raised stage. Many cars and trucks sported Wallace stickers, whip antennas, gun racks, and Confederate flags. Except that half the crowd was African American, it might have been a Wallace or even a Klan rally.

We parked where the union guard said to park and walked toward the stage. M. O. spied some of his old union buddies, maybe his old Klan buddies, too, and wandered off toward them. As soon as he was out of earshot, Susan wheeled on me and hissed, "Did you hear what he said?"

I replied calmly, "You mean about Negroes?"

"Exactly," she exploded, "How can you work with people like that?"

"What kind of people would you want us to work with?" I asked.

She found it difficult to answer.

"These are the people we need to be reaching," I explained, trying not to patronize. "But I don't think you are getting the full picture."

I whistled in the direction of McCarty and motioned for him to rejoin us. He ambled over and asked, "Yeah, what?"

"M. O.," I asked, "Where did you have dinner today?"

"Over there at the committee house, why?"

"Was the food good?" I asked, "and did you stand up to eat or did you sit down?"

"Sure was," he said, "My wife made a whole bunch of it this morning, started frying that chicken at four this morning. She served and then sat with us there at the table, remember?"

"I do remember," I assured him. "Do you remember, M. O., who was sitting there at the table with you?"

"Yeah, I was sittin' with my running buddies," M.O. happily recounted, "Ivory Garrett was sitting on my left and James Nealy was on my right side."

Throughout this colloquy, our guests for the day were looking at us like what in the world are these two nuts up to. Given McCarty's last answer, I began to close my case. "What color is Mr. Garrett?" I asked.

"He's black," M. O. answered innocently.

I felt like a prosecutor leading the witness. "And what color is Mr. Nealy?"

"He's black, too."

"Well, M. O.," I sprung the trap, "remember what you said back in the car about the Negroes?"

"Yeah?" he kind of strung it out like he, too, was beginning to wonder where this was going.

"Well, my friend," I grinned at McCarty, "If you don't have any better luck with you daughter than you are having with your eating, then you better look out."

M. O. slapped his knee with a huge laugh and shouted, "Bob, I see what you mean!" Still laughing, he headed back to his buddies.

I DID THINGS DURING that organizing project that were even more hair-raising than some of the things we did in SNCC. A lot of the pulpwood cutters were in peonage to a local wood dealer. In backwoods areas of Mississippi, this guy was the lord of the manor and a law unto himself. Sometimes, I had to go by myself to meetings. We'd be having a meeting of black and white woodcutters, and the man himself would walk in, and I had to absolutely Bogart. Even James Simmons, president of the Gulfcoast Pulpwood Association, who was an old Wallace supporter from Alabama, had said, "These people would just kill you without a flicker of an eye." I would have to get up at the meeting in front of his men and say, "Mr. So-and-so, I am an organizer for the Gulfcoast Pulpwood Association, and we're glad to have you here, and we'd love for you to say a word, but this meeting will be private."

There were some attempts on my life. I had my car windows shot out several times, and attempts were made to run my car off the road. I did start carrying a weapon. Philosophically, I had decided that even the strongest advocates of nonviolence always said that if you have to choose between nonviolence and not functioning at all, do whatever you have to do. One night, a guy in a pickup was trying to force me off the road. I took out my pistol, a big old Webley .45, a British officers' revolver, formidable with its long barrel. When he pulled up beside me, the guy put his window down and started shouting at me, "You dirty communist, nigger-loving Jew, son of a bitch, blah, blah, blah." We were on a double-lane highway going from Laurel back to New Orleans, and he was trying to keep my attention so he could run me into a bridge abutment or the water. The minute I realized what he was doing, I just raised the gun up, and he turned his truck so fast that he spun around and went across the median. The next meeting we had in Laurel, a friend of M. O. McCarty's, who I knew was still going to Klan meetings, came up to me and said, "That was fantastic last weekend."

I knew what he was talking about, but I didn't want to say anything. I said, "The speech I gave?"

"No, not that speech. That was good, too, but on the way home. They talked about it in the meeting. They were all flabbergasted, because they were all saying, 'Well, that S.O.B. is supposed to be nonviolent.'"

I told him, "Look, if you see those guys again. Tell them I have absolutely nothing against them—me and you and M. O. get along all right. But if people threaten me, I will shoot them. I'm not going out of my way to hurt anybody, but if they shoot at me, goddam right I'm gonna shoot back."

He told me, "Bob, I don't care what you say about nonviolence but that has done more good for the union movement than anything I have seen happen for a long time."

When you take up the weapon, you have taken into your hands your own protection, while in the nonviolent mode your protection is in the hands of a higher power, whatever it may be. It was like when I was captured by the Klan, every time I thought they were going to kill me, I was okay. If I had any chance to escape or maybe survive, then things got shaky.

GROW LASTED A DECADE, and the years with black and white workers from Masonite and pulpwood yards across the South proved GROW could change hardened racists. GROW caught fire in 1968, just as Democrats turned their backs on workers in a new class-based elitism that scorned hard hats and poor people and forgot the MFDP '64 Convention challenge. It was ironic that while Wallace, then Reagan, urged white workers to vote against their own economic interests, white and black common people in Mississippi, Alabama, Georgia, Florida were demonstrating that progressive populism is, as Norman Corwin said, "not so wild a dream as those who profit by postponing it pretend." GROW brought organizing expertise (developed in SNCC) to white people suffering from low wages, poor schools, health care, and housing—all in the name of white supremacy.

GROW recruited and trained over a dozen staff. Like SNCC, we saw our role as "working ourselves out of a job" by making grass roots interracial organizing become self-sustaining. As soon as pulpwood cutters, white and black together, could run the saw shop cooperatives GROW helped them establish, the jobs went to woodcutters. The Gulfcoast Pulpwood Association enrolled hundreds of black and white Southerners by conducting strikes involving thousands, electing officers, and running their own affairs. Our political campaigns, run by candidates and supporters, helped local people get trained; they branched out to organize successful unions of poultry workers and catfish skinners.

We put hundreds of workers through residential workshops in our New Orleans center and at the end of GROW the big house was sold for exactly what we paid for it. The staff moved on. Jack Minnis had a successful career as a political commentator; our photographer, Robert Analavage, wrote a novel, then killed himself; Walter Collins, our most effective black organizer, went to prison for draft resistance; Mike Higgson, an Englishman who became an experienced organizer, is a successful builder in New Orleans; Toni Algood and Charlie Gillespie became mainstream union organizers. Marie and Steve Martin continued their political work. After his wife died, Steve organized teachers in Alabama and campaigned for Senator Barack Obama. John and Vicki Koeferl helped organize the Holy Cross Neighborhood Association in New Orleans' Lower 9th Ward, continuing the physical and political work of recovery from Katrina and President George Bush's neglect.

DOTTIE AND I BEGAN drifting apart towards the end of the GROW Project. After GROW, I first worked in the oil field, but left so I could be home every night and went to work as a union carpenter, making the best pay of my life, at the Shell Refinery in LaPlace, Louisiana. Dottie went back to school to become a licensed practical nurse, and later went to work at the New Orleans Home for Incurables, a brick-walled enclave near the monastery on Magazine Street. To me, Dottie had been one of the original new-wave feminists, some of whom came out of SNCC. We separated in 1979, and although I moved to New York, I kept an apartment in New Orleans to be with Maggie and Katie as much as possible. Dottie and the girls then moved to New York in the summer of 1983 after Maggie graduated from high school and before Katie started the ninth grade.

22

FUNDI: PASSING IT ON

In 1980, I moved to New York to start a small construction company. Over that decade I also did some work in the film industry and I was traveling, writing, and lecturing. As the nineties began, I was thinking about writing a memoir, a process which unexpectedly led to graduate school and then eventually to this book. These were interesting and productive years.

My New York building company was called Big Apple Design. Looking for clients, I went to the people I had known for twenty years in the movement. I built a new law office of ten thousand square feet at 800 Broadway in exactly ninety days for my friend Victor Rabinowitz and his partners at Rabinowitz, Boudin, Standard, Krenski, and Lieberman. I built a deck for Bill Kunstler's home on Gay Street in the Village and he liked it so much I did another one and a tree house for his summer place on Peek a Moose Road near the Shandankin reservoir in upstate New York. Other clients included artist Helen Frankenthaler and art historian Barbara Rose. John Koeferl from New Orleans helped me I renovate the Hudson River mansion of the poet John Ashbery.

I managed the construction of Harry Belafonte's new Italianate office in the theater district and did some work on his country lake house. I enjoyed driving upstate with Harry and hanging out at his house. He said I ate an apple like a rich guy. I asked what he meant, and he showed me his core. It looked like a caricature of an apple core. There was not an atom of white left, just the stem, the seed pod in the center and two little specks of peel at each end. He said if you grew up in the islands poor like him, you'd eat an apple that way, too. I told him I did grow up poor, then I lied and said we were so poor we didn't even know what an apple was. Harry laughed and said I could signify as much as I wanted but there was no way, no way, I was ever as poor as he had been.

I thought I would have the last word when I told him that I was certainly poorer now than he was. Belafonte said to remind him when we got to the house that he had something for me. At the house he took me to the finished attic which he had converted into a giant air-conditioned walk-in closet. In neat rows there were highly polished pairs of shoes arranged from black on one end of a row through to pure white on the opposite end of another row.

"What size you wear?" he inquired like a shoe salesman. I told him ten and a half or eleven.

"Just my size," he crowed. "Zellner, poor boy, this is your day! Take your pick, start with five pairs."

I wore Belafonte shoes for years after that. They were good ones. I guess he had every pair he had purchased since the fifties. When Townsend and the rest of us listened to "Banana Boat" and "Matilda" while we were at Huntingdon College, I could not have imagined that one day I would be wearing Harry Belafonte's shoes!

JOANNE GRANT RABINOWITZ WAS very close to our SNCC founding mother, Ella Baker, and when I moved to New York Joanne was working on a film to be called *Fundi* (a Swahili word meaning one who passes on a craft or specialized knowledge; a teacher). Hearing that I was in NYC, Joanne asked me to work with her and cinematographer Judy Irola. They needed me to suggest filming sites and individuals in Mississippi for an important segment of the movie. I did location work for Joanne's movie and later worked with her and Judy on a half-dozen features and documentaries. We traveled all over the world doing films about women in Frelimo, the revolutionary freedom army in Mozambique; the Mariel boatlift in Cuba; the Mexican view of the Battle of the Alamo; a feature film with Eddie Almos; and many more.

I was also traveling, writing, and lecturing. In the late eighties while on a trip to New Orleans I talked to Lance Hill about the challenges of doing carpentry work in New York to earn enough money to support brief writing periods in a little cabin upstate. Lance and I had worked with Tulane

University professor Larry Powell on campaigns opposing David Duke's forays into Louisiana politics. Lance was in a similar will-work-for-writing-time situation with a small lawn service he ran in New Orleans. He asked, "Why don't you come to Tulane for a PhD?" When I said I couldn't afford it, he said, "Hell, Bob, they will pay you to come to Tulane—they pay me." Lance was then doing a dissertation on the self-defense side of the Southern struggle, using as his topic the legendary Deacons for Defense and Justice.

In 1991, with Hill's encouragement and Powell's support, I enrolled in a PhD program in the Tulane history department to write a dissertation on my experiences as a civil rights worker. My doctoral committee, chaired by Powell, approved the somewhat unusual proposition that I would write three chapters of a memoir of the civil right movement as the equivalent of a master's thesis. Should I finish a complete memoir of my experiences, it could serve as my doctoral dissertation. On the first day of orientation, Powell told the class that only a small percentage of us would ever actually receive the PhD. So far I have proven his words to be prophetic. Maybe finishing this book will inspire me to persevere.

Dr. Powell and Professor Patrick Maney gave me similar writing advice: Tell it like it was—don't be theoretical or too analytical. Historians will be asking their own questions of the material. You just tell the story. You are a primary source, let others do the historiography. Maney mumbled under his breath that Newt Gingrich had gotten a doctorate from their department—maybe mine would somewhat compensate.

I continued graduate work at Tulane for the requisite two years of course work through 1992. As an older student—also older than many of the professors—I didn't need to socialize and party all hours of the night, so I was able to keep up with the exceptional young minds around me. The reading and research load was so staggering that I took a course in speed reading.

When I handed in the opening chapters of the dissertation, Larry Powell gave me more advice: "Leave out the 'wow factor' in telling about your first mass meeting. Readers will provide the 'wow!' from your description of the scene."

Two years of course work and another two as a resident teacher and scholar gave me a start on my story. From 1993 to 1995 I began the preliminary research and writing for the dissertation while teaching undergraduate history. I also served as a graduate assistant to my professors and others in the department, proctored, graded tests, and recorded attendance. I sometimes lectured in the Sociology Department.

I was a teaching assistant for a professor who had lost his sight. The history field I plowed, Civil War and Reconstruction through the Modern Civil Rights Movement, looked like current events compared to his work on medieval history. The reading machine he used got its "voice" from a Moog synthesizer and it sounded like the robot it was. The professor, though grateful for his little robot, preferred the human voice, which I provided. Feeling sorry for my puny period of history, he spent hours recreating the Romaioi defense of Constantinople to play on my mind's big screen. He traced sparkling arcs of Greek Fire coursing high above enemy ships held at bay by the giant iron chain stretched across the straits. I could almost hear the hiss of the napalm-like goo exploding at the water line next to the hull.

I was only supposed to write three chapters while at Tulane. The rest of the book was to be done as the full dissertation. I did my practice teaching at Tulane and later at Long Island University/Southampton College, where I moved after Tulane.

THE JOB AT SOUTHAMPTON College was providential, because in the early 1990s the Higher Power demonstrated that there is life after SNCC by enabling me to fall in love with a dear friend whom I had met some years before. Linda Miller and I were married on June 18, 1994, at the Rams Head Inn on Shelter Island, near Southampton, New York.

The Southampton wedding gathering united our families and friends and reunited a number of movement veterans. Naturally, there was lots of talking, not all of it about the past. Some interesting and challenging ideas germinated, including the notion of building a North–South alliance, based on issues still facing us. These ideas later developed into a national conference on social justice and the development of a Freedom Curriculum.

Linda and I worked with Julian Bond, Pat Sullivan, Joanne Grant, Kathleen Cleaver, Howard Zinn, Maggie Donovan, Reggie Robinson, Matthew Jones, and others to organize the conference around the theme, "The SNCC Experience—Passing It On." The conference took place in 1997 at Wheelock and Simmons colleges and was also supported by MIT and Harvard. The meeting laid the basis for a Freedom Curriculum for public schools and other projects which have since been launched under the slogan, "Teaching Social Justice, Living Social Justice."

The 1997 conference in Boston also served as a joyful reunion for movement people, and, more importantly, their children. I especially remember the workshop organized and led by our daughter Margaret especially for movement offspring and their parents. Matthew Jones, a SNCC Freedom Singer, sat in the room with his kids and was moved to tears hearing Margaret and other black and white movement babies talk about missing their moms and dads while the parents were on the picket line, in jail, or otherwise away from home. The freedom struggle so engulfed us that we sometimes neglected our kids even though we were aware of it at the time and felt a great sense of guilt.

Maggie Donovan and her colleagues have done the writing, perfecting, and vetting of the Freedom Curriculum, which became a project of the National Civil Rights Coordinating Committee (NCRCC), co-chaired by Julian Bond and me. The Freedom Curriculum is an umbrella term covering a set of ideas on how to explore the lessons of the civil rights movement with young children. These ideas include considering racism as an institution; understanding the history of African American resistance; and connecting the civil rights movement to other struggles of oppressed peoples. The curriculum emphasizes collaboration and perseverance. The intent is always for children to see themselves as activists in a democracy.

Spinoffs from North-South work and that 1997 conference, along with the Freedom Curriculum, have meant new directions in training teachers to teach the movement, racial and ethnic sensitivity, and diversity. Providing a focus for the new NCRCC, the Boston experience strengthened our determination to put civil rights into American education. A fluid group of activists, educators and business people formed around New England, while the most collective work centered in Boston; it evolved into a rotating unpaid staff of students, teachers, and community activists.

Maggie Donovan, a first-grade teacher and graduate school professor, has become an international expert in experiential learning. In 2000 Maggie and Cheryl Sutter were invited as teacher researchers to the "Making Learning Visible Project at Project Zero," a research institute within the Harvard

Graduate School of Education. Maggie and Cheryl used the Freedom Curriculum as their research subject and have documented students' responses to it. With their colleagues they have integrated the Freedom Curriculum into literacy and social studies curricula and aligned it with state standards. Project Zero published this work in the monograph, "Making Teaching Visible." Maggie and Cheryl were also invited to present the Freedom Curriculum in Havana, Cuba, in 2004.

In 2004 the Washington-based Teaching for Change published a book, *Putting the Movement Back Into Civil Rights Teaching*, which includes many selections from the Freedom Curriculum. These stories, written by Maggie, are based on work done in her first-grade classroom in Harwich, Massachusetts. One of my favorites is "Pssssst! Hey Mister!" by a seven-year-old boy. I had told the boy's class about "the troubles" in Danville during the exceptionally bloody summer of 1963. I made an adventure story of how a small boy had rescued me from some marauding policemen. Afterwards, one little boy wrote me a letter. He said, "Bob, I really liked that story you told about 'psst, hey mister' and getting shot at and falling in the stickers. I told my teacher it shows that little people can help big people sometimes."

Maggie and I are especially excited about the educational work being done in Mississippi, the state where the movement struggle was most intense and deadly and where SNCC played such a central role in developing local organizers. The curriculum uses real stories from real people in real situations during the freedom movement, and some schools there have courageously decided to face their own past and help children learn their own history. Working with the William Winter Institute for Racial Reconciliation at the University of Mississippi and its director, Susan Glisson, several of the communities where the struggle was most explosive, including Philadelphia, McComb, and Oxford, have hosted conferences for elementary teachers where Maggie presented the Freedom Curriculum. During these conferences many teachers have approached Maggie to tell her their own stories, which are now included in the curriculum.

Some portions of the New York City school system under Chancellor Joel Klein are involved and have done field testing along with Sean Devlin through the American Civil Rights Education Services. "ACRES" organizes three-week tours of historical sites across the Deep South. Students raise money for the trip while attending an eight-week intensive course at Medgar Evers College in Brooklyn or the City Academy at City Hall in Manhattan. Devlin recruits movement veterans as master teachers and traveling instructors during the tours. Diane Nash, James Bevel, Bernard Lafayette, Barbara Bland, Amelia Boynton, Elizabeth Eckert, James Meredith, John Seigenthaler Sr., Matthew Jones, Hollis Watkins, Dave Dennis, and Bob Moses are among those who have served.

My weeks with Sean Devlin as a master teacher have been rewarding. I use the Freedom Curriculum a lot as I have watched him build an experiential learning instrument employing videos, movies, live heroines and heroes, drama, poetry, rap, bands, and freedom music. Devlin got hooked on freedom while working with Jane Pauley producing documentaries on the sixties.

Some exciting events on the road to the Freedom Curriculum have been small ones. Maggie's first graders in Harwich performed a play they wrote about the Montgomery boycott. One little girl played the bus driver, another was Martin Luther King, and a small boy played Rosa Parks, the favorite role. Others set out chairs in the shape of a bus. The rest became policemen and women or parts of the crowd shouting encouragement or abuse at "Mrs. Parks." They thoroughly enjoyed doing their play for me, "the visitor." After the delightful play, I told them about meeting Dr. King and Mrs. Parks while I was a student in Montgomery. Classwork included writing to the visiting "speaker." One first-grader wrote to thank me, "Bob, I was so excited when you said you met Martin Luther King and Rosa Parks, do you mind if I ask if you met Harriet Tubman?" I read it perfectly in spite of small misspellings or uncertain grammar. I wrote and asked Maggie to show him my letter saying I missed meeting Tubman, but that she was in the same movement as me—just earlier.

As our teaching plan has been studied in real class rooms, we have documented children's engagement with the movement through storytelling, drama, artwork, poetry and music. We have collected evidence of children's growth as readers, writers, and historians as well as their passion for justice. Children have an innate sense of justice—"It isn't fair!" They prove to be at home using metaphor and love the adventure of the movement, easily identifying with the heroines and heroes. Freedom songs, which they sing with gusto, become as important in the plan as freedom stories. Students pile up a large number of books they have read, and they and their teachers add a small pebble to the story tin can as each is added to their repertoire. Songs and poetry they write in class are amazing and the plays they produce and the hand-bound books they make are inspiring. Student responses to the curriculum are being used by a number of school systems as a proven experiential learning tool. In 2005, Teaching For Change made a professional development film in Maggie's classroom of the class's original play about the Montgomery Bus Boycott and how to teach the movement in the ways we have developed. They also have some of our lessons on their website.

Educators recognize the value of civil rights teaching material produced by actual participants in the events they are describing and analyzing. Movement veterans support a Freedom Teaching Plan because we want our story to be told by us, since others who are writing curricula have learned of the movement from secondary sources. We, who made and lived the freedom movement, are now facing our mortality and realize that in a short quarter-century, few if any of us will be left to tell the story. It is crucial that those who made this history be involved in passing it on and interpreting our movement to children and students. Already many "experts" are putting their spin on our history. That's why the Freedom Curriculum is destined to make a major contribution to American education for the rest of this century.

23

UP SOUTH

As I mentioned, Linda and I were married on Shelter Island, near Southampton, New York. We still live in Southampton, and our home is not far from the Shinnecock Indian Reservation. There on February 24, 2000, three Native Americans were arrested on St. Andrews Road. Some confrontations had occurred between tribe members and Parrish Pond Associates, a real estate developer attempting to develop reservation land. At the time, Linda and I were in New York City for a preview of the movie, *Freedom Song*, so I had no knowledge of these arrests. When I checked my messages on Friday morning I had a call from Ben Haile, a friend and member of the tribe. He asked me to contact him about the arrests. When I returned the call I spoke to someone on the reservation who asked if I could go to a construction site on St. Andrews Road and talk to Ben.

I was called as co-chair of our local anti-bias task force. This group is appointed by the town board, and it's a respected organization of business people and concerned citizens who monitor and investigate charges of bias in the area. There is strong bias in the local area against both African Americans and Native Americans. I told them I would come down and stay fifteen or twenty minutes and at least talk to the State Police and make sure they were not going to hurt anybody. I had no intent to participate in the demonstration—just to mediate between the police and the activists on this reservation, who were protecting their burial site from desecration. The person explained that there was a large contingent of State Troopers at the site, and based on their experience the day before they were concerned that events not be repeated.

The Shinnecock Reservation had dwindled from hundreds of thousands of acres to the smallest that it was ever supposed to be, thirty-six hundred acres. That minimum was guaranteed to the Shinnecocks a century ago by way of a thousand-year lease from the Town of Southampton. Then the railroad came through. It's strange to think of railroad land grabs from Indians on Long Island. It sounds so Western. But it happened right here, and it's still with us, taking egregious advantage of the Native Americans. The tribe gave a right of way to the Long Island Railroad. Then the white people took advantage by taking everything north of the railroad. They argued that since the railroad separates the thirty-six hundred acres into two parts, the tribe will no longer own or control all lands north of the right of way. The reservation was thus effectively reduced to eight hundred acres.

In 1959 a developer laid the foundations for several houses on reservation land along the Montauk highway. The ruins of the foundations are there still, but the New York state attorney general went into court and stopped the buildings from being constructed on reservation land. The tribe has not always been so lucky. The attorney general, under ancient laws, is charged with the responsibility of defending the rights of the Indians under the ward-of-the-state theory and law. But things have changed drastically now that "The Hamptons" is a world-famous destination. In recent years, then-Attorney General Eliot Spitzer filed cases *against* the Shinnecocks.

Still the developers come and try to take a few acres here and there. The development attempt in 2000 was on sixty-two acres contiguous to the reservation—a traditional hunting ground and ceremonial burial area. Under cover of night developers brought in a bulldozer and started destroying the trees. Even the ecologists were upset. Finally, on February 24, the young activists said they had had enough and were going to stop the bulldozers by sitting in front of them. The police then came with riot gear, equipment, and forty vehicles. They started beating the small picket line of old men and women and children and a few young activists.

Arriving at the site on February 25, the day after the initial arrests, I observed half a dozen state police cars at the entrance to St. Andrews Road. At the protest site I observed another dozen or so state police vehicles and more troopers than there were demonstrators. I spoke briefly to the people on the picket line, some of whom carried signs. The tribal historian, Harriet Gumbs, mother of the tribal chairman, Lance Gumbs, gave me a briefing on the confrontation between the Nation and the developers. She told me that the developers were in a frenzy of tearing down trees and ripping up the ground and that a chain-link fence had been constructed overnight, to try to get as much done before a restraining order came. The tribe was concerned that the developers were attempting to make the protection of the land a moot point by making the site development into a fait accompli. Gumbs also said the state police were in no way acting as disinterested peace-keepers but were openly hostile to the interests of the Native People and seemed to be friendly to the developers. Then they told me that their lawyers had obtained a stop-work order, or temporary restraining order, and that it was on the way to the site. She asked if I would communicate with the state police in an attempt to maintain the peace until the stop-work order arrived. They asked me to reiterate to the police that material or equipment could leave the area but they did not want any other machinery to enter the site since it was being shut down by court order.

I asked who was in charge, then I introduced myself to State Police Major Thomas Weber as co-chair, along with Oscar Byrd, of the Southampton Town Anti-Bias Task Force. I told Major Weber I had been asked by people from the Shinnecock Reservation to contact the state police to facilitate communication between the Nation and the state police. I told the major that there had been complaints of mistreatment and injuries from the day before, February 24, and I wanted to be sure that there was a clear understanding between the parties. I asked the major if he was aware that a restraining order had been granted by the court stopping work at the site. He said he had been informed of that. While I was talking to the major, I learned later, a truck had pulled up to the picket line. I suggested to the major that, as the person in charge, he could set a good tone of even-handedness by asking truck drivers not to cross the line until the order was served, at which time the builders could peacefully remove their equipment.

I asked if we could go to talk to the developer about the fact that the work had been officially stopped by the court and that the restraining order was even now being driven to us from the New York State Supreme Court and was only a few minutes away.

He said he couldn't do it—that he had to keep the road open, and that I was standing in the middle of it. I was not aware of standing in a "road" at that moment. While I was literally still shaking the major's hand, I was grabbed by several state troopers from behind, pulled backwards, and wrestled to the ground. I have had experiences with the police in the South when they have lost control of themselves during demonstrations and have exercised more force than necessary to make an arrest. This experience with the New York State Troopers had the same feeling. They were out of control.

They were attempting to handcuff me, and I relaxed my arms so they would be able to handcuff me, and they took advantage of that by holding me by the elbow and the wrist and literally turning my arm backwards. I could hear the cartilage and tendons snapping in my elbow, and I screamed "You're breaking my arm." They intended to, because when I said that they gave it another twist. I turned and looked over my right shoulder and said, "I want your name. You're breaking my arm."

When I did that, they said, "Oh, you're resisting arrest." That's when they began to kick me. They kicked me in the jaw and knocked it out of place so that my teeth would not fit together, and my left knee, weak from previous surgery, was re-injured. Then they dragged me between two cars. I had experienced police brutality and knew they were really going to work me over, but a brave photographer, a woman from the Southampton paper, came right over with a camera. The cops told her she couldn't take photos, but she told them that she was the press and started taking pictures, and that's when they stopped beating me. When they allowed me up, I stood and walked to the police van with my hands cuffed behind my back. I was not told I was under arrest and from that time until my release after arraignment the next morning I was not read my rights against self-incrimination, though there were numerous attempts to interrogate me. I had done nothing to warrant arrest, but the constitutional principle was lost on these police officers.

I was placed in a police utility vehicle with my hands still cuffed behind my back and the cuffs cutting into my arms. The officer slammed the door on my already painfully injured right arm. The pain was so excruciating that they finally handcuffed me in front and allowed me to stand for a moment in the rain so I could get my breath. I asked the driver to take me to Southampton Hospital as soon as possible because of my heart condition; I was feeling faint with a terrific headache. It was all so Southern. It's incredible. When I talk on the lecture tour, I talk about moving from Down South to Up South.

Much later I was taken to Suffolk Central Hospital where the trooper said I "claimed to be injured." The attendants casually X-rayed my right arm, noted "no injuries," and released me with medication for pain and swelling. My blood pressure was very high but I was taken to the trooper barracks on Flanders Road, where I was cuffed to a steel bench with Doreen Arundel, who had also been arrested, until late at night and then taken to town lock-up for the night. While waiting at the trooper barracks, the Diallo verdict came in and the troopers made a big show of clapping and laughing that their fellow officers were acquitted. "Next time we go on the reservation, we're bringing our bullet-proof vests."

At town lock-up I was refused access to my medication even though the state police had given it to the jailer. At breakfast time Saturday morning a guard opened the door and asked, "Can you catch?" And then he threw a sandwich and a carton of fruit punch at me which I attempted to catch with my left hand, unsuccessfully. I don't know if that was a routine indignity or if the officer was trying to see if my right arm would function. My right arm was too stiff to move.

This was February 26. The development was stopped for several weeks. Then they had a court hearing, and the judge ruled on a technicality that the tribe had not responded in a timely fashion. Obviously, the town officials were in on the deal. Welcome to America in the twenty-first century in the beautiful Hamptons, and that is part of the irony. The Hamptons is considered one of the great garden spots of the world. Rich people from all over come there, and we have the most backward and the most embarrassingly reactionary government that you can imagine

After the Shinnecock episodes, I ran for town supervisor and although I lost, my campaign work helped to elect, for the first time in history, a majority-Democratic town board. We have now been through a number of two-year election cycles and Southampton is reverting to Republican cronyism. We do still have enough influence, however, that activist members of the tribe and community supporters have gotten an agreement from the town to buy and preserve some land that used to be part of the reservation.

During the incident on the reservation land, my elbow was permanently dislocated, and I will probably be in some pain for the rest of my life. It had been a long time since anything like that had happened to me, and I realized I'm not willing to be beaten up any more—I'm getting too old for that, and you don't bounce back from it when you are in your sixties like we did when we were young people in the fifties and sixties. The episode was indeed reminiscent of the South, because the police were in such a fury over the young activists on the reservation. You could tell the police wanted to hurt people.

In the end, we did not let them get away with it. We filed a federal court lawsuit and a jury found that I and the Shinnecock Nation members were victims of false arrest, malicious prosecution, denial of civil rights, and unlawful physical injury (though it found we were not subject to "excessive violence"). The state appealed, but the verdict was upheld and we collected damages. Most importantly, we demonstrated again that truth crushed to earth will always win in the end.

LINDA MILLER AND I were married on June 18, 1994, at the Rams Head Inn on Shelter Island, near Southampton, New York. Julian Bond was again my best man, and family and many old friends, including Joe Thomas and the late Townsend Ellis from Huntingdon College days, came to the wedding. Townsend, who had been my roommate at Huntingdon, had the voice of an angel and was our soloist. His renditions of "Amazing Grace" and "O Promise Me" brought everyone to tears.

I wrote a piece about our marriage and celebrations called "Twelve Days that Shook the World—June 15–26, 1994." The activities indeed lasted twelve days and covered four states—from New York to New Orleans and crawfish, to Mississippi and the thirtieth anniversary of Freedom Summer, to Alabama and my family, with another wedding ceremony, and a great Southern feast.

Linda and I lived and still live in Southampton. She was prepared for my work, being a great organizer herself, and we do many projects together.

I FORMERLY TAUGHT HISTORY at Long Island University's Southampton College (now Stoneybrook Southampton). My course was the history of activism with emphasis on the freedom movement, including the women's struggle, the fight for gay liberation, Native American rights, environmentalism, and various ethnic and religious rights movements. I hope my course did not contribute to the demise of Southampton College.

Linda sold the publishing business she and her brother Jim had built over a twenty-year span. *Homes of the Hamptons* became the standard against which all other real estate publications are measured. Linda and I finished our beautiful house on Peconic Bay and moved in with Pooh Bear, our huge black dog and his younger sister Lulu, both retrieved from ARF, the Animal Rescue Fund of the Hamptons. Pooh is now circling the great fire hydrant in the sky while Lulu continues to chase her beloved ball.

I gallivant around the country, while Linda finds third and fourth careers. First was Goldman Sachs, then Miller Publishing. She then bought a store on Southampton's Jobs Lane, the "Rodeo Drive" of the Hamptons. Linda and her founding partner of the fashionable boutique, Cynthia Kolbenheyer, are now metamorphosing that store, "Clothes Minded," into an expanded business called "Open Minded," a community concierge for the upbeat Hamptons.

Cynthia's husband and his business partner, along with Linda and I through Miller+Zellner Associates, have designed and completed for sale a five-bedroom "cottage" overlooking the Atlantic and Shinnecock Bay.

Miller+Zellner Associates also owns and operates The Level Woodworks, my cabinet shop on North Main Street, our consulting service on Building and Design, Education, and Politics, and the lecture series I do around the country every year. Writing a book and making a movie sounds like high cotton for a preacher's boy from lower Alabama. It only goes to show to that a lifelong revolutionary, usually never making a penny, can have a soft landing.

Since Southampton College and finishing this book with the able assistance of my friend of forty-eight years and scholar of the movement, Connie Curry, I have learned a lot. All of us who were together in the struggle carry a deep love for each other and we meet whenever we can. Sometimes it is for a comrade's memorial service, or reunions and conferences.

We take time to celebrate. I was honored to attend Chuck McDew's retirement event from his years of teaching at Community College in St. Paul, Minnesota, in 2005. He told us to make our comments as if it were his memorial service—he wanted to hear the stuff while he was still alive. McDew was and is one of my boon running buddies. My first emotional bond with him and Bob Moses was formed when I was attacked in McComb and the two of them came over and absorbed some of the blows that were directed at me. McDew and I had to show up for various trials, and we sometimes traveled together to college campuses, both north and occasionally south. McDew was the first real traveling executive of SNCC. His job was to translate nationally what was happening locally—to tie together the bus boycott, the lunch counter sits-ins, the freedom rides, and the voter registration work in Mississippi which met with such brutal treatment. Besides publicizing our work, his speeches and meetings with students helped form SNCC support groups across the country, which eventually brought offices in Boston, New York, Chicago, San Francisco, and Los Angeles.

When I first met Chuck, I thought of him as a brash northerner—with a wonderful, droll sense of humor, a dry wit. He would have been a great comedian, or great at anything he did, because he is a person of great talent. One of the things that he spoke of in SNCC was his double vision of the church, because so many white racists were imbued with church doctrine. He also had some ambivalence about the North and South in general. He was raised in the steel town of Massillon, Ohio, but his parents were from the South, and at his parents' insistence, he enrolled in South Carolina State in Orangeburg. He started going to church but soon found he couldn't go to whatever church he wanted with so-called Christians. Then he went to a synagogue and was welcomed. He would talk about the concept from the Talmud—if not me, who; if not now, when—and how that had helped propel him into the movement. He had found some people in the movement who would stand up—in the tradition of social justice in the Jewish faith that he didn't find elsewhere. This caused Bob Moses to make a very famous statement about McDew when we were all in jail in McComb. Moses was writing about each person, and he wrote a wonderful letter called "The Center of the Iceberg." He says, "McDew is a revolutionary who dares to stand in a strong light. He was a black man by birth, a Jew by choice, a revolutionary by necessity." It is one of the great poetic passages from the movement.

For Reggie Robinson's birthday, in the fall of 2006, we had a fine fishing party in Martha's vineyard. I took my Ram 2500 4WD pickup to the island so we could drive on the sand. There I met Reggie, McDew, and other fishing friends at a rented mansion. Reggie planned the trip to coincide with the Vineyard fishing derby, but the weather was so hot the stripers were late coming down from the north. We caught barely enough fresh fish to eat, but we had fun grilling steaks and telling lies late into the night.

For years and years, whenever Reggie and I would see each other, one of us would jump into the other's arms. Reggie was from Baltimore. He was a street guy in lots of ways—a wonderful, funny, upbeat person and with a philosophy sometimes different from a lot of other SNCC people. Most of them had never had any brushes with the law—we were a nice middle-class group, whether black or white. Reggie had no illusions about run-ins with the law, because he ran on the streets of Baltimore. Reggie never got arrested with us. He would tell us, "You guys go get arrested. I'm out here doing the work. I'll take care of you." Indeed his strength was knowing what had to be done in emergency situations, and he was willing to stay in the background. He made phone calls, arranged for bail, did a lot of basic good community organizing. He has worked in D.C. since the movement and has lived in the same house for years and years, which has become a kind of safe house for all of us and a place to stay when we are in town.

I CONTINUE TO TRAVEL around the country talking about the movement and how we must continue to promote justice and freedom for the people in the United States and the rest of the world.

My friend Maggie Donovan and I were talking about the mess our society is in since Hurricane George struck America's shores eight years ago and the huge mess that continues today. We take comfort from Ella Baker's words — "We Who Believe in Freedom Cannot Rest Until it Comes." Maggie said she was really tired and having some health problems and was going to have to take some time off from a heavy teaching load. She was feeling bad about this turn of events but had reinterpreted Ms. Baker's words to mean that if she has to rest for a while, there are others who will take up the slack. We do this for each other and we will not rest "until freedom comes."

EPILOGUE AND ACKNOWLEDGMENTS

People say that I must have suffered a lot for my principles. They are often surprised when I laugh and tell them that my family suffered more than me. Far from suffering for my beliefs, I count it as a blessing that I was privileged to participate in one of our country's greatest struggles. Until I began to question my brothers about their experiences during the upheavals of the sixties, I never understood how they and Mom and Dad had simply sucked it up and endured the slings and arrows from my outrageous fortune. If you think the British are the owners of the stiff upper lip, you don't know my part of the South. The endless courage and support from my family is reflected in this book. I am forever humbled and grateful to them.

My father developed a brain tumor and entered a steady decline. He had retired from the ministry and two years later collapsed in the pulpit while preaching as guest minister at the Government Street Methodist Church in Mobile. After a nonmalignant tumor was removed, he and Mom moved in with Suzanne and Mal, who aided them with love and dedication. From the time Dad collapsed with the brain tumor until he died, Mom took care of him. The tumor and surgery left him with scrambled speech—a particularly bitter pill after a lifetime of delivering exactly the right word at the right time with the right modulation. I always thought rather cynically that the Lord had played a trick on Dad. He had served God faithfully for more than forty years and now, Job-like, he was being tested instead of enjoying twenty years of retirement ease.

Mother was a saint in the face of Dad's black moods and his ever-present frustrations. The only time he could put words in the correct sequence was when he was furious. At these times he would lash out! In a detached part of my brain I would say, "Oh yes, the speech center of Dad's brain is scrambled, not his anger center."

Mom watched Dad slowly give up the fight to live. As his death approached, Mom called us to the Seven Z's cabin to give him permission to leave. The hospice nurse told us that several days before, Dad had seemingly made a rational decision to stop eating and drinking. He was ready to meet the deity he had labored for all these years, and I'm sure he expected to receive a commendation from his Commander-in-Chief for a job well done. He died October 5, 1996. After his death, Mother began to show signs of frailty and Alzheimer's disease. She lived with Mal and Suzanne until she died on April 19, 2005.

Years before I had asked Dad if he expected to see some of his fellow preachers of the segregationist faith up there. He thought before saying he knew he would see Fletcher McLeod, Garner, and the others who had fought the righteous fight for equality in the church, but he wasn't sure that Red Hildreth and the Bob Jones crowd would make it through the pearl-studded doors. Then he laughed and said, "What the heck, I won't be surprised at all if God forgives those suckers and has them playing harps right along with the rest of us."

While Daddy was fading away and later when Mom was beginning her own decline, we had many joyful family gatherings. Suzanne would cook up a storm and Mal would fire up the outdoor fireplace and barbeque pit which he built in their courtyard under a huge live oak. While the well-cured oak and hickory burned down to magenta and gray coals, he and I and his boys would drive down to the fish shack on Fly Creek in Montrose for fresh shrimp and crabs.

Whenever I went down home for a visit, I would walk with Mom past Mal's tin-roofed cabinet-making shop, toward the grape vine which had remained for sixty years in the same place curling around the old cedar sapling runners. We would pause and remember the good times the Zellners and the Phillipses and all the Hardy-Zellner clan had enjoyed while gathered near the old arbor for all-day singing and dinner on the grounds, with the food spread on white table cloths over wide boards laid across sawhorses.

Mom could remember the old days better than the present. As we approached the old cabin I thought how small and forlorn it looked. It was a bit saggy then, being vacant, but Mom's eyes would brighten and her pace quicken. Past the ancient azalea bushes, now thick and tall, she retrieved the mail from the battered mailbox by the road, then she'd turn to enter the Seven Z's. Inside it was the way she left it when she reluctantly moved across the yard to Mal and Suzanne's. The oversized fireplace with its ten-foot mantle exuded the same elegance and utility it demonstrated when its first fire was proudly laid by Dad some fifty years before. Swallows have now built mud nests in the massive chimney and their red dirt droppings cover the cold hearth.

During each visit I would take Mom for a drive in the country. When Margaret and Katie were along we would pile into one of the many vehicles around the Zellner compound and head out. Baldwin County roads made Mom reminisce about her years driving the dirt tracks when she served as a visiting teacher to handicapped and shut-in children. Driving to Dad's grave just outside Loxley, Alabama, where Mom's mother and dad lived and had died in their retirement home, she would point to a country cabin high on a hill. "Margaret and Katie, that's where little Clyde lived," she'd say, "He would always be in his chair on the front porch waving and clapping. He'd always smile so big, he was that happy that 'teacher was here.'"

At the cemetery, Mom would softly say, "Here they are," pointing to a low stone that was inscribed "Rev. James Abraham Zellner and James Hubert Zellner" (Brother Jim). The last name on the three-person plot read "Ruby Rachael Hardy Zellner."

Mom always said the same thing: "It does make me feel funny to see my name there already, but it was cheaper to have them put it on at the same time as Daddy's and Jim's." Then, pointing to four little plots near Dad's and Jim's feet, she said, "Bob you are over here. Doug, David, and Mal are next to you over there." It gave her comfort to think we'd all be together after the last of us entered the fog bank.

After "seeing" Daddy and big brother Jim in their red-dirt plot overlooking a small creek and a cotton field, Mom, the girls, and I would wend our way among the modest headstones to pick out the graves of Granddaddy and Grandma Hardy lying next to Uncle Hubert and Aunt Rosetta. Uncle Harvey slumbered a few yards away beneath an incongruously large headstone adorned with a very handsome ceramic of him in his Sunday best. They said his likeness would last for a thousand years, but Cousin Jane and Aunt Lois were told they paid way too much for it.

MY BROTHER JIM, THE oldest of the five Zellner boys, had entered the ministry like Dad and strove mightily to live up to Dad's expectations. Jim excelled at Duke Divinity School and served a small country church in Rocky Mount to hone his preaching skills and make a little money for graduate school. Jim started drinking and smoking, but the good church folks didn't take kindly to their preacher drinking or, even worse, smoking tobacco. Jim laughed and pointed out that tobacco grew right up to the church door, being about the only cash crop worth raising in those parts. The hypocrisy he saw was enough to run him out of the ministry. After Duke, Jim figured the right thing for a well-educated young single man was to make leather sandals, belts, and purses for the wealthy young flower children not attending classes in Durham and Chapel Hill. Listening to progressive jazz, brother Jim hung out at the Null and Void coffee house giving occasional readings and acting in little plays. A fierce anger was building in him about the way black people and misfits were treated and about the growing obscenity of Vietnam.

My beloved big brother then became an expatriate in Germany and returned to the U.S. only for short visits. He worked on his little farm, making leather goods and developing a thriving antiques and repair business. In the early 1980s, he and his German wife came to spend some days with me with me and my partner, Judy Irola, in Paris. The last time I saw Jim, we stood for a picture in front of Notre Dame on the banks of the Seine. I later received a tape he recorded as he suffered through the last days of lung cancer. His voice, still strong, talked about his struggle to understand. He died February 8, 1991, in Wartburg, Germany, after telling us, "I don't know what might be on the other side, but I am interested to see."

Using that Southern metaphor of the great beyond, I hope our beloved brother Jim and our underestimated and often-unappreciated parents, James Abraham Zellner and Ruby Rachael Hardy Zellner, will look down with approval on my effort at telling this story. Since Jim led the way to Huntingdon in 1955, my treasured old-fashioned, happy nuclear family has scattered to the winds. I thank my remaining brothers and their wonderfully giving and forgiving wives for the excitement and concrete assistance they have brought to this project.

Doug, my next brother, is a retired social worker. He followed the family tradition of willingness to tackle almost any job by working in almost every setting, client group, and program in the health and human services field. In both direct service and administrative positions he was an advocate for disadvantaged individuals and groups. Doug married his college sweetheart, Judy, a gifted photographer and the mother of my nephews, Davey, a builder, and Mike, the marine. Doug and Judy lived in the South until his retirement, then moved to Indiana and later to La Jolla, California. For this book, Doug and Judy corrected much of the family history and offered their photos and extensive family archives.

Brother David served in the Air Force in Guam in 1964 before the bombing began in Vietnam. He lives in Rockford, Tennessee, with his wife, Ruth. They met in New Orleans while David worked as head mechanic at a paper plant. He and Ruth have two boys, Mark and Jason, and have recently adopted Ruth's great-niece. While I worked on the book, David and Ruth provided photos, family lore, and joyful enthusiasm, and played host to the entire writing and publishing team. They fed Chuck McDew and me more than once. Thanks to the good food and fellowship, Chuck adopted our Tennessee family branch as his own.

Mal, the youngest, was drafted into the Army in 1966. He was an MP serving at Fitzsimmons Army Hospital in Denver. The military considered him a a security risk because of my civil rights work, prompting an investigation that took so long that he did not have enough time left in service to be sent to Vietnam. He now lives in Daphne at Mom and Dad's old home place where he works as a builder, designer, and cabinet maker. Malcolm's wife Suzanne works with Catholic Charities, most recently aiding victims of Hurricane Katrina. Mal is a Catholic deacon, and performs weddings and funerals. I feel immense gratitude to Malcolm and Suzanne. They cared for Mom and Dad with love during their last years while preserving the core of the family archive in the old Seven Z's cabin. They have become the darlings of the Wisconsin State Archives in Madison and, incredibly, the library and archives at Bob Jones University. When Mal carried pictures of Dad with Bob Jones in Europe to the BJU library in South Carolina, the archivists said they had the same pictures but could not identify the young men in the pictures. Mal said, "Well that's Dad right there standing next to Dr. Bob Jones." Mal and Suzanne have five children, Francis, Ashley, Rachael, and the twins, Peter and Stephen, all of whom graduated from Alabama's super-advanced state boarding high school for science in Mobile.

DOTTIE ZELLNER LIVES IN Manhattan and I am proud that she is the mother of our two fine daughters, Margaret Rachael and Cathrin Ruby. Dottie fights for the rights of all people, including the Palestinians, showing the courage she consistently displayed during the gloomiest days of the freedom struggle in this country. In the years we were a family, Dottie, Margaret, Katie and I were a team of sculptors chipping away the granite of Southern segregation. A redneck Southern scalawag romanced the beautiful Northern Jewish school-marm-red-diaper-baby. With the resulting two movement diaper babies, Marg and Katie, the four of us sallied forth to battle the bloody dragon of American apartheid.

I could write a whole book about the accomplishments of our super daughters. This history is for them and their generation; I hope they will someday pass it along. My love and gratitude goes to them.

Katie and Margaret are doing well in their careers and I am proud of them. Both live on the upper west side in Manhattan. In the family tradition, they have chosen to serve others. Katie worked for a number of years as a staff assistant in a day treatment program for developmentally disabled adults. She now works in a nonprofit organization taking care of homeless and disadvantaged people in New York City. Katie also uses her skills in computer medical record keeping and research.

After graduating from Brown University, Margaret got a master's in Latin-American studies. Following psychoanalytic training, she was certified as a practicing psychoanalyst, conducting much of her therapy in Spanish. She has now completed a PhD in neuropsychology at Queens College, which happens to be the alma mater of both her mother and her step-mother. She is active in a growing movement to bring together neuroscience and psycho-analysis with practical application in addiction therapy. Abby Rockefeller and the Brothers Fund supported the GROW Project. Margaret worked with Peggy Rockefeller and Roberto Mizrahi while working her way through

Brown. With her new degree, Dr. Maggie Zellner is now ensconced in the Rockefeller Laboratories in Manhattan.

I HAVE BEEN SADDENED over the years by the loss of people dear to all freedom lovers and to me. Deaths now come with quickening regularity. Clifford Durr died in 1975; Virginia in 1999. They are memorialized with an annual civil rights lecture series in Montgomery. My mentor and great friend, Anne Braden, died in 2006; Anne set a high-water mark of dedication that has no equal in the movement. Catherine Fosl, her biographer, has founded an institute in Louisville to honor Anne, her family, and her work. It is often said of soldiers that when they go off to war, the family goes with them. Families of civil rights workers also served. James Forman died in 2005, as did Jack Minnis. Joanne Grant Rabinowitz died in 2005 and Victor Rabinowitz in 2007; they were longtime friends and co-midwives of my memoir, not to mention stalwarts of the movement. There are many, many more I could mention here and some of us are working to make sure that they are known and celebrated through the Freedom Curriculum project.

Thankfully still among the living are many to whom I owe debts of gratitude for friendship and support. I have already mentioned the chair of my dissertation committee, Professor Larry Powell, along with an activist friend, Lance Hill (now Dr. Hill), who were responsible for getting me into the History graduate program at Tulane University. They set me on the path leading to completion of this book.

Even before Tulane, however, I was already thinking about writing a memoir. Jeff Jones was the first to help me pull it together. He and fellow SDS Weather Underground activist Eleanor Stein shared a country hide-away with Bill Ayers and Bernadine Dohrn in upstate New York. They gave cinematographer Judy Irola and me the use of a converted chicken coop down the hill from their estate, Red Hawk. The tiny cabin had lights and a small refrigerator, but no running water. I spent winters there writing close to the wood stove where Judy and I cooked. The years I spent planting the vegetable garden with the help of the Ayers-Dohrn and the Jones-Stein kids, along with Katie and Margaret, helped me survive some severe post-traumatic stress disorder. The freedom to roam the woods harvesting meals of squirrel and venison, while spending priceless time with Katie and

Margaret provided the serenity I needed to join a twelve-step program and become a real friend of Bill's.

Jeff Kisseloff of Sleepy Hollow, New York, was a skilled doula for this book. Afternoons at his mountain retreat talking about the olden days produced transcripts, which expanded into chapters. *Generation on Fire*, his oral history of the sixties, includes a chapter incorporating parts of this book.

Harry Belafonte helped over the writing years, subsidizing my ailing economy by hiring me for construction jobs on his New York office and his country lake house. More importantly, Harry reminded me of stories I had forgotten, some of which were actually true.

Actor Joan Rosenfeld of Modern Times Theater and Vinceremos Brigade founder Julie Nickerman nurtured and gave me encouragement.

Michael Ratner, Bill Kunstler, and Margie Ratner provided jobs and encouragement while Dr. Gwendolyn Midlow Hall provided criticism, support, and priceless insight into early movement mentality. Her children were a great inspiration during my first long writing sessions, accomplished at her mountain home in Effort, Pennsylvania.

Rose and Ralph Fishman of Brookline, Massachusetts, are key to much of the flavor in my story. In Boston with Maggie Donovan for work on the Freedom Curriculum, we often visited the Fishmans. Rose, bringing out her pictures of SNCC folks and her diaries, made the sixties pulse and sing again. Images of Margaret and Katie as little kids, Dottie, Maggie and Ed, Rose and Ralph and their little ones, along with Mrs. Hamer. Jim Forman appeared young, vibrant and very much alive.

Danny Lyon, aka in SNCC as "Dandelion," was one of the coolest cats in our very cool organization and he has stood the test of time. His photographs are the best the movement has to offer and his bravery under fire is legend. He once snuck through the woods to take pictures of teenage girls imprisoned in an abandoned dungeon in the middle of a snake-infested swamp near Albany, Georgia. He had to shush his many fans in the standing room-only stockade when they spotted Danny. They could have alerted the authorities when they screamed, "Dandelion is here! We will all be saved." After the bad old SNCC days began to fade, to avoid sinking into lethargy and in the interest of keeping his hand in as an ace photographer, Danny went to Haiti to take pictures of the Tonton Macoutes. The man lives dangerously and it is gratifying to see him reach the stratosphere in his field. Thank you, Danny for letting me use your historic pictures in *Murder Creek*. Danny, you are in good company as I also express deep gratitude to my friend and teacher, Richard Avedon, and to the Richard Avedon Foundation for the use of his gorgeous image of the young SNCC.

Scholars have interviewed me over the years, including Howard Zinn, Clay Carson, Kerry Taylor, John Dittmer, Charles Payne, Judy Richardson, John Hampton, Pat Sullivan, Bruce Nelson, Jerry Thornbery, Taylor Branch, the late David Halberstam, and Dan Carter. Clay, Kerry, and others were kind enough to forward transcripts of interviews for use in my memoir. Halberstam talked me through a way to see the book as a rounded story with a theme, a beginning and an end. I hope I have done justice to the memory of my friend and SNCC chronicler David Halberstam.

Thanks to publisher Daniel H. Fiske of *Verdict* magazine, the official organ of the National Coalition of Concerned Legal Professionals, for excerpting three chapters my book during 2006 and '07.

John Dittmer, scholar and writer on the freedom movement, read for corrections and additions, actually volunteering to do so. Others checked specific references—Dottie Miller, Maggie Donovan, Joan Browning, Tom and Casey Hayden, Lawrence Guyot, as well as SNCC buddies Chuck McDew and Reggie Robinson. Special kudos to Julian Bond for writing the foreword despite tremendous demands—his teaching schedule and his invaluable leadership of the NAACP.

At NewSouth Books, editor Randall Williams, publisher Suzanne La Rosa, managing editor Brian Seidman, and Lisa Emerson, Lisa Harrison, Mary Katherine Pappas, and Ashley Hockensmith could not have been more encouraging and committed to the book. Attorney Will Campbell of Lancaster, Pennsylvania, a longtime NewSouth friend, proofread the manuscript and made helpful suggestions.

This tale has taken so long to write and produce that new helpers have been added along the way like Marla Schwenk. She has kept my schedule and me on track so I can devote more time to finishing "the book."

Our friends Jeff Weinstein, Lisa Kombrink and Rita White were pressed into service as proof readers; for their selfless work I am eternally grateful. Thanks to our attorney, Kathryn Dalli, who was always there with sage advice. Rose and John Dios have been valuable advisors and, along with Roberta LaRosa, have helped us with endless encouragement, hope and good humor. Beloved friends like Ed Stateman and our neighbor across the street, Jerry Chalem, provided the necessary spiritual sustenance needed to persevere, while Richard Lawless and Bobby Onco have guided Linda and me into the mysteries of the very demanding Shinnecock sweat lodge, where the beautiful Linda Miller-Zellner bore the heat much better than I did, and I am the Southerner!

I could not have completed this book without Linda, who came into this marriage on with her eyes wide open. Even so, she has been astounded at the baggage my past has brought to our Eden. To her immense credit she and her large, very progressive extended family and friends have welcomed me and Margaret and Katie into their lives. My loving and lovely Linda, who I call "Boo" because she was such a happy surprise in my life, is an astute and successful businesswoman with the spirit of a life-long movement person. Needless to say, our business together, Miller+Zellner Associates, is more efficient than mine alone has ever been.

AND WHAT TO SAY about my co-writer, Connie Curry, confidante, sister and comrade of fifty years. Authors often claim their tome wouldn't have existed without their editor. It's true for me. Many tried pulling these stories out of me—Connie succeeded. I enjoy telling war stories on the rubber chicken circuit—the funny ones, that is, but Connie declared in her calm, no bullshit manner that I was avoiding the painful parts of the story—"now get on with it!" I can't blame her, gentle soul, for screaming she would never again collaborate with a "movement man" on a book. I try to soothe by pointing with pride to her irreplaceable role. An accomplished and lionized writer in her own right, she's become a movement Svengali, the Henry Higgins of movement literature, more than Samuel Johnson's Boswell.

To the thousands of my closest friends and relatives who are left out of this lengthy acknowledgment, please forgive me. The vital roles you have played in my life are intertwined to form the silken thread holding the pearls of this book together. Remember, it has been almost twenty years in the making. More importantly, as Connie and other comrades of the sixties remind me, brain drain is commencing. I thank you all.

INDEX

Experience the music of the civil rights era . . .

Sing for Freedom unites two classic collections of freedom songs in one volume, with a new introduction by editors Guy and Candie Carawan. The Carawans are long-time associates of the Highlander Research and Education Center, which factored heavily in the civil rights movement, including spreading and preserving freedom songs.

Sing for Freedom contains sheet music for over one hundred freedom songs—including "We Shall Overcome," "I'm Gonna Sit at the Welcome Table," and "We Shall Not Be Moved"—but this volume is more than just a song book. The pages contain numerous firsthand reports from participants in the freedom rides, protests, and sit-ins, many of them young students. *Sing for Freedom* includes a bevy of photographs, making this an invaluable collection for anyone interested in the civil rights era.

ISBN 978-1-58838-193-4 • Trade Paper • $21.95

Available in bookstores or at www.newsouthbooks.com